Territorial Governance across Europe

This book provides a comprehensive framework for analysing, comparing and promoting territorial governance in policy relevant research. It reveals in-depth considerations of the emergence, state-of-the art and evolution of the concept of territorial governance. A unique series of ten case studies across Europe, from neighbourhood planning in North Shields in the North East of England to climate change adaptation in the Baltic Sea Region, provides far-reaching insights into a number of key elements of territorial governance. The book draws generalised empirically-based conclusions and discusses modes of transferability of 'good practices'. A number of suggestions are presented as to how the main findings from this book can inform theories of terrritorial governance and spatial policy and planning.

This book will be of considerable interest to scholars around the world who are concerned with European studies, regional policy, urban and regional planning, and human and political geography. It provides a solid debate on discourses, theories, concepts and methods around the notion of territorial governance as well as a number of empirical findings from various contexts across Europe. It specifically targets scholars involved in policy-relevant research.

Peter Schmitt is Associate Professor at the Department of Human Geography at Stockholm University and Senior Research Fellow at Nordregio, the Nordic Centre for Spatial Development. He has a PhD in Spatial Planning from Dortmund University. His areas of expertise are in the fields of territorial governance and regional planning.

Lisa Van Well is a Senior Researcher at the Swedish Geotechnical Institute. She has a PhD in Regional Planning from KTH, Royal Institute of Technology in Stockholm. Her areas of expertise and publication are in the policy relevant fields of climate change adaptation governance, regional development and European territorial cooperation.

Routledge Research in Planning and Urban Design
Series editor: Peter Ache
Radboud University Nijmegen, Netherlands

Routledge Research in Planning and Urban Design is a series of academic monographs for scholars working in these disciplines and the overlaps between them. Building on Routledge's history of academic rigour and cutting-edge research, the series contributes to the rapidly expanding literature in all areas of planning and urban design.

Brand-Driven City Building and the Virtualizing of Space
Alexander Gutzmer

Deconstructing Placemaking
Mahyar Arefi

The Empty Place
Democracy and public space
Teresa Hoskyns

Dealing with Deindustrialization
Adaptive resilience in American Midwestern regions
Margaret Cowell

Public Space and Relational Perspectives
New challenges for architecture and planning
Chiara Tornaghi and Sabine Knierbein

Heteroglossic Asia
The transformation of urban Taiwan
Francis Chia-Hui Lin

Building the Inclusive City
Theory and practice for confronting urban segregation
Nilson Ariel Espino

The Robust City
Tony Hall

Planning Urban Places
Self-organising places with people in mind
Mary Ganis

Planning for the Material World
Laura Lieto and Robert Beauregard

Planning and Citizenship
Luigi Mazza

Paris Under Construction
Building sites and urban transformation in the 1960s
Jacob Paskins

Territorial Governance across Europe
Pathways, practices and prospects
Peter Schmitt and Lisa Van Well

Territorial Governance across Europe

Pathways, practices and prospects

Edited by Peter Schmitt
and Lisa Van Well

LONDON AND NEW YORK

First published 2016
by Routledge
2 Park Square, Milton Park, Abingdon, Oxon OX14 4RN

and by Routledge
711 Third Avenue, New York, NY 10017

Routledge is an imprint of the Taylor & Francis Group, an informa business

© 2016 Peter Schmitt and Lisa Van Well

The right of Peter Schmitt and Lisa Van Well to be identified as the authors of the editorial material, and of the authors for their individual chapters, has been asserted in accordance with sections 77 and 78 of the Copyright, Designs and Patents Act 1988.

All rights reserved. No part of this book may be reprinted or reproduced or utilised in any form or by any electronic, mechanical, or other means, now known or hereafter invented, including photocopying and recording, or in any information storage or retrieval system, without permission in writing from the publishers.

Trademark notice: Product or corporate names may be trademarks or registered trademarks, and are used only for identification and explanation without intent to infringe.

British Library Cataloguing-in-Publication Data
A catalogue record for this book is available from the British Library

Library of Congress Cataloging in Publication Data
Names: Schmitt, Peter, 1971- editor of compilation. | Well, Lisa Van, editor of compilation.
Title: Territorial governance across Europe : pathways, practices and prospects / edited by Peter Schmitt and Lisa Van Well.
Description: Abingdon, Oxon ; New York, NY : Routledge, 2016. | Series: Routledge research in planning and urban design | Includes bibliographical references and index.
Identifiers: LCCN 2015026432
Subjects: LCSH: Regionalism--Political aspects--European Union countries. | Regionalism--Political aspects--Europe--European Union countries--Case studies. | Subnational governments--European Union countries. | Subnational governments--European Union countries--Case studies. | Intergovernmental cooperation--European Union countries. | Intergovernmental cooperation--European Union countries--Case studies.
Classification: LCC JN34.5 .T47 2016 | DDC 320.94--dc23
LC record available at http://lccn.loc.gov/2015026432

ISBN: 978-1-138-86087-2 (hbk)
ISBN: 978-1-315-71622-0 (ebk)

Typeset in Sabon
by HWA Text and Data Management, London

Contents

List of figures	x
List of tables	xii
List of contributors	xiii
Preface and acknowledgements	xvii

PART I
Exploring territorial governance pathways across Europe   1

1   Territorial governance across Europe: setting the stage   3
    LISA VAN WELL AND PETER SCHMITT

2   Shifts in governance and government across Europe   21
    DOMINIC STEAD AND ILONA PÁLNÉ KOVÁCS

3   Territorial governance challenging government   36
    ANDREAS FALUDI

4   Guiding principles of 'good' territorial governance   48
    SIMIN DAVOUDI AND PAUL COWIE

PART II
Territorial governance in practice: ten European cases   61

5   Territorial governance at play: methodological
    introduction to the case studies   63
    PETER SCHMITT AND LISA VAN WELL

viii *Contents*

6 Hyper-local planning in England: territorial governance
at the neighbourhood scale 67
PAUL COWIE, GEOFF VIGAR, SIMIN DAVOUDI
AND ALI MADANIPOUR

7 The 'European Capital of Culture – Pécs': territorial
governance challenges within a centralised context 81
ILONA PÁLNÉ KOVÁCS AND ZOLTÁN GRÜNHUT

8 Planning for resource efficiency in Stockholm: 'good'
territorial governance practices without consistency 95
MITCHELL REARDON AND PETER SCHMITT

9 Territorial governance faces complexity: the South
Loire Plan for territorial cohesion 111
ALBERTA DE LUCA AND NADIA CARUSO

10 Integrating public transport and urban development
in the southern Randstad 126
MARJOLEIN SPAANS AND DOMINIC STEAD

11 Maintaining stable regional territorial governance
institutions in times of change: Greater Manchester
Combined Authority 141
PAUL COWIE, ALI MADANIPOUR, SIMIN DAVOUDI
AND GEOFF VIGAR

12 Limited involvement: the role of local and regional
actors in the Hungarian Structural Fund management 157
CECÍLIA MEZEI

13 The rise of a new territorial governance domain: flood
management in the Rhine river basin 171
WIL ZONNEVELD AND ALEXANDER WANDL

14 The trilateral nature park Goričko-Raab-Őrség: a
project-based mode of territorial governance 189
MARKO PETERLIN AND MAJA SIMONETI

Contents ix

15 A role for macro-regions: climate change adaptation
  in the Baltic Sea Region 204
  STEFANIE LANGE SCHERBENSKE AND LISA VAN WELL

PART III
Prospects on territorial governance across Europe **219**

16 Revisiting territorial governance: twenty empirically
  informed components 221
  PETER SCHMITT AND LISA VAN WELL

17 Transferring 'good' territorial governance across
  Europe: opportunities and barriers 238
  GIANCARLO COTELLA, UMBERTO JANIN RIVOLIN
  AND MARCO SANTANGELO

18 Towards future territorial governance 254
  LISA VAN WELL, SIMIN DAVOUDI, UMBERTO JANIN RIVOLIN,
  ILONA PÁLNÉ KOVÁCS AND PETER SCHMITT

  Index 268

Figures

1.1	Defining territorial governance – 'five key dimensions'	13
5.1	The ten case studies' main territorial scope	65
5.2	Exploring territorial governance: the research framework in a nutshell	65
6.1	Location of case study area	69
6.2	Boundaries of the neighbourhood plan area	78
8.1	The territorial scope of the case study: the city of Stockholm and Stockholm Royal Seaport	97
9.1	The territorial scope of the Territorial Cohesion Plan of South Loire	113
9.2	Types of actors involved in the Territorial Cohesion Plan governance process	114
9.3	Cross-sectoral integration and participation platforms	118
10.1	Relation between regional rail stations and urban development	127
10.2	Public transport network in the southern Randstad	128
10.3	Boundaries of the administrative platform for the South Wing	129
10.4	City regions in the Netherlands (as defined in 2003)	130
11.1	The territorial scope of the Greater Manchester Combined Authority	144
11.2	The 'institutional embeddedness' of the Greater Manchester Combined Authority	148
12.1	The territorial scope of the South Transdanubia Region in Hungary	158
13.1	The Rhine river basin and its sub-basins	173
13.2	The area of the main partners in the German–Dutch Working Group on High Water	178
14.1	The Trilateral nature park Goričko-Raab-Őrség	193
16.1	The 20 components of territorial governance	222
16.2	Inter-relations between the five dimensions of territorial governance	233

		List of figures xi

16.3	The operative field of multi-level governance and the 'added territorial elements to multi-level governance'	236
17.1	The dynamic and changing framework of territorial governance	244
17.2	Process of change of 'European' territorial governance	244
17.3	Modes for the transfer of (good) territorial governance in Europe	245

Tables

1.1	Characterisation of two types of multi-level governance	9
4.1	Overview of the dimensions and indicators of territorial governance	54
9.1	Framework of cross-sector objectives in the South Loire Plan for territorial cohesion	117
13.1	International conventions, declarations and relevant organisations	175
13.2	Structure of the water management administration in Germany (here NRW) and the Netherlands	177
14.1	Facts and figures of the three parks	191
17.1	A policy transfer framework	242
17.2	A typology for the transfer of good territorial governance in Europe	249

Contributors

Nadia Caruso is a Postdoctoral Research Fellow at Politecnico di Torino, Italy. As a spatial planner, her research interests focus on territorial governance, the evolution of the planning field, housing policies and social housing. She is working on a research project funded by the Italian Ministry of Education, University and Research. Nadia is a member of the Coordination Team of the Young Academics within AESOP (Association of European Schools of Planning).

Giancarlo Cotella is Assistant Professor for Spatial Planning at Politecnico di Torino, Italy. His research focuses on European territorial governance, in particular on the mutual influence between the EU and the member states in the field of planning. He has been visiting professor at various institutions, including the Wroclaw University of Technology, the University of Tartu, the Polish Academy of Science, and the University of Kaiserslautern.

Paul Cowie is a Research Associate within the Global Urban Research Unit at Newcastle University, UK. The focus of his research is on governance within both local communities and at the regional scale. His research also involves long-term governance issues and foresight methodology.

Simin Davoudi is Professor of Environmental Policy and Planning and Associate Director of the Institute for Sustainability at Newcastle University, UK. Her research focusing on spatial planning, environment and governance has been published widely. Recent books include: *Conceptions of Space and Place* (2009, Routledge), *Planning for Climate Change* (2009, Earthscan), *Reconsidering Localism* (2015, Routledge), *Justice and Fairness in the City* (2016, Policy Press).

Andreas Faludi is Professor Emeritus and Guest Researcher at Delft University of Technology, the Netherlands. He has held various other teaching positions in the United Kingdom and the Netherlands and has published on planning theory, comparative planning and, for the past 20 years, on European spatial planning and EU territorial cohesion policy.

xiv *List of contributors*

Zoltán Grünhut is a Research Fellow at the Centre for Economic and Regional Studies at the Hungarian Academy of Sciences. His research concentrates on social capital, the issue of trust and the interplay between sociocultural specificities and public policy efficiency especially in Eastern Europe and Israel.

Umberto Janin Rivolin is Full Professor of Spatial Planning at Politecnico di Torino, Italy, where he is Deputy-head of the Inter-university Department of Regional and Urban Studies and Planning (DIST) and Coordinator of the PhD Programme in Urban and Regional Development. His research is focused on planning theory, spatial planning systems and EU territorial governance.

Stefanie Lange Scherbenske is a Research Fellow at Nordregio, the Nordic Centre for Spatial Development in Stockholm (Sweden). Stefanie's research focuses on understanding policy and planning processes for climate change adaptation and maritime spatial planning in the Baltic Sea Region from a governance perspective.

Alberta de Luca is a Postdoctoral Research Fellow at Éupolis Lombardia, the Institute for Research, Statistics and Training of the Lombardy Region, Italy. Her research interests focus on urban and regional development, territorial governance and smart cities. Currently, she is working in a research project within the Alpine Space Programme.

Ali Madanipour is Professor of Urban Design and Director of Global Urban Research Unit (GURU), School of Architecture, Planning and Landscape at Newcastle University, UK. His latest (co-)authored books include *Public Space and the Challenges of Urban Transformation in Europe* (2014), *Reconsidering Localism* (2015), and the four-volume *Planning Theory: Critical Concepts in Built Environment* (2015), all published by Routledge.

Cecília Mezei is Associate Professor and Head of Department at the Centre for Economic and Regional Studies of Hungarian Academy of Sciences. Her research is focused on the theory and practice of local and regional development in Europe, particularly on institutional and financial questions.

Ilona Pálné Kovács is Research Professor and Director of the Institute for Regional Studies, Centre for Economic and Regional Studies at the Hungarian Academy of Sciences and full-time Professor at the Department for Political and International Studies of University of Pécs, Hungary. Her scientific interests are local and regional governance and regional policy.

Marko Peterlin is trained as an architect and urban planner. He is the Director of the Institute for Spatial Policies based in Ljubljana, Slovenia. Through work at the institute, he supports public participation and networking of NGOs in the fields of spatial and urban development, and engages with related policies at various levels. His particular interest is in urban and territorial governance and related topics.

Mitchell Reardon is a city-maker informed through urbanism and research. He is a planner and Founding Principal at Metropolitan Collective, a city-making office in Vancouver, Ottawa and Shanghai, and contract Research Fellow at Nordregio, in Stockholm. Exploring potentials for holistic urbanism, Mitchell's interdisciplinary work focuses on how people live, work and move in the city.

Marco Santangelo is Assistant Professor for Geography at the Politecnico di Torino, Italy. His research has focused on territorial governance and on multi-scalar interactions among different territorial and institutional levels, in particular regarding the European Union and in the field of development policies. He is currently working on the smart city concept and on socio-techno-territorial hybrids.

Peter Schmitt is Associate Professor at the Department of Human Geography at Stockholm University and Senior Research Fellow at Nordregio, the Nordic Centre for Spatial Development, Sweden. His research is focused on territorial governance, EU spatial policies and transnational cooperation, self-governance in urban areas and strategic spatial planning in metropolitan regions.

Maja Simoneti is a licensed landscape architect and spatial planner. After 25 years in planning practice, she joined the Institute for Spatial Policies based in Ljubljana, Slovenia in 2009 as a Project Manager and Research Fellow. Her main topics of interest are urban green space, public participation, community-based governance, spatial policies and spatial literacy.

Marjolein Spaans is a Senior Researcher at the Faculty of Architecture and the Built Environment at Delft University of Technology, the Netherlands. Her fields of expertise cover governance and urban and regional development. Her research often has an international comparative dimension and she carries out both academic research and contract research. She regularly publishes in academic and professional literature.

Dominic Stead is Associate Professor of Urban and Regional Development in the Faculty of Architecture and the Built Environment at Delft University of Technology, the Netherlands. He has published widely in international peer-reviewed journal articles and book chapters and has been principal investigator of a large number of national and international research projects. He is a member of the editorial board of four international peer-reviewed journals.

xvi *List of contributors*

Lisa Van Well is a Senior Researcher at the Swedish Geotechnical Institute in Stockholm. Her research is focused on the intersection between territorial and technical knowledge and climate change adaptation governance. At her current employment and previous employment at Nordregio her areas of interest also include territorial cohesion policy and territorial cooperation in the EU and the Baltic Sea Region.

Geoff Vigar is Professor of Urban Planning at Newcastle University, UK. His research focuses on two key areas: the politics of mobility, infrastructure supply and demand; and plan-making in theory and practice, focusing particularly on institutional design questions in making spatial strategies.

Alexander Wandl is a Research Fellow at the Department of Urbanism at the Faculty of Architecture and Built Environment at Delft University of Technology, the Netherlands. His research focuses on the relationship between urban form and sustainable development to inform urban planning and design. He has contributed to a number of national and internal research projects, like 'Rural Future Networks' (EU-FP7) and 'Climate Proof Cities' (NWO).

Wil Zonneveld is Professor of Urban and Regional Planning in the Department of Urbanism, Faculty of Architecture and the Built Environment at Delft University of Technology, the Netherlands. He is co-leader of the departmental research theme on regional design and governance. His research includes strategic planning and conceptualisation of space and territory in relation to governance complexity.

Preface and acknowledgements

The conception of this book and much of the data for the empirical chapters was based on the ESPON 2013 programme project 'Territorial Approaches for New Governance' (TANGO). For this volume, the material and reports elaborated within the 'TANGO project' have been revised, updated and presented in a more academic context as well as accessible style.

The editors would like to acknowledge the funding and support of the ESPON 2013 programme and the ESPON Coordination Unit during the TANGO project which made this volume possible.

The TANGO project and most of the work on this volume were performed while both editors were employed at Nordregio, the Nordic Centre for Spatial Development, in Stockholm, Sweden. We would like to extend thanks to Nordregio and our colleagues there for their comments and discussions on the topic of territorial governance, in particular Linus Rispling for assistance with the maps.

The views expressed in this book are those of the authors and the editors and do not represent those of the ESPON Monitoring Committee or our respective employers.

Part I

Exploring territorial governance pathways across Europe

1 Territorial governance across Europe

Setting the stage

Lisa Van Well and Peter Schmitt

Introduction

Since the early 1990s, the concept of 'governance' has been commonly used as a framework for describing the various types of interplay between the state, market actors and civil society. The concept has been employed particularly to explain the ongoing shifts in public policy- and decision-making characterised, among other things, by the increased involvement of non-state actors and the formation of new interaction pathways in formerly established policy processes. This shift has been necessary in order to address societal challenges such as climate change, regional economic development, or the provision with public services, which are no longer solvable by the state itself. Within the European Union the related concept of 'multi-level' governance has been recognised in order to understand the system of nested relationships among primarily governmental levels (e.g. supra-national, national, regional and local). This was largely entwined in the policy and academic debate of the early 1990s on European integration and inter-governmentalism (see e.g. Hooghe and Marks 2003, Stephenson 2013). In recent years the literature on the concept has expanded to various types and characteristics of multi-level governance. Yet the role of territory, as Faludi (2012) criticises, has been hardly incorporated at all into this body of research.

The notion of multi-level governance has already penetrated policy and research agendas in Europe; however the related concept of 'territorial governance' seems to be a somewhat 'new animal'. In recent years, the term has appeared in a number of transnational policy documents (as exemplified below), but a robust conceptualisation, be it in a more strict academic or policy perspective, is still missing. Thus the concept of 'territorial' governance appears rather blurred, which can be at least partly explained by confusion around the various notions associated with the terms 'territory', 'space' and 'place'. Hence it is not surprising that the concept of territorial governance is not used in a consistent way. This development has led to several gaps in the existing knowledge and methods to study territorial governance. Clear denotations are lacking and many contributions to the debate on what

4 *Lisa Van Well and Peter Schmitt*

territorial governance actually is (and how we can capture it in research) are left to develop their own notions (cf. the endeavours undertaken by Davoudi *et al.* 2008 and in this volume).

Much of the policy analysis today focuses on governance or multi-level governance in the sense of tracing vertical and horizontal linkages and integration of relevant stakeholders (particularly from the bottom-up) into decision-making and policy-making processes. Thus far, little attention has been paid to the more specific 'territorial' dimensions of governance or how knowledge of territorial specificities and the territorial impacts of various courses of action are used in decision-making. This includes ways in which the need for territorial knowledge (for instance, technical knowledge of the impacts of climate change or statistical data on demographic trends) is identified, understood and integrated (or not) into governance processes.

The level of territorial knowledgeability can thus help to improve transparency or even support clarifying who is accountable to the public for making place-based decisions. But in order to be able to sufficiently understand and use such knowledge, actors and institutions need to be adaptive and reflexive enough to convey territorially informed understandings of knowledge into governance processes. In particular the interplay between the use of territorial knowledge and the capacity of institutions and organisations to be able to utilise such knowledge is a gap in governance-oriented research that should be addressed further. The conceptualisation of territorial governance in this book and how it is played out in the case studies in Part II specifically addresses these shortcomings and helps to assess institutional processes around achieving explicitly defined territorial development goals.

One of the main objectives of this book is thus to delve deeply into the conceptualisation of territorial governance with the goal to operationalise the term as a guide for future empirical and analytical case studies. Based on a theory-driven, pragmatic and consensual definition and operationalisation of territorial governance, the focus is to understand the processes by which actors and institutions at different levels formulate and implement policies, programmes and projects to achieve a certain territorial goal. In the final chapters (cf. Part III) a number of conclusions will be drawn about territorial governance throughout Europe. The evidence base of territorial governance processes is gleaned from ten in-depth and comparable case studies across Europe. In addition, a number of policy-relevant implications are carved out to support future spatial planning and territorial development policies in general and Cohesion Policy in particular as they relate to issues such as regional competitiveness, social inclusion and sustainable and balanced development of the European territory. To that end, conclusions are provided on not only how spatial planning and regulatory instruments are involved in territorial governance, but also how broader policy processes such as coordination of actors and institutions, cross-sectoral integration, stakeholder mobilisation, adaptive capacity, and

Setting the stage 5

realising territorial specificities and impacts, have contributed to 'good' territorial governance.

Many of the research efforts on 'governance', irrespective of what kind of further modifier chosen (territorial, multi-level, city-regional, etc.), take an inductive approach, using methods such as constructing narratives and storylines around particular processes and components of governance (such as Buček and Ryder 2015, Pradhan *et al.* 2013, Hooper and Kramsch 2004 and Paraskevopoulos *et al.* 2006). Inductive approaches have certainly contributed greatly to our understanding of the role that governance plays in achieving a certain outcome and confirming that, indeed, governance matters. But there remains a need to revisit the feedback loop by use of grounded theory, from the theoretical starting point that 'governance matters' to generating hypotheses about 'how', 'why' and under 'which circumstances' it matters a little, a lot or not at all. This sort of reflection is provided here and shall in particular help to meet the specific objectives of this book, namely to synthesise current trends of territorial governance, to identify those practices which can be considered 'innovative' and, finally, to discuss the extent of their transferability into other contexts.

Thus the main research questions that will be explored in this book are:

- What is territorial governance and why does it matter?
- How does territorial governance differ from 'governance of territories'?
- What are recent shifts and what is the current state of territorial governance in Europe?
- What are the inherent challenges of territorial governance in relation to government?
- How can we operationalise territorial governance?
- Informed by ten case studies, how does territorial governance differ across Europe?
- Based on the analysis of the case studies, what elements of territorial governance can be synthesised?
- How can we re-conceptualise territorial governance in respect of related concepts such as multi-level governance and spatial planning?
- How can the study of territorial governance be pursued more systematically in research programmes?
- To what extent and how can lessons from 'good' territorial governance be transferred across Europe? What are the barriers and opportunities?
- What futures for territorial governance across Europe can we discern? Which prospects for territorial governance research can we see?

This book is organised in three parts. The first part presents a conceptual framework for exploring territorial governance pathways across Europe. It problematises the conceptual distinction between government, 'regular', 'multi-level', and finally, 'territorial' governance. This part also presents key trends, policy and academic discourses and methods of analysing territorial

6   Lisa Van Well and Peter Schmitt

governance, with a specific focus on how the concept is operationalised. The second part illustrates territorial governance practices throughout Europe in ten in-depth case studies from a number of policy areas. The third part reflects key elements of territorial governance informed by the evidence base from the case studies. The framework for exploring territorial governance will be revisited and discussed in the light of the related concept of multi-level governance. It also considers the different modes of transferability of 'good' territorial governance in a European perspective. Finally some prospects will be discussed in view of future trends and research themes for territorial governance across Europe.

Before presenting the three parts in more detail and the contents of the chapters therein, we briefly consider the extent to which this rather new animal 'territorial governance' has thus far permeated the EU spatial policy discourse. After that, some of the theoretical underpinnings of territorial governance will be synthesised. It should be noted that these theoretical perspectives do not represent a comprehensive review of all literature, but rather the theoretical and analytical body of knowledge that has informed our conceptualisation and methodology for operationalisation of territorial governance.

A brief history of territorial governance in the EU spatial policy discourse

Although the term territorial governance stems primarily from the EU spatial policy discourse, the Organisation for Economic Cooperation and Development (OECD) was a pioneering institution in promoting the concept of territorial governance (cf. Stead 2014, OECD 2001), defining it as

> the manner in which territories of a national state are administered and policies implemented, with particular reference to the distribution of roles and responsibilities among the different levels of government (supra-national, national and sub-national) and the underlying processes of negotiation and consensus-building.
>
> (OECD 2001, p. 142)

This definition, which perhaps more clearly alludes to 'governance of territories' (see below), has later been echoed in a European context, in the Resolution on Territorial Governance of 2006 by the Council of Europe (in the Council of Europe Conference of Ministers responsible for Spatial/ Regional Planning, cf. CEMAT 2006) and by the expert advisors to the Ministers responsible for 'Urban Development and Territorial Cohesion within the EU' in the 2007 report 'The Territorial State and Perspectives of the European Union' (cf. Ministers of Urban Development and Territorial Cohesion of the European Union 2007). Additional references to the notion of territorial governance are also seen in the 'Green Paper on Territorial

Cohesion' elaborated by the European Commission (cf. CEC 2008) and in the so-called 'Barca Report' (Barca 2009). The Barca Report, which was a prime influence on the EU Cohesion Policy period 2014 to 2020, did not specifically refer to the term territorial governance, but claimed that a place-based approach to development policies

> refers both to the context-dependent nature of the efficiency and equity problems that the policy deals with, and to the fact that the design of integrated interventions must be tailored to places, since it largely depends on the knowledge and preferences of people living in it.
>
> (Barca 2009, pp. 5–6)

More recently the notion of territorial governance is seen to be a process by which territorial cohesion can be achieved, as reflected in the 'Territorial Agenda of the European Union 2020' from 2011 (Ministers responsible for Spatial Planning and Territorial Development of the European Union 2011) and the Network of Territorial Cohesion Contact Points in a report from 2013 (NTCCP 2013). Both of these policy documents call for a place-based, territorially sensitive and integrated approach to policies, to improve the performance of actions on all levels and create synergies between different types of policy interventions.

Theoretical and methodological underpinnings of territorial governance

From government to governance

Governance as a concept has permeated social science research for the last few decades, whereby research has chronicled the shift in policy-making from state-dominated 'government', coordinated through formal and hierarchical public sector agencies and bureaucratic procedures, to 'governance' characterised by overlapping and complex competencies and the introduction of new types of actors into the political arena (Painter and Goodwin 1995). This shift has led to modifications in representative and jurisdictional government (Pierre 2000, Jessop 1997), as well as to a disruption of traditional channels, networks and alliances through which government is interconnected to citizens and private interests. The challenge of governance in addressing governmental pitfalls is in creating new forms of integration out of fragmentation, and new forms of coherence out of inconsistency (Davoudi *et al.* 2008). As Stoker (2000, p. 93) succinctly summarises, governance is 'a concern with governing, achieving collective action in the realm of public affairs, in conditions where it is not possible to rest on recourse to the authority of the State'.

Governance has been approached in social science and spatial planning both normatively and descriptively. As a normative construct, governance has been used as a conceptual tool to make sense of the increasing emergence of intersectoral issues such as climate change adaptation (cf. Kern and Bulkeley 2009) or to provide input into deliberate policy-making processes in spatial planning (cf. Healey 1997, 2010) that can no longer be adequately addressed by traditional governmental efforts. Linked to the idea of governance as a post-political project is the use of governance as a normative framework for questions involving long-term strategies that can outlast political periods (Giddens 2005). Normative interpretations of governance have also been concerned with features of 'good' governance, for instance in connection with the work of the OECD (OECD 2001) or the EU White Paper on Governance from 2001 (CEC 2001).

The literature on governance as a descriptive concept (e.g. Pierre and Peters 2000, Jessop 1997) often uses empirical observation to show how a specific type of territory, such as a metropolitan region (e.g. Salet *et al.* 2003), is shaped by decision-making and planning processes by the inclusion of new actors, networks and constellations. In this vein, Stoker promotes the value of a governance perspective as an organising framework for understanding these types of processes (Stoker 1998, p. 18).

As mentioned earlier, most comparative studies of governance are inductive and governance research could be complemented by more analytical/deductive studies emphasising the historical-institutional and socio-political context of the issue. Van Kersbergen and van Waarden (2004, p. 166) conclude that a further distinction should be made between empirical-analytical governance issues, or descriptions of what is happening, and why, and the normative evaluations of governance – prescribing or proscribing courses of action. Jordan (2008) and Kooiman (2003) allege that we are still in a state of 'creative disorder' about governance; while there is a wealth of research on governance, the concept is being used in basically three different ways – as an empirical phenomenon, as normative prescription and as theory.

More recently there have been a number of efforts to problematise the governance concept as an analytical construct. For instance, Nuissl and Heinrichs (2011) propose four general governance-inspired categories for investigating spatial planning actions – actors, their relationships, institutional frameworks and decision-making processes. They conclude rather sceptically that many issues discussed under the label of governance are already integral elements of current thinking about spatial planning. Nevertheless, they remark that within the governance discourse 'the notion of "good governance" can serve as a reality check for the expectations regarding the efficacy of [....] approaches to participatory, transparent, and proactive spatial planning' (Nuissl and Heinrichs 2011, p. 55). Harrison (2013) approaches the understanding of territory and networks by looking at spatial strategies and sociological interactions and asking if the 'fit between academic conceptualisation and on-the-ground developments' is really so neat (Harrison 2013, p. 71). We consider these as research efforts that are

Setting the stage 9

moving into the direction of deductive inquiry, or to put it plainly, into the nuts and bolts of how and why (territorial) governance really matters.

Multi-level governance and its types

As a concept, multi-level governance describes and aids in understanding the system of nested relationships among supra-national, national, regional and local governmental levels within the EU policy-making apparatus. This was largely entwined in the policy and academic debate of the early 1990s on European integration and inter-governmentalism. In this vein of research, several scholars, notably Marks, problematised the different types of multi-level governance in terms of allocations of responsibilities and competencies and described how various layers of government are nested or 'enmeshed in territorially overarching policy networks' (Marks 1993, pp. 402–403). Later, Hooghe and Marks (2001, 2003, 2010) distinguish between Type I governance systems with a limited number of non-overlapping multi-issue jurisdictions and Type II governance systems composed of many flexible, sometime overlapping jurisdictions that are often task-specific. Type I governance, stemming from federalism studies (Hooghe and Marks 2001, p. 4), illuminates various types and processes of formal decentralisation or devolution of government levels and sees territorial boundaries as fixed and non-intersecting. Type II governance is more ad hoc in nature and informal and can be used to address specific tasks that transcend a number of fixed administrative levels. Hooghe and Marks (2001, p. 26) call for further empirical and comparative studies to show how these types of governance can co-exist.

Faludi asserts that most multi-level governance discourses actually refer to Type I where levels of government are nested 'Russian doll-like' in territorial arrangements (Faludi 2012, p. 203). Even Type II jurisdictions have some characteristics of nested levels, which according to Hooghe and Marks (2003, p. 240) 'share some geographical or functional space and who have a common need for collective decision-making'. Nevertheless, the malleable design of Type II governance helps to 'respond flexibly to changing citizen preferences and functional requirements' (Hooghe and Marks 2003, p. 238).

Table 1.1 Characterisation of two types of multi-level governance

	Type I	Type II
Jurisdictions	General-purpose	Task-specific
Boundaries	Non-intersecting memberships	Intersecting memberships
Scales	Limited number of levels	Unlimited number of levels
Organisational Structure	System-wide architecture	Flexible design

Source: Authors' own adaptation based on Hooghe and Marks (2003, p. 236).

10 *Lisa Van Well and Peter Schmitt*

Thus Type II governance arrangements, with their non-fixed jurisdictional boundaries may be edging closer to what we would call 'territorial governance' (see below), whereby no overarching governmental sovereignty is apparent. Nonetheless, we concur with Faludi (see Chapter 3), who states that there is still the need to problematise the conception of territory: 'What is missing in the literature on this topic is any awareness of different notions of underlying territory' (Faludi 2012, p. 205).

Distilling elements for conceptualising 'territorial' governance in this book

Moving on from 'regular' and 'multi-level' governance, and spurred by the political debate across the EU on 'territorial cohesion', territorial governance itself has been conceptualised as a means to achieve endogenous territorial development via the organisation of new 'constellations of actors, institutions and interests' (Gualini 2008, p. 16). 'Territorial governance' can thus be understood as a more encompassing way of understanding relationships and linkages among actors within a territory, than can either of the types of multi-level governance as characterised by Hooghe and Marks. Territorial governance might be said to encompass both the Type I (formal governance/ government) arrangements of multi-issues within a specific territory, as well as Type II (informal governance) processes among territories and with regard to issue-specific as well as more cross-sectoral issues (see Table 1.1).

Another key aspect of territorial governance is participation, mobilisation and inclusion of relevant stakeholders into policy-making processes to activate their place-based knowledge and concerns in the formulation and implementation of public policies, programmes and projects. As Davoudi *et al.* characterise territorial governance, it is 'the process of territorial organisation of the multiplicity of relations that characterise interactions among actors and different, but non-conflictual, interests' (Davoudi *et al.* 2008, p. 37). It implies horizontal and vertical coordination within the structural context, the policies of the institutional realm, and the results and processes of actions, programmes and projects for territorial cohesion (ibid., pp. 37–38).

Our territorial governance concept encompasses these first three dimensions – coordinating actions of actors and institutions, integrating policy sectors and mobilising stakeholder participation – into its framework. Yet it also incorporates the dimension of adaptability of institutions, as related to the concept of resilience of social systems and their adaptation to changing contexts (e.g. economic crisis, natural disasters). This dimension focuses on flexibility and adaptability of governance structures that are driven by social learning processes. The level of adaptability is thus dependent on the ability to self-organise, reflect and learn. In this sense, according to Gupta *et al.* (2010), 'adaptive institutions' can encourage learning among the actors by questioning the socially embedded ideologies, frames, assumptions, roles, rules and procedures that dominate problem-solving efforts. Maru (2010) more explicitly notes in this context that while the capacity to self-organise and adapt are shared properties of social (and ecological) systems, 'learning' is an essential human (and thus individual) capability.

The final dimension we add is related to the notion that territory is often absent in the literature, as expressed above. Jordan (2008, p. 21) earlier had stated that

> in fact, its lack of geographical specificity [in regards to the conceptualisation of 'governance'] has allowed scholars operating at totally different spatial scales – international, national, and/or sub-national – or even across many scales [...], to use it. This ability to 'bridge' disciplines and distinct areas of study has undoubtedly boosted the popularity of governance (van Kersbergen and van Waarden, 2004), but has also contributed to the lack of precision noted above.

The research approach presented here is sensitive to how place-based/territorial specificities and characteristics are addressed within territorial governance practices. We emphasise that territory and/or place are considered as social constructs, and not as purely physical artefacts, and are thus not necessarily limited by jurisdictional boundaries. In this vein, we further argue that territorial governance (i.e. employing a territorial approach in the development of strategies and in decision-making) should be carefully distinguished from the 'governance of territories' (as largely being addressed in Chapter 2 for instance). The latter is inevitably present, in particular with regard to multi-level governance (here Type I), since it reflects how a territorial entity is governed. However, the former offers, according to our conceptualisation (see also Figure 1.1), a high degree of sensitivity in regards to 'how' territorial dynamics and challenges as well as prevailing perceptions and knowledge may feed into various processes within (multi-level) governance for achieving a certain territorial goal. Hence these considerations refer to the often hidden territorial dimension of governance. As discussed above, governance is often studied without due attention to its spatial characteristics and inherent spatiality as an integral part of any social process (Lefebvre 1991). Indeed the fluidity of relations and the fuzziness of boundaries make it difficult to illustrate the spatiality of governance processes. However, new light can be shed on governance processes by honing in on some of the underlying causes for forms of decision-making and implementation that may otherwise remain unnoticed. Namely in the fifth dimension (cf. Figure 1.1) one key question is whether the actors in governance processes are aware of the territorial dimensions of their actions, such as knowledge of territorial diversity and an advanced understanding of the territorial and place-specific impacts of their policies, programmes or projects.

However, by incorporating the latter two perspectives we are entering a kind of grey zone between a pure analytical understanding of governance and a more prescriptive-normative of what constitutes 'good' (territorial) governance (cf. Chapter 4). Nevertheless, we argue that these additional dimensions further our understanding of territorial governance as a 'process', as they highlight not only actors and institutions but also their inherent knowledge and learning capabilities.

This brief stocktaking of the emerging body of territorial governance research has furthered our understanding of the concept as an elaboration and expansion on the more commonly accepted notions of 'regular' governance and 'multi-level' governance. In this light, the proposed five dimensions that form our definition of territorial governance (see Figure 1.1) reflect and emphasise this by accentuating explicit notions such as territory, process, change, inclusion and context. The rationale for this, as we would call it, 'holistic approach towards understanding territorial governance' is summarised in the following understandings that are seminal to the research presented in this book:

- Territorial governance is a 'process' that is influenced by structural contexts and institutions. Nevertheless the study of territorial governance must be linked to how the process contributes to the achievement of a specific territorial goal.
- Territorial governance is a way of helping to define or reify new types of 'softer' or 'functional' territories. Thus it can potentially help to analytically 'unravel the territory' much in the same way that multi-level governance has helped to re-conceptualise and 'unravel the state' (cf. Hooghe and Marks 2003).
- Territorial governance concerns more flexible territorial arrangements, but also the interplay between informal networks and formalised jurisdictionally-bounded spaces. The potential complexity involved makes it important for actors and institutions to be adaptable and to consider the territorial pre-conditions that inform a specific policy or task.
- Territorial governance should be carefully distinguished from the governance of territories. The latter is inevitably there, in particular in regards to multi-level governance. However, the former offers, as will be further illustrated in Chapter 16, a high degree of sensitivity to 'how' territorial dynamics and challenges as well as prevailing perceptions and knowledge may feed into various processes within (multi-level) governance.
- Hence, territorial governance as a concept and a way of framing research is enriched by the additions of dimensions concerning adaptability and territorial specificities. Following up on Faludi's observation (2012), while the idea of territory may be implicit in studies of multi-level governance, the research presented here shall indicate that it should be made very explicit and tangible in analytical terms.

Territorial governance is the formulation and implementation of public policies, programmes and projects for the development* of a place/territory by

1)   co-ordinating actions of actors and institutions,

2)   integrating policy sectors,

3)   mobilising stakeholder participation,

4)   being adaptive to changing contexts,

5)   realising place-based/territorial specificities and impacts.

* We define development as the improvement in the efficiency, equality and environmental quality of a place/territory.

Figure 1.1 Defining territorial governance – 'five key dimensions'

Source: Own adaptation based on ESPON and Nordregio (2013, p. 8)

Conceptualising territorial governance: five dimensions

Based on the ten case studies presented in this book, we argue that territorial governance does matter for better comprehension of the role of territory and its dynamics, including its territorial knowledge and perception, in view of achieving a certain territorial goal. We assert that territorial governance is evolving as a new breed of 'animal', partly distinct from, yet bred from its forefathers: the concepts of 'regular' governance and 'multi-level' governance. To this end, we have established our own conceptual and operational definition of territorial governance. Based on a literature review, briefly summarised above, and extensive discussion and negotiation with the experts contributing to this book and the original research project upon which it is based (ESPON and Nordregio 2013), the definition of territorial governance presented in Figure 1.1 has been derived to further develop the analytical framework for the empirical research (cf. Chapters 4 and 5) as well as to synthesise, reflect and conclude upon the findings from the case studies (cf. Part III).

Outline of the book

Part I: exploring territorial governance pathways across Europe

After this introductory chapter, Stead and Pálné Kovács consider the territorial aspects of shifts in government and governance across Europe in Chapter 2. Many of these shifts are linked to the rescaling of government and its functions, often brought about either by reforms that affect the dominant decision-making level (or levels) at which different public policy issues are addressed and at which public services are delivered, or by shifts in the dominant actors involved in public policy formulation and delivery (e.g. as a result of the deregulation of service delivery). The chapter illustrates that although many of the shifts in governance and government are common to many countries, an increasing diversity, variation and even asymmetry of governance in Europe is apparent.

In Chapter 3, Faludi shows how the concept of territorial governance puts the very nature of the state into sharp relief. This chapter draws on international relations as well as geography and planning literature, challenging the exclusive responsibility of the state for its territory and its people. Where does this leave cherished forms of democratic legitimacy relying on territorially-defined constituencies? The chapter challengingly asks for re-imagining democratic legitimacy in non-territorial terms and problematises the notions of 'place' and 'territory'.

Chapter 4 switches the focus onto operationalising 'good' territorial governance. In this chapter, Davoudi and Cowie present an analytical framework and a number of qualitative indicators for guiding the assessments of territorial governance. The relevance and practicality of these indicators were tested and refined through a Delphi survey of a policy and practice expert panel from different European countries and subsequently used in the case studies in Part II. While being aware of the situated nature of governance practices, the framework and the indicators presented provide a useful guide for understanding and judging the quality of territorial governance, as shown by their utilisation in the case studies presented in this book.

Part II: territorial governance in practice: ten European cases

The second part of the book is devoted to the empirical investigation of territorial governance practices based on the framework discussed and outlined in Part I. The first chapter in Part II introduces the research methodology used to guide and conduct the case studies. In this chapter, Schmitt and Van Well recap how the selected case studies were conducted and reported so as to enable analysis and synthesis.

The ten cases in the book were carefully chosen in accordance with the size of their geographic scope – from the micro-local (neighbourhood) level to the transnational macro-regional level. They also represent different geographical areas of Europe and are representative of the commonly depicted spatial planning families of Europe – Nordic, British, Germanic, Napoleonic and Eastern European. The ten cases can be read as 'stand alone' empirical chapters, portraying how territorial governance processes have unfolded in a specific context. In this way, the individual chapters will be relevant for policy-makers and decision-makers who wish to benchmark their territorial governance processes against an example of a similar situation. On the other hand, the ten cases are structured and written according to the same case study methodology and analytical framework and thus have several comparable elements, making the collective cases interesting objects of study for academics and students.

Setting the stage 15

In Chapter 6, Hyper-local planning in England: territorial governance at the neighbourhood scale, Cowie, Vigar, Davoudi and Madanipour show how the 'Localism' agenda in England and Wales has opened up new opportunities for communities to undertake spatial planning at the neighbourhood scale. This hyper-local planning presents interesting territorial governance opportunities and challenges for neighbourhoods. These relate to the legitimacy of both the process and institutions involved. These challenges and opportunities are examined in detail and some conclusions drawn on the future of hyper-local territorial governance.

Pálné Kovács and Grünhut address how an overwhelmingly centralised governance context and the lack of social capital have challenged the implementation of the Pécs European Capital of Culture project in Chapter 7. The case of Pécs illustrates that the normative development interventions of the European Union which require effective multi-level cooperation, bottom-up logic, place-based spirit, and endogenous activities, cannot be applicable in member states as standardised models. Not just territorial governance as an approach matters, but the complex social, cultural, institutional specificities of each 'territory' are also essential.

Exploring territorial governance as resource efficient urban development in Stockholm in Chapter 8, Reardon and Schmitt look at both the city and project scale, zooming into the eco-district, Stockholm Royal Seaport. A lack of consistency between projects and interactions, coupled with an emphasis on marketisation are the most significant territorial governance challenges to greater resource efficiency. A silver lining is that Stockholm Royal Seaport demonstrates that the territorial governance capacity and competencies to achieve greater resource efficiency exist in Europe's first Green Capital. Readers will learn about Stockholm's territorial governance strengths and what to avoid in a quest for urban sustainability.

Chapter 9, by de Luca and Caruso describes the territorial governance process that led to the Territorial Cohesion Plan (Schéma de Coherence Territoriale, or SCOT) of South Loire in France. The authors highlight the strengths and weaknesses of this process following the main territorial governance dimensions. The chapter shows the complex process of territorial governance and highlights the importance of many effective operative tools, but also the sometimes problematic character of relationships among institutions.

Spaans and Stead, in Chapter 10, demonstrate how the Dutch Stedenbaan initiative in the southern Randstad aims to promote greater integration between public transport and urban development. The initiative primarily has a platform function where coordination and promotion activities for provincial and local politicians are central, utilising soft instruments and modes of governance. In this case, the development of a coherent, high-frequency public transport network is seen as an important prerequisite for increasing the competitiveness of the Netherlands.

16 *Lisa Van Well and Peter Schmitt*

Regional governance in the UK has been in a state of flux for a number of decades. Regional territorial governance institutions have come and gone over this period. In Chapter 11, Cowie, Madanipour, Davoudi and Vigar show how in spite of these difficulties Greater Manchester has managed to maintain a strong regional territorial governance capacity. This chapter outlines how they have done this and looks at some of the challenges for the future.

Chapter 12 by Mezei analyses the planning, institution building and partnership making processes of the Hungarian South Transdanubia region related to the management of Structural Funds in the 2007 to 2013 programme period. Due to the ongoing centralisation in Hungary. the regional stakeholders were insufficiently involved in the processes, The regional knowledge could not be utilised in an optimal manner as the regional interests and territorial specificities mostly were not represented in the Regional Operational Programme.

In Chapter 13, Zonneveld and Wandl chronicle the rise of a new territorial governance domain: flood management in the Rhine river basin. Over the course of years cooperation in relation to the Rhine river basin became dominated by water quantity issues especially after the (near) floods during the first half of the 1990s. This chapter deals with the results of cross-border cooperation through the German–Dutch Working Group on High Water. It shows how the activities of this Working Group can be interpreted as an implication of 'solidarity between people upstream and downstream'.

Chapter 14, by Peterlin and Simoneti, profiles the Trilateral Nature Park Goričko-Raab-Őrség, a cooperation structure in Slovenia, Hungary and Austria, aimed at coordinating protection and management of natural areas across national borders. The park currently operates as three separate parks, each following its own national policy system and governance culture. Joint projects, either trilateral or bilateral, are thus the main basis for effective governance. Park administrations informally coordinate applications for new joint projects in a way to further knowledge and experiences gained from previous projects, which is a key aspect of organisational learning in the trilateral nature park.

Finally in Chapter 15, Lange Scherbenske and Van Well argue that the exchange of 'best practices' and good examples of territorial governance processes for climate adaptation within a transnational context are helping actors to define and respond to their own particular problems and opportunities. The added value of climate change adaptation within the macro-regional strategy of the Baltic Sea Region is seen in providing a platform for exchange of technical and process-oriented knowledge and as a learning vehicle between actors working in different countries (transnational) and at different levels (e.g. local and national authorities).

Part III: prospects on territorial governance across Europe

The empirical cases in the book demonstrate that there is no 'one-size-fits-all' approach to territorial governance, but instead there is a set of opportunities for innovation in territorial governance practices at different levels/in different contexts. These opportunities are distilled as a number of components which then demonstrate how the territorial governance framework can inform the further methodological study of territorial governance in Chapter 16 by Schmitt and Van Well. This chapter is devoted to synthesising the case studies in order to provide a concise, but evidence-informed summary. It presents 20 distilled 'components of territorial governance' and critically revisits the robustness and validity of the five key dimensions of territorial governance (see Figure 1.1). It is argued that the concept of territorial governance, as defined and investigated in this volume, helps to capture knowledge-related and territorial/place-based elements, which would be otherwise neglected or even overlooked in other governance research frameworks.

Policy transfer is a complex issue, and further complexities emerge if territorial governance is the subject of transfer. In Chapter 17, Cotella, Janin Rivolin and Santangelo present a conceptual framework to understand the potentials for spreading 'features' of good territorial governance in Europe. It presents an analytical model suitable to identify 'paths and means' through which features of good territorial governance can pass from one place to another. To that end, a 'dialogic mode', an 'operational mode' and an 'institutional mode' for the transfer of good territorial governance in Europe are identified and discussed. Apart from purposes of practical application, the proposed model may cast further light on the nature of 'European' territorial governance as a continuous process based on articulated and interwoven forms of policy transfer between the EU and its member states.

In the concluding Chapter 18, Van Well, Davoudi, Janin Rivolin, Pálné Kovács and Schmitt explore the future prospects for how territorial governance can better inform spatial policy and planning on all levels. To this end the prospects will be discussed of how territorial governance can be facilitated not only at different levels, but also in different parts of Europe and various spatial planning and governmental systems. The chapter concludes with some ideas about territorial governance within future research programmes.

References

Barca, F., 2009. *An Agenda for a Reformed Cohesion Policy.* A Place-based Approach to Meeting European Union Challenges and Expectations. Independent Report Prepared at the Request of Danuta Hűbner, Commissioner for Regional Policy, Brussels: Directorate General for Regional Policy, European Commission. Available from http://ec.europa.eu/regional_policy/archive/policy/future/pdf/report_barca_v0306.pdf [Accessed 17 January 2015].

Buček, J. and Ryder, A. eds., 2015. *Governance in Transition*. Dordrecht: Springer,

CEC – Commission of the European Communities, 2001. *European Governance. A White Paper*, Communication from the Commission, COM (2001) 428, Brussels, 25 July.

CEC – Commission of the European Communities, 2008. *Green Paper on Territorial Cohesion: Turning Territorial Diversity into Strength*. Communication from the Commission to the Council, the European Parliament, the Committee of the Regions and the European Economic and Social Committee, COM (2008)616 final, Luxembourg: Office for Official Publications of the European Community.

CEMAT – European Conference of Ministers Responsible for Regional Planning, 2006. *Resolution no 2 on Territorial Governance: Empowerment Through Enhanced Coordination*. 14 CEMAT (2006) 13 Final. Strasbourg, France: Regional Planning and Technical Cooperation and Assistance Division, Council of Europe.

Davoudi, S., Evans, E., Governa, F. and Santangelo, M., 2008. Territorial governance in the making. Approaches, methodologies, practices. *Boletin de la A.G.E.N.*, 46, 33–52.

ESPON and Nordregio, 2013. ESPON TANGO – Territorial Approaches for New Governance. Final Report. Available from: http://www.espon.eu/export/sites/default/Documents/Projects/AppliedResearch/TANGO/FR/ESPON_TANGO_Main_Report_Final.pdf [Accessed 20 April 2015].

Faludi, A., 2012. Multi-level (Territorial) governance: Three criticisms. *Planning Theory & Practice*, 13 (2), 197–211.

Giddens, A., 2005. The world does not owe us a living! *Progressive Politics*, 4 (3), 6–12.

Gualini, E., 2008. 'Territorial cohesion' as a category of agency: the missing dimension in the EU spatial policy debate. *European Journal of Spatial Development*, Refereed Articles 28, Available from: http://www.nordregio.se/EJSD/refereed28.pdf [Accessed 18 January 2015].

Gupta, J., Termeer, C., Klostermann, J., Meijerink, S., van den Brink, M., Jong, P., Nooteboom, S. and Bergsma, E., 2010. The Adaptive Capacity Wheel: a method to assess the inherent characteristics of institutions to enable the adaptive capacity of society. *Environmental Science & Policy*, 13 (6), 459–471.

Harrison, J., 2013. 'Configuring the new 'regional world': On being caught between territory and networks. *Regional Studies*, 47 (1), 55–74.

Healey P., 1997. *Collaborative Planning: Shaping Places in Fragmented Societies*. London: Macmillan.

Healey, P., 2010. *Making Better Places*. Basingstoke: Palgrave Macmillan.

Hooghe, L. and Marks, G., 2001. *Multi-level Governance and European Integration*. Lanham MD: Rowman & Littlefield.

Hooghe, L. and Marks, G., 2003. Unraveling the central state, but how? Types of multi-level governance. *The American Political Science Review*, 97 (2), 233–243.

Hooghe, L. and Marks, G., 2010. Types of multi-level governance. In: H. Enderlein, S. Wälti and M. Zürn, eds. *Types of Multilevel Governance*. Cheltenham: Elgar, 17–31.

Hooper, B. and Kramsch, O., 2004. *Cross-Border Governance in the European Union*. New York: Routledge.

Jessop B., 1997. The entrepreneurial city: re-imaging localities, redesigning economic governance or restructuring capital. In: N. Jewson and S. Mc Gregor, eds. *Transforming Cities. Contested Governance and New Spatial divisions*. London: Routledge, 28–41.

Jordan, A., 2008. The governance of sustainable development: taking stock and looking forwards. *Environment and Planning C: Government and Policy*, 26 (1), 17–33.

Kern, K. and Bulkeley, H., 2009. Cities, Europeanization and multi-level governance: governing climate change through transnational municipal networks. *Journal of Common Market Studies*, 47 (2), 309–332.

Kooiman, J., 2003. *Governing as Governance*. London: Sage.

Lefebvre, H., 1991. *The Production of Space*. Oxford: Blackwell.

Lidström, A., (2007) Territorial governance in transition, *Regional and Federal Studies*, 17 (4), 499–508.

Marks, G., 1993. Structural policy and multi-level governance in the EC. In: A. Cafruny and G. Rosenthall, eds. *State of European Community*. Boulder, CO: Lynne Rienner, 391–410.

Maru, Y., 2010. *Resilient Regions: Clarity of Concepts and Challenges to Systemic Measurement*. Working Paper Series from CSIRO Sustainable Ecosystems, No. 2010-04, Socio-Economics and the Environment in Discussion, Available from: http://core.ac.uk/download/pdf/6616696.pdf [Accessed 26 March 2015].

Ministers of Urban Development and Territorial Cohesion of the European Union, 2007. Territorial State and Perspective of the European Union: Toward a Stronger European Territorial Cohesion in the Light of the Lisbon and Gothenburg Ambitions. Based on the Scoping Document Discussed by Ministers at Their Informal Ministerial Meeting in Luxembourg in May 2005 – A Background Document for the Territorial Agenda of the European Union. Available from http://www.eu-territorial-agenda.eu/Reference%20Documents/The-Territorial-State-and-Perspectives-of-the-European-Union.pdf [Accessed 17 January 2015].

Ministers of Urban Development and Territorial Cohesion of the European Union, 2011. *Territorial Agenda of the European Union 2020: Towards an Inclusive, Smart and Sustainable Europe of Diverse Regions*. Agreed at the Informal Ministerial Meeting of Ministers responsible for Spatial Planning and Territorial Development on 19 May 2011 Gödöllő, Hungary. Available from http://www.eu-territorial-agenda.eu/Reference%20Documents/Final%20TA2020.pdf [Accessed 17 January 2015].

NTCCP – Network of Territorial Cohesion Contact Points, 2013. *Place-based Territorially Sensitive and Integrated Approach*. Ministry of Regional Development, Warsaw, Poland.

Nuissl, H. and Heinrichs, D., 2011. Fresh wind or hot air – does the governance discourse have something to offer spatial planning? *Journal of Planning Education and Research*, 31 (1), 47–59.

OECD – Organisation for Economic Co-operation and Development, 2001. *OECD Territorial Outlook*. 2001 Edition. Paris: OECD.

Painter J. and Goodwin, M., 1995. Local governance and concrete research: investigating the uneven development of regulation, *Economy and Society*, 24 (3), 334–356.

Paraskevopoulos C., Getimis, P. and Rees N., eds., 2006. *Adapting EU Multi-level Governance: Regional and Environmental Policies in Cohesion and CEE Countries*. Aldershot: Ashgate.

Pierre J., 2000. Understanding Governance. In: J. Pierre, ed. *Debating Governance. Authority, Steering, and Democracy*. Oxford: Oxford University Press, 1–10.

Pierre, J. and Peters, B., 2000. *Governance, Politics and the State*. Basingstoke: Macmillan.

20 *Lisa Van Well and Peter Schmitt*

Pradhan, P.K., Buček, J, and Razin, E., 2013. *Geography of Governance: Dynamics for Local Development.* International Geographical Union Commission on Geography of Governance. Available from: http://www.igu-gog.org/download/Pradhan_Bucek_Razin.pdf [Accessed 12 April 2015].

Salet, W., Thornley, A. and Kreukels, A. 2003. *Metropolitan Governance and Spatial Planning. Comparative Case Studies of European City-Regions.* London: Spon Press.

Stead, D., 2014. The rise of territorial governance in European policy. *European Planning Studies,* 22 (7), 1368–1383.

Stephenson, P., 2013. Twenty years of multi-level governance: 'Where does it come from? What is it? Where is it going?' *Journal of European Public Policy,* 20 (6), 817–837.

Stoker, G., 1998. Governance as theory: five propositions. *International Social Science Journal,* 50 (155), 17–18.

Stoker G., 2000. Urban political science and the challenge of urban governance. In: J. Pierre, ed. *Debating Governance. Authority, Steering, and Democracy.* Oxford: Oxford University Press, 91–109.

Van Kersgergen, K. and Van Waarden, F., 2004. ´Governance´ as a bridge between disciplines: cross-disciplinary inspiration regarding shifts in governance and problems of governability, accountability and legitimacy. *European Journal of Political Research,* 43 (2), 143–171.

2 Shifts in governance and government across Europe

Dominic Stead and Ilona Pálné Kovács

Introduction

The governance of territories is closely linked to the quality of democracy and public services. For this reason, various attempts have been made to reform governance arrangements in order to increase the effectiveness and quality of government policy. Recent decades in particular have witnessed key changes in the governance of territories across Europe and beyond. Many of these changes, although certainly not all of them, are linked to the rescaling of government and its functions (OECD 2001, Lidström 2007, Loughlin 2007). In some cases, policy responsibilities, sometimes together with revenue-raising capacities (but not always), have shifted downwards from central to sub-national government. In other cases, powers and responsibilities have shifted upwards to the supra-national level. Both of these directions of change (i.e. upwards and downwards) have had significant impacts for governance arrangements in Europe's member states. Not only have specific tasks been re-allocated to different agencies and revenue allocations reformed, a wider range of actors, both governmental and non-governmental (including the voluntary and private sector), have become involved in territorial governance arrangements. A number of other key features are associated with these new governance arrangements, including new cooperation arrangements between government bodies, more public participation in decision-making and greater emphasis on partnerships and contracts.

Formal mechanisms of horizontal and vertical cooperation between governmental bodies and partnerships with non-governmental actors have become more commonplace. Government authorities have become increasingly interlinked and networked with each other, as well as with other levels of government, social partners and NGOs. At the same time, new spatial structures for territorial governance (e.g. inter-communal frameworks, regional platforms, territorial pacts) have been created in order to promote policy coordination between sub-national authorities, more coherent allocation of public resources across territories, and greater transparency of resource use (Lidström 2007).

The role of citizen participation has increased over recent decades. In part, this has been in response to criticisms that public administration in the past was often distant and poorly adapted to the needs of local and regional constituencies. As a result, there has been a growth in initiatives to involve representatives of local and regional communities and interest groups in order to increase the responsiveness of public policy delivery. These include initiatives designed to promote empowerment, associative democracy and stakeholder democracy. Today, these types of bottom-up approaches are increasingly rooted in territorial governance in most countries in Europe although they have rarely delivered the kind of balanced, participative and inclusive governance that they sought to achieve.

The importance of negotiation and contract has grown in establishing new governance structures and in transforming existing structures. This trend is rooted in the notion that cooperation between levels of decision-making can help to provide a better assessment of relative need and allocate resources more effectively and accountably. Contracts are not only being used as a way of formalising cooperation arrangements between actors, but are also being used as management tools to promote and monitor the efficiency and quality of service provision.

Although territorial governance is generally evolving in response to common societal challenges (such as sustainable development, climate change, social exclusion, territorial cohesion and competiveness), the responses to these challenges have been far from homogeneous across Europe's member states. The diversity of the governance of territories in Europe is still very much apparent and seems unlikely to disappear since it is rooted in the specific histories and geographies of particular places, and the way these interlock with national institutional structures, cultures and economic opportunities (see also Healey and Williams 1993). While changes in the governance of territories are increasingly being influenced by European policy, national and sub-national communities of actors still play a crucial role in shaping its nature and form (Stead 2013, Stead and Cotella 2011).

In examining the shifts in governance and government (primarily in Europe), this chapter is structured in five main parts. It begins by considering the notion of rescaling, both upwards and downwards, in relation these shifts. Second, it identifies a number of key contemporary trends in the governance of territories and government. Third, it looks specifically at the impacts of European integration on the rescaling of governance. Fourth, the specific impacts of these shifts in governance for countries in Eastern and Central Europe are considered. The fifth and final part of the chapter contains our conclusions.

Rescaling government and governance

European integration is creating new territorial boundaries for various policy fields whereby nation-states are losing their old monopolies on some areas of policy-making. However, this does not mean that powers are simply shifting to the European level: Europe is not so much suppressing state borders as changing their meaning and impact for different social, economic and political systems (Bartolini 2005, Keating 2009). European integration has not only been accompanied by changes in powers across existing layers of decision-making but also by new scales of intervention, new actor constellations, and new geometries of governance (Jessop 2005, Lidström 2007). These changes are all part of the general process of the rescaling of governance, which McCann (2003, p. 162) defines in terms of

> the process in which policies and politics that formerly took place at one scale are shifted to others in ways that reshape the practices themselves, redefine the scales to and from which they are shifted, and reorganise interactions between scales.

Various trends in the rescaling of government and governance (both upwards and downwards) can be found across Europe (Keating 2009). These rescaling processes are producing new policy spaces which vary in their configuration according to their functional or political logic. In these new spaces, there may be little coincidence between functional, political and institutional boundaries, and there may be no strict hierarchies of collective action. The result is that these new spaces are often contested, since the level at which issues are managed can, by including certain actors and excluding others, affect policy outcomes (ibid.). The contested nature of these new spaces is reflected in geographical studies on the politics of scale, processes of rescaling and impacts on the distribution of power (see for example Baldersheim and Rose 2010, Herod and Wright 2002, Loughlin *et al.* 2010, Keil and Mahon 2008, Sheppard and McMaster 2004). These studies illustrate how actors gain or lose influence as a result of authority being reconfigured around new spaces and territories.

The ideal construct of the nation-state with a fixed set of policy boundaries and a perfectly hierarchical structure is being eroded by processes of rescaling and the emergence of new boundaries above and below the national level, as well as transnational spaces cutting across the state system (Keating 2009). Some of the roles or tasks of the nation-state are being transferred to these new spaces, where different actors, agendas and resources prevail (ibid.). Rescaling is arguably leading to broader and more inclusive processes but is on the other hand contributing to more fragmented and differentiated approaches as different groups participate in different contexts, according to their interests (Meadowcroft 2002). Processes of rescaling are by no means leading to uniform changes across different territories: substantial variations in the nature of new territorial spaces are apparent across Europe but, whatever their form is, these new policy spaces and territories pose significant challenges for democratic legitimacy and social equity (Keating 2009, Moss and Newig 2010). Moreover, new governance arrangements, new scales of interaction and/or new actor constellations resulting from rescaling are not always more participatory or more integrated or better able to respond to complex problems involving different policy sectors (Cohen 2012).

The emergence of *soft spaces* – multi-area regions in which spatial strategy is being made between or alongside formal institutions and processes – is a phenomenon associated with contemporary processes of rescaling. According to Haughton and Allmendinger (2007, p. 306), these soft spaces are

> 'fluid areas [...] between formal processes where implementation through bargaining, flexibility, discretion and interpretation dominate' in contrast to 'hard spaces' that are 'formal visible arenas and processes, often statutory and open to democratic processes and local political influence (ibid.).

Also associated with recent processes of the rescaling of governance is the use of 'fuzzy boundaries', which, as Allmendinger and Haughton (2009, p. 619) argue, functions, as a means of breaking away from 'the shackles of pre-existing working patterns which might be variously held to be slow, bureaucratic, or not reflecting the real geographies of problems and opportunities'. On the one hand this trend can be considered to represent a more place-based approach to planning – responding to the territorial specificities of particular places. On the other it can be seen as a form of neoliberalism – trying to shortcut democratic processes that may be considered as inefficient (Haughton *et al.* 2009).

Waterhout (2010) contends that many examples of *soft spaces* can already be found across much of Europe, citing French *Projets du Territoire*, German Überregionale Partnerschaften and Italian *Sistemi Macroregionali Funzionali* as examples at the sub-national scale, and initiatives in the Saar-Lor-Lux (Saarland, Lorraine, Luxembourg), Basel Eurodistrict, Øresund and Vienna-Bratislava-Gyor regions as cross-border examples. In many cases, governments are not the main initiator or the leading actor behind the strategies. Instead, they primarily play a role in promoting and coordinating public and private initiatives that are concerned with either fostering or managing spatial development. This form of territorial governance with less state involvement represents a break from traditional government-led approaches and an attempt to establish cooperative arrangements and delivery mechanisms for promoting and/or managing spatial development via the public and private sector. The implementation of European strategies for territorial cooperation can also be seen as another scale of planning in soft spaces (Metzger and Schmitt 2011, Faludi 2012). Gualini (2006) observes that many areas of experimental or informal governance are characterised by *ad hoc*, problem-oriented forms of governance through partnerships and policy exchange, and based on loose forms of institutionalisation. These new types of governance often overlap established jurisdictions and can even encompass non-contiguous territories (e.g. via networks of actors concerned with specific issues/problems or types of territories).

More generally, it is argued that these new areas of soft spaces often better reflect the geographies of problems or potentials than areas defined by 'hard' administrative boundaries. The distinction between hard and soft spaces is closely related to the two different forms of multi-level governance set out by Hooghe and Marks (2003) and the distinction between Euclidean and relational planning discussed by authors such as Friedman (1993) and Healey (2006). The governance of hard spaces often closely resembles Euclidean planning or Type I multi-level governance as defined by Hooghe and Marks (2003) (see Table 1.1), where decision-making takes place in uniform, general-purpose, nested administrative units. Governance of soft spaces on the other hand more closely resembles relational planning or Type II multi-level governance as defined by Hooghe and Marks (2003), where decision-making occurs in flexible, functionally-defined, overlapping decision spaces. While soft spaces offer a more functional or relational approach to decision-making, they pose significant problems of accountability and responsibility (see for example Keating 2009, Faludi 2012 and the discussion in Chapter 3) and may exacerbate problems of sectoral integration (Cohen 2012).

Key trends in governance and government across Europe

Building on the work of Lidström (2007) and Fürst (2009), a number of closely interlinked contemporary trends across Europe can be identified. These trends are summarised below under five sub-headings: (i) redefining of the role of the nation-state; (ii) the strengthening of lower levels of self-government; (iii) increasing diversity, variation and even asymmetry of governance; (iv) increasing marketisation of the public domain; and (v) shifting rationales for intervention.

Redefining of the role of the nation-state

The establishment and gradual expansion of the EU has limited the role of national borders and transferred decision-making powers to supra-national bodies. According to Loughlin (2007), actors such as the Council of Europe and the European Union have been instrumental in strengthening the trend towards greater political decentralisation in Europe: the former via initiatives such as the European Charter of Local Self-Government, adopted in 1985; the latter via European regional policy, primarily through the Structural Funds and Cohesion Funds, whose resources were substantially increased in the mid-1980s, leading to the establishment of new regional bodies (or the strengthening of existing bodies) in various countries (e.g. Greece, Ireland) to administer European regional policy resources (see below). At the same time, territorial management and planning approaches in member states are being increasingly shaped by European policies and initiatives (e.g. structural fund rules, environmental management and nature protection directives). This in turn has impacts on the procedures and practices of territorial governance (Dühr *et al.* 2007). Meanwhile, the role of the nation-state has been challenged from inside in some cases where demands for separatism or self-government have been made, motivated by regional culture or identity arguments (e.g. Belgium, Spain, the UK).

Strengthening lower levels of self-government

In many European countries, examples can be found where functions have been decentralised from central government to local and regional levels of government. In some countries, this has happened as a result of the reorganisation of sub-national government, either by amalgamating municipalities or regions, or by creating new regional levels of self-government. Reforms in sub-national government have been enacted in various countries (e.g. Greece and Denmark) where comprehensive reforms of the whole structure of local and regional government have taken place, including amalgamations of municipalities and regions, and the transfer of functions between different levels of government (see for example Galland and Enemark 2013). In some cases, however, reforms to government structures and competences have not always been accompanied by corresponding shifts in funding allocations for a variety of reasons including the political difficulties or complexities of fiscal reforms (Maier 1998, OECD 2001). Sub-national governments have become increasingly linked, both nationally and internationally, via organisations representing regional and local authorities across a variety of themes and arenas (such as United Cities and Local Governments, Council of European Municipalities and Regions, Eurocities, Eurotowns). However, the claim that sub-national levels of government are gaining power is not unchallenged. There are also tendencies of upward rescaling (powers shifting to the supra-national level) and recentralisation. EU institutions are now taking decisions that were previously national matters, which limit the scope for municipalities and regions. Centralisation of national policies is also occurring in some cases. Feltenius (2007), for example, describes how government reforms in Sweden have led to the decentralisation of powers in certain policy areas at the same time as greater centralisation in other policy areas.

Shifts in governance and government across Europe 27

Increasing diversity, variation and even asymmetry of governance and government

This tendency towards diversity can be seen as the result of empowerment of lower levels of government. Not only is the scope for variation between sub-national units greater, some units are also permitted to follow their own paths that may differ from the general national pattern. Various types of asymmetry can be distinguished: political, administrative and fiscal (Loughlin 2007). The 'special' and 'ordinary' regions in Italy provide one example of political asymmetry and diversity within a state. Different forms of territorial administration within the UK provide one example of administrative and fiscal asymmetries, where the three territorial offices representing Scotland, Wales and Northern Ireland have distinct relations and arrangements with London. Meanwhile, in Spain, the Basque Country and Navarre have more financial (and legal) autonomy than the rest of the country, and exhibit fiscal asymmetry. One of the arguments used to support the existence (and/or the creation) of diversity and asymmetry of territorial governance within nation-states is the need to respond to specific local/regional conditions (adopting a more 'place-based' approach), where sub-regional governments are given more autonomy to shape policies according to their own circumstances (e.g. culture, economy). Policy experiments can also contribute to more asymmetrical governance arrangements. In Sweden, for example, the regions of Skåne and Västra Götaland, which were established on an experimental basis in 1999 and made permanent in 2011, are divergent from other Swedish counties in several respects: they are not only larger in size and population than most other counties, they also have additional responsibilities for regional development that other counties do not have (Feltenius 2007, Stegmann McCallion 2014). Following this development, a further regional governance entity, the region of Östergötland, was established on 1 January 2015.

Increasing marketisation of the public domain

The increased involvement of non-state actors (including the private sector) is one of the central dimensions of the shifts from government to governance (see for example Kooiman 1993). Many functions that were seen as typical public responsibilities during the peak of the welfare state era (when government rather than governance prevailed) have more recently either been privatised or are run jointly by public and private providers. Public organisations are increasingly taking an 'enabling' role where other actors are the providers of public services. In many countries, the welfare state has been reconfigured in ways that makes it less centralised and less redistributive, and more oriented to promoting the role of the market. Outsourcing is one of the ways in which non-state actors (including private and non-profit) are increasingly involved in delivering goods and/or services, a trend closely associated with the emergence of new public management. Over recent years, the amount of outsourcing has increased significantly across most countries: government spending on outsourcing typically amounts to more than 10 per cent of the total Gross Domestic Product in many European countries (OECD 2011). In general, there has been a wider acceptance of liberal economic systems, with more reliance on market-oriented solutions, private investment, and increasing competition between cities. These trends have had profound territorial effects, including increasing the polarisation of economic disparities with concentration of services, education and know-how in favoured metropolitan regions and increased social and economic segregation within cities (see also Kunzmann 2008).

Shifting rationales for intervention

Territorial governance is being redefined in the light of important societal challenges, new powers and responsibilities (see above) and new attempts to increase the societal relevance of planning. Across Europe, territorial governance is being recast as a way of managing the increasing interdependencies of actors involved in territorial development (Stead and Meijers 2009). New forms of participative governance are being introduced and promoted as a way of strengthening local influence over sub-national policy-making and promoting a more 'place-based' approach (according to the rhetoric at least, see also Chapter 1). Globalisation is another challenge that new forms of governance attempt to address. Because the competition for various goods and services often extends well beyond national boundaries, the pressure to introduce governance reforms to respond to these challenges has increased. Moreover, the internationalisation of trade, education and communication is also contributing to shifts in the way in which territorial governance is practised and conceptualised.

Rescaling in the light of European Cohesion Policy

As mentioned above, recent governance reforms in Europe have been influenced by a range of societal challenges. According to Sykes (2008), these reforms have been accentuated by the general processes of European integration. In this regard, European Cohesion Policy – the European Union's regional policy – has been a key driver of change. From the 1970s, the EU's regional policy budget grew steadily in size and importance in the European Union for a period of around two decades, and now represents a third of the EU-budget (Allen 2010). In order to utilise and manage these funds, member states of the European Union were required to adapt existing institutional structures and/or create new ones. EU Cohesion Policy demanded increasing public involvement in economic development, closer links to the business sector and new market-oriented systems of economic support. It also required new arrangements for cooperation between different sectors and

Shifts in governance and government across Europe 29

tiers of government. As a result, the 1980s and 1990s witnessed various decentralisation and regionalisation reforms in many member states (Larsson *et al.* 1999). Preparations for the 2004 and 2007 accession waves also meant that similar processes took place in Eastern and Central European countries in the late 1990s and early 2000s (see for example Chapter 12).

New administrative arrangements

The advent of EU Cohesion Policy led to the creation of development agencies across Europe. These new institutional structures presented a challenge for many member states in terms of administrative arrangements, new programming procedures and new coordination mechanisms. In many countries, quasi-governmental or non-governmental tripartite/corporate organisations (e.g. councils, assemblies, chambers, fora) were set up, specifically designed for the preparation and implementation of regional policy decisions and for the harmonisation of interests of the central state, local governments, NGOs and citizens.

By introducing different categories of development objectives in EU regional policy, national governments were required to designate eligible areas at the regional level. This process led to a series of reforms in the territorial structure of the meso-tier governance and the establishment of new, larger administrative tiers or the amalgamation of old ones. As such, the Structural Funds were an important accelerator of change to territorial governance in Europe (Keating 1998).

New cooperation and partnership mechanisms

Since 1988, decisions about the operational programmes for EU regional policy have been taken in partnership between the European Commission, member states, regional organisations, other public bodies and non-governmental organisations (Allen 2010). Commentators are divided about the effects of these joint programming arrangements. Some argue that these arrangements have facilitated substantial regional and local government involvement in the policy process, and have resulted in a shift of power away from the national level (ibid.). Others however argue that the involvement of different parties in joint programming has mainly been symbolic and has not led to any real shifts of power away from the national level (Hughes *et al.* 2004). In some cases, it is argued, states were able to control, manipulate or cooperate with newly enfranchised sub-national actors in order to consolidate, rather than weaken, their central authority (ibid.). Irrespective of the extent of power shifts that have (or have not) taken place, the principle of partnership posed challenges to the national public administrative systems, especially for those models that lacked a tradition of cooperation between different governmental tiers or sectors (see also Chapter 12). According to Kelleher *et al.* (1999), the

30 Dominic Stead and Ilona Pálné Kovács

introduction of the partnership principle resulted in diverse and varyingly efficient solutions across EU member states. More generally, a diversity of public administrative arrangements is still very much apparent in European member states despite all the administrative reforms that have taken place over recent years. These changes – both in Eastern and in Western Europe – were partly related to political transformations and partly to the socio-economic and political development within national frameworks.

Specific challenges in Eastern and Central Europe

Significant changes in governance occurred in the new Eastern and Central European democracies during the period of post-socialism and pre-accession. First, they had to establish a democratic state and a new political system. The new democracies, hoping for accession to the European Union, were keen to identify a suitable state institutional model to match the requirements of the *acquis communautaire* within the EU. However, the general governance model from Western democracies did not generally fit with local needs and conditions.

For some countries, such as the Baltic States of Estonia, Latvia and Lithuania, entirely new institutional, economic and political systems were required (Downes 1996). Progress has been made since the late 1990s in overhauling planning legislation and institutional structures but many countries and regions are still in the process of developing transparent, accountable decision-making processes and clear political leadership at the urban and regional levels. The implementation of governance reforms, often involving decentralisation, was often driven by internal political demands and the requirements of pre-accession EU regional policy funding (Pallagst and Mercier 2007) although the driving force of regionalisation was not exclusively linked to Structural Funds: in some cases, it was also motivated by cultural and historical differences and/or efficiency arguments.

Many candidate Eastern and Central European countries preparing for accession were convinced that 'regions matter' (Pálné Kovács 2014). Even though national governments were given relatively wide scope by Brussels for deciding on suitable governance arrangements to administer regional policy, many new member states did not make full use of this scope. For example, the new Nomenclature of Territorial Units for Statistics, which are instrumental in the European Union's Structural Fund delivery mechanisms, became the territorial basis of public administrative reforms in most Central and Eastern European countries (here in particular regarding the NUTS 2 level). Had this strict territorial requirement of the EU not existed, other territorial sub-divisions may have been more rational in terms of functional relationships.

The dramatic economic and political changes in Eastern and Central Europe since 1990 have had far-reaching consequences for spatial development and the institutional arrangements that were meant to guide them (Altrock *et al.* 2006, Stanilov 2007). Entry into the Single Market enhanced the prosperity of regions close to the west, but it also reinforced competition and helped lead to massive restructuring of both urban and rural economies. New member states enjoyed some economic growth (although from a very low baseline and concentrated in a few main cities) but unemployment rates remained generally higher than in the old member states. While there is some evidence of economic convergence at European level, there is often increasing divergence within member states, especially in Central and Eastern Europe (CEC 2007, Ezcurra *et al.* 2007). Interregional spatial inequalities deepened during the crisis which presented a serious challenge for EU Cohesion Policy and national spatial policies. In the Central and Eastern European countries, national goals for competitiveness are often in conflict with European cohesion goals, particularly since the economic crisis (Márkusné Zsibók 2013).

A further difficulty was that new member states, with their distinct administrative cultures and strong histories of centralisation, were unfamiliar with certain styles of governance in Western Europe. For example, the logic of *new public management*, prominent in Western Europe at the time of pre-accession, was alien to most Eastern and Central European countries. In most cases, countries formulated and established their territorial public administration parallel to the institutions of the regional support system of the European Union. However, the two systems were not always harmonised. Organisational cultures often remained unchanged, and structural reforms were only partial. As a result, reforms led to some changes to institutional structures but not often to shifts in the values, attitudes and ways of working of civil servants (Lazareviciute and Verheijen 2000).

Conclusions

Over recent decades European governance and government has undergone significant transformations (both structural and functional) and will undoubtedly continue to do so in the future. Various trends are shared by many countries across Europe. These include the redefinition of the role of the nation-state, the strengthening of lower levels of self-government, increasing diversity, variation and even asymmetry of governance, increasing marketisation of the public domain, and shifting rationales for intervention. There is however much variation in the timing and extent to which these trends have occurred within the countries. Over the last two decades, sub-national governments in most European countries have gained responsibilities and power. The share of sub-national expenditure has grown as a proportion of total government expenditure but sub-national governments remain highly dependent on central government. More recently, there are signs of new governance models emerging in some European countries (e.g. Hungary, Bulgaria and Romania), partly as a result of the recent economic crisis and the accompanying social tensions, which are moving away from neoliberal models of governance towards greater bureaucracy and centralisation of governments (Pálné Kovács 2014). Clearly, all of these trends have implications for the above described rescaling processes, both upwards and downwards. Rescaling has not only meant shifts in powers across existing layers of decision-making but also the creation of new scales of intervention, new actor constellations, and new geometries of governance. Rescaling is sometimes associated with the emergence of soft spaces – multi-area regions in which spatial strategy is being made between or alongside formal institutions and processes.

The modernisation of national public administrations and local governments has frequently been led by structural reforms in Europe during the last decades. Cohesion Policy has been a key driver of change in territorial governance. Many of these policies involve multi-level governance constructions which bring together the European Commission, national states, local and regional authorities and a variety of non-governmental agencies. This has necessitated new institutional arrangements for policy development and implementation. A key aim of Cohesion Policy funding has been to encourage member states to increase national and sub-national expenditure on regional policy and to stimulate private-sector involvement in certain projects. More recently, however, particularly since the financial crisis, co-funding from the private sector and national and sub-national government has become increasingly difficult, especially in much of Eastern and Central Europe. In many cases, states are increasingly unwilling or unable to match EU-funding. Partly because of this, the convergence of economic development among regions remains limited. While disparities between EU countries have reduced over the past 20 years, regional differences have not. Regional differences in economic growth within some countries are substantial and show few signs of convergence.

References

Allen, D., 2010. The Structural Funds and Cohesion Policy. Extending the bargain to meet new challenges. In: M.A. Pollack, H. Wallace and A.R. Young, eds. *Policy-making in the European Union*. 6th ed. Oxford: Oxford University Press, 229–252.

Allmendinger, P. and Haughton, G., 2009. Soft spaces, fuzzy boundaries and metagovernance: the new spatial planning in the Thames Gateway. *Environment and Planning A* 41 (3), 617–633.

Altrock, U., Günter, S., Huning, S. and Peters, D., eds., 2006. *Spatial Planning and Urban Development in the New Member States: From Adjustment to Reinvention*. Aldershot: Gower.

Baldersheim, H. and Rose, E.L., eds., 2010. *Territorial Choice. The Politics of Boundaries and Borders*. Houndmills: Palgrave Macmillan.

Bartolini, S., 2005. *Restructuring Europe*. Oxford: Oxford University Press.

CEC – Commission of the European Communities, 2007. *Growing Regions, Growing Europe: Fourth Report on Economic and Social Cohesion*. Luxembourg: Office for Official Publications of the European Communities.

Cohen, A., 2012. Rescaling environmental governance: watersheds as boundary objects at the intersection of science, neoliberalism, and participation. *Environment and Planning A*, 44 (9), 2207–2224.

Downes, R., 1996. Regional policy development in Central and Eastern Europe. In: J. Alden and P. Boland, eds. *Regional Development Strategies: A European Perspective.* London: Jessica Kingsley and Regional Studies Association, 256–272.

Dühr, S., Stead, D., and Zonneveld, W., 2007. The Europeanization of spatial planning through territorial cooperation. *Planning Practice and Research*, 22 (3), 291–307.

Ezcurra, R., Pascual, P., and Rapun, M., 2007. The dynamics of regional disparities in Central and Eastern Europe during transition. *European Planning Studies*, 15 (10), 1397–421.

Faludi, A., 2012. Multi-level (territorial) governance: three criticisms. *Planning Theory and Practice*, 13 (2), 197–211.

Feltenius, D., 2007. Relations between central and local government in Sweden during the 1990s: mixed patterns of centralization and decentralization. *Regional and Federal Studies*, 17 (4), 457–474.

Friedmann, J., 1993. Toward a non-Euclidian mode of planning. *Journal of the American Planning Association*, 59 (4) 482–485.

Fürst, D., 2009. Planning cultures en route to a better comprehension of 'planning processes'? In: J. Knieling and F. Othengrafen eds. *Planning Cultures in Europe: Decoding Cultural Phenomena in Urban and Regional Planning*. Farnham: Ashgate, 23–38.

Galland, D. and Enemark, S., 2013. Impact of structural reforms on planning systems and policies: loss of spatial consciousness? *European Journal of Spatial Development*, Refereed article No. 52. Available from: http://www.nordregio.se/Global/EJSD/ Refereed articles/refereed 52.pdf [Accessed 16 April 2015].

Gualini, E., 2006. The rescaling of governance in Europe: new spatial and institutional rationales. *European Planning Studies*, 14 (7), 881–904.

Haughton, G. and Allmendinger, P. (2007). Soft spaces in planning. *Town and Country Planning*, 76 (9), 306–308.

Haughton, G., Allmendinger, P., Counsell, D. and Vigar, G., 2009. *The New Spatial Planning: Territorial Management with Soft Spaces and Fuzzy Boundaries*. London: Routledge.

Healey, P., 2006. Relational complexity and the imaginative power of strategic spatial planning. *European Planning Studies*, 14 (4), 525–546.

Healey, P. and Williams, R.H., 1993. European planning systems: diversity and convergence. *Urban Studies*, 30 (3/4), 701–720.

Herod, A. and Wright, M., eds., 2002. *Geographies of Power: Placing Scale*. Oxford: Oxford University Press.

Hooghe, L. and Marks, G., 2003. Unraveling the central state, but how? Types of multi-level governance. *American Political Science Review*, 97 (2), 233–243.

Hughes, J., Sasse, G. and Gordon, C., 2004. *Europeanization and Regionalization in the EU's Enlargement to Central and Eastern Europe: The Myth of Conditionality*. London: Palgrave.

Jessop, B., 2005. Multi-level governance and multi-level meta-governance. In: F. Kratochwil, and E. Mansfield., eds. *International Organisation and Global Governance: A Reader*. London: Pearson Longman, 355–367.

Keating, M., 1998. *The New Regionalism in Western Europe: Territorial Restructuring and Political Change*. Cheltenham: Edward Elgar.

Keating, M., 2009. Rescaling Europe. *Perspectives on European Politics and Society,* 10 (1), 34–50.

Keil, R. and Mahon, R., eds., 2008. *Leviathan Undone? The Political Economy of Scale.* Vancouver: University of British Columbia Press.

Kelleher, J., Batterbury, S. and Stern, E., 1999. *The Thematic Evaluation of the Partnership Principle: Final Synthesis Report.* Evaluation Development and Review Unit, London: The Tavistock Institute.

Kooiman, J., ed., 1993. *Modern Governance: New Government-Society Interactions.* London: Sage.

Kunzmann, K., 2008. Futures for European space 2020. *Journal of Nordregio,* 8 (2), 12–21.

Larsson, T., Nomden, K. and Petiteville, F., eds., 1999. *The Intermediate Level of Government in European States: Complexity versus Democracy?* Maastricht: European Institute of Public Administration Report.

Lazareviciute, I. and Verheijen, T., 2000. Efficient and effective government. In: G. Péteri and O. Simek, eds. *European Union Enlargement and the Open Society Agenda. Local Government and Public Administration.* Budapest: Local Government and Public Service Reform Initiative, Open Society Institute, 149–163.

Lidström, A., 2007. Territorial governance in transition. *Regional and Federal Studies,* 17 (4), 499–508.

Loughlin, J., 2001. *Subnational Democracy in the European Union: Challenges and Opportunities.* Oxford: Oxford University Press.

Loughlin, J., 2007. Reconfiguring the state: trends in territorial governance in European states. *Regional and Federal Studies,* 17 (4), 385–403.

Loughlin, J., Hendriks, F. and Lidström, A., eds., 2011. *The Oxford Handbook of Local and Regional Democracy in Europe.* Oxford: Oxford University Press.

Maier, K., 1998. Czech planning in transition: assets and deficiencies. *International Planning Studies,* 3 (3), 351–365.

Márkusné Zsibók, Z., 2013. Methodologies to measure the impacts of territorial cohesion policies – what's new in Brussels? In: I. Pálné Kovács, I., J. Scott, and Z. Gál, eds. *Territorial Cohesion in Europe.* Pécs: Institute for Regional Studies, Centre for Economic and Regional Studies, Hungarian Academy of Sciences, 99–108.

McCann, E., 2003. Framing space and time in the city: urban policy and the politics of spatial and temporal scale. *Journal of Urban Affairs,* 25 (2), 159–178.

Meadowcroft, J., 2002. Politics and scale: some implications for environmental governance. *Landscape and Urban Planning,* 61 (2/4), 169–179.

Metzger, J. and Schmitt, P., 2012. When soft spaces harden: the EU strategy for the Baltic Sea Region. *Environment and Planning A,* 44 (2), 263–280.

Moss, T. and Newig, J., 2010. Multilevel water governance and problems of scale: setting the stage for a broader debate. *Environmental Management,* 46 (1), 1–6.

OECD – Organisation for Economic Cooperation and Development, 2001. *OECD Territorial Outlook.* 2001 Edition. Paris: OECD.

OECD – Organisation for Economic Co-operation and Development, 2011. *Government at a Glance 2011.* Paris: OECD.

Pallagst, K.M. and Mercier, G., 2007. Urban and regional planning in Central and Eastern European countries: from EU requirements to innovative practices. In: K. Stanilov, ed. *The Post-Socialist City Urban Form and Space Transformations in Central and Eastern Europe after Socialism.* Dordrecht: Springer, 473–490.

Pálné Kovács, I., 2014. Failed rescaling of territorial governance in Hungary. What was the gist? In: C. Nunes Silva and J. Bucek, J., eds. *Fiscal Austerity and Innovation in Local Governance in Europe*. Aldershot: Ashgate, 95–111.

Sheppard, E. and McMaster, R.B., eds., 2004. *Scale and Geographic Inquiry. Nature, Society, and Method*. Oxford: Oxford University Press.

Stanilov, K., 2007. Urban development policies in Central and Eastern Europe during the transition period and their impact on urban form. In: K. Stanilov, ed. *The Post-Socialist City Urban Form and Space Transformations in Central and Eastern Europe after Socialism*. Dordrecht: Springer, 347–359.

Stead, D., 2013. Convergence, divergence or constancy of spatial planning? Connecting theoretical concepts with empirical evidence from Europe. *Journal of Planning Literature*, 28 (1), 19–31.

Stead, D. and Cotella, G., 2011. Differential Europe: domestic actors and their role in shaping spatial planning systems. *disP – The Planning Review*, 47 (186), 14–22.

Stead, D. and Meijers, E.J., 2009. Spatial planning and sectoral policy integration: concepts, facilitators and inhibitors. *Planning Theory and Practice*, 10 (3), 317–332.

Stegmann McCallion, M., 2014. *Regionalism in Sweden. Report for the Assembly of European Regions*. Karlstad: Department of Political, Historical, Religious and Cultural Studies, Karlstad University.

Sykes, O., 2008. The importance of context and comparison in the study of European spatial planning. *European Planning Studies*, 16 (4), 537–555.

Waterhout, B., 2010. Soft spaces and governance: the transformation of planning. *Paper presented at the 24th AESOP Conference*, Helsinki, 7–10 July 2010. Available from: http://repository.tudelft.nl/assets/uuid:247daffa-2240-492f-a091-f979fab1dd9c/262482.pdf [Accessed 16 April 2015].

3 Territorial governance challenging government

Andreas Faludi

Introduction

These days, when preparing and implementing their policies, governments depend on a range of other actors. Thus the art of government becomes what is called governance. This is particularly so where governments deal with their territories and with territorial development. If land use regulations and public spending on projects were sufficient to ensure that the territories for which they are responsible develop as intended, then governments would not need to obtain the acquiescence of and/or the active support from other actors. But they do, and their appeals to various other actors and the related structures, mechanisms and processes are captured by the term territorial governance. However, since control over its territory is one of the defining features of the sovereign state, the advent of the concept of territorial governance raises fundamental questions about the very nature of the state.

States, the state system and state sovereignty are commonly regarded as issues for international relations theory. 'All sovereign states […] have territory, people, and a government', say Fowler and Bunck (1996). Likewise, Shaw (2003, p. 178) notes that states have a permanent population living in a defined territory and a government with the capacity to manage its relation with other states. But when other actors have the possibilities to influence how states discharge their duties, can governments still be held responsible? More in particular, if acquiescence and/or support from outside are indispensable for success, their own territories are no longer the exclusive geographic frame of reference of states, what does this mean?

The geographic frame of territorial governance may be wider or smaller than the state unit, depending on the issue at hand. This challenges the notion of territory as the area under sovereign state control. Territory is thus embedded in multiple, sometimes overlapping spatial configurations, each with its own governance arrangement depending on the spatial scale on which problems and solutions are defined and addressed.

The same as has been said about states and their territories applies to subnational authorities as well: arrangements for the governance of what are increasingly being described as 'places' criss-cross jurisdictional boundaries.

Challenging government 37

Place is an umbrella term for spatial formations that reside both inside and outside of formal jurisdictions. Place can also embrace one or more jurisdictions, as for instance in the case of the EU macro-regional strategies (see also Chapter 15). In this sense, it might even be better that territorial governance is called 'place' governance.

The first section of this chapter further explores the notions of government, the state and territory and their relationships. It shows that even the traditionally dominant role of the paradigmatic French state is now being questioned. The second section points out that the way this book conceptualises territorial governance raises the same fundamental issues as outlined above. The third section brings relevant human geography and planning literature to bear on the discussion of territorial governance. Where it questions notions of space as absolute and permanent, the challenge as outlined to government and its exclusive responsibility for territory and its people is implied. The fourth section deals with an explosive issue. Where does the questioning of territory as a relevant geographic frame leave established forms of democratic legitimacy, reliant as they are on territorially-defined constituencies? The conclusions point to there being no immediate resolution in sight.

'The end of territories'

The French national anthem, the *Marseillaise* recalls a citizen army defending French territory against foreign monarchs colluding with the internal forces of restoration. This has been as defining a moment as any for the French Republic. Since then, territory, citizenship and government have become constitutive elements of any state under international relations theory. Nonetheless, in '*La fin des territoires*' (the end of territories), Badie (1995) noted some inherent challenges to territory. The reasons for these challenges he noted at the time were globalisation, the end of the Cold War and the crisis of the welfare state. The review by David (1976) eloquently says that territory as the organisational principle of political formations and the frame of reference of international society 'suffers agony' (*le territoire agonise*). This raises issues about sovereignty, about the locus of decision-making and importantly also about territory as the focus of the state's concern as such.

Up until the early 1990s there had not been much concern about territory, as Badie (1996) related at a conference presentation of his book. True, there had been recognition of the state's diminishing importance in regulating international relations. Because of this, the function of territory as uniting and transcending singular concerns and ethnic loyalties had already been coming into focus. But territory was a political construct, a cultural and historical fact and not an eternal truth, Badie continued. What was at issue was whether the deconstruction of territory would lead to new forms of solidarity. Here Badie was referring to new European or Far Eastern spaces emerging. He also noted new complex and volatile territorial geometries under which individuals defined themselves as belonging to several spaces, prioritising their allegiance from case to case. This new marketplace for territorial identities was perhaps a portent of tomorrow's social order, one unlike the Westphalian order which had defined the principles of territorial sovereignty in the mid-seventeenth century.

This raises questions about the very concept of the state. Its supreme responsibility for the development of its territory and for its population is no longer self-evident. The challenge is keenly felt in France where an official government websites says: 'Traditionally, the State in France has an important role in providing public services, and thus in developing the country, since the time of Colbert' (translation by the author). Referring to a 'Republican model', Peyrony (2007) points out that, rooted in a social contract based on solidarity and equality, the public service is linked to the history of the French state. Already under Louis XIV, its territory was conceived as an organic whole. Vauban, the king's military engineer fortifying France's borders invoked the human body as a metaphor. So did Saint Simon inspiring generations of engineers organised in the *corps d'état,* the elite public services. To meet the new challenges of industrialisation, social policies were added (Chevallier 2012). These social policies became an essential part of national identity. Threats to them due to globalisation, European integration and policies of liberalisation also threaten the republican model. Under the republican model, the state considers itself responsible for contributing to the well-being of citizens by means of public services

> [...] defined and regulated principally in a national framework by the administration subject to the control of the political power accountable to the nation, the community of citizen-voters-users-taxpayers, from which it derives its legitimacy. The public service is required to be, in theory if not in practice, homogenous throughout the whole of the national territory.
> (Peyrony 2014, pp. 307–308, translation by the author)

In the same mode, the opening paragraph of a work by Chevallier (2012) on the public service says that, whereas one finds in all societies' activities considered to be of common interest and for this reason being a joint responsibility,

> the French notion of public service [...] has very specific implications. The public service has in fact been elevated in France to the lofty height of a veritable *myth,* which means one of these foundational images polarising beliefs and condensing emotions on which collective identities thrive. [...] This mystical dimension forbids all assimilation with like notions which one can find abroad: behind the words there is a whole conception of the status of the State [...]; the public service constitutes in France one of the 'sensitive questions' at the core of social cohesion.
> (Chevallier 2012, pp. 3–4, translation by the author)

Challenging government   39

However, both Peyrony and Chevallier note that in the market economy the public services lose their privileged position, a development which threatens social integration. The threat, Chevallier suggests, has played a role in the referendum going against the Constitution of Europe. He nonetheless talks about the inevitable decline of a concept which forms the foundation of French collective identity, implicating at the same time a threat to territorial cohesion, a concept reflecting specifically French concerns as they relate to, amongst others, spatial planning (Faludi 2007). Apparently as a response, French national planning, called *aménagement du territoire* is now under a new *Commissariat général à l'égalité des territoires* [General Commissariat for the Equality of Territories].

Lascoumes and Le Gales (2012) in *Sociologie de l'action publique* [Sociology of public action] relate such challenges to the rise of governance under the headline: *De l'État-nation aux sociétés ingouvernable* [From the nation state to ungovernable societies]. Historically, they say, policies had been linked to the progressive construction of the state until after the Second World War when the welfare state expanded rapidly. However, since the end of the 1970s, the state's share in spending has ceased to grow, leading to transformations in the manner of governing, the position that the state occupies and the resources at its disposal (Lascoumes and Le Gales 2012, p. 22).

In this vein, the concept of 'governance' relates to the shortcomings of government, the failures of classic public policies, and the proliferation of new forms of exchanges and of organisation. Inspired by the social science focus on institutions and on markets, governance puts the horizontal interaction between actors, their interdependencies, the growing autonomy of sectors and networks, the coordination of political and social actors and new forms of negotiations, constraints and incentives on the agenda. Governance thus stands for coordinating actors, social groups, and institutions so as to achieve collectively discussed and defined ends. It relates to the multi-actor dynamics which produce the stability of a society and of a political regime, its orientation and its capacity to provide services and to assure its legitimacy. Lascoumes and Le Gales (2012, p. 23) add that, rather than signalling the disappearance of government, governance means its completion.

Where Lascoumes and Le Gales note how interdependence leads to the re-composition of spatial scales, the argument becomes particularly relevant to territorial governance. Thus, the national scale loses in importance as non-state networks constitute themselves. Under European governance in particular, Lascoumes and Le Gales point to the interpenetration of levels of government, the diversity of actors and interests organised outside the state, and the outcomes of negotiations that are imposed on all participants. Where public policies are well entrenched, this makes for tensions with their champions amongst member states.

The process of governing, rather than remaining a monopoly of government, is now the object of a growing literature on governance (Bevir 2011, Levy-Faur 2012). European governance in particular has

40 *Andreas Faludi*

been the topic of a White Paper (European Commission 2001). As this volume shows, there is also much to do about territorial governance. This is all but inescapable, given the changes as outlined above that have taken place. Lascoumes and Le Gales do not answer the implicit question they pose themselves. Is society becoming ungovernable? Government appears to stand for order, for transparency. Governance, including territorial governance, with its focus on fleeting compromises and relationship to ephemeral spaces, is messy, creating issues for democratic legitimacy to be discussed in the last section.

Territorial governance as conceptualised in this volume

In Chapter 1 the notion of territorial governance is further defined by depicting five dimensions. Opting for a broad definition of what territorial governance involves, the dimensions and the given explanations do not offer any further indication of a careful distinction between territory and place. This becomes obvious by adding that 'territorial governance is the formulation and implementation of public policies, programmes and projects for the development of a place/territory' (see Figure 1.1), amplifying that development is understood to refer to measures to enhance efficiency, equality and environmental quality of a place/territory. It is further specified that territorial governance can take distinct forms. The chapters in this volume give evidence of this wide variety.

Turning more specifically to the identified five dimensions of territorial governance (see Figure 1.1) the following comments can be made. The first dimension of territorial governance in this book relates to the coordination of actors and institutions. Now, without this being spelled out, as argued, such coordination implies crossing institutional boundaries, but also and importantly boundaries between territories. The second dimension which territorial governance takes is integrating policy sectors. This could refer to sectors operating within one and the same territorial jurisdiction. However, where sectors operate in functional areas rather than within jurisdictions, integrating policy sectors may once more imply crossing boundaries between territories. The third dimension is mobilising stakeholder participation. Here the same observation can be made: where, as is often the case, relevant stakeholders come from outside the jurisdictional boundaries, this means transcending the fixation on territories. The fourth dimension of territorial governance is what is called 'being adaptive to changing contexts'. Needless to say, where that changing context is shaped by globalisation and the emergence of a network society, the same issues arise as discussed in the previous section and which are to be further elaborated below of how to deal with an increasingly interconnected world. Lastly, territorial governance, as dimension five suggests, seeks to reflect place-based/territorial specificities and impacts. At first sight, this may seem to suggest a focus on the local scale. However, as a concept 'place' is not necessarily defined as local, though it is often connoted as such. Its defining characteristic is that it is not encased by jurisdictional boundaries.

The conclusion is that the definition of territorial governance as further conceptualised and empirically applied in this volume implies that governance, and even more so territorial governance, transcends territorial boundaries and, as has been argued, challenges governments. How it will be challenged, what sorts of conflicts (solved or unsolved) and eventually 'trade-offs' may occur will be discussed and illustrated in a number of case studies (see Part II, Chapters 6 to 15). Nonetheless, as touched upon above, concepts such as territory and place, and related ones such as space, can be easily conflated, in particular in policy related empirical studies as it is the case in this volume. Since there is much discussion in the literature on the relationship and distinction of these concepts, it is therefore useful to delve a bit deeper into this.

Territory, space and place

In the first section of this chapter it has been argued that territorial governance brings the notion of territory as such into focus. This section brings to bear on this issue some thinking in human geography and in the planning literature. It suggests that this thinking can be organised around two, to invoke a term coined by Murphy (2008), 'metageographies', one which will be described, invoking Scholte (2000) as 'territorialist' and the other for which there is no ready-made label.

Before going into this issue, Murphy's notion of metageography needs explaining. Murphy invokes the notion to criticise the literature on EU multi-governance for what he calls an 'institutional-cum-political-economic emphasis'. This one-sidedness needs to be corrected by adding '[...] a concern for the ways in which territorial understanding and arrangements are shaping how things are organised on the ground'. Doing so '[...] challenges the territorial logic of the modern state system'. The system, Murphy further argues,

> [...] can no longer be understood in terms of the sovereignty norms of the modern state system because governmental competencies are no longer concentrated in discrete political spaces organised at a single scale or level.
>
> (Murphy, 2008, p. 7)

Without spilling much ink on the alternative, Murphy says one should contemplate another metageography, one that avoids falling into what Agnew (1994) in a much-quoted paper identifies as the 'territorial trap.' Conventional thinking in international relations theory, the object of Agnew's and also of Bardie's concern above, assumes that states are fixed units of sovereign space, that there is a clear dividing line between domestic and foreign policy, and that states are 'containers' of societies.

42   Andreas Faludi

Without invoking the term metageography, Scholte (2000, p. 47) characterises this view as 'territorialism'. Under territorialism,

> [...] macro social space is wholly organised, in terms of units such as districts, towns, provinces, countries and regions. In times of statist territorialism more particularly, countries have held pride of place above the other kinds of territorial realms [...].

However, Scholte points out that some connections are at least partly detached from this territorial logic. In global transactions, place is not territorially fixed; territorial distance is covered in effectively no time, and territorial boundaries present no particular impediment.

In these terms, the metageography which Murphy criticises is territorialist. Murphy also points out that the current 'cartography of social life' is the outcome of historic choices, more in particular '[...] of efforts to achieve particular ends with concrete implications for how things are organised and how people think about the world around them.' Murphy claims that the territoriality of the European state system, being his central concern, '[...] helped to produce a geographical imagination that privileges the "nation-states" over river basins, vegetation zones, population concentrations, or other possible regionalisations [...]' (Murphy 2008, p. 9). So, much like with the concept of the state to which it is wedded, there are alternatives, and in the fullness of time, territorialism may change into some other non-territorialist metageography. Indeed, Scholte (2000, p. 57) who once again does not talk in terms of metageography, argues for an alternative, non-territorialist cartography of social life that does not treat fixed territories as the immutable building blocks. Thrift used neither metageography nor territorialism as terms, but he, too, in pointing out the historicity of the existing system, opens up the possibility of change. The existing system is after all the

> [O]utcome of a series of highly problematic settlements that divide and connect things up into different kinds of collectives which are slowly provided with the means which render them durable and sustainable.
> (Thrift 2003, p. 95)

Another important geographer speaks about

> [A] process of carving out 'permanences' from the flow of processes [that are] creating spaces. But the 'permanences' – no matter how solid they may seem – are not eternal; they are always subject to time as 'perpetual perishing'.
> (Harvey 1996, p. 261)

In the same spirit, Davoudi and Strange (2009) advocate a relational conception of space, one that depends on the processes and substances that

Challenging government   43

make it up. In this relational perspective '[D]ifferent spaces and places are not seen as hierarchical (global, national, local) but as 'nodes in relational settings'. It is the length of relation that counts, Davoudi and Strange (2009, p. 36) add. From this they conclude that

> [P]ost-structuralism and its relational conceptions of spatiality put the emphasis on fluidity, [....] far from the apparent reified fixities and certainties that are conveyed by the spatial imaginaries of traditional planning practices.
>
> (Davoudi and Strange 2009, p. 37)

Further down in a passage reminiscent of Hooghe and Marks (2010) distinguishing multi-level governance of Type I and Type II (see Table 1.1), they say that scale should be

> [C]onceived of in terms of interconnections with places seen as elements in a web of contingent boundaries, constantly territorialised and open to political contestation. The organising spatial principle here would be one of multiple overlapping networks with continuous flows of people, resources and knowledge.
>
> (Davoudi and Strange 2009, p. 38)

To sum up, the existing metageography based on statist territorialism is the outcome of historic processes and as such is subject to change. Countries in times of statist territorialism have not only held pride of place, as Scholte says. They have tried and continue to try to counteract transgressions of, and even threats to state sovereignty. It is proposed to label this 'absolutistic territorialism'. This type of territorialism sees space overall as filled with fixed territorial containers and regards state control over them as absolute. For the far less well articulated, and admittedly vague alternative, 'relativist constructionism' may be appropriate as a term: constructivism because central to the alternative, non-territorialist cartography which Scholte advocates (and Thrift *and other authors* have been shown to agree), is the recognition that spatial units are socially constructed, the product of actors dealing with space and spatial development in ways reflecting their changing positions and aspirations in and with space. So 'relativist constructivism' sees space as filled with malleable, overlapping constructs, each the more or less fleeting outcome of interaction between social actors.

Relativistic constructivism takes a leaf out of the book of, amongst others, Amin (2004) in his programmatic article 'Regions unbound: Towards a new politics of place'. The butt of his criticism has been a 'new regionalism' prevalent in the United Kingdom at the time of the then Labour government and based on the mainstream view of cities and regions as fixed territorial entities. However, 'cosmopolitan forces' had produced a world of cities and regions without prescribed or proscribed

44 *Andreas Faludi*

boundaries, so Amin was proposing a relationally imagined regionalism freed from territorialism.

It will be clear once again that government as traditionally conceived tends towards absolutistic territorialism. It is only so that, if it ever has, absolutistic territorialism no longer works. So government tends to turn into governance which in turn rests on relativist constructivism fundamentally at odds with absolutistic territorialism. On a fundamental level, compromise seems impossible, which is why the challenge to government of governance is serious. Governments answer by invoking democratic legitimacy as an apparently unassailable point justifying their continuing supremacy.

A threat to democratic legitimacy?

Drawing on more human geography literature, Faludi (2013a) pursues the themes of territorialism and territoriality further. The studies discussed are innovative in conceptualising new territories criss-crossing existing jurisdictions leading to an 'unusual regionalism', the term coined by Deas and Lord (2006, p. 1850). New imaginative configurations being constructed in response to new perceptions of new problems straddling national and regional boundaries challenge absolutistic territorialism.

However, in a paper dealing with subsidiarity, this author also recognises that territorialism has a strong point in its favour which is that 'neatly defined jurisdictions are the basis for producing democratic legitimacy' (Faludi 2013b, p. 1603). He points out though that there are alternative notions. Sabel and Zeitlin (2010, p. 2) for instance describe the EU as a functional novel polity without a state and further down (on page 8) as a forerunner of 'new forms of governance suited to the temper of our times at both national and global levels'. At the same time, Sabel and Zeitlin also counter the concern about its 'democratic deficit'. They point out that accountability can no longer be seen as the democratic sovereign setting the goals for the administration to implement. Rather, actors 'have to learn what problem they are solving and what solution they are seeking, through the very process of problem solving' (Sabel and Zeitlin 2010, p. 11). Expert opinion comes into this, a point also made by the French author Rosanvallon (2008) writing on issues in democratic theory. This only goes to show that democratic legitimacy through elections is perhaps not quite as self-evident as one may think.

Sabel and Zeitlin (2010) do not discuss a basic assumption about representative democracy of relevance here, which is that accountability is to territorial constituencies and thus articulated in terms of closed territories. The assumption is 'that territories, and also the constituencies defined on this basis, are self-contained and that the field overall consists of contiguous units of this kind: territorialism' (Faludi 2013b, p. 1604). In this vein, democratic legitimacy is wedded to absolutistic territorialism. However, while closed territories as political units may up to a point have made sense in the past, the fact that they have been naturalised, making people believe that there is no alternative, is a problem. Kersten (2010) argues that territorial governance should be a synthesis of representative, participatory and associative, or what Sabel and Zeitlin (2010) call deliberative democracy. So the challenge is 'to combine territorial representation with other forms reflecting the real interdependence that characterises the world' (Faludi 2013b, p. 1306). In the terms of the discussion here, the challenge is to combine territorial representation with territorial governance. However, there is an implication that may be unpalatable to representatives of absolutistic territorialism. It is that they have to let go the exclusive claim to legitimacy, in other words, abandon absolutistic territorialism. To put it in another way, combining territorial representation with territorial governance implies relativist constructivism as the only defensible alternative. It is merely the simple fact that the trajectories of the construct of the nation state have already a long tradition that which gives states their weight and staying power.

The greater the staying power of states, the more they establish themselves in people's minds. Based on shared national histories and cultures, states enjoy the loyalty of their people. They actively re-enforce their sense of identity, and the institution of democratic representation greatly contributes to this. Unfortunately, it also tends to work towards exclusionary practices, towards identification with territories as if they were not historic constructs but fixed and eternal truths. There is a fundamental incompatibility here with today's world but, unless one takes flight into fantasies of global government, there is no resolution of this issue within sight. Challenging government, territorial governance remains a weak sparring partner and at a disadvantage.

Conclusions

Varró and Lagendijk (2013) and Harrison (2013) both refer to the example of England's 'regional problem' and regional governance and the 'relational versus territorial debate' involving 'radicals' and 'moderates'. To the disappointment of 'radicals', the regional policy of the Labour government around the turn of the millennium stuck to a container-view of socio-economic processes, causing Amin and others to criticise regional and urban policies based on, in the terms of this chapter, absolutistic territorialism. 'Moderates' as against this 'have pointed out the need to be aware of the persisting relevance of the territorial dimension of socio-spatial processes' (Varró and Lagendijk 2013, p. 21). It is not clear, however, why the persistence of territorial units needs to be recognised. Presumably, it is because these units are the producers of democratic legitimacy through elections.

Harrison (2013) takes this somewhat further. He, too, discusses UK regional planning in terms of 'territorially embedded' and 'relational and unbounded' conceptions, referring to Jessop, Brenner and Jones (2008) talking about a 'polymorphy' of social enquiry, territory, space, scale

46 *Andreas Faludi*

and network. Harrison's case study of North West England leads him to conclude: '[N]etworks and their institutional forms have clearly been unable to escape the existing territorial mosaic of politico-administrative units and their boundaries in the way that relationists argue they can' (Harrison 2013, p. 68). What is needed are

> [e]ver-more-complex configurations in order to make emergent strategies compatible with inherited landscapes of sociopolitical organisation, and for new conceptual frameworks capable of theorising the 'inherently polymorphic and multidimensional' nature of social relations.
>
> (ibid., pp. 71–72)

This chimes well with the observation of territorial governance being complex. Anyhow, elected representatives having to cope with the opaque arrangements to deal with a likewise opaque situation are likely to concur. Thanks to an electoral system which embeds representatives firmly in the 'territorial mosaic', rooted as this system is in absolutistic territorialism, they have a strong power base. In the terms of this volume discussing territorial governance, government has a claim to exercising ultimate control over the outcomes. The alternative would perhaps be to rethink democratic legitimacy in non-territorial terms.

References

Agnew, J., 1994. The territorial trap: the geographical assumptions of international relations theory. *Review of International Political Economy*, 1 (1), 53–80.

Amin, A., 2004. Regions unbound: towards a new politics of place. *Geografiska Annaler B*, 86 (1), 33–44.

Badie, B., 1995. *La fin des territoires*. Paris: Fayard.

Badie, B., 1996. La fin des territoires Westphaliens (Transcript of oral presentation). In: *Le territoire, lien ou frontière?* Conference, Paris, 2–4 octobre 1995. Available from: http://horizon.documentation.ird.fr/exl-doc/pleins_textes/divers08-09/010014865-80.pdf [Accessed 16 November 2014].

Badie, B. and Smouts, M.-C., 1999. *Le retournement du monde: sociologie de la scène international*. 3rd ed. Paris: Presses de Sciences Po/Dalloz (Amphithéâtre).

Bevir, M., 2011. Governance as theory, practice, and dilemma. In: M. Bevir, ed. *The Sage Handbook of Governance*. London: Sage, 1–16.

Chevallier, J., 2012. *Le service public*. Paris: Presses Universitaires de France.

David, D., 1976. Bertrand Badie: 'La fin des territoires'. Essai sur le désordre international et l'utilité sociale du respect. *Politique étrangère*, 61 (1), 220–221.

Davoudi, S. and Strange, I., 2009. *Conceptions of Space and Place in Strategic Spatial Planning*. London: Routledge.

Deas, I. and Lord, A., 2006. From new regionalism to an unusual regionalism? The emergence of non-standard regional spaces and lessons for the territorial reorganisation of the state. *Urban Studies*, 43 (10), 1847–1877.

Faludi, A., 2007. *Territorial Cohesion and the European Model of Society*. Cambridge, MA: Lincoln Institute of Land Policy.

Faludi, A., 2013a. Territorial cohesion, territorialism, territoriality, and soft planning: a critical review. *Environment and Planning A*, 45 (6), 1302–1317.

Faludi, A., 2013b. Territorial cohesion and subsidiarity under the European Union treaties: a critique of the 'territorialism' underlying. *Regional Studies*, 47 (9), 1594–1606.

Fowler, M.R. and Bunck, J.M., 1996. What constitutes the sovereign state? *Review of International Studies*, 22 (4), 381–404.

Harrison, J., 2013. Configuring the new 'regional world': on being caught between territory and networks. *Regional Studies*, 42 (1) 55–74.

Harvey, D., 1996. *Justice, Nature and Geography of Difference*. Oxford: Blackwell.

Hooghe, L. and Marks, G., 2010. Types of multi-level governance, In: H. Enderlein, S.Wälti, and M. Zürn, eds. *Types of Multilevel Governance*. Cheltenham: Elgar, 17–31.

Jessop, B., Brenner, N., and Jones, M., 2008. Theorising sociospatial relations. *Environment and Planning D: Society and Space*, 26 (3), 389–401.

Kersten, J., 2010. Europäische Raumentwicklung nach dem Lissabon-Urteil des Bundesverfassungsgerichts. *Umwelt und Planungsrecht – Zeitschrift für Wissenschaft und Praxis*, 6, 201–208.

Lascoumes, P. and Le Gales, P., 2012. *Sociologie de l'action publique*. 2nd ed. Paris: Arman Colin.

Levy-Faur D., 2012. *The Oxford Handbook on Governance*. Oxford: Oxford University Press.

Murphy, A.B., 2008. Rethinking multi-level governance in a changing European Union: why metageography and territoriality matter, *GeoJournal*, 72 (1–2), 7–18.

Peyrony, J., 2007. Territorial cohesion and the European model of society. In: A. Faludi, ed. *Territorial Cohesion and the European Model of Society*. Cambridge, MA: Lincoln Institute of Land Policy, 61–79.

Peyrony, J., 2014. La 'modernisation de l'action publique territoriale' en perspective européenne at transfrontalière'. In: *GIS Collège international des sciences du territoire*, Paris, 307–316. Available from: http://www.gis-cist.fr/wp-content/uploads/2014/02/peyrony.pdf [Accessed 17 May 2015].

Rosanvallon, P., 2008. *Counter-Democracy: Politics in an Age of Distrust*. Cambridge: Cambridge University Press.

Sabel, C.F. and Zeitlin, J., 2010. *Experimentalist Governance in the European Union: Towards a New Architecture*. Oxford: Oxford University Press.

Scholte, J.A., 2000. *Globalization: A Critical Introduction*. Houndsmill: Macmillan.

Shaw, M.N., 2003. *International Law*. Cambridge: Cambridge University Press.

Thrift, N., 2003. Space: the fundamental stuff of geography. In: S.L. Halloway, S. Rice and G. Valentine, eds. *Key Concepts in Geography*. London: Sage, 95–108.

Varró, K. and Lagendijk, A., 2013. Conceptualizing the region: in what sense relational? *Regional Studies*, 47 (1), 18–28.

4 Guiding principles of 'good' territorial governance

Simin Davoudi and Paul Cowie

Introduction

This chapter addresses the questions, what is 'good' territorial governance and how might it be assessed. It presents an analytical framework and a number of qualitative indicators for examining territorial governance. It discusses how their relevance and practicality were tested and refined through a Delphi survey of an expert panel whose members came from policy and practice from different European countries. While acknowledging the situated nature of governance practices, we believe that the framework and the indicators provide a useful guide for understanding and judging the quality of territorial governance, as was shown in their application to a dozen of case studies across Europe, ten of which are presented in Part II of this volume.

Good territorial governance

What constitutes 'good' territorial governance? What criteria can be used to assess the quality and nature of territorial governance systems? In addressing these questions, our aim is not to come up with one definition of 'good' territorial governance that would be suitable for different contexts and circumstances. Rather, it is to provide a set of guiding principles which can be used in different contexts. The aim is not to develop an 'ideal type' or a desired standard of practice for which common values or norms could be identified, but rather to suggest a number of guiding principles which could inform judgment about particular governance practices in a specific time and place.

The main point of departure for identifying such principles is the work undertaken by international organisations and the European Union. The United Nation defines good governance as 'an efficient and effective response to urban problems by accountable local governments working in partnership with civil society' (UN-Habitat 2009, p. 74). Its Development Programme (UNDP) considers governance as the exercise of economic, political and administrative authority to manage the affairs of any country at all levels, and the mechanisms, processes and institutions through which citizens and groups articulate their interests, exercise their legal rights, meet their obligations and mediate their differences (UNDP 1997). Similar to other international organisations, the UNDP considers that good governance requires participation, transparency and accountability, and that it should promote the rule of law. Governance encompasses the state, but also the private sector and civil society organisations. In its Global Campaign on Urban Good Governance launched in 2002, the UN considered the seven main characteristics of good governance as follows (UN-Habitat 2002):

- 'Sustainability': balancing the social, economic and environmental needs of present and future generations.
- 'Subsidiarity': assigning responsibilities and resources to the closest appropriate level.
- 'Equity' of access to decision-making processes and the basic necessities of urban life.
- 'Efficiency' in delivery of public services and in promoting local economic development.
- 'Transparency' and 'accountability' of decision-makers and all stakeholders.
- 'Civic engagement' and 'citizenship': recognising that people are the principal wealth of cities, and both the object and the means of sustainable human development.
- 'Security' of individuals and their living environment.

Similarly, the World Bank (1994) has set the following three goals for good governance: empowering citizens to hold governments accountable through participation and decentralisation; enabling governments to respond to new demands by building capacity; and enforcing compliance with the rule of law and greater transparency. Similar objectives are advocated by the EU White Paper which identifies five principles that underpin good governance (CEC 2001, pp. 10–11). These are:

- 'Openness': better communication and accessible language.
- 'Participation': wide participation throughout the policy chain.
- 'Accountability': greater clarity and responsibility.
- 'Effectiveness': delivering what is needed on the basis of clear objectives, an evaluation of future impact and past experience.
- 'Coherence': consistent approach between various policies and political leadership.

The application of these five principles reinforces two other EU principles of:

- 'Proportionality': checking whether public intervention and regulation is really necessary and the measures chosen are proportionate to those objectives.

- 'Subsidiarity': Checking whether the level of governance in which action is to be taken is the most appropriate one.

While each principle is considered to be important for establishing more democratic governance, they cannot be achieved through separate actions. Furthermore, the principles apply to all levels of governance at the global, European, national, regional and local levels. In addition to the above definition and in the context of radical uncertainties, a new dimension has been added to principles of 'good' governance which emphasises the significance of resilience and adaptive capacity, defined by Gupta *et al.* (2010, pp. 461–462) as:

> The inherent characteristics of institutions that empower social actors to respond to short and long-term impacts either through planned measures or through allowing and encouraging creative responses from society both ex-ante and ex-post.

Developing and implementing flexible territorial strategies requires governance institutions that are capable of supporting social actors and enabling them to respond proactively (Davoudi *et al.* 2013). Building societal and institutional adaptive capacity is therefore a critical part of good governance. In the context of hazard mitigation, for example, Godschalk (2003, p. 139) argues that, in order to create resilient cities, the following principles should be taken into account for the design and management of cities:

- 'Redundancy': systems designed with multiple nodes to ensure that failure of one component does not cause the entire system to fail.
- 'Diversity': multiple components or nodes versus a central node, to protect against a site-specific threat.
- 'Efficiency': positive ratio of energy supplied to energy delivered by a dynamic system.
- 'Autonomy': capability to operate independent of outside control.
- 'Strength': power to resist a hazard force or attack.
- 'Interdependence': integrated system components to support each other.
- 'Adaptability': capacity to learn from experience and the flexibility to change.
- 'Collaboration': multiple opportunities and incentives for broad stakeholder participation.

In the context of climate change, Birkmann *et al.* (2010, p. 185) stress the significance of governance in effective implementation of adaptation strategies and call for

> new forms of adaptive urban governance that goes beyond the conventional notions of urban (adaptation) planning [...] and move from

the dominant focus on the adjustment of physical structures towards the improvement of planning tools and governance processes and structures themselves.

They identify the following key elements for 'adaptive urban governance' (Birkmann *et al.* 2010, p. 203):

- integration of strategies and tools at 'multiple scales',
- consideration of multiple 'timeframes',
- new methodological tools that go beyond cost-benefit analysis,
- 'more 'flexible' and 'inclusive' governance structures, moving from management of administrative units to applying flexible units for specific problems'.

In the wider context of urban (territorial) governance, Gupta *et al.* (2010) identify six dimensions of adaptive capacity including:

- 'Variety': multiple problem framing, multi-sector and multi-level solution seeking.
- 'Learning capacity': trust, double loop learning and institutional memory.
- 'Autonomous change': access to information, acting according to plan, capacity to improvise, non-hierarchical flexibility.
- 'Leadership': visionary, entrepreneurial, collaborative, action-oriented.
- 'Resources': authority, human capital, financial resources.
- 'Fair governance': legitimacy, accountability, equity, transparency, responsiveness.

This brief overview of the literature shows that there appears to be a degree of confusion between process (inputs) and substance (outcomes) of good governance. Examples of the former are principles such as: efficiency, learning capacity, effectiveness and transparency while examples of the later include sustainable development, equity and territorial cohesion. The former is about good processes while the latter is about good outcomes. While in practice they are clearly interrelated, for analytical purposes we may need to treat them separately. The ambition in the TANGO project, on which this is volume based, was mainly to assess the quality of territorial governance in terms of its processes. As far as outcomes are concerned, we use the overarching goals of the EU 2020 strategy to which European territories should aspire to. These include: smart, sustainable and inclusive growth. As regards inputs, our starting point was the principles derived from our literature review and discussed in the next section. The review also confirmed a lack of attention to the significance of 'territoriality' in achieving good governance. We therefore proposed that a sound awareness of the territorial dimension of decision-making should be a key guiding principle of good governance.

Qualitative indicators of good territorial governance

We use the working definition of 'territorial governance' presented in Chapter 1 and its five dimensions as our departure point and draw on the wider literature on good governance to identify and develop indicators of good territorial governance. Below are brief descriptions of the dimensions and the indicators.

Dimension 1: co-ordinating the actions of relevant actors and institutions

This dimension reflects how coordination of actions is managed and how competencies are distributed at various territorial levels. We consider 'governing capacity', 'leadership' and 'subsidiarity' as key indicators of the ability of territorial governance to coordinate the actions of relevant actors and institutions. *Governing capacity* is a key pre-requisite for effective coordination of the actions of multiple and diverse actors in particular places/territories. It is about the ability to: a) organise, deliver and accomplish; b) review, audit, and monitor; and c) integrate various platforms/forums. It, therefore, requires access to human, financial and knowledge resources. Hendriks (2014) calls the first ability 'the productive' and the second one 'the corrective' capacity. All three require institutional capacity at appropriate scale or scope for accommodating and marshalling the salient, necessary and non-obvious stakeholders at all governance levels. This indicator is loosely connected to the notion of distributed or shared leadership and the development of the scope of territorial actors within a given place to learn together. *Leadership* is about oversight, vision and the ability to secure stakeholders' participation and ownership of the place-specific goals. It is about the ability to drive change, show direction and motivate others to follow. Leadership may be performed by individual actors or institutions. It can be concentrated or diffused among the actors collectively. Power, in this account, refers not just to power over action of others, but also power to get things done (Davoudi and Evans 2005). It can be wielded collectively and mobilised through collaboration among actors. *Subsidiarity* is about ensuring that decisions are made at the territorial level which is as close to citizens as strategically and practically possible, while taking into account the multi-level nature of territorial governance. European literature on subsidiarity is large and controversial. Action at 'best fit' should frame good territorial governance intervention. In a sense, this refers to appropriate scale for intervention, taking into account the multi-level interplay (Faludi 2012).

'Good' territorial governance 53

Dimension 2: integrating relevant policy sectors

Integrating policy sectors means developing linkages among different policy sectors (such as land use and transport) and creating synergies among public, private and civil society sectors. We consider 'policy packaging' and 'cross-sector synergy' as key indicators of the ability of territorial governance to integrate different policy sectors. *Policy packaging* refers to strategic oversight for enabling the bundling of relevant policy areas in order to add value. This includes avoiding policy 'silos' and combining various interventions in such a way that they mutually reinforce one another. An effective way to achieve strategic policy packaging is to focus on the needs and opportunities of places. *Cross-sector synergy* is about seeking horizontal cross-fertilisation and coordination between public, private and civil society sectors, so that they work in favour of a particular place/territory.

Dimension 3: mobilising stakeholder participation

Mobilising stakeholder participation is the ability to engage with relevant stakeholders by providing them with insights into the design of territorial governance processes and opportunities for shaping them. We consider 'democratic legitimacy', 'public accountability' and 'transparency' as key indicators of the ability to mobilise diverse stakeholder participation in decision-making. *Democratic legitimacy* is about ensuring that relevant interests are represented and given voice in territorial governance processes. It should be noted that there are various forms of legitimacy and representations (Cowie and Davoudi 2015) which include both representative and participative democracy. *Public accountability* is about ensuring that those in positions of authority are accountable to the public for making place-based decisions that affect their lives. *Transparency* is about ensuring that the composition, procedures, and tasks of territorial governance are open and visible to the public. It is about avoiding the 'black boxing' of territorial governance and making its procedures and policies informative, accessible and legible to the public.

Dimension 4: being adaptive to changing contexts

This dimension is about the extent to which territorial governance is sensitive to the changing contexts and has various learning and feedback mechanisms in place. We consider 'reflexivity' and 'adaptability' to be key indicators of the ability of territorial governance to cope with and seize opportunities from changing circumstances. These capacities are essential for governing under the condition of uncertainty. *Reflexivity* is about social learning and the ability to reflect on, review and revise the territorially specific ideas, routines, instruments, inputs, outcomes and processes in the face of new information, opportunities, and threats arising from both endogenous

54 Simin Davoudi and Paul Cowie

and exogenous factors. It refers both to individuals acting as reflective practitioners and to governance as a whole. *Adaptability* is about flexibility and resilience (Davoudi 2012a) in the face of territorial change and crisis. It is also about seeking opportunities for transformation through creativity and imagination as well as territorial knowledgeability, discussed below.

Dimension 5: realising place-based/territorial specificities and impacts

This dimension acknowledges that territory is a socio-spatial construct rather than a mere physical entity. It acknowledges the various overlapping notions of place/territory and the need for management of knowledge about place-related/territorial characteristics and impacts. We consider 'territorial relationality' and 'territorial knowledgeability' as key indicators of this dimension. *Territorial relationality* is about acknowledging the porous boundaries of territories and the fluidity of their relations with other places in an increasingly interconnected world (Davoudi 2012b). Actors should be able to address the territorial scale of governance in relation to the issues at hand rather than being constrained by administrative boundaries. An example is using a network approach to governance for matching the purpose and objective of the intervention and the interests of those who have a stake in the decision(s). Place-related *territorial knowledgeability* is about utilising multiple sources of knowledge, including local knowledge, about the territory. It is about dealing with the territorial impacts of policies and programmes on the territory.

Table 4.1 Overview of the dimensions and indicators of territorial governance

Dimensions of territorial governance	Indicators of good territorial governance
Co-ordinating actions of actors and institutions	Governing capacity
	Leadership
	Subsidiarity
Integrating policy sectors	Public policy packaging
	Cross-sector synergy
Mobilising stakeholder participation	Democratic legitimacy
	Public accountability
	Transparency
Being adaptive to changing contexts	Reflexivity
	Adaptability
Realising place-based/territorial specificities and impacts	Territorial relationality Territorial knowledgeability

Source: Authors' own adaptation based on ESPON and Nordregio (2013, p. 20)

Validating the indicators through a Delphi method

We used a Delphi survey to test the 'relevance' and 'practicality' of the above 12 indicators. The Delphi method (or technique) is widely recognised as a robust process of eliciting expert views in which the judgments collected in one round of the survey are fed back to the participants in the subsequent rounds with the aim being to move towards a consensus of opinion among the participating experts.

In the TANGO Project we used a two-round Delphi survey to test the relevance and practicality of the indicators. The first step was to establish a Delphi Panel by using the network of country-based contacts held by the ESPON Coordination Unit (CU), EPSON Monitoring Committee and ESPON National Contact Points. This resulted in a panel of approximately 80 experts from different disciplinary and cultural backgrounds. Before seeking the panel's views, we undertook a number of validation and piloting exercises during project workshops. This led to the revision of the initial ten indicators which were derived from the literature and the addition of two new indicators (cross-sector synergies and territorial knowledgeability). Second, the Delphi survey was piloted with members of the ESPON CU to test the legibility of the questionnaire and the time required to complete the survey. Taking into account the outcome of these exercises, we conducted two rounds of the survey. Round one took place in October 2012 in which 22 individuals from across the EU member countries completed the survey. The panel was provided with the 12 indicators (listed in Table 4.1) and their brief descriptions and their views were sought about the relevance and practicality of the indictors for judging 'good' territorial governance. The questionnaires were conducted using the publicly available online survey software, Survey Monkey. The analyses of the responses from the first round showed an overall strong agreement that the indicators were relevant for 'measuring' the related dimensions of territorial governance. The outcome was less clear with regard to their practicality. The reason for the low scores in relation to the practicality was that the panel equated measurement with quantification, and the indicators with quantitative indicators.

The second round of Delphi was undertaken in November 2012 in which only nine out of the 22 experts fully completed the survey. This gave a second round response rate of 41 per cent which was slightly below the second round response rate found in other similar Delphi Surveys (e.g. Frewer *et al.* 2011). The inability to do a non web based survey could have also affected the response rate. The panel members were provided with the following feedback from round one: the statistical information about the relevance and practicality of each of the indicators, a synthesis of the comments and a note about the meaning of practicality. The latter made clear that practicality should not be equated with quantification and should include qualitative assessments of a particular indicator. Overall, there remained a strong

56 Simin Davoudi and Paul Cowie

support for the proposition that all 12 indicators were relevant and most were practical indicators for assessing good territorial governance.

What did experts think about the indicators?

The following account provides the summary of the main comments made by the Delphi Panel members during both rounds of the survey with regard to the relevance and practicality of the 12 proposed indicators for examining the nature and quality of territorial governance processes and outcomes. These are organised according to the relevant 'dimensions' discussed above.

Co-ordinating the actions of relevant actors and institutions

Governing Capacity had the highest score for relevance but the joint lowest score for practicality. As with public policy packaging, a number of experts questioned whether the indicator is about analysing the process of territorial governance or its outcomes. They argued that high capacity does not necessarily produce a desired outcome. The counter argument was that governing capacity is a pre condition for territorial governance and without it any decision (good or bad) would be difficult to take. In terms of 'practicality', the reason for its low score was the difficulty of measuring it quantitatively and the possibility of placing a higher weighting on spurious factors such as the speed of decision-making which may not be the same as 'good' decision-making. Some experts suggested that qualitative measures can be used, such as attitudinal surveys, to consider factors such as stability and confidence in decision-making. *Leadership* had similar scores to Governing Capacity. The experts highlighted how leadership featured repeatedly in qualitative research as a factor of 'good' territorial governance and the need to distinguish between the process of leadership and the outcomes associated with it. It was recognised that process was as important as outcome. This subjectivity of the judgment about leadership was considered by many of the experts as the reason for the indicators to be seen as non- practical. *Subsidiarity* scored highly for both relevance and practicality. However, as regards the former, the panel suggested that the devolution of decision-making should be to the appropriate level rather than the lowest possible level. This begs the question: who should determine the scale to which territorial governance should be devolved? The panel's answer was that it should be up to the territory to determine what kind of devolved powers and responsibilities (competencies) it requires for effective governing.

Integrating relevant policy sectors

Public Policy Packaging scored high for relevance but low for practicality. The latter was due to the difference between process and outcome. A number of experts pointed out that it was possible to have public policy packaging as a process with poor outcome. This was a key theme which came out in relation to nearly all the indicators. *Cross-sector Synergy* received a good deal of support in terms of relevance and practicality. As regards the latter, it was seen to offer opportunities for both quantitative and qualitative analysis.

Mobilising stakeholder participation

Democratic Legitimacy scored the same as subsidiarity in terms of both practicality and relevance. Many experts highlighted the fundamental need for democratic processes to underpin other aspects of territorial governance. For example public accountability and transparency are both enhanced by the presence of strong democratic legitimacy as is another indicator, leadership. A number of practical measures were proposed for the indicator, ranging from an assessment of the legal framework for democratic legitimacy, the presence of a free press and vibrant civic society, to quantitative measures around voter turnout in elections and participation rates in public consultations. *Public Accountability* scored fairly high on its relevance and practicality. For some experts, it was closely associated with democratic legitimacy and elected representation. For others it was more associated with transparency and the ability of civic society to scrutinise the governance processes and hold the decision-makers to account. *Transparency* was the highest scoring indicator both in relation to its relevance and practicality. The ability of those affected by the decision-making process to have access to and understand all aspects of the process was seen as critical.

Being adaptive to changing contexts

Reflexivity showed an increase in its score for practicality between the first and second rounds of the Delphi survey. Most of the experts agreed that reflexivity is a highly desirable trait when considering governance in general. The ability to learn from past experiences and, as one expert put it, 'not constantly reinvent the wheel' leads to efficiency and effectiveness. Some suggested that it should be a cross-cutting indicator. *Adaptability* received the same scores as reflexivity. It was also seen as a cross-cutting indicator which affects all aspects of territorial governance. As one expert commented, 'adaptability is complementary to reflexivity [...] the capacity to adapt to change without creating instability in the system and procedures'. To be able to determine whether a system of territorial governance is adaptable requires analysis over time and this should be reflected in the indicator. The long-term perspective was seen as difficult and costly to manage at a large territorial scale.

Realising place-based / territorial specificities and impacts

Territorial Relationality had the lowest score for relevance due to concerns about the abstract nature of the indicator. The expert panel perceived it to be a technical terminology and academic concept which would be hard to use in everyday practice. Despite this, the majority of the experts agreed that territorial relationality is a practical indicator for analysing territorial governance because it helps connect governance processes to the territory and the community. *Territorial Knowledgeability* was the second highest scoring indicator with the joint highest score for its practicality and joint second highest score for its relevance. Put bluntly, one expert commented that, 'if you don't have a clue about the kinds of impacts your decisions are having on the ground you probably shouldn't be making those decisions in the first place'. A number of experts felt the only way to investigate territorial knowledgeability would be through culturally specific qualitative criteria.

Concluding remarks

Our literature review and the resuts of our Delphi survey have confirmed the difficulty of defining what is 'good' territorial governance. This is largely due to the situated nature of territorial governance and the inherently normative and political nature of what 'good' is. It is therefore important to reiterate that the selected five dimensions of territorial governance are useful mainly for analytical purposes and should not be taken as prescriptive and fixed. Similarly, the selected 12 indicators should be taken as guiding principles for exploring the quality of territorial governance within a specific time and place and taking into account the context within which a certain governance system operates. Indeed, our own understanding of these dimensions and indicators stem from values and norms that are largely rooted in (Western) European societies. So, it is paramount that caution is exercised and appropriate adjustments are made in using them. Furthermore, two crucial points came out the Delphi exercise. First is there need for more clarity regarding what a given indicator seeks to measure, the process or the outcome? Second is the emphasis on the interrelatedness of the indicators and the fact that they are designed to work together? This was confirmed repeatedly by the expert panel who suggested that many of the indicators should have been taken as cross-cutting and related to all five dimensions. This is an important point and was reflected in the final analysis of empirical evidence generated by the case studies.

References

Birkmann, J., Garschargen, M., Kraas, F. and Quang, N., 2010. Adaptive urban governance: new challenges for the second generation of urban adaptation strategies to climate change. *Sustainability Science*, 5 (2), 185–206.

CEC – Commission of the European Communities, 2001. *European Governance: A White Paper.* COM (2001), 428 final, Brussels: Commission of the European Communities.

Commission on Global Governance, 1995. *Our Common Neighbourhood*, Oxford: Oxford University Press.

Cowie, P. and Davoudi, S., 2015. Is small really beautiful? The legitimacy of neighbourhood planning. In: S. Davoudi and A. Madanipour, eds. *Reconsidering Localism.* London: Routledge, 11–30.

Davoudi, S., 2012a. The legacy of positivism and the emergence of interpretive tradition in spatial planning. *Regional Studies*, 46 (4), 429–441.

Davoudi, S., 2012b. Resilience, a bridging concept or a dead end? *Planning Theory and Practice,* 13 (2), 299–307.

Davoudi, S. and Evans, N., 2005. The challenge of governance in regional waste planning. *Environment and Planning C: Government and Policy*, 23 (4), 493–517.

Davoudi, S., Brooks, E. and Mehmood, A., 2013. Evolutionary resilience and strategies for climate adaptation. *Planning Practice and Research,* 28 (3), 307–322.

ESPON and Nordregio, 2013. ESPON TANGO – Territorial Approaches for New Governance. Final Report. Available from: http://www.espon.eu/export/sites/default/Documents/Projects/AppliedResearch/TANGO/FR/ESPON_TANGO_Main_Report_Final.pdf [Accessed 03 April 2015].

Faludi, A., 2012. Multi-level (Territorial) governance. three criticisms. *Planning Theory & Practice*, 13 (2), 197–211.

Frewer, L., Fischer, A., Wentholt, M., Marvin, H., Ooms, B., Coles, D. and Rowe, G., 2011. The use of Delphi methodology in agrifood policy development: Some lessons learnt. *Technological Forecasting & Social Change,* 78 (9), 1514–1525.

Godschalk, D.R., 2003. Urban hazard mitigation: Creating resilient cities. *Natural Hazards Review,* 4 (3), 136–143.

Gupta, J., Termeer, C., Klostermann, J., Meijerink, S., van den Brink, M., Jong, P., Nooteboom, S. and Bergsma, E., 2010. The Adaptive Capacity Wheel: a method to assess the inherent characteristics of institutions to enable the adaptive capacity of society. *Environmental Science & Policy*, 13 (6), 459–471.

Hendriks, F., 2014. Understanding good urban governance: essentials, shifts and values. *Urban Affairs Review*, 50 (4), 553–576.

Hendriks, F., Lidström, A. and Loughlin, J., eds., 2010. *The Oxford Handbook of Local and Regional Democracy in Europe.* Oxford: Oxford University Press.

OECD – Organisation for Economic Co-operation and Development, 2001. *Best Practices in Local Development.* Paris: OECD.

UN-Habitat – United Nations Human Settlements Programme, 2002. *The Global Campaign on Urban Governance.* Nairobi: UN-Habitat.

UN-Habitat – United Nations Human Settlements Programme, 2009. *Best Practices and Local Leadership Programme.* Nairobi: UN-Habitat.

UNDP – United Nations Development Programme, 1997. *Governance and Sustainable Human Development.* New York: UNDP.

World Bank, 1994. *Governance: The World Bank's Experience.* Washington, DC: World Bank.

Part II

Territorial governance in practice

Ten European cases

5 Territorial governance at play

Methodological introduction to the case studies

Peter Schmitt and Lisa Van Well

Validating the indicators was the first step in operationalising the five dimensions of territorial governance. Yet the task remained how to trace territorial governance in the ten case studies that are presented in Part II of the book (see Chapters 6 to 15). We contend that territorial governance processes can only be truly understood by performing research using qualitative methods that involve tracing processes within a specific territorial context. If applied to an individual case this will provide a rich description and analysis of how territorial governance processes actually works within a setting and generate lessons from each specific case. However our challenge was to undertake a series of case studies from very different types of territories on a number of different levels – from the macro-regional to the neighbourhood level – which would provide both specific and comparable results. These could then lead to some generalised observations about territorial governance within Europe. This meant that we had to carefully construct a framework for analysis which could allow comparisons and syntheses from the ten various cases.

The case studies were designed according to a multi-case study method whereby all cases 'serve a specific purpose within the overall scope of inquiry' (Yin 2003, p. 47). The multiple-case study design also facilitates exploration of the differences and similarities in territorial governance processes within and between cases. While we have not used a 'strict' comparative case study method, the chosen cases do allow a comparison of territorial governance processes, structures or mechanisms (cf. Chapter 16).

Operational criteria for identifying and selecting the cases have been that the pair or group of researchers had an intimate knowledge of the government/governance context at hand and established contacts with a critical mass of key informants for interviews. In addition, the idea had been to cover a wide spectrum of territorial governance practices in regards to different planning and governance cultures and systems across Europe (cf. Howlett 2009, Treib *et al.* 2007, Stead and Nadin 2009, Reimer *et al.* 2014), different territorial development goals and sectoral policy areas (e.g. water management, public transport, resource-efficient urban planning, climate change adaptation, culture-based development, natural protection and tourism, etc.), and different levels and spatial scopes of territorial governance across Europe. The

64 Peter Schmitt and Lisa Van Well

governance practices were to bridge at least two political/administrative levels and range from neighbourhood issues to larger cross-border regions or even macro-regional strategies as the map in Figure 5.1 indicates.

That said, most of the cases address a perceived tension between 'hard' and 'soft' spaces (cf. also Chapters 2 and 3). The former relates to jurisdictional boundaries, which is normally represented by some sort of government. Soft territories are often loosely defined. In some cases functional or geographic criteria (such as a labour market, river catchment area or expanse of a nature park) set the scope of the case. In other cases, the inherent territorial logic of a specific project, policy or programme to address some specific territorial goal or challenge to be overcome (such as developing a climate change adaptation strategy for the Baltic Sea Region) provided the boundaries of the case. In Figure 5.1 the dominating territorial logic is highlighted for each case study.

All case studies are based on initial desk research, as well as in-depth interviews with key stakeholders and policymakers from October 2012 to December 2013. Those presented in this volume have been revisited during 2014 and subsequently updated where relevant. The cases were undertaken in two stages. The first stage was a preliminary analysis of the five dimensions of territorial governance within the cases to confirm their usefulness as a rough analytical framework and to gain an initial understanding of territorial processes at play. This stage also served to identify interviewees as actors and institutions involved in working towards a territorial objective and their contextual room for manoeuvre. After the initial phase the 'thick descriptions' provided by each case study were further analysed in view of how to design stage two.

The second and more in-depth stage involved testing the hypotheses about 'good' territorial governance that were generated in the first phase in a series of eight to twelve semi-structured interviews with key informants in each case. In order to guarantee anonymity, they will be referred to only as 'personal communications' in the following case studies. The five dimensions as well as the twelve indicators of territorial governance were employed again to further 'trace' the initial assumptions of the cases by carving out the various practices, routines or even critical views within each case study's specific territorial and institutional context. To that end, the method of process tracing was used to stress 'the temporal unfolding of causality', since 'the basic unit of analysis is not an individual variable, but a multi-level model or configuration of densely linked causal factors' (Blatter and Blume 2008, p. 29). This method has often been used in social science as a way to discover the 'links between possible causes and observed outcomes' (George and Bennett 2005, p. 6). In this way, the process tracing is able to test not only hypotheses, but also generate them together with other new variables that may have been previously overlooked (George and Bennett 2005, Falleti 2006).

To guide the researchers in performing the interviews, the five dimensions and twelve indicators were de-constructed into a total of 42 'core' questions. These questions thus formed the general guideline and structure for the interviews for all cases. As such they provided a common framework of

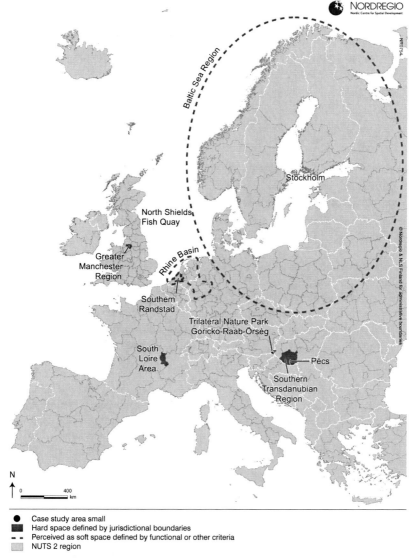

- ● Case study area small
- ■ Hard space defined by jurisdictional boundaries
- - - Perceived as soft space defined by functional or other criteria
- ▨ NUTS 2 region

Figure 5.1 The ten case studies' main territorial scope

Source: Own elaboration

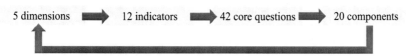

Figure 5.2 Exploring territorial governance: the research framework in a nutshell

Source: Own adaptation based on ESPON and Nordregio (2013, p. 8)

66 *Peter Schmitt and Lisa Van Well*

analysis for each case and allowed the findings from the cases to be re-constructed and analysed later. But the guidelines also allowed the researchers the freedom to explore how the dimensions and indicators were intertwined or even suggest new indicators which were external to the framework. Each case extracted a number of 'features' of territorial governance which could be seen as either promoters or inhibitors with regard to achieving a certain territorial development goal (as defined in the policy, programme or project at hand). These included innovative practices but also how certain barriers to territorial governance were (or were not) overcome. The identified features were then used to analyse the transferability of lessons and experiences of territorial governance processes among the cases (see Chapter 17).

While the 'features' had a more 'normative' function indicating some lessons for designing territorial governance, the re-constructed 'components of territorial governance' were more of an objective character in the process of synthesising comparable results. These twenty distilled components are presented in Chapter 16 and are related to the observed practices, routines, but also mechanisms and partly structures of territorial governance. The results for each component were finally synthesised in order to provide a concise, but evidence-informed summary of the ten case studies and to critically re-visit the five dimensions of territorial governance (see Chapter 16). This research framework for the empirical exploration of territorial governance at play is summarised in Figure 5.2.

References

Blatter, J.K. and Blume, T., 2008. Co-variation and causal process tracing revisited: clarifying new directions for causal inference and generalization. *Qualitative Methods – Newsletter of the American Political Science Association Organized Section for Qualitative and Multi-Method Research*, 6 (1), 29–34.

Falleti, T.G., 2006. Theory-guided process-tracing in comparative politics: something old, something new. *American Association of Political Science Newsletter*, Fall 2006, 9–14.

George, A. and Bennett, A., 2005. *Case Studies and Theory Development in the Social Sciences*. Cambridge, MA: MIT Press.

Howlett, M., 2009. Governance modes, policy regimes and operational plans: a multi-level nested model of policy instrument choice and policy design. *Policy Sciences*, 42 (1), 73–89.

Reimer, M., Panagiotis, G. and Blotevogel, H.H., 2014. *Spatial Planning Systems and Practices in Europe. A Comparative Perspective on Continuity and Changes*. New York: Routledge.

Stead, D. and Nadin, V., 2009. Planning cultures between models of society and planning systems. In: J. Knieling and F. Othengrafen, eds. *Planning Cultures in Europe. Decoding Cultural Phenomena in Urban and Regional Planning*. Aldershot: Ashgate, 283–300.

Treib , O., Bähr, H. and Falkner, G., 2007. Modes of governance: towards a conceptual clarification. *Journal of European Public Policy*, 14 (1), 1–20.

Yin, R.K., 2003. *Case Study Research: Design and Methods*. London: Sage.

6 Hyper-local planning in England

Territorial governance at the neighbourhood scale

Paul Cowie, Geoff Vigar, Simin Davoudi and Ali Madanipour

Introduction

Since taking office in 2010, neighbourhood planning has been part of a suite of mechanisms connected with the UK Coalition government's broader agendas of 'Localism' and the 'Big Society'. They chime with global agendas of subsidiarity, participation and citizen engagement, but have particular manifestations in the UK context. As expressed by the Localism Minister the agenda seeks to 'hand over power and responsibility so that local communities have real choices, and experience the real consequences of those choices' (Clark 2010). This statement reflects one of the key critiques of the current planning system, that it is overly centralised, and top-down with the planning professional seen as being distant and technocratic without any idea of what goes on in the 'real world' (Farnsworth 2011). However critics of the Coalition's manifestation of localism are sceptical about its commitment to genuine local empowerment, seeing it as an opportunistic window to roll back the state (e.g. Parvin 2011).

The Localism Act 2011 gives new plan-making powers, within important constraints, to local communities. This devolution of plan-making power seeks to both reduce the distance between those making the plans and the communities affected by them (Gallent 2013) and increase the legitimacy of the resulting plans through a process of participatory democracy (Cowie and Davoudi 2015). Once adopted as policy, neighbourhood plans are legally binding and have to be taken into consideration in any subsequent planning decision. Neighbourhood plans are advocated by central government to be light touch, empowering of communities, led by neighbourhoods, innovative, and permissive with regard to development. The last point highlights one important constraint on the plan-making process; neighbourhood plans are required to take a positive approach to development. They are not permitted to state what cannot be developed, only the type and where new development should take place.

Neighbourhood plans create a number of novel features to the English planning system. First they introduce a new planning institution, the neighbourhood forum. Second they allow business interests direct input and involvement in the preparation of these plans. Previously the development of strategic plans at the local level was restricted to elected councillors who were required to be residents of the locality and professional planning officers. Both these novel features of neighbourhood planning are discussed in this chapter.

At this stage it is perhaps worth saying a word or two by way of background on territorial governance and planning at the local scale in England. It should be noted that, in England and Wales, the smallest geographical governance institutions are Parish and Town Councils. These Councils, which cover small local communities of 500–5,000 individuals, are given the power to produce neighbourhood plans. It should be noted, however, that not all areas in England are covered by a Parish Council.

There is no equivalent institution in major urban areas. This lack of a competent body in urban areas allowed the Coalition government to create a new governance institution, the neighbourhood forum. A neighbourhood forum can be formed whenever at least 21 individuals from a locality decide to form a group with a view to preparing a neighbourhood plan. The group must be representative of the local community although there is no guidance as to what constitutes representativeness (Davoudi and Cowie 2013). The neighbourhood forum is responsible for the preparation of the local plan only. Once it has completed this task it ceases to exist. This can be contrasted with Parish and Town Councils who have a continuing governance role after the completion of the plan.

In the following this case of hyper-local planning will be investigated by examining the territorial governance opportunities and challenges at the North Shields Fish Quay area in the North East of England.

Background to the case study area

North Shields is at the mouth of the River Tyne in the North East of England. The fish quay has been the focus of economic activity in the area for centuries. In more recent decades there has been a general decline in the UK fishing industry arguably caused by increased competition from cheap imports of white fish and the limits to fishing imposed through the Common Fisheries Policy quota system which has affected the quay both economically and physically. Many of the traditional buildings associated with the fishing industry are either now redundant or have been replaced by modern industrial units away from the immediate quayside area. At the turn of the millennium therefore many of the buildings had become derelict and new uses needed to be found for them.

The area has been subject to a number of previous regeneration projects stretching back as far as the 1970s. The prevailing understanding of the local authority responsible for the North Shields Fish Quay area was that they were planning for a post-fishing industry future. In common with many post-industrial areas in the North East the problem seemed to be how can buildings which are no longer required for their original purpose be reused.

Hyper-local planning in England 69

Figure 6.1 Location of case study area
Source: Own adaptation based on OS Open data

Related to this was the question of sustainability of the community. How can the diversity of community businesses, residential and recreational activity, be maintained in the neighbourhood? The previous regeneration efforts had led to some changes with some of the redundant building being converted into residential or live-work units. The area had also started to develop an economy based around tourism with a number of cafés and restaurants opening on the quayside and a major redevelopment of the historic elements of the quay. What is perhaps different about the latest effort was the degree to which control was passed to the community itself rather than the community being consulted on plans prepared by higher authorities.

Coordinating the actions of actors and institutions: making planners out of fishermen

The North Shields Fish Quay Neighbourhood Forum was one of the first to embark on the process of neighbourhood plan-making in England. It therefore offers a suitable case study to investigate territorial governance issues at this micro scale. Being an urban area there was no Parish or Town Council to take on responsibility for the plan. It was therefore necessary to form a neighbourhood forum.

As outlined earlier one of the main issues facing the North Shields Fish Quay was the reuse of redundant industrial buildings. To protect and preserve the industrial heritage of the area a partnership had previously been formed between a group of individuals with an interest in the historic environment and the local authority, North Tyneside Council. The partnership, the Fish Quay Heritage Partnership, had gone on to produce a conservation area character statement. This is a statutory planning document which seeks to protect and preserve the historic environment. It forms part of the local planning framework and is managed by the local authority.

The core of the North Shields Fish Quay Neighbourhood Forum was formed from the members of the Fish Quay Heritage Partnership. It seems to be a common occurrence within neighbourhood planning that there needs to be a source of civic capacity within a neighbourhood to carry forward the impetus to start the plan-making process (Cowie and Davoudi 2015). The North Shields Fish Quay Neighbourhood Forum was also slightly different from the process envisaged by the localism legislation in that it was North Tyneside Council who suggested to the community that they should prepare a neighbourhood plan. Normally a neighbourhood would decide themselves to prepare neighbourhood plans where and when they felt the need for one, namely a bottom-up process. The reason for this slightly top-down approach will never fully be known but a number of the stakeholders interviewed for the case study were of the opinion that local politics had a lot to do with the decision. North Tyneside Council was at that time controlled by the governing Conservative Party with most of the region around it controlled by the opposition Labour Party. Neighbourhood planning was seen as a priority by the national Liberal Democrat/Conservative government and it was felt to be a good thing politically if a neighbourhood plan in the urban North East could be instigated. This perhaps shows how quickly the broad rhetoric around bottom-up territorial governance can be subverted when practical implementation issues and local political interest come into play.

Using a pre-existing community group, the Fish Quay Heritage Partnership, could have raised issues of representativeness for the neighbourhood forum. This partnership was primarily concerned with the built environment whilst the neighbourhood plan had the express aim to encompass all aspects, social, environmental and economic, of the neighbourhood. It was therefore decided to actively seek out other stakeholders and persuade them to participate in the planning process. Open meetings were held and widely advertised. Initially 80 members of the community attended the meetings of the neighbourhood forum. From this pool of people a core team was chosen to drive forward the process. This self-selection of neighbourhood representatives raises interesting issues of democratic legitimacy. This representative claim, as Saward (2010) has highlighted, shifts how the issue of democratic representation and legitimacy can be established, away from electoral mandates, to one based on participation. In the case of neighbourhood forums, their legitimacy relies on both the claims made by the neighbourhood forum and the acceptance of those claims by the community within the neighbourhood. In the case of neighbourhood plans

Hyper-local planning in England 71

this is formalised through the use of a referendum as the final step in the process of producing a neighbourhood plan. The success, or otherwise, of this claim to be representative was particularly relevant as the North Shields Fish Quay Neighbourhood Forum sought to integrate the various policy sectors and stakeholders as we will explore in the next sections.

Integrating policy sectors

The quayside area around the fishing port in North Shields has experienced several decades of decline. Many of the buildings in the area had become vacant and a number derelict. Previous attempts to regenerate the area looked to diversify the economy away from the fishing industry into tourism and the knowledge economy. Efforts had also been made to convert the redundant buildings into mixed use properties with small commercial units on the ground floor and residential dwellings above. This was the background to the formation of the neighbourhood planning group. Essentially they were assuming they were planning for a post-fishing area. This assumption on the part of the group's core members, and to a lesser extent the local council, did cause some mistrust with fishing industry stakeholders. Whilst in general fishing in the UK has been declining, North Shields is one of the remaining active fishing ports on the North East coast and therefore had been growing in recent years as it won business from other ports as they closed. In addition, previous investments in the fish processing industry locally had also boosted that sector. Initially the focus of the proposed neighbourhood planning process was to be the area occupied by the fishing industry. As is outlined later this was extended as the local members of the neighbourhood forum started to take ownership of the process.

Once the various parties started to engage in the process of plan-making it became clear that the fishing industry was going to continue playing a major economic and cultural role in the area. This highlights the need for both an open mind when seeking to integrate various policy sectors and to have a period of time to allow the various stakeholders to gain a mutual understanding of each other's situation. Allowing time to coalesce as a group also provided space to establish the formal structures of the group. A series of officials, a chairman and secretary had to be appointed by the group.

During this 'getting to know you phase' the stakeholders established each of their priorities. For the fishing industry it was the message that they were here to stay and had certain operational requirements. The fishing industry is still the major employer in the area and the quayside and associated processing industry occupies a significant amount of the land and buildings in the area around the fish quay. For example, the fact that their working practice was linked to the state of the tide had been perhaps overlooked by some of the other stakeholders. A particular area of conflict was around the unsocial working hours of the port. Once all stakeholders understood the necessity of working with the tide, which may mean late nights or early starts, a way forward could be discussed. In fact the necessity for the fishing port to operate on a 24 hours a day basis was written into the preamble of the final plan. This group forming process can be seen as a necessary preamble for territorial governance institutions which do not necessarily derive their authority from existing democratic institutions, either directly or indirectly.

Once the challenges had been identified, work started on negotiating a strategic spatial plan for the future. This planning work has previously been the preserve of professional planners working within local authorities. There was therefore a need to endow the members of the neighbourhood forum with a significant level of specialist planning knowledge. For the North Shields Fish Quay this was undertaken in two ways: first, a planning professional from a local planning organisation was appointed as mentor for the group; second, a period of time was set aside within the planning process for the group to get to grips with the technical aspects of preparing such a plan. The North Shields Fish Quay Neighbourhood Forum was perhaps fortunate in their novelty. A significant number of external stakeholders had an interest in being a part of a front-runner plan. It was therefore relatively easy for the neighbourhood forum to engage with bodies such as the Environment Agency, English Heritage and other strategic stakeholders who were able to provide expert advice from their particular point of view.

There was not universal approval however from the members of the neighbourhood forum. A number felt this process acted to constrain the group and led to a narrow set of policy agendas. They argued that to restrict the remit and process of the group in this way risked losing what is important about bottom-up neighbourhood planning and the ability of communities to think creatively about their future. The inability to think creatively was also due to the constraints imposed on neighbourhood planning from the centre. The Localism Act specifically restricts neighbourhood plans to positive statements around development. It was specifically designed to prevent neighbourhood plans being used to block or hamper development, so called NIMBYism (e.g. Matthews *et al.* 2015). In addition to the restriction on the scope of neighbourhood plans, there is also a requirement that they do not conflict with spatial plans produced at local authority level. This further restricts the scope for neighbourhood forums to produce radical and innovative plans for their local area.

Having highlighted the restrictions and limits to policy integration within neighbourhood planning it should be pointed out that there were examples from North Shields Fish Quay Neighbourhood Plan as to how stakeholders were able to coordinate certain aspects of policy. One area where there was a degree of agreement in policy terms and stakeholder agreement was around the redevelopment of redundant buildings. At issue in the plan were two plots of land; the first a derelict warehouse at the centre of the neighbourhood; the second a plot of land between the fish quay and a residential area, which had previously been redeveloped and was used by fish processing businesses.

The warehouse land was owned by a property developer. There had been a longstanding debate about the land and its possible redevelopment. Each of the various stakeholders, the local authority, the developer, local residents and businesses all had slightly different aspirations for the site. One of the main conflicts was between the financial viability of any proposed development and the need for a development to complement the future vision for the neighbourhood. In practical terms it was a choice between a purely residential development, favoured by the developer and a mixed used development, favoured by the local authority and other business stakeholders in the area. During the planning process the developer was able to impress upon the neighbourhood forum the need to bear in mind the commercial viability of any specific use for the site within the plan. As such the final plan did not specify a particular use for this site but give broad guidance on the type of development needed in the area.

The second plot also highlights the various trade-offs that resulted from the neighbourhood planning process. This site contained poor quality industrial units and had been selected for redevelopment by the local authority. During the neighbourhood planning process a group of residents residing in a converted building overlooking the site successfully argued the land should be left open as green space with alternative accommodation found for the remaining businesses. Whilst both these examples of policy integration and agreement between stakeholders were a result of negotiation and debate it is not hard to imagine situations where there will not be such an easy win-win solution. In this case the role of individual stakeholders as 'representatives' of their particular policy interest could cause significant problems in producing a meaningful plan if such a plan could be produced at all. The role of stakeholders in territorial governance is therefore critical and this is the focus of the next section.

Mobilising stakeholder participation

As outlined in the previous section, there was an initial period during which the structure and the participation of stakeholders were developed. In the case of the North Shields Fish Quay Neighbourhood Plan there were three key sets of stakeholders involved in the process. These could be categorised as primary, secondary and tertiary stakeholders. The primary stakeholders were those making up the neighbourhood forum itself. These stakeholders tended to have a direct interest in the neighbourhood and/or were located within the neighbourhood. Secondary stakeholders were drawn from a much wider geography and range of interests. They represented different policy sectors and political interests within the plan-making process. Finally the tertiary stakeholders are those people who have an interest in the future of the North Shields Fish Quay, but were not members of the neighbourhood forum. These could be residents or businesses in the neighbourhood or else visitors or those with a cultural connection to the neighbourhood. Each of these categories of stakeholder will be considered in turn.

Primary stakeholders

The process which led to the formation of the North Shields Fish Quay Neighbourhood Forum had the effect of including two key stakeholders from the start, the local authority and the North Shields Heritage Partnership. Early in the process it was realised that to be successful the neighbourhood forum had to reach out to a wider spectrum of stakeholders. There was a concerted effort to contact and include as many of the stakeholders relevant to the future of the fish quay. One of the key stakeholders was the fishing industry and those associated with it. To begin with there was a degree of mistrust and weariness on the part of the fishing stakeholders. This was based on a, probably legitimate, concern that this was yet another regeneration project which would inevitably fail just as the previous versions had. It was also founded on a feeling of isolation and pressure the fishing industry had felt as a result of past issues of noise and smell from the fish quay. However once it was understood what the process involved and the potential for a significant input into the future spatial plan for the area, fishing stakeholders felt necessary to become directly involved in the planning process. In the end the representative of the fishing sector played a major role in the drafting of the final version of the neighbourhood plan. The involvement of the fishing industry did secure a greater understanding of their continuing role and relevance to the community, a fact which is clearly reflected in the plan itself.

Another stakeholder with a direct interest in the plan's contents was the owner of the major redevelopment site. As with the fishing stakeholder there was arguably a dual purpose to their involvement. The primary purpose was to secure a favourable provision in the plan for their land which they achieved through involvement in the process to the end. The secondary purpose of their involvement was to make local people aware of the need to ensure that commercial viability is considered when planning decisions are made. This argument reflects the national government's concerns with a lack of commercial sensitivity in planning decisions which then act as a barrier to development.

Both these examples highlight how difficult it can be to mobilise stakeholders but also the fact that just mobilising them is not the end of the problem. The implicit aim of neighbourhood planning is for those with an interest in the future of a particular place to work together for the common good. If individual stakeholders engage in the process with their own specific agendas and strategic goals, the ability of the group to achieve this common purpose is undermined. This is made worse if there are power and capacity differences between the relevant stakeholders. In any governance process of this kind there needs to be a degree of understanding between the stakeholders and sensitivity to each other's interests and goals. In the case of North Shields Fish Quay the two commercial stakeholders had both the human and financial capital to continue their engagement in the planning process through to the end. They also had the experience in their everyday lives of dealing in similar strategic plans, being it business planning or in the land use planning system itself. This could be contrasted with the other stakeholders representing the general community. Many had other competing interests, demands on their time and had little or no experience in strategic planning. These somewhat covert differences between stakeholders in relation to their relative power and capacity need to be made overt and the planning process needs to mediate between them in a way that power is shared equally. This calls into question the role of professional planners in these new forms of territorial governance (Allmendinger and Haughton 2012).

Secondary stakeholders

In the context of neighbourhood planning and localism, secondary stakeholders are those with a general interest in the neighbourhood planning process and the impact of a neighbourhood plan in a wider context. In the case of the North Shields Fish Quay Neighbourhood Plan they include non-departmental government bodies such as the Environment Agency or English Heritage as well as the local authority. Although these secondary stakeholders do not have a direct role in the neighbourhood forum, they do have significant influence in the way the process is conducted. This is partly due to the fact that the neighbourhood in question is not an island, cut off from its surroundings. It is connected physically and in other ways, socially and culturally, to the surrounding areas. The impact of the neighbourhood plan will extend beyond its boundaries. For this reason there needs to be a degree of strategic context provided to the neighbourhood forum. Once the structure of the group had been settled there was a period of time devoted to 'making planners out of fishermen' with secondary stakeholders presenting their views on the content of the neighbourhood plan. North Shields Fish Quay Neighbourhood Forum were lucky in that as a front-runner there was a certain novelty value attached to being involved in this project.

It remains to be seen to what extent such secondary stakeholders will, want, or have the capacity, to engage with the hundredth neighbourhood plan as they are produced in many other areas. There is also a potential conflict of interest between the primary and secondary stakeholders. The secondary stakeholders will have their own corporate and political priorities which may not coincide with the priorities of the primary stakeholders. This again raises questions as to the balance of power. Given the status of neighbourhood plans at the bottom of the hierarchy of plans, is it conceivable that secondary stakeholders could have undue influence over neighbourhood forums given their capacity and experience of planning at all levels.

76 Cowie, Vigar, Davoudi and Madanipour

Tertiary stakeholders

Tertiary stakeholders can be differentiated from primary stakeholders through their participation in the plan-making process. Tertiary stakeholders may form the community of place, that is they live and/or work in the neighbourhood. Alternatively they may form a community of interest, namely have a cultural or social connection with the neighbourhood. The North Shields Fish Quay Neighbourhood Plan case study highlighted the role of two tertiary stakeholders: non-participating residents and businesses, and tourists interested in visiting the area. One of the difficulties with any planning process is how to engage those who have a general interest in the plan. Scholars such as Healey (1997 and 2006) have highlighted the need for greater public participation in place making and planning. On the face of it neighbourhood planning seems to fit the bill but they still faced familiar consultation problems.

To engage the tertiary stakeholders the neighbourhood forum adopted more traditional consultation methods. The two methods used to engage tertiary stakeholders were a door-to-door questionnaire and a drop-in consultation day. The response rate from the questionnaire was just over 25 per cent. The local authority stakeholder was delighted with this level of response. A typical response rate to their planning consultations is below 10 per cent. However some members of the North Shields Fish Quay Neighbourhood Forum felt this was not sufficient when considering community planning:

> The idea of reaching out, the idea that a questionnaire was suitable and [name removed] reassuring people that 25% was a fantastic percentage back, well the council never achieve that ... but that's the Council, we're not the Council and we are the neighbourhood. It's not acceptable to say 25% is okay.
>
> (personal communication 2012)

The feeling was that everyone should have a chance to have a direct say in the plan, not just be consulted.

The three types of stakeholder highlight the complexity in mobilising stakeholder engagement. It is not just a question of getting everyone involved. Different stakeholders will need and want to have a different role at different stages of the process.

Being adaptive to changing contexts

The adaptability of neighbourhood forums is perhaps their weakest feature. As outlined in the introduction, a neighbourhood forum has a finite lifespan. Once it has completed its task, to draft and publish a neighbourhood plan, it is finished and ceases to exist. The rationale for this way of structuring the process is that once the plan is produced and adopted as a statutory document it will speak for itself. All future planning decisions will need to be decided in accordance with the provisions of the neighbourhood plan. However, as more and neighbourhood plans are published and adopted it is likely that they will be debated and contested. In particular neighbourhood plans will be subject to legal challenges by interested parties such as landowners and developers whose interests are affected by plans. This process, by which a new set of stakeholders engage in the process through legal challenges, has been termed 'judicialization' (Hirschl 2006). Legal challenges to statutory plans, including neighbourhood plans, are often founded on the process by which the plan was produced as much as they relate to the provisions of the plan itself. This can of course work both ways with the neighbourhood forum challenging decisions which they feel do not conform to the provisions of the neighbourhood plan, as was the case with the Exeter St James neighbourhood forum where the local group challenged a planning decision by the local authority which they felt did not take into account their neighbourhood plan (Exeter St James Forum 2014).

This shows therefore a need for a continuing interest on the part of the community in the life of the plan. To maintain this capacity both financial and human capital both of which are lacking in neighbourhood forums are needed. The current government has acknowledged this failing within the current system and has proposed the introduction of a fast-track method for neighbourhood forums to convert themselves to Parish Councils if they wish (Sandford 2014).

In addition to lacking capacity to react to changed circumstances, the current system is also wasteful. Significant amounts of social and cultural capital have been built up over the process of drafting the neighbourhood plan. The stakeholder from the local authority commented that it had helped developing strong ties with the community over the period which could be valuable in the future. However, as the members of the neighbourhood forum have now gone their separate ways and no longer have any permanent contact with each other this capacity risks being lost. Any spatial plan will inevitably become out of date and irrelevant in the face of changed local and extra-local circumstances. In most planning situations there is provision to regularly review and update plans in light of changed circumstances. There is no such provision with neighbourhood plans. In this age of technological connectivity, there is a case to have something akin to a living document. It should be possible to produce a version of the plan which is subject to an ongoing debate and update by the general public. This ongoing debate and discussion would allow a degree of engagement and transparency within the process of plan-making.

Realising place-based/territorial specificities and impacts

The North Shields Fish Quay Neighbourhood Forum was undertaken at the instigation of the local authority, who also proposed the initial boundary of the neighbourhood plan (shown in cross-hatched black in Figure 6.2). The area was restricted to the operational fish quay and the associated fish processing premises to the north. This focus on the economic activity of the area is perhaps understandable given the national policy priorities of economic growth.

However, once the process became a partnership between the local authority and the Fish Quay Heritage Partnership, concern was raised about the narrow focus of the plan boundary. After discussion it was agreed that the neighbourhood plan boundary would be extended to include the area covered by the previous conservation area character statement produced by the Fish Quay Heritage Partnership (the areas shown hatched black in Figure 6.2). The area now included significant residential areas and the tourism and other new businesses to the south of the main fishing quay. This greater diversity was felt to be necessary to ensure a broad coalition of stakeholders were included in the plan-making process. It also reflects an understanding by the stakeholders of the importance of the various elements within the neighbourhood which need to act together to ensure a secure future. Past initiatives around the fish market have already highlighted the benefit of tourism to the fishermen. Many of the fish merchants who were previously wholesalers only have now opened stalls selling directly to the visiting public. In addition the restaurants in the area have started to specialise in seafood again, targeting tourists. This integration

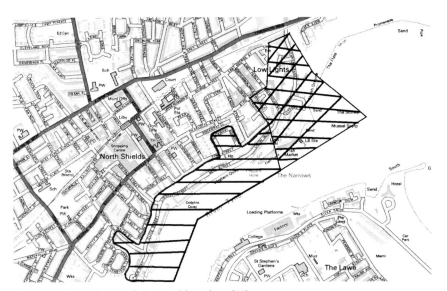

Figure 6.2 Boundaries of the neighbourhood plan area
Source: Own adaptation based on OS Open data

of activity has had both direct and indirect benefits. Whilst the volume of sales to direct customers is only a fraction of the overall turnover of the businesses it carries a greater profit margin. At the same time it raises the profile of fish as an affordable and local food source. This place-based knowledge of the area has arguably worked to produce a much more holistic plan for the area as well as increasing the mutual understanding between the various stakeholders involved in the plan as outlined above.

Conclusions

The North Shields Fish Quay case study highlights the level of support and capacity building needed to ensure territorial governance at the local level is successful. To ensure all the relevant dimensions of territorial governance are adequately developed, those undertaking governance at a very local level need to have a degree of civic capacity. This includes the ability to constitute the group in a way that is recognised by other institutions and the ability to conduct a formal planning process which is open and transparent. In many cases this civic capacity can be co-opted from existing civic groups, as was the case here with the Fish Quay Heritage Partnership forming the core of the neighbourhood forum. In other examples of neighbourhood planning it can result in the 'usual subjects' taking control of the process (Gunn *et al.* 2015).

This potential for the process to be dominated by existing powerful groups can be avoided by providing time and resources to develop the capacity from within the community. Spatial planning even at the neighbourhood scale is a complex and technical undertaking. There needs to be a period during which the community can construct the required governance structures and then endow them with the requisite knowledge needed to conduct a planning process.

This period of development also allows a recalibration of the relationship between the planning professionals and the community undertaking the neighbourhood plan. As was outlined in the introduction, part of the reason for the introduction of neighbourhood plans was to tackle to the top-down bureaucratic nature of planning. This change has significant implications for the role of professional planners. Planners are now required to fulfil the role of facilitators rather than experts. This combination of local knowledge with the professional support of professional planners should enhance a number of key characteristics of territorial governance: realising place-based specificities and safe-guarding transparency and legitimacy.

The major concern for neighbourhood plans and neighbourhood forums is their lack of continuity. Once the plan has been completed the community capacity gained during the process may be lost. The recent changes to allow neighbourhood forums to form Parish Councils more easily goes some way to addressing this shortfall but its voluntary nature means those that need to retain the hard-won community capacity are the one least likely to proceed to form a Parish Council.

References

Allmendinger, P. and Haughton, G., 2012. Post-political spatial planning in England: a crisis of consensus. *Transactions of the Institute of British Geographers*, 37 (1), 89–103.

Clark, G., 2010. *Community engagement and the planning system: speech to the Town and Country Planning Association*. Available from: http://www.gregclark. org/articles~speeches/community-engagement-and-the-planning-system/15 [Accessed 1 January 2015]

Cowie, P. and Davoudi, S., 2015. Is small really beautiful: the legitimacy of neighbourhood planning? In: S. Davoudi and A. Madanipur, eds. *Reconsidering Localism*. Abingdon: Routledge, 168–189.

Davoudi, S. and Cowie, P., 2013. Are English neighbourhood forums democratically legitimate? *Planning Theory and Practice*, 14 (4), 562–566.

ESPON and Nordregio, 2013. ESPON TANGO – Territorial Approaches for New Governance. Final Report. Available from: http://www.espon.eu/export/sites/ default/Documents/Projects/AppliedResearch/TANGO/FR/ESPON_TANGO_ Main_Report_Final.pdf [Accessed 20 April 2015].

Exeter St. James Forum, 2014. Improved scheme at Cricket Club: Explanation of legal action. *ESLF Newsletter 24*. Available from: http://www.exeterstjamesforum. org/news/esjf-newsletter-24 [Accessed 17 December 2014].

Farnsworth, D., 2011. A network route to localism in planning. *Town & Country Planning*, 80, 128–132.

Gallent, N., 2013. Re-connecting 'people and planning': parish plans and the English localism agenda, *Town Planning Review*, 84 (3), 371–396.

Gunn, Z., Vigar, G. and Brooks, E., 2015. The community's capacity to plan: is it there, and is it enough? In: S. Davoudi and A. Madanipur, eds. *Reconsidering Localism*. Abingdon: Routledge, 168–189.

Healey, P., 1997. *Collaborative Planning: Shaping Places in Fragmented Societies*. London: Macmillan.

Healey P., 2006. Transforming governance: challenges of institutional adaptation and a new politics of space. *European Planning Studies*, 14 (3), 299–320.

Hirschl, R., 2006. The new constitutionalism and the judicialization of pure politics worldwide. *Fordham Law Review*, 75 (2), 721–753.

Matthews, P., Bramley, G. and Hastings, A., 2015. *Homo economicus* in a big society: understanding middle-class Activism and NIMBYism towards new housing developments. *Housing Theory & Society*, 32 (1), 54–72.

Parvin, P., 2011. Localism and the left: the need for strong central government. *Renewal*, 19 (2), 37–49.

Sandford, M., 2014. *Parish and town councils: recent issues*. London: House of Commons Library. Available from: http://www.parliament.uk/briefing-papers/ sn04827.pdf [Accessed 17 December 2014].

Saward, M., 2010. *The Representative Claim*. Oxford: Oxford University Press.

7 The 'European Capital of Culture – Pécs'

Territorial governance challenges within a centralised context

Ilona Pálné Kovács and Zoltán Grünhut

Introduction

The title 'European Capital of Culture' (ECoC) is annually awarded by the European Union to grant the nominated city the opportunity to present its cultural life and developments. The idea originates from Melina Mercouri, and 2010 was the 25th anniversary of this popular 'project'. The scheme has not been changed since the last regulation (1622/2006 EC), so the honoured cities will carry out 'their projects' in accordance with the same framework until 2019 (Selection Panel 2009). A new framework has subsequently been adopted by the European Parliament and Council in April 2014 and will be applied for the post-2019 period, which also includes the chronological list of member states that may host the title from 2020 until 2033.

A number of European cities have used this title to transform and improve their cultural life as well as their national and international reputation. Formally, this kind of project belongs to the European Communities' Cultural Policy, since the designated cities implement dozens of cultural programmes and events. However, in the last decade the scheme could rather be characterised as a complex urban development project with strong ties to culture and knowledge-based investments (Palmer 2004, Palmer *et al.* 2011, Sykes 2011).

This shift was also characteristic for the European Capital of Culture project implemented in Pécs in 2010. Pécs is a medium-sized Hungarian city with about 150,000 inhabitants near the Croatian border and is considered a regional centre in Hungary. The former coal-mining city started to decline after 1990 when industrial activities were almost completely eliminated. The Balkan war worsened the economic situation even further, along with the city's historically poor accessibility to the Hungarian capital, Budapest. Therefore the European Capital of Culture project was a key opportunity for Pécs to catch up and generate economic growth. The town is the centre of an economically declining NUTS-2 region receiving priority in the Regional Operatioipnal Programme (ROP) of the National Development Plan (2007–2013) designed for the application of the then called European Structural Funds (ESF).

When the bid for the title of European Capital of Culture was formulated, the project was thought to be an excellent chance for the city to launch a 'cultural turn of urban development'. Constructing new cultural infrastructures (like a concert hall, library and exhibition centre), regenerating an old industrial district for cultural functions and renovating public places were all based on the assumption that these investments would launch subsequent economic growth in the fields of creative and cultural industries (ECoC Bid of Pécs 2005). The other conceptual element was to become a 'gate to the Balkans', by cooperating with neighbouring regions beyond the national borders in the spirit of a 'borderless Europe'. Hence, the newly built cultural infrastructure, the renovation of public space, and the new motorway between Pécs and Budapest were relatively large and important investments in Hungary.

Nonetheless, this almost five-year process was hectic and full of conflicts. Local struggles ensured with time pressure, media, central government departments, development agencies and European offices, as well as among local stakeholders, politicians and civil society. These provide ample evidence on the mechanisms and determinants of a complex urban development programme in a territorial governance context characterised by a centralised financing and decision-making system, and also by an 'Eastern' paternalistic political culture.

The European Capital of Culture project was challenging in several aspects: vertically, because European, national and local levels of governance had to collaborate with each other; and horizontally, since public actors had to align to the partnership model, that is, to cooperate with civil society and the creative communities in this context. Multi-level governance and the partnership model are conceptual pillars of the European Cohesion Policy. These requirements were set as conditions for the new member states, and the European Capital of Culture project can be thus seen as another episode of the so-called Europeanisation process, or rather, as Hughes *et al.* 2004 put it, the 'Eastern version' of conditionalism, since the respective stakeholders are almost obliged to use a governance model fitting these principles. In addition, the European Capital of Culture Pécs as such has to be considered as a large-scale project that drastically influenced the development of the city with all its risks (Häussermann and Simons 2000).

Co-ordinating the actions of actors and institutions

In order to understand what happened in Pécs one has to know that, like most of the other Eastern European countries, Hungary is still a centralistic state, and though local autonomy is a frequently mentioned principle in official political documents and reform programmes, neither the regions nor the cities or civil society are generally able to reconcile and enforce their interests (Hendriks *et al.* 2011). In spite of the Eastern European countries having implemented administrative reforms under the flag of 'subsidiarity

The 'European Capital of Culture – Pécs' 83

and regional decentralisation', almost all of them have remained centralised (Scott 2009).

Similar to Sykes' (2011) observations, the vertical dimension of the governance system proved to be crucial in the European Capital of Culture case as well. Formally, the local government was the 'owner' of the project, but it lacked both the legal and the financial preconditions for controlling the whole process, confirming the old rule: 'He who pays the piper calls the tune'. In other words, there were no local resources for the local programmes from the very beginning. Hence, the dependence on national and EU funds, filtered through national bodies, remained constant during the whole project cycle. Not only the investments, but also the cultural programmes were managed centrally, that is, the national government paid for the cultural programmes through a central cultural agency (the so-called Hungarofest) that was commissioned to manage the local cultural events performed in 2010. The local management, the artistic director and local artists were almost completely excluded, which can be considered as being unique in the history of European Capital of Culture projects so far (Palmer 2004, Palmer and Greg 2011). The external dominance limited the local discretion, which made the decision-making process slow and difficult as well as less transparent and unpredictable, and, finally, greatly contributed to the loss of trust locally. The central actors mostly tried to avoid any risk, and this also limited local innovations and flexibility. The representative of the Ministry of Culture said cynically about the cultural programme: 'It wasn't bad, but it had no face!' (personal communication 2012).

The urban development investments were also controlled externally by the European Structural Funds regime. Both the National and the Regional Development Agencies were obliged to control the entire process (application, planning, public procurement, etc.) following the strict EU regulations and regular reporting to the EU Commission. While their decision-making processes were extremely slow, they prescribed feasibility studies and eliminated the exhibition hall from the 'list of dreams', declaring it to be unsustainable. Experts of these EU regulations tried to keep the project close to the European standards and provided special skills for the project managers, but most of the domestic stakeholders regarded these frames rather as obstacles than guarantees for quality and efficiency (personal communication 2012).

The process was not clearly planned for the whole governance cycle from the beginning. Problems were 'solved' by *ad hoc* solutions lacking any regulated channels of feedback. Although monitoring was prescribed by EU regulation, these reports were written for the 'European audience' and not from an implementation perspective in order to learn from it. We also have to mention that Hungarian governance culture is generally weak on evaluation practice, not having any professional and institutional background for the task. Unfortunately, this was the case with the *ex post* evaluation of this project as well (cf. Ágoston *et al.* 2011). The central government completely

84 *Ilona Pálné Kovács and Zoltán Grünhut*

forgot this evaluation due to the election in 2010 and the new cabinet with its comprehensive government and public administrational reform.

Integrating policy sectors: requirements and limits of the integrative approach

The goal of European Capital of Culture projects in general is, as mentioned before, to link the one-year series of cultural events with long-term urban development. This integrative approach was also supported by the logic of the EU Cohesion Policy requiring complex plans at different territorial levels and scales for the 2007–2013 programming period. This double European challenge aimed to integrate sectoral and territorial needs in appropriate general institutional frames and processes. But to what extent is the respective territorial governance framework able to adapt to these challenges? The Hungarian government system is traditionally very centralised and fragmented at the same time in the sense that government does not act as a collective body, but instead, it is the ministries and informal groupings of leaders that constitute the real power centres. Although the central government and its units controlled the project from the beginning, there was no designated body at the national level to coordinate the various sectors and levels. This meant that the cultural, economic and financial elements of the project belonged to different actors at state level. Thus local actors had to build separate channels to communicate with them as there was no platform to bring the dispersed ambitions and actions together.

To understand the role of the local self-government of Pécs, it is worth outlining the essence of the Hungarian local governance system (Pálné 2012a). Following the systemic change in the 1990s, local governance had high political relevance. Local freedom and independence were the most important aims of the Parliament to loosen state control and broaden their responsibility for local affairs. This initial enthusiasm towards a decentralised power structure has eroded over time. During the European Capital of Culture project the local government already enjoyed less respect and less financial scope of action, so Pécs had no other choice but to adapt to the wishes of the central and the European actors in order to subsidise its aims.

Both the general public government frames and the special management system of the project were problematic from the point of view of sectoral integration. Actions during the project were obstructed by the confused competences of the managers in the permanent office of the local government and also by the often changing managers in the newly created temporary management organisation. The local government of Pécs would have been appropriate for the overall project management. However, the majority of the tasks were outsourced to a management company and therefore the local government was not involved in the overall co-ordination and implementation. This management organisation could have had many advantages, as compared to the rigid and bureaucratic routines, but as an 'outsider' having no legitimacy it was less able to integrate other actors. This principal dilemma emerged in the relations among the local government, local politicians and the 'technocrats' of the project management company.

Although mostly with no formal decision-making competences, there were several collective bodies, committees, councils set up and roundtables held separately for the cultural programmes and for the development projects. No one single body had an overview of the entire European Capital of Culture project. Individual commissioners were also nominated in order to help the formal (in practice usually informal) top-down and bottom-up information flows. As they were often active in the 'grey zone' of governance, this supports the view that the role and impact of trust in networks of local elites can easily become a negative factor (Sik 2012, Uslaner 2002). These commissioners symbolised the centralistic attitude of the government. The central government insisted on its representation even in local bodies. Thus, every member of the artistic council, and consequently the local members too, had to be assigned by the minister.

Another dilemma was how the chain of *ad hoc* single projects could be integrated into the general institutional framework. According to experiences of other European Capital of Culture projects, both short-term success and long-term sustainability require integration into the overall context of city-marketing and cultural industry, or more generally, of creative cities (Cook and Lazzeretti 2008). The territorial dimension is also important in successful integration. Project-based organisations can only be efficient if they are embedded in the spirit and traditions of the place at hand (Belussi and Sedita 2008). However, a centralised European Capital of Culture structure, like the one in Pécs, did not support the realisation of this rather theoretical expectation.

Packaging urban culture and economic development policies

The general European Capital of Culture regulation recommends the combination of cultural events and broader urban and regional development investments, acknowledging that culture can be a driving force for local/regional development. The relatively soft cultural policy of the EU supports regional identity, combining socio-economic and cultural development and opening up new ways of participation for the local/regional civil society. The synergy, however, is still missing among the different policy fields and cultural aspects (During *et al.* 2009), although these driving forces are recognised as an innovation potential in economic development policy. Paradoxically, at the time of the European Capital of Culture Pécs project, the European Structural Funds (2007–2013) regulation did not favour integrated solutions, since it is difficult to coordinate and finance an integrated project from different funds. The first phase of policy packaging in this project was the preparation of the bid for the title of European Capital of Culture. The bid was prepared by a team of a limited number of experts representing different organisations, profiles and disciplines. Only a few persons – such as those affiliated with local civic organisations, artists and academic scholars – worked mostly informally together at the beginning in order to collect some ideas and create elements for the programme. This face-to-face method was ideal to prepare a cultural strategy. However, as business actors and urban planners were absent from this group, the result was lacking a comprehensive development plan (Takáts 2011).

The relatively independent local civil elite worked on the new version of the bid in the second round of the selection as well (Tarrósy 2011). Although the local government of Pécs financed the bid, it did not intend to take part in it and to cooperate with the writers of the concept. At the same time, the mayor started to use the competition between the candidate cities to promote his own political career and granted political and financial support for the huge additional infrastructural investments, such as the motorway mentioned above or the airport near Pécs (Takáts 2011). This means that 'policy packaging' could be found in both formalised planning and informal lobbying.

After winning the title the third phase of planning started by preparing some of the investments more professionally. That was the real programming within the frame of the Regional Operational Programme financed by the European Structural Funds. When this preparation started in 2005 to 2006, the national plan for the programming period of 2007–2013 was not ready yet. So it is no wonder that the integration of the European Capital of Culture project into the general policy programme was hindered. Although the project was officially prioritised by a government decree, during programming and implementation each investment of the development package had to appear as a separate application (of around 3,000–4,000 pages each).

Policy packaging can be promoted or hindered by means of financing. Sources from the European Structural Funds were available, as Pécs was eligible as part of a 'lagging behind' NUTS 2 region. However, the slow processes and the difficulties in integrating money from different operational programmes proved to be an obstacle rather than an advantage for the integration of the various elements of the project.

During the European Capital of Culture project the original culture-based economic development aims were gradually weakening at the expense of urban regeneration projects. Almost all of the energy of the local government was used in struggling with time in order to complete the huge buildings and the reconstruction of public places. It appeared that the most powerful actors were more interested in achieving visible success in the short term than in launching long-term development processes.

It is no wonder then that not much synergy seemed to emerge among the different investments. The two (urban development and cultural) lines of programming and their public institutional frameworks were separated and even the actors able to locally represent a holistic, integrated approach (like the civic and the business sectors) were almost completely excluded. Neither the dominant governance level (the central one) nor the involved (mostly public) sectors were properly chosen and the transmitting mechanisms proved insufficient to bridge the gaps.

The European Capital of Culture project had great expectations concerning tourism since, according to Kundi (2012), the effect of larger festivals can be positively evaluated and measured at least in the short term. Thus, marketing the cultural events and 'selling' the city would have been important. The tourism figures for these years, however, were not convincing. Centralised marketing activities were apparently not effective enough and the city itself was also unable to integrate the other attractive places into a common package.

Mobilising stakeholders to participate

The political and administrative sector dominated the whole project as almost everything was financed from public (national and EU) resources. The lack of private investors was due not only to the lagging behind of the city and its region, but also to political decision-makers ignoring real economic development problems. The whole process was over-politicised since actors with publicly elected legitimacy or party affiliation insisted on their 'responsibility' and 'power'.

Within the local arena the mayor personally dominated the decision-making process (Takáts 2011). Acting as a 'spider in the web', his power was based not only on his democratically gained mandate, but also on informal, personal networks built upon two other positions as a party leader and a member of parliament. This is a typical Hungarian political constellation; in order to be successful as a local politician it is necessary to lobby at the central level to be able to exert influence within the party and in the national government.

The overwhelming dominance of the central government was coupled with the centralised management system of European Structural Funds. The connection between the National Development Agency (and its regional branch) and the Pécs 2010 Management Centre was another non-political decision-making channel. This formal mechanism was strictly regulated (by EU procedural requirements) defining the roles and the frames of activities, so the actors did not have much chance to evade them.

Lack of social capital as a barrier to stakeholder mobilisation

As mentioned above, the logic of the European Capital of Culture project, as Sykes (2011) argues, requires a bottom-up spirit in general and local/regional social capital in particular. This means that local actors should have a relatively high level of trust and willingness to cooperate and to appreciate collective commitment and responsibility as well as collective participation and voluntary actions (see for example, Coffé and Geys 2005, Guiso et al. 2011, Kapucu 2011, Newton 2001, Putnam 2000).

88 *Ilona Pálné Kovács and Zoltán Grünhut*

In the early period of the bidding procedure these social capital factors seemed to have a central role, since the submitted proposal envisaged a well-functioning, enthusiastic local milieu and a bottom-up organisational structure. The preparatory activities were controlled and managed by a small number of committed persons from the local elite. However, they did not publicise the European Capital of Culture project's idea and they neglected to involve local stakeholders from the civic and business sectors. So it was not a broad network based on social capital, but rather a particular civil elite group with informal ties. In light of this, it is not surprising that during the elaboration phase all the tasks were managed by a civic organisation taking full responsibility, namely, the Pécs 2010 Management Centre. Although this structure was made up of several platforms – such as Bidding Cabinet, Bidding Office, Board (for consultations with the city leadership), Programme Council, Development Council and many working-groups involving more than a hundred persons (Somlyódy, 2010) – it was strongly dominated by the 'original owners of the idea' who intended to share neither their functions nor their information. After the unexpected success of the bid, the local government of Pécs 'awakened' and immediately centralised most of the relevant competences (Rampton *et al.* 2011). It took advantage not only of the traditional Hungarian political-administrational constellation, but also of the lack of social capital, the weak civic network and the missing general trust.

At the very beginning the mayor categorically expressed his intention to concentrate all relevant functions related to infrastructure development. This approach hampered the integration of the business sector, and it was drastically contrary the original intent to involve external financial sources as noted in the European Capital of Culture Pécs 2010 evaluation report of 2011 (cf. Ágoston *et al.* 2011). Although some company leaders were involved in preparing the key investments mentioned above, they had tight connections to the mayor, so this cooperation was not about obtaining business-like thinking. Despite the intent of the proposal to target a change of economic model by the dynamic emergence of cultural and creative industry, this attempt failed completely (Pálné 2012b). Local stakeholders, mainly from small and medium-sized enterprises were excluded from both planning and implementation. These local enterprises were weak and struggled with capital and capacity shortages. Actors from the local business sector were rather disorganised and thus not able to compete with large firms at the national level. The few – overall insignificant – involvements resulted from informal agreements and personal connections, which strengthened the still prevalent opinions about corruption (personal communication 2012).

The group of prioritised consortium partners acting as stakeholders related to infrastructural development was formed just after the local government of Pécs had realised that the operating costs of the new infrastructure would be unacceptably high. After lengthy and sometimes complicated negotiations, two key partners emerged: the county self-government and the University of Pécs. The consortium partners had unequal influence on the planning process, and both of them tried to moderate the role of the 'outsider' stakeholders as the large investments were in need of ideas, innovation and business development to reflect the local interests. That is why the consortium partners tried to integrate several (mainly cultural) public or semi-public organisations into the new institutions, but this was done primarily for cost-saving purposes. Consequently, just after the planning phase closed down the involved actors could no longer influence the preparatory processes anymore (personal communication 2012).

In the preparatory years there were various bodies and forums involving independent professionals. However, these fulfilled consultative functions only and had no decision-making competence. Later most of these bodies were dissolved and thus the legitimacy of the planning and implementation activities rapidly decreased with the result that the inhabitants of Pécs became ambivalent towards the European Capital of Culture project (Takáts 2011). Local intellectuals, artists and professionals also became frustrated and disappointed. They gave up the chance of effective participation, and 'locked' themselves into the role of independent critics (Takáts 2011). Presumably, the local government of Pécs had just imitated the intention to create networks and partnerships. In addition to these circumstances, the civil sector itself remained disorganised despite the common interests and frustrations and failed to demonstrate unity or to present alternative methods, structures and strategies (Pálné 2010). The continuous arguments and scandals, the acute uncertainties about the infrastructural investments, the perpetual personnel changes at the different levels of structures and, finally, the critical articles, statements and interviews in the local and national media affected civic participation negatively (Koltai 2011). The mobilisation and integration of the local population failed and the attempts of the local government were not sufficient to overcome this challenge. In some cases the locals were asked about general issues, but not in an organised way and just via online sites. In addition, access to public information and data was insufficient and belated, which hampered transparency (Somlyódy 2010).

Being adaptive to changing contexts: forced adaptation, learning and the trap of sustainability

During the preparatory phase and in the year of project accomplishment, there was constant pressure to immediately solve the continuously arising organisational and financial challenges. Two aspects must be underlined here. First, that largely unprepared *ad hoc* crisis management happened in the name of 'adaptation'. And second, decision-makers could not practically cope with the challenges of multi-level governance, since related principles as claimed by the EU were rejected by the central and local governments alike (cf. Ágoston *et al.* 2011). Both governmental levels wanted to heavily interfere in the functions of the independent management actors. This attitude adversely influenced the slow progress of infrastructural developments as well as the cultural programming.

Local stakeholders, namely actors of the local civic and business sector, were quite well-informed about how the EU's general bidding, financing, reporting and monitoring system worked. Although this knowledge was not completely comprehensive, it could have been useful for the local government. This was a serious mistake to ignore this basic knowledge as two of the interviewees argued (personal communications 2012). The management structure had to struggle with professional deficiencies because the necessary knowledge was not available institutionally, but only individually, and the continuous personnel changes blocked the accumulation of intellectual and technical capacities. However, even though the operational autonomy of the management was not expanded formally, its independence was strengthened informally and resulted in a reduced employee turnover and incidents of personal conflicts (personal communications 2012). The relationship between the local government and the management therefore became consolidated after some informal status-compromises (cf. Ágoston *et al.* 2011). In addition one could discern that while the management and the organisational frameworks adapted to the EU criteria, the political decision-making bodies did not.

Nonetheless, there is no doubt that the Regional Development Agency, just like the Pécs 2010 Management Centre, acquired a fairly well-functioning human resource and operational culture. This organisational learning could have been an important outcome for the local government as well. Unfortunately, this was not the case with regard to long-term learning, since the intention to evaluate the lessons of the European Capital of Culture project is still lacking. But the problems of the city (economic crisis, lack of money to maintain the new infrastructure, etc.) were too big to neglect past experience, and because the expectations considering the European Capital of Culture were too ambitious, the re-elected mayor asked independent experts to investigate the impacts of the project. Although the report is an honest account, it has not proven to be an appropriate basis for comprehensive learning and planning the future (cf. Ágoston *et al.* 2011).

Unfortunately, the aspect of sustainability disappeared due to the weaknesses of local actors. The financial sustainability of the newly created infrastructure had also generated a lot of problems, as the management could not influence the strategic conceptions of the investments. The feasibility studies already emphasised this, but the decision-makers mostly neglected the different recommendations (personal communication 2012). In addition the exclusion of local civil and business actors has also had ramifications more recently: the local government could not integrate external resources to maintain the new facilities, so the only available funding was via national contributions, which threatened local ownership.

Realising place-based/territorial specificities and impacts

The most important governance challenge for any European Capital of Culture project is that the implementation should be designed in a bottom-up manner, or as Barca (2009) calls it, a 'place-based' manner. In our case, however, the city was only formally in focus, as the centralised decision-making system did not give enough scope of activity for the local government to behave in a 'place-based' fashion. It was not only the copying of the centralised government system which characterised project in Pécs, but also the deficiency in the required 'horizontal, co-operative governance' model, as the Hungarian political environment is dominated by public actors while civil society is weak. Several surveys (Giczi and Sik 2009, Halman and Luijkx 2006, Mihaylova 2004, Papaioannou 2013) show that the Eastern European political culture and the social context is characterised by a lack of trust and low willingness for collective actions, so it was assumed that participation would be limited despite the involvement of locals being a core factor in the place-based approach.

The intended territorial integration, namely cooperation with the surrounding area, also diminished over time, regardless of the special programmes launched for the settlements in the regions. Since the representatives of the region were just formally involved in decision-making, the original promises for cooperation were forgotten and the city (called the 'borderless city' in the bid, cf. ECoC Bid of Pécs 2005) became an island that implemented its own investments. Although the so-called urban poles scheme 'officially' required territorial embeddedness in the frame of the Regional Operational Programme, and the official political slogans also emphasised regionalism. In practice no one insisted on accomplishing territorial integration.

Conclusions

The case of Pécs exemplifies how the dominance of a centralised governance context made it impossible to implement the original European Capital of Culture project according to a multi-level governance logic. The project would have been a very effective external motivation to initiate a bottom-up and complex development programme involving in particular horizontal governance elements. But these ideas were not sufficient to change the traditional administrative structures or the general social norms, values and attitudes of the prevailing local milieu.

The logic of multi-level governance is crucial for the success of European Cohesion Policy, but as our analytical framework to study 'territorial' governance along the five dimensions has revealed (see Chapters 1 and 4) it has many obstacles in centralised countries. In principle, the asymmetric power structure could be counterbalanced by a much stronger European role. However, our analysis has shown that a better 'anchoring' at the local level seems to be even more important, because without the responsibility for the so-called place-based projects this level degenerates to be the puppets of other levels and actors and institutions (here the national government). It remains to be seen whether the two new instruments within the EU Cohesion Policy 2014–2020, the so-called 'Community led local developments' and 'Integrated territorial developments', will provide more opportunities for local implementation and control of place-based projects.

The efforts of Pécs regarding the management of this particular project were ambitious, but the external forces strongly limited local room for manoeuvre. The city was the audience rather than the provider of its 'own' cultural events. Even more important is that the new governance challenges have not yet penetrated the local government structure, thereby providing no lessons to be learned the future. As a result, the original long-term goals about sustainable economic development based on a cultural event have failed and what remained from the project are large, underused cultural infrastructures.

References

Ágoston, Z., Berkecz, B., Faragó, L., Horváth, A., Kovács, K., Müller, P., Rappai, G. and Szijártó, Z., 2011. *Elemző értékelés a Pécs 2010 Európa Kulturális Fővárosa program tapasztalatairól [Evaluation report about the experiences of ECOC Pécs 2010]*. Pécs: Pécs MJV Önkormányzata. Available from: http://ekf.afal.hu/userfiles/file/ekf_elemzes.pdf [Accessed 12 January 2015].

Barca, F., 2009. *An Agenda for a Reformed Cohesion Policy. A Place-based Approach to Meeting European Union Challenges and Expectations*. Independent Report Prepared at the Request of Danuta Hűbner, Commissioner for Regional Policy, Brussels: Directorate General for Regional Policy, European Commission. Available from: http://ec.europa.eu/regional_policy/archive/policy/future/pdf/report_barca_v0306.pdf [Accessed 6 March 2015].

Belussi, F. and Sedita, S.R., 2008. The management of 'events' in the Veneto Performing Music Cluster: bridging latent networks and permanent organisations. In: P. Cook and L. Lazzeretti, eds. *Creative Cities, Cultural Clusters and Local Economic Development*, Cheltenham: Edward Elgar, 237–258.

Coffé, H. and Geys, B., 2005. Institutional performance and social capital: an application to the local government level. *Journal of Urban Affairs*, 27 (5), 485–501.

Cook, P. and Lazzeretti, L. eds., 2008. *Creative Cities, Cultural Clusters and Local Economic Development*. Cheltenham: Edward Elgar.

During, R., van Dam, R. and van der Zande, A., 2009. A missing link in the cultural evolution of the European Union: confronting ideology with INTERREG III practice concerning cultural diversity. In: J. Knieling and F. Othengrafen, eds. *Planning Cultures in Europe: Decoding Cultural Phenomenon in Urban and Regional Planning*. Burlington: Ashgate, 255–269.

ECoC Bid of Pécs, 2005. *Borderless City. European Capital of Culture – Pécs, 2010*. Pécs: Europe Centre.

Giczi, J. and Sik, E. 2009. Trust and social capital in contemporary Europe. In: *TÁRKI European Social Report 2009*, 63–81. Available from: http://www.tarki.hu/en/research/european_social_report/european_social_report_2009_full.pdf [Accessed 18 January 2015].

Guiso, L., Sapienza, P. and Zingales, L., 2011. Chapter 10 – civic capital as the missing link. In: J. Benhabib, A. Bisin and M. O. Jackson, eds. *Handbook of Social Economics, Volume 1*, New York: North Holland Press, 417–480.

Halman, L. and Luijkx, R., 2006. Social capital in contemporary Europe: evidence from the European Social Survey. *Portuguese Journal of Social Science*, 5 (1), 65–90.

Häussermann, H. and Simons, K. 2000. Die Politik der grossen Projekte – Eine Politik der Grossen Risiken? *Archiv für Kommunalwissenschaften*, 39 (1), 56–71.

Hendriks, F., Loughlin, J. and Lidström, A., 2011. European subnational democracy: comparative reflections and conclusions. In: J. Loughlin, F. Hendriks and A. Lidström, eds. *The Oxford Handbook of Local and Regional Democracy in Europe*. Oxford: Oxford University Press, 715–743.

Hughes, J., Sasse, G. and Gordon, C., 2004. *Europeanization and Regionalization in the EU's Enlargement to Central and Eastern Europe*. London: Palgrave Macmillan.

Immler, N.L. and Sakkers, H., 2014. (Re)programming Europe: European capitals of culture: rethinking the role of culture. *Journal of European Studies*, 44 (1), 3–29.

Kapucu, N., 2011. Social capital and civic engagement. *International Journal of Social Inquiry*, 4 (1), 23–43.

Koltai, Z., 2011. Európa Kulturális Fővárosa – Pécs 2010 program megítélése Pécsett és Budapesten. *Tudásmenedzsment*, 7 (2), 84–94.

Kundi, V., 2012. Fesztiválok gazdasági hatásmérésére alkalmazott nemzetközi és hazai modellek bemutatása. *Tér és Társadalom*, 26 (4), 93–111.

Mihaylova, D., 2004. *Social Capital in Central and Eastern Europe. A Critical Assessment and Literature Review*. Budapest: Policy Studies Series of CEU. Available from: http://pdc.ceu.hu/archive/00002064/01/pub_polstud_soccap.pdf [Accessed 13 February 2015].

Newton, K., 2001. Trust, social capital, civil society and democracy. *International Political Science Review*, 22 (2), 201–214.

Palmer, R., 2004. *European Cities and Capitals of Culture*. Study Prepared for the European Commission Brussels: Palmer/Rae Associates. Available from: http://ec.europa.eu/programmes/creative-europe/actions/documents/ecoc/cap-part1_en.pdf [Accessed 20 October 2014].

Palmer, R., Richards, G. and Dodd, D., 2011. *European Cultural Capital Report 3*. Arnhem: ATLAS.

Pálné Kovács, I., 2010. Tudás, közösség, kormányzás – EKF párhuzamok. *Echo – Pécsi Kritikai Szemle*, 13 (5–6), 12–14.

Pálné Kovács, I., 2012a. Roots and consequences of local governance reforms in Hungary. *Revue d' etudes comparatives East-Ouest*, 43 (3), 173–199.

Pálné Kovács, I., 2012b. Nagyvárosi fejlesztési koalíciók. In: E. Somlyódyné Pfeil, ed. *Az agglomerációk intézményesítésének sajátos kérdései*, Pécs: Publikon, 135–153.

Papaioannou, E., 2013. *Trust(ing) in Europe*. Brussels: Centre for European Studies.

Putnam, R., 2000. *Bowling Alone: Collapse and Revival of American Community*. New York: Simon & Schuster.

Rampton, J., McAteer, N., Mozuraityte, N., Lévai, M. and Akçali, S., 2011. *Ex-post Evaluation of 2010 European Capitals of Culture – Final Report for the European Commission, DG Education and Culture*. London: Ecorys UK. Available from: http://ec.europa.eu/programmes/creative-europe/actions/documents/ecoc/ecoc-2010-report_en.pdf [Accessed 20 October 2014].

Selection Panel, 2009. *Designation of a European Capital of Culture for 2014.* Pre-selection report, European Commission. Available from: http://ec.europa.eu/programmes/creative-europe/actions/documents/ecoc/2014/preselection-report-latvia_en.pdf [Accessed 16 May 2015].

Scott, J., ed., 2009. *De-coding New Regionalism: Shifting Socio-political Contexts in Central Europe and Latin America.* Farnham: Ashgate.

Sik, E., 2012. *A kapcsolati tőke szociológiája.* Budapest: ELTE Eötvös.

Somlyódy, N., 2010. *A Balkán kapujában.* Budapest: Kalligram.

Sykes, O., 2011. Introduction. European cities and capitals of culture – a comparative approach. *Town Planning Review*, 82 (1), 1–12.

Takáts, J., 2011. *Az újragondolt város. EKF-iratok.* Pécs: Publikon.

Tarrósy, I., 2011. Az együttműködés politikai kultúrájának sajátosságai. *Civil Szemle*, 8 (3), 29–41.

Uslaner, E., 2002. *The Moral Foundations of Trust.* Cambridge: Cambridge University Press.

8 Planning for resource efficiency in Stockholm

'Good' territorial governance practices without consistency

Mitchell Reardon and Peter Schmitt

Introduction

The built form, and population density in particular, can have a significant impact on urban resource efficiency through the size of living spaces, achieving viable ridership on public transit and proximity to jobs and services (Schremmer *et al.* 2011). Numerous factors influence how our city-regions develop, most central are the array of actors with cooperative and competitive interests from the public, private and third sectors. This chapter explores how the City of Stockholm promotes and achieves its relatively high rate of resource efficiency while managing this range of interests at both the city level and in its ongoing flagship project, Stockholm Royal Seaport, known in Swedish as *Norra Djurgårdsstaden*. By studying two scales of territorial governance simultaneously (planning at the city level and at the neigbourhood level), the aim is to assess the consistency of the 2010 European Green Capital's approaches, while identifying territorial governance strengths and weaknesses at district and citywide levels.

Infrastructure for vehicles and public transit both influence the amount of energy consumed for commuting and other journeys. Access to efficient and high quality public transport has a considerable influence on ridership and the consumption of energy for transportation. In the face of dispersed development, more resources are needed for the construction and maintenance of mobility infrastructure (Schremmer *et al.* 2011). Conversely, mixed-use areas allow in principle for shorter distance access to many services, goods and jobs. In contemporary urban planning, such areas are considered to be more resource efficient than their single use counterparts. Finally, buildings account for 40 per cent of final energy consumption in Europe (Jaeger *et al.* 2011), a figure that can be influenced by building standards and retrofitting activities.

Throughout the case study, the City of Stockholm, which currently counts 870,000 residents and is expecting a growth rate of + 17 per cent between 2011 and 2021 (Landstingsstyrelsens förvaltning and Tillväxt, miljö och regionplanering 2012, p. 36), refers to the jurisdictional boundaries of the Stockholm municipality, unless otherwise noted.

Stockholm Royal Seaport is an environmental flagship development situated at the north-eastern edge within the city of Stockholm boundaries (see Figure 8.1) that builds on its eco-district predecessor *Hammarby Sjöstad* (cf. Svane 2008, Pandis Iverot and Brandt 2011). Construction formally began during the winter of 2010 and the project has a tentative completion date of 2030. Once completed, it will offer 12,000 new apartments, 35,000 office units and 600,000 m² of commercial space, thereby having a considerable impact on growth in a location just three kilometres from the city centre (Stockholm Royal Seaport 2013).

Key policy documents

The central guiding document for development in the city is 'Vision 2030: A Guide to the Future' (City of Stockholm 2007). All urban development should be in line with the general strategies outlined in it. It is stated that the city should be fossil-fuel free by 2050 through reductions in energy consumption, smart transport solutions and energy efficient buildings; solutions that are developed in concert with companies working in Stockholm. Further, the vision highlights the importance of regional cooperation, cooperation with the business community and international cooperation.

'The Walkable City: Stockholm City Plan' (City of Stockholm 2010) is the non-binding comprehensive plan for the city. A planner for the City described it as a 'flexible game plan' (personal communication 2012). The plan underlines the importance of environmental and climate issues. In meeting these challenges, the plan focuses on strengthening central Stockholm, strengthening specific districts beyond the inner city, connecting different city areas and creating a vibrant urban environment. In terms of urban development, the intensification of activities in the city centre and the strengthening of urban cores are seen as ways to foster greater resource efficiency in the city's urban form.

Following up on 'The Walkable City: Stockholm City Plan', the transport department of the city created an accessibility strategy and cycling plan in 2012 (Stockholms stad 2012a and 2012b). The accessibility strategy (*Framkomlighetsstrategin*) has four key goals, which are to make more room for buses and cyclists, to ensure that that travel times for public transport and other traffic are more reliable, to improve conditions for pedestrians, and to reduce the negative effects of traffic in the city. Closely linked to the accessibility strategy, the cycle plan (*Cykelplan*) identifies actions and interventions to increase cycling in Stockholm. It also takes account of the regional cycling strategy, which was developed in cooperation with neighbouring municipalities, the county administration and national government. Finally, the city released the 'Stockholm Environment Programme 2012–2015' (City of Stockholm 2012) which has core goals related to the above mentioned plans, such as to promote environmentally efficient transport and to ensure sustainable use of land.

Resource efficiency in Stockholm 97

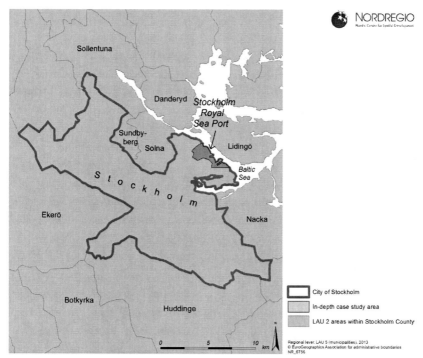

Figure 8.1 The territorial scope of the case study: the city of Stockholm and Stockholm Royal Seaport

Source: Own elaboration

It is important to note that none of the abovementioned policy documents is legally binding. Rather, they serve as guides for various aspects of Stockholm's development. This enables a more flexible approach that can respond to changing conditions. However, it also bears the risk of inconsistency if not arbitrariness, where binding detailed plans use the correct language, but eventually lack the substance to achieve the aims stipulated in these 'guiding policy documents'.

Coordinating the actions of actors and institutions

The City of Stockholm plays a central role in urban development and resource efficiency, in large part due to its significant land ownership and planning monopoly within its territory. A number of actors are relevant stakeholders within the City administration. Relevant to this case study are the following departments; the Development Office (*Exploateringskontoret*), the City Planning Administration (*Stadsbyggnadskontoret*), the Traffic Office (*Trafikkontoret*) and the executive board (*Stadsledningskontoret*). In the following when talking about these actors, we will collectively refer to them as 'the City', unless a further specification is made.

98 *Mitchell Reardon and Peter Schmitt*

Larger projects, such as Stockholm Royal Seaport also have a steering group, which consists of a number of decision-makers from the aforementioned departments, as well as other public and private organisations. There are other actors, such as the Stockholm Beauty Council (*Stockholms Skönhetsråd*) which is concerned with maintaining and developing the city's urban design. Beyond the city, key private actors include a number of development architecture and planning companies as well as firms that deal with related activities. Further, grassroots organisations with an interest in Stockholm's development include YIMBY ('Yes In My BackYard') and *Samfundet St. Erik* (specifically concerned with maintaining Stockholm's historical heritage). The regional planning agency (*Tillväxt- och regionplaneförvaltningen*) and the regional public transport agency (*Storstockholms Lokaltrafik*) also have roles of varying relevance within Stockholm's municipal boundaries. In addition one needs to mention the County Administrative Board (*Länsstyrelsen*), who has the role of monitoring the municipal planning work in the Stockholm region as well as safeguard the integration of national interests. Many of these actors were interviewed during the course of our research.

In Stockholm, where a range of public and private actors contribute to development, it is important to understand the key interactions that influence the city's resource efficiency. The City of Stockholm is itself made up of numerous departments that are not always focused on the same goals. Given the city's planning monopoly and the fact that they own about 75 per cent of developable land within their boundaries (Metzger and Rader Olsson 2013), the city and its respective departments are central to this issue. However, before zooming in on the internal mechanisms of the City of Stockholm, this section will focus on the relations and dealings between the city and private actors (primarily developers).

Prior to considering this external interaction, a key factor that informs urban development in Stockholm is the sequential process through which the city's development decisions are taken. In the standard situation, according to the 'Stockholm model', planning proposals, usually initiated by the city or developers, are assessed based on their economic feasibility and profitability by the Development Office, which is responsible for city-owned land and which is guided by a strong economic logic. If the transfer of land rights is approved, the City Building Office then addresses the issue of building and design quality. This risks creating a disparity in decision-making power between departments and reduces considerations about building and design quality, both important aspects to achieving resource efficiency.

A challenge that results from this model is that economy is considered before quality. Most urban development projects are expected to be 'self-feeding', which means that in addition to meeting the city's general strategic requirements, the city should not incur any debt in selling the land and establishing the infrastructure (personal communication 2012).

This means development is likely to occur where the city can make an immediate return, not necessarily where resource efficiency standards are best met. Nevertheless, it is important to note that the city's strategic aims for urban development emphasise mixed-use development, which is widely seen to be more resource efficient than single or uniform land use planning. Further, the Traffic Office focuses almost exclusively on roads and mobility (personal communications 2012 and 2013), limiting cross-cutting solutions between mobility and the built form. Finally, it is important to note that the County Administrative Board's responsibilities cover a range of issues, including the environment, the labour market and business community, transport and infrastructure, and housing. In maintaining a focus on these diverse topics, while also working among 26 municipalities on a regional platform, the County Administrative Board contributes to the coordination of actors and institutions.

The city's relationship with private actors, and large developers in particular, strongly influences efforts to promote resource efficiency in Stockholm. The context in which these interactions take place has undergone a considerable shift in recent years. This results primarily from a national, but also municipal, political focus on liberalisation, away from the traditional welfare state, and is reflected in the 'Stockholm Model'. Stockholm's rapid population growth, which has led to an acute housing shortage, has also contributed to this shift. Such efforts are also evident in the increasing prominence of private developers, who are taking larger roles in Stockholm's urban development. The position large developers have in Stockholm's development is also bolstered by population growth. In responding to the acute housing shortage, the previous governing coalition promised that 20,000 new dwellings would be constructed during their 2010–2014 mandate, a goal that, within the context of liberalisation, necessitates a large role from private developers. The need to encourage housing construction by private developers limits the City's power, which, given their dominance in the ownership of available land and an official monopoly on planning, would otherwise be very strong in this relationship.

Contested and shifting leadership

One of the most interesting aspects of our research in this dimension was the contrasting perspectives on leadership in urban development in Stockholm. Several individuals we spoke to felt that the current dynamics were very much in favour of large developers, while others felt that the city continued to have a strong leadership role. During the study, the multifaceted nature of the relationship between developers and the city arose time and time again.

Planners working for the city felt that the planning administration remained in a strong position.

The planning architect from the Development Office is (formally) leading meetings to develop specific parcels of land and thus is in a powerful position. Of course his or her leadership is contested in particular by the developers. We are powerful due to the planning monopoly and that we have to take care that the process is going according to the rules/policy documents.

(personal communication 2012, translated by the authors)

Regardless of which actors are leading development, most interviewees felt that there was a lack of consistency in the city's application of strategic objectives in practice, to the detriment of the city's resource efficient urban development. For most actors we spoke to, this variation resulted from a number of factors, including the lack of specific steps and measures for achieving the city's strategic aims for urban development, the time-consuming and costly process, public and political interest in the project and the personalities in charge of the respective projects (personal communications 2012 and 2013).

Limited consistency in urban policy limits coordination

Of particular interest to resource efficient urban development was the issue of clarity for how strategic aims are concretely applied to projects (personal communications 2012 and 2013).

In Stockholm, the City has worked well at defining profiles for a number of areas [like Stockholm Royal Seaport]. They work very hard in such areas but much less so in other areas with lower profiles. There are significant differences between projects.

(personal communication 2013)

Difficulties in integrating the goals of the environmental programme more widely and consistently appear to stem from the emphasis on immediate economic solvency (personal communication 2012). One positive step in favour of greater resource efficiency was the city's recent increase in energy standards to an impressive 55 kWh per m^2 in all new developments. This follows a trajectory in resource efficiency catalysed in Hammarby Sjöstad, where a 'twice as good' ambition was set for building energy consumption in the mid-1990s (Pandis Iverot and Brandt 2011).

Transparent distribution of power and influence among actors and institutions

The importance of the lead planner from the city on a project was also underlined during several conversations.

I'm still a bit amazed, when talking about dominance, that the responsible planner has so much to say. If there's a strong personality, and I think this is the heritage from the modernist era, when the architect was this 'genius' who had solutions for everything. But I'm amazed that if you look at the plans that become physical, there is lots of power for the planners themselves.

(personal communication 2012)

The variation in how the planner guides a process, the political support the project enjoys, and the relationship with private actors influence the outcome. From a citywide perspective, this reduces the outwardly perceived consistency between projects in Stockholm.

Other arenas for coordination between many actors have developed as well. The Regional Planning Office, which has developed one of only a handful of regional plans in Sweden, is encouraging municipalities to talk to one another, to identify common objectives and challenges. Conferences and other planning related events are also occurring. A good illustration of this type of arena was an exhibition at a multifaceted community, culture and discussion centre, *Färgfabriken*, called 'Stockholm at Large' in the early 2000s. This exhibition helped to broaden the urban development discussions while also making it more inclusive (personal communication 2013).

How to better integrate actors and institutions: Stockholm Royal Seaport

Efforts to coordinate the actions of actors and institutions in Stockholm Royal Seaport went further than in many other developments in Stockholm. There, developers and architecture companies have been more integrated in many aspects of the project throughout the process. Only in the first two stages of the project, approximately 40 different developers and a similar number of architecture companies were involved (personal communication 2013). Making detailed plans for the area has also involved a broader range of other actors as well, including the district administration, the Traffic Office and the County Administrative Board (personal communication 2013).

Many meetings have taken place; discussing strategic issues such as how the development will look, as well as more detailed aspects, including specific greenspaces (personal communication 2013). Other initiatives included a competence programme for the developers and architects. Through lectures and seminars, private actors, together with the city, looked at issues that affect construction and architecture (personal communication 2013). It is also noteworthy that few factors have influenced urban development patterns, and thus resource efficiency, to the extent that transport planning does. In Stockholm Royal Seaport, it is the municipality who clearly leads the question what kind of public transport is suitable (personal communications 2012 and 2013). This is not the case for all public transport projects in Stockholm, however.

Integrating policy sectors

In considering the integration of policy sectors for resource efficient development in Stockholm, the city planning and development departments have considerable responsibility for dealing with the complexity of urban planning. As briefly mentioned in the previous section, the interaction and integration between the various actors within the city is important to consider. Further, the expanding role of private actors, and the interactions between them, is an essential part of planning for resource efficiency in Stockholm. As such, integration of policy sectors is hardly exclusive to the City of Stockholm; however given the detailed discussion of how various external actors interact in the previous chapter, there is no need to rehash these findings here.

Competing motivations limit cross-sectoral synergies

As mentioned before, the city' urban planning and development apparatus is divided into various divisions with different responsibilities. For decades, the departments have operated quite distinctly from one another and although there have been recent efforts to reduce barriers between these divisions (personal communication 2013). Changes in political direction at the City Hall can also have an impact on the trajectory of planning and development in Stockholm. Through the interviews, it became apparent that the 'silo effect' continues to pervade urban planning at the City of Stockholm in large part because of the size of each department and the complexity of the issues at hand. There are internal politics in each department; each is positioning itself in regards to other departments. Politicians also have a role in decisions concerning development; however the majority of their decisions are at arm's length from the departments (personal communications 2012 and 2013).

Inconsistent urban policy packaging

The need for integration and a more holistic approach to urban development is recognised in Stockholm Royal Seaport, as well as other prominent projects. In recent projects of this nature, the city executive has strongly encouraged departments to cooperate. This top-down process is evident in projects that have widespread public and political attention. In addition to Stockholm Royal Seaport, this was exemplified by a project in the inner city where the Executive Office took charge because the city felt that the project was too important to be the responsibility of a department with a specific disciplinary focus (personal communication 2013). In Stockholm Royal Seaport, the area's designation as Stockholm's newest eco-district ensured that quality was considered simultaneously with economy. Stockholm Royal Seaport illustrates how a project's prominence, and thus political interest, can influence its aims. A flagship projects like this is not expected to be economically 'self-feeding' (at least in the short term), as it also serves to promote Stockholm's environmental profile while providing an example of best practice for the city and private actors to follow for continued urban development. It is only through political support that a project does not need to make rapid economic returns within the paradigm of the politically approved 'Stockholm Model' (personal communications 2012 and 2013).

Again: about the growing role of private actors

Although the city plays an essential role in planning for resource efficiency, it is easy to recognise that private actors have taken an increasingly proactive role in integrating policy sectors dealing with this issue and more generally with urban development. This reflects the efforts of private actors, developers in particular, to fill the void in two steps – economy, then quality – Stockholm Model, by 'selling' their development proposals as thought out contributions to Stockholm's built form. In doing so, private actors can play a greater role in shaping the detailed plan and quality aspects of their prospective development.

Mobilising stakeholder participation

Legitimacy through participation – a remaining challenge

A central challenge in terms of communication and stakeholder mobilisation are the barriers inherent in the formal rules for engagement in the detailed plans. This happens later in the process, once the decision-making process has come quite far (personal communications 2012 and 2013). This is underlined by the fact that there is no formal requirement for the involvement of concerned stakeholders during the time in which the Development Office or Building Office are considering plans, thus leading to situations where stakeholders are informed about, rather than consulted on plans (personal communication 2013). This is a source of considerable frustration for many stakeholders seeking to be engaged in development (Reardon 2010).

Transparency versus complexity

The mobilisation process is restricted by the complexity of the projects at hand. In the wider context of development, it was also noted that, 'Stockholm is doing a lot, but I think it is also important to communicate the big picture, how Stockholm as such will develop and not only project by project' (personal communication 2013). This further contributes to a lack of outward consistency in how projects are carried out within the territory of the entire city. The city is working to improve engagement however. In larger or more strategic projects, the City of Stockholm has introduced new participation approaches before starting the formal planning process (including comprehensive opinion surveys, brochures, and social media like Facebook). This goes beyond what is legally required (personal communication 2012). The cost of carrying out these processes is regarded as the number one reason that such efforts do not take place in smaller projects (personal communication 2012). This suggests that the city has good intentions in promoting citizen engagement and participatory planning; however it also underlines the variation between projects and also a division between 'larger or more strategic projects' and others.

A critical focus on the city's efforts is sharpened by local grassroots organisations that have a strong interest in Stockholm's development. YIMBY and Samfundet St Erik are two well-known groups that frequently voice their opinions and make efforts to influence Stockholm's development. YIMBY, which stands for Yes In My BackYard, is an organisation that is often in favour of dense development and more provocative projects, while Samfundet St Erik tends to focus on preserving Stockholm's traditional built form. Beyond these organisations, there is a host of smaller groups that are often focused on a very local area and/or a specific issue that work to lobby for specific outcomes.

Enhanced practices in Stockholm Royal Seaport

In Stockholm Royal Seaport opposition to the development was not assuaged with early, and legally mandated, efforts at participation. In response to the opposition, the city chose to embark on a strategy of greater cooperation with area residents and other concerned stakeholders in 2007. Beyond this, the manner in which such engagement took place was altered to create an atmosphere whereby information could be more easily diffused and concerns addressed (Reardon 2010). These meetings also served to underline the need from the planners' perspectives to better present and inform the public of their plans, something that led to a mail survey involving the residents of surrounding neighbourhoods and to several walking tours of the development area (Claesson 2009).

Being adaptive to changing contexts

Throughout the course of our case study, it became clear that there were no institutionalised mechanisms for reflection of adaptation. This is due in large part to a firm belief in long-term population growth and demand for housing. It also suggests that the city can weather an economic downturn (personal communications 2012 and 2013).

Limited reflection, but signs of knowledge transfer

Although the City of Stockholm is heavily focused on ongoing projects, there were no standardised routines and time available for feedback or

Resource efficiency in Stockholm 105

process evaluations to distill lessons that could be transferred (personal communication 2013). It also became clear that, as with other aspects of projects and plans, the level of experimentation (if at all) was dependent on the responsible planner, who then needed permission from the City's Real Estate Office (*Fastighetskontoret*).

It was also noted that even in the case of flagship projects, the city moves on fairly quickly. This was illustrated in Hammarby Sjöstad by the creation of 'HS2020', a community group in the district. HS2020 was created as a response to the perceived shortsightedness of planning in Hammarby Sjöstad, arguing that development is an ongoing process and that such a perspective would allow the eco-district to sustain its globally recognised success if such a position were adopted (Sjöstadsföreningen 2013). According to a planner in Stockholm Royal Seaport, there has been some knowledge transferring however,

> You can say that we've learned a fair amount from Hammarby Sjöstad. In terms of being goal oriented and having a fairly long-term perspective, but it wasn't really a model to build a community on. We've added the requirements and people can also write in with proposals, which hasn't been the standard process.
> (personal communication 2012, translation by the authors).

Reflecting on what has been learned in Stockholm Royal Seaport, it was also noted that

> We've learned that it's important to have a good dialogue with those already living in the area. We've also worked to refine the requirements, either because we missed something or because they weren't applicable. We will re-evaluate the requirements throughout the life of the project.
> (personal communication 2013, translation by the authors).

A planner in Stockholm Royal Seaport assessed that the City Planning Administration is looking into how this decision-making body can be applied in other projects (personal communication 2012). This indicates that efforts are being undertaken to promote learning and knowledge exchange to a greater extent and beyond Stockholm's flagship projects.

An academic with a great deal of experience in many aspects of Stockholm's urban development over the last half century adopted a long-term, and critical, perspective on the importance of being adaptive to changing contexts and the current growth paradigm.

> I would say there is too little capacity for reflection; we are too stuck in the growth euphoria and almost take for granted the forecast of endless growth, instead of being more cautious. I think it is possible that we could see an abrupt turnaround as in 1971 again.
> (personal communication 2013, translation by the authors)

Realising place-based/territorial specificities and impacts

It is important to note that the City of Stockholm is a small territory by Swedish standards, something that increases the need for interaction with neighbouring municipalities. Further, this means that there is only limited room for further greenfield development, putting a greater onus on densification efforts for accommodating population growth. At the regional level, Stockholm County includes 26 municipalities. Therefore, considerable effort is necessary to coordinate activities between these various levels of governments.

Territorial relationality – container versus network approach

Stockholm's cooperation with neighbouring municipalities was perceived as under-developed. While there are examples of cooperation (e.g. Kista-Sollentuna, Stockholm-Huddinge, Bromma-Sundbyberg), there seems to be little individual capacity for strategic regional thinking within the various administrative departments within the city (personal communication 2013). The strong decision-making capacity that municipalities enjoy in Sweden, best illustrated in this case by a planning monopoly within their territories, which was described as 'sacred', challenges coordination and cooperation as well. This results from the fact that numerous larger urban development projects (e.g. large retail centres) are dealt with by a single municipality (personal communications 2013). Yet the strategic regional development plan (Regionplanekontoret 2010) suggests many areas for further densification, which are based on a number of investigations together with the municipalities and criteria (close to public transport, maintaining green wedges, cultural heritage, etc.), many of which are close to municipal borders. However, due to its non-binding character, this policy document cannot be used to align strategic municipal land use planning within the Stockholm region. It is designed to support regional consensus-building and inter-municipal cooperation (personal communications 2012 and 2013). However, criticism of municipal coordination efforts by the City of Stockholm should be qualified by the fact that they were described as a willing partner who took an active role in financing some regional efforts (personal communications 2012).

In this light, it has been also mentioned that the regional public transport agency (*Storstockholms Lokaltrafik*, SL), for instance, follows a different territorial logic from the regional development plan. This plan is more aligned to the plans of the City of Stockholm, when it comes to determining the nodes and axes for future development. As such it rather suggests prioritising the improved accessibility of so-called 'regional urban cores' that are located at a distance of 15 to 40 km around the municipality of Stockholm (Regionplanekontoret 2010) (personal communications 2012 and 2013). Also on the neighbourhood level, a kind of territorial blindness has been criticised, since in terms of the provision of public transport the Stockholm Royal Seaport project has been solely discussed in a more narrow municipal perspective, instead of considering it in a more systemic, larger regional context (personal communication 2013). As a result, it appears that the capacity for territorial relationality to overcome the barriers of municipal jurisdictions is hard to conceive in this case. A more soft or functional understanding of urban planning is restricted by the strong tradition of local government.

Utilising territorial knowledge – to some extent

In regards to the utilisation of multiple sources of territorial knowledge, nearly every interviewee stated that a number of ex-ante evaluations are integrated to support the planning and decision-making process, but that ex-post assessments are rather rare. This applies to various aspects of urban development, including territorial, social, economic or environmental, but also public transport.

One specific issue regarding territorial knowledge seems to be the different territorial mind-sets within the city's planning authority. This is seen in the tensions between the physical planners within the Development Office, who follow a more project and design-based approach and the more strategic planners within the Building Office, who have a more holistic perspective in mind (personal communications 2012 and 2013).

Further, due to the planning monopoly and the fact that the city owns lots of land, there are numerous opportunities for making comprehensive territorial strategies, in particular regarding resource efficient urban planning throughout the city (personal communications 2012 and 2013). Stockholm Royal Seaport was again mentioned as a positive example, since here numerous forums and platforms have been installed to bring together various experts, in particular architects and the developer, to discuss various possibilities as regards a more resource efficient approach to urban planning (personal communications 2012 and 2013). The mobilisation of expert knowledge (at least to verify the positive impacts of the project) should also be considered in the light of Stockholm's quest to promote itself internationally as a Green City (personal communications 2012 and 2013).

Conclusions

The case study has given numerous insights into the territorial governance practices related to urban planning in Stockholm in general and one flagship project, Stockholm Royal Seaport in particular. The fact that a project that we initially hypothesised to be representative of how projects take place in Stockholm has had to be considered distinctly from wider urban development efforts, highlights the lack of consistency between projects in the city. This lack of consistency appears to be the most significant territorial governance challenge limiting the city's capacity to promote greater resource efficiency.

A silver lining to this finding is that Stockholm Royal Seaport demonstrates that the city does in fact have the territorial governance capacity and competencies to achieve greater resource efficiency and that there is a strong potential for a greater exchange of learning experiences between planning projects.

Stockholm Royal Seaport demonstrates that there is political will to develop urban projects that are characterised by a high degree of resource efficiency and that help to promote Stockholm's green profile internationally. The extent to which the ambitious resource efficiency standards, as well as other environmental standards, which are set in the various local policy documents, are applied elsewhere in the city is limited by economic considerations, however. The strong role enjoyed by the city through its planning monopoly and the Swedish building and planning code, and augmented by the fact that the City of Stockholm (still) owns a lot of land, gives the city, in principle, a considerable scope for action. Despite these strengths in steering decision-making, the city's role in setting environmental standards and principles for a project is limited by an acute housing shortage, a high degree of liberalisation in Sweden and the 'Stockholm model', which requires direct economic solvency for the majority of projects. This has led to a situation where development leadership is contested on an almost case-by-case basis.

Greater integration and coordination between various city departments (and thus sectors), which has been encouraged top-down, can be taken further. Variation between projects in the dominance of specific public policies and/ or sectors continues to limit the knowledge transfers and learning between projects. The same applies to other territorial governance indicators, which are intertwined, namely governing capacity and subsidiarity, the latter implicitly addressed through the Stockholm Royal Seaport case.

In terms of mobilising stakeholder participation, the city follows what is stipulated in Swedish planning legislation. In specific projects, such as Stockholm Royal Seaport and certain others, the city made efforts to go beyond the business-as-usual approach by adding additional platforms, including more open hearings or social media. Nonetheless, it seems that engagement and communication could be taken considerably further. This was also evident in the analysis of the three related indicators of (good) territorial governance in this respect (democratic legitimacy, public accountability and transparency), where the results were rather disappointing, particularly in regards to the latter two indicators.

In the fourth dimension of territorial governance, a number of practices were distilled that also have to be assessed as rather negative. There are minimal institutionalised mechanisms for adaptation or reflection. In terms of specific knowledge that should feed into the planning process, numerous ex-ante studies and evaluations are conducted to 'oil the political machinery', as one critical voice mentioned (personal communication 2012). Ex-post evaluations, any kinds of feedback-loops or the definition of alternative paths (plan B) and fields for experimentation, amongst other things, are uncommon. Besides remarking on the scarce resources to implement such mechanisms, the majority of the interviewees pointed to the considerable time pressure to build new houses and infrastructure, because of the immense local and regional growth in Stockholm (at European standards). This suggests that a number of the interviewed stakeholders support increased capacity for being adaptive to changing contexts, but that this is dropped in favour of other priorities.

Finally, the results regarding the fifth dimension confirm earlier investigations regarding the limited capacity for inter-municipal coordination in Stockholm (see Schmitt *et al.* 2013). In addition, it became obvious that urban projects are considered rather in an isolated manner or at best within the municipality, but hardly in a regional context. The fact that ex-post analysis (e.g. regarding various territorial impacts) is scarcely used in urban planning work in Stockholm, suggests that the integration of specific territorial knowledge is somewhat limited too.

As a final note, individual capacities, attitudes, logics and routines are a bit overlooked in our research framework, which rather seeks to detect institutional practices. Throughout our interviews it was uttered many times for instance, that the modernist planning tradition with its various implications (strong belief of the projectable society, appreciation of clear power-relations, the car as the norm for mobility and accessibility) has not withered away totally. Another example is the role of charismatic personalities in key positions, which to some extent, influences governance practices and outcomes. The City of Stockholm has a number of strengths in regards to territorial governance for resource efficient planning, something that is particularly well highlighted in Stockholm Royal Seaport; however more can be done to ensure that this goes beyond specific projects. Greater outward consistency can enhance resource efficiency, project economics, competitiveness and a host of other aspects that shape urban development.

References

City of Stockholm, 2007. *Vision 2030*. Stockholm: City of Stockholm Executive Office. Available from: http://www.stockholm.se/PageFiles/266315/SthlmStad_Vision2030.pdf [Accessed 24 March 2015].

City of Stockholm, 2010. *The Walkable City: Stockholm City Plan*. Stockholm: The City of Stockholm Planning Administration. Available from: http://international. stockholm.se/globalassets/ovriga-bilder-och-filer/the-walkable-city---stockholm-city-plan.pdf [Accessed 24 March 2015].

City of Stockholm, 2012. *Stockholm Environment Programme* 2012–2015. Stockholm: The City of Stockholm. Available from: http://international. stockholm.se/globalassets/ovriga-bilder-och-filer/the-stockholm-environment-programme-2012-2015.pdf [Accessed 24 March 2015].

Claesson, J., 2009. *Fördjupat Program för Hjorthagen*. Stockholm: The City of Stockholm Development Office.

Jaeger, C.C., Paroussos, L., Mangalagiu, D., Kupers, R., Mandel, A. and Tabara, J.D., 2011. *A New Growth Path for Europe*. Commissioned by the German Federal Ministry of Nature Conservation and Nuclear Safety. European Climate Forum. Available from: http://www.globalclimateforum.org/fileadmin/ecf-documents/publications/reports/A_New_Growth_Path_for_Europe_-_Synthesis_Report.pdf [Accessed 13 January 2015].

Landstingsstyrelsens förvaltning and Tillväxt, miljö och regionplanering, 2012. *Huvudrapport, Befolkningsprognos 2012–2021*. Demografisk rapport. Stockholm: Landstingsstyrelsen.

Metzger, J. and Rader Olsson, A., eds., 2013. *Sustainable Stockholm*. New York: Routledge.

Pandis Iverot, S. and Brandt, N., 2011. The development of a sustainable urban district in Hammarby Sjöstad, Stockholm, Sweden? *Environment, Development and Sustainability*, 13 (6), 1043–1064.

Reardon, M., 2010. *An Opportunity for Renewal: The Participatory Process and Social and Income Diversity in Brownfield Developments*. Master's Thesis, Stockholm University. Available from: http://su.diva-portal.org/smash/get/diva2:321893/FULLTEXT01.pdf [Accessed 18 November 2014].

Regionplanekontoret, 2010. *RUFS 2010 – Regional Utvecklingsplan för Stockholmsregionen 2010*. Rapport 1:2010, Available from: http://www.trf.sll.se/Global/Dokument/publ/2010/RUFS10_hela.pdf [Accessed 7 March 2015].

Schmitt, P., Greve Harbo, L., Tepecik Diş, A., Henriksson, A., 2013. Polycentricity and urban resilience – the case of the Stockholm urban agglomeration. In: A. Eraydin and T. Tasan Kok, eds. *Resilient Thinking in Urban Planning*. Berlin: Springer, 197–209.

Schremmer, C., Mollay, U., Pinho, P., Santos Cruz, S., Stead, D., Schmitt, P., Davoudi, S., Megginson, C., Gaube, V., Heinz, M., Steinberger, J., Pichler, P. and Weisz, H., 2011. *Planning Resource-efficient cities*. SUME Synthesis Report. Available from: http://www.sume.at/project_downloads [Accessed 23 January 2015].

Sjöstadsföreningen, 2013. *HS2020*. Accessed at http://sjostadsforeningen.se/hs2020/, May 15, 2015 (Formerly www.hs2020.se).

Stockholm Royal Seaport, 2013. *Stockholm Royal Seaport*. Available from: http://www.stockholmroyalseaport.se. [Accessed: January 10, 2013].

Stockholms Stad, 2012a. *Framkomlighetsstrategin*. Available from: http://www.stockholm.se/PageFiles/237245/framk%20svensk.pdf [Accessed 18 November 2014].

Stockholms Stad, 2012b. *Cykelplan*. Available from: http://www.stockholm.se/PageFiles/227195/Cykelplan%202012.pdf [Accessed 18 November 2014].

Svane, Ö., 2008. Situations of opportunity – Hammarby Sjöstad and Stockholm City's process of environmental management. *Corporate Social Responsibility and Environmental Management*, 15 (2), 76–88.

9 Territorial governance faces complexity

The South Loire Plan for territorial cohesion

Alberta de Luca and Nadia Caruso

Introduction

This chapter describes the territorial governance process that led to the Territorial Cohesion Plan (*Schéma de Coherence Territoriale*, or SCOT) of South Loire, an area in the Loire Department of the Rhône-Alpes region. The capital of the Loire Department is Saint-Étienne, a city of nearly 178,000 inhabitants, is located 60 km southwest of Lyon, the second largest metropolitan area in France and capital of Rhône-Alpes region. Saint-Étienne is the driving city for the whole surrounding region, and has been deeply connected to the region's industrial growth since the nineteenth century, witnessing its decline and the following attempts to recover. Many efforts, in fact, were made in the 1990s and the early 2000s to mitigate the deep economic decline that occurred from the 1970s to the beginning of the 1990s. Nevertheless, these efforts have been largely considered unsuccessful. According to a number of experts, this failure is due to the strong role played by the central state and its decentralised structures, which seems to have inhibited local institutional resources and their autonomy (Béal *et al.* 2010, Vant and Gay 1997). Thus, Saint-Étienne has inherited a structure of social, economic and political relations that still prove unable to build both a capacity for collective actions and shared strategies to face various crises.

Against this framework, national regulations impacting on territorial planning and management were set up in the mid-1990s. Among them, are the Territorial Planning Directives, which highlight the central state's interests in specific territories in terms of planning and land management and are legally binding for all the other documents and plans referring to the same area. The Territorial Planning Directive for the Lyon Metropolitan Area (which also includes the South Loire territory) was adopted in 2007 after a lengthy process, which started in 1998. Furthermore, a turning point occurred in the early 2000s with the introduction of the 'Solidarity and Urban Renovation Law', that particularly stressed social issues in urban planning and provided a framework for shared projects such as the 'Agglomeration Project' and the 'Local Agenda 21'. In 2010 the so-called 'Grenelle II Law' revisited the 'Solidarity and Urban Renovation Law' focusing on environmental matters.

Since the early 2000s the development strategies of Saint-Étienne and the surrounding area have been grouped under the Territorial Cohesion Plan, the new planning instrument tasked to strengthen innovations in terms of inter-institutional cooperation, stakeholder involvement and territorialisation of policies. According to the 'Grenelle II Law', all the French territories will have a Territorial Cohesion Plan by 2017 (in early 2015 about 40 Territorial Cohesion Plans were adopted).

The role of the Territorial Cohesion Plan is to ensure a better balance between the development and the protection of urban, rural and natural areas as well as promoting the sustainable use of the land. It ties together various public urban planning policies, particularly concerning private and low-income housing, transport and infrastructure, commercial premises and environmental protection. Territorial Cohesion Plans are prepared by an Inter-Municipal Cooperation Structure (*Établissement public de cooperation intercommunale*, or EPCI), or by a group of them (as in South Loire), usually committed to joint activities in fields such as mobility, environment, and so on. France has a highly centralised government and it has only been during the decentralisation processes of the last century that municipalities have gained autonomy. Since then they have started to look for inter-municipal arrangements, performed on voluntary basis, in order to maintain public services at reasonable costs.

A Territorial Cohesion Plan is elaborated through a wide negotiation process that engages governmental and non-governmental actors. Its approval is submitted to a public consultation which involves the local community, collecting different opinions and obtaining the authorisation of independent advisors. It is implemented by a structure called *Syndicat Mixte* (henceforth referred to as Syndicat), a joint venture between various public authorities, which has no budget of its own. The territory of the Territorial Cohesion Plan must encompass a continuous area, which stretches beyond the municipalities' borders. At first glance, the Territorial Cohesion Plan area could be considered as a 'soft space' which is, however, still defined by the outer borders of the selected set of municipalities, see Figures 9.1 and 5.1. The perimeter should take into account existing Inter-Municipal Cooperation Structures, other plans or programmes, and consider economic and territorial characteristics. Municipalities and/or Inter-Municipal Cooperation Structures are in charge of submitting the Territorial Cohesion Plan proposal to the Prefect (representing the state), who approves it after having received acceptance from a qualified majority of the municipalities involved.

The process of developing a Territorial Cohesion Plan for the South Loire officially started in 2004 (though several consultations had taken place since 1999), and was approved in 2010 only to be revoked two years later. The cancellation was due to a legal appeal presented by a powerful commercial stakeholder, which contested some environmental actions concerning green corridors for wildlife preservation. The Administrative Court found that the green corridors were neither extensive enough nor adequately preserved

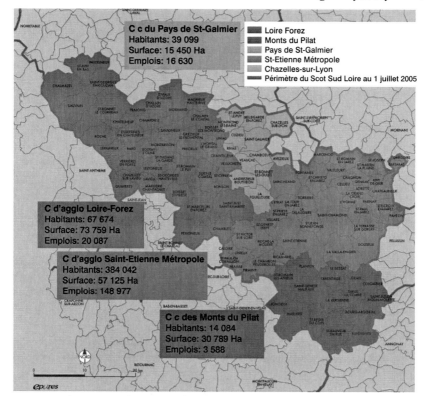

Figure 9.1 The territorial scope of the Territorial Cohesion Plan of South Loire
Source: Syndicat Mixte SCOT Sud Loire (2010e, p. 9). Reproduced by permission.

and withdrew the plan. In July 2012, a new Territorial Cohesion Plan was deliberated and finally, in December 2013, the plan was approved.

Co-ordinating actions of actors and institutions

The Territorial Cohesion Plan is, by its nature, a multi-level instrument that involves 'a new constellation of actors, institutions and interests', as stated by Gualini (2008, p. 16). The South Loire Plan's 'constellation' is represented in Figure 9.2. The distribution of power among the actors was formal, because it derived from the statutory mandate entrusted to the Syndicat. The power was exercised over a soft territory, which was proposed by the Inter-Municipal Cooperation Structures and approved by the Prefect, transcending the prevailing administrative organisation of space.

Four types of actors were involved in the Territorial Cohesion Plan governance process: the project management (the Syndicat), the operative actor (EPURES, the local Urban Planning Agency), the members (the Inter-Municipal Cooperation Structures and one municipality) and a number of institutional partners.

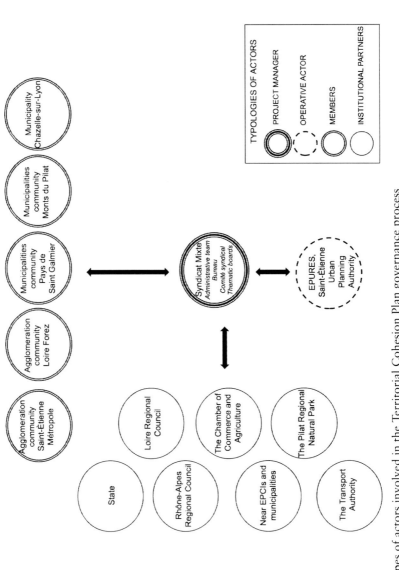

Figure 9.2 Types of actors involved in the Territorial Cohesion Plan governance process

Source: Own adaptation based on information gathered from SCOT Sud Loire (2015)

The Syndicat, the keystone of the governance system, was the contact point among all the actors. As project manager, it worked in close connection with EPURES, the local Urban Planning Agency, one of the 52 non-profit associations in France stated by the National Planning Law committed to support local spatial planning. Formally the Syndicat was composed of a simple structure:

- a restricted administrative team (only three persons) that worked together with the technicians, EPURES and the state decentralised services within a technical committee,
- a *comité syndical,* the managing board and decision-making body that involved representatives of 26 municipalities,
- a *bureau* of nine members which exercised political steerage and was intimately linked to the institutional members,
- and, finally, five thematic boards that analysed the documents and plans proposed by municipalities and the community.

The Territorial Cohesion Plan members are four Inter-Municipal Cooperation Structures and a municipality: the Agglomeration Communities (*Communautés d'Agglomeration*) of Saint Étienne Métropole and of Loire Forez; the Municipalities Communities (*Communautés de Communes*) de Pays de Saint-Galmier and of Monts du Pilat and the Municipality of Chazelles-sur-Lyon, in total 117 municipalities (cf. Figure 9.1). This inter-municipal partnership was only recently established and few previous shared projects existed. This means that there was neither institutional memory nor collaborative traditions or reciprocal knowledge upon which to base the inter-municipal territorial governance process.

As regards institutional partners, some are by law associated with the Territorial Cohesion Plan. Their role is only marginal during the process: they can be consulted on specific issues, and at the end of the process they need to be consulted for its final validation. The Syndicat can choose to take into account their advice or not. But it has to justify the grounds for the rejection of the advice. After the approval of the Territorial Cohesion Plan, the central state guarantees its implementation by monitoring the adaptation of the local urban development plans, which have to be revisited within three years after approval. In South Loire, the institutional partners are: the central state, the Rhône-Alpes Regional Council, the Loire Regional Council, the nearby Inter-Municipal Cooperation Structures and Municipalities, the Regional Transport Authority, the Chambers of Commerce and Agriculture and the Pilat Regional Nature Park.

The only economic actors involved in the process were the Chamber of Commerce, the Inter-Municipal Cooperation Structures' economic services and, solely in specific phases, the Regional Development Council and the Agency for the Economic Development of Loire. In other words, no private economic actor was directly involved in the territorial governance process.

116 *Alberta de Luca and Nadia Caruso*

Exercising leadership

From the operative and managing point of view, the Syndicat together with the local Urban Planning Agency exercised leadership, which was recognised and accepted by all the other involved actors. From the political point of view, leadership was articulated by the *comité syndical*, the closed committee within the Syndicat. However the *comité syndical* faced some difficulties. Most of the problems occurred in particular regarding three aspects: the representativeness system, the presence of different interests within the inter-municipalities organisations, and the supposed centrality of Saint-Étienne.

As for the first problem, it is worth remembering that only 26 out of the 117 members' municipalities involved were part of the decision-making body. Such a restricted system of representativeness would have required that the participating representatives should inform non-participating mayors continuously in order to share the whole elaboration process instead of imposing their final choices. Nevertheless, interviews with key informants showed that this occurred in only a few cases. In the renewed Territorial Cohesion Plan the mechanism was indeed revised, improving the communication with the mayors (see section 'Being adaptive to changing contexts').

The second problem that affected actors' interactions was the presence of different interests and territorial development visions. For example, some municipalities of the Agglomeration Community of Saint-Étienne (in particular those located in the Plaine Area and generally with a different political colour compared to Saint-Étienne) hindered the process in order to defend their own interests concerning, in particular, urbanisation, enterprise localisations etc. (personal communication 2012).

Other frictions among the municipalities occurred as some of them felt their interests not adequately represented due to the dominance of Saint-Étienne in the Territorial Cohesion Plan. This circumstance occurred in particular when the plan provided new housing constructions around Saint-Étienne. The negotiation was hard and, after having decided to establish a robust threshold that quantified the minimal residential stock to be built in each municipality, the Syndicat committed itself to revise the quota after five years (when a new analysis would be conducted). In this way, the Syndicat proved not only that it had problem-solving skills (in one of the more complex domains of the plan's interventions), but also the willingness to introduce reflection and integration of feedback routines (personal communication 2012).

To deal with these issues, the Syndicat decided to organise a number of public meetings. Forums, conferences and workshops were put in place in order to facilitate the exchange among actors. These tools were institutionalised, that is formally and officially part of the plan's process and in some cases actually mitigated the frictions among actors (see also sections 'Integrating policy sectors' and 'Mobilising stakeholder participation') (personal communication 2013).

Integrating policy sectors

The Territorial Cohesion Plan has been conceived to promote cross-sectoral integration, as stated in article L-122 of the French Urban Code (*Code de l'urbanisme*):

> The SCOTs [Territorial Cohesion Plans] provide a diagnosis of the territory in terms of economic and population projections and needs identified in terms of economic development, agriculture, spatial and environmental planning, social balance in housing, transportation, arrangements and services. They present the adopted sustainable development planning, which establishes the public policy objectives of planning in terms of housing, economic development, recreation, mobility of people and goods.
>
> (authors' own translation)

Therefore, by law, the Territorial Cohesion Plan is a 'territorial project' aimed at giving coherence to the sectoral policies concerning residential,

Table 9.1 Framework of cross-sector objectives in the South Loire Plan for territorial cohesion

Introductory report main axes	Planning and sustainable development project priorities	General guidelines document trends
• Development based on a preserved natural environment and on a high quality of life • Attractiveness and sustainable urban development as the region's challenges • Consolidation of the South Loire identity in the Lyon metropolitan area	• Developing the South Loire as one of the most important hubs in the metropolitan area of Lyon-Saint Étienne, in connection with the wider area of the Massif Central • Improving the quality of life, enhancing and protecting natural resources of the South Loire • Meeting the territorial development needs (a 'new development model') • Improving accessibility and mobility • Preserving resources and preventing risks • Equipping the area for urban development	• Spatial balance • Public policies • Safeguard of resources and risk prevention

Strategic aims of the development process

1. Safeguarding the environment in order to guarantee high standard of life.
2. Guaranteeing a sustainable territorial development by improving the governance of territories.
3. Improving the attractiveness of the South Loire region to ensure its dynamism.

Source: Authors' own adaptation based on Syndicat Mixte SCOT Sud-Loire (2010c)

commercial and tourist development, environmental conservation and green recreational areas promotion for future years. In the South Loire case, the cross-sectoral integration can be observed on two levels: on the formal (structural) and on the procedural levels, that is, in the general framework of the objectives and in the cross-fertilisation of groups, platforms and practices. Formally, the horizontal integration was built around cross-sector axes, priorities and trends collected in the different Territorial Cohesion Plan documents (the Introductory Report, the Planning and Sustainable Development Project and the General Guidelines Document) and merging into the three strategic aims of the development process (see Table 9.1).

Procedurally – beyond the formal statements – the integration of policy sectors can be mainly seen as taking place within two platforms: the technical committee within the Syndicat and the working groups coordinated by the local Urban Planning Agency. In these important platforms, sectoral frictions were dealt with by gathering information and knowledge. This process also had the effect of promoting and strengthening the links among the managerial, technical and political bodies and stakeholders (see Figure 9.3). Thus, these platforms can be understood as the main forums for coordination.

Political bodies (the *comité syndical,* the *bureau* and the six commissions) worked together in the technical committee composed of the state's and Inter-Municipal Cooperation Structures' technicians. The committee was organised into thematic boards, in the fields of economy, housing, natural and agricultural environment, mobility and urban planning. In the diagnostic

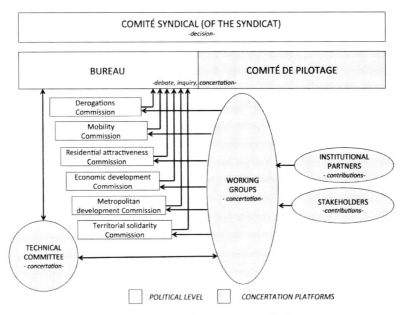

Figure 9.3 Cross-sectoral integration and participation platforms

Source: Own adaptation based on Syndicat Mixte SCOT Sud Loire (2005)

phase, the thematic boards worked quite separately, by examining documents and plans coming from the municipalities in order to take into consideration territorial needs in different fields. In the policy-making phase, exchanges were organised to fine-tune sectoral policies and bring them together into a common strategy.

The working groups, coordinated by the Urban Planning Agency, were the second platform for horizontal integration. These groups worked for six commissions, which operated at the political level, and gathered institutional and social actors (see also section 'Mobilising stakeholder participation').

In terms of dealing with conflicts, the dominant sectors were the 'harder' ones, namely those concerning housing and commercial settlements, where there were many conflicts concerning, in particular, coordination among municipalities (see also sections 'Co-ordinating actions of actors and institutions' and 'Realising place-based territorial specificities and impacts') (personal communication 2012).

Mobilising stakeholder participation

The reforms of the French Urban Code legal framework in the mid-1990s have widened the policy-making context by allowing multiple actors to participate in the process. Thus, elected representatives can be supported by public and private legal bodies, technicians, experts and inhabitants, which then become part of the Territorial Cohesion Plan process. The concertation aims at both driving a common strategy about the future of the territory among all local actors and institutions and informing residents in order to share with them the final project.

It has already been stated that the identification of actors was mainly achieved by conventional methods. The identification of stakeholders, instead, was the result of explicit decisions taken at a political level. In South Loire the exclusion of economic representatives can be seen both in the actor system and in the stakeholder arena. Indeed, it was decided to leave out the private economic stakeholders, both local and national ones, and this represents one of the weakest aspects of the process. Because of this exclusion, economic stakeholders considered the Territorial Cohesion Plan to be a threat against their own interests. In particular, as one of the interviewed policy-makers stated, they feared that new planning rules would be unfavourable for new commercial establishments. Economic stakeholders for this reason presented a number of legal appeals. One of them was IMMOCHAN, a branch of the Auchan Group responsible for real estate management, which needed a pretext to invalidate the plan. By referring to some environmental issues, IMMOCHAN presented a legal appeal. The Administrative Court evaluated that actually the plan did not adequately safeguard some green corridors, as stated by the Territorial Planning Directive for the Lyon Metropolitan Area, and revoked the plan (personal communication 2012).

Beyond this crucial exclusion, an advanced system of participation was planned. The working groups represented the main forum for the participation of social stakeholders, coordinated by the local Urban Planning Agency. In addition to this formal and institutional structure, different tools were put in place to guarantee transparency and foster participation. Various media channels were utilised during the development of the plan, thus making territorial governance more visible to residents. To improve exchange and communication among inhabitants and municipalities, the Syndicat published a dossier, set up a website and organised public communications and forums.

Being adaptive to changing contexts

Due to the complexity of the plan-making process, analysing this dimension is not a simple task. Commenting on the extent to which the plan was 'adaptable', one of the respondents denounced the effectiveness of the Territorial Cohesion Plan (personal communication 2012). In his opinion, changes in society are occurring too rapidly to be reflected in the public action connected to the elaboration of the plan. As a tool the Territorial Cohesion Plan is considered to have a lengthy gestation period which is incompatible with the rapidity of changes and limits its capacity to be effective (personal communication 2012). This statement gains weight as coming from the person representing one of the most important institutional public partners. The presence of such different points of view poses some serious problems to the territorial governance process.

Actually, beyond the (presumed) rigidity of the Territorial Cohesion Plan, institutional learning had little room in the process. It was especially due to the fact that the structures of inter-municipal coordination were quite new. The Inter-Municipal Cooperation Structure was born in 2004 in connection with the Territorial Cohesion Plan. The structure of the individual inter-municipal members are also recent: the Municipalities Community Structure of Saint-Étienne was established in 1995 and became Agglomeration Community in 2001, thus widening its territorial area; the Municipalities Community of Loire Forez was established in 2003 and enlarged in 2005; the Municipalities Community of Monts du Pilat was born in 2004 from the union of Drôme and Sivom Communities; finally the Municipalities Community of Pays de Saint-Galmier, the oldest, was established in 1996. Except for a few projects shared by some members, there was no previous collaborative planning experience. In one of the first official documents related to this Territorial Cohesion Plan, the Syndicat states: 'The territorial inter-municipal organisation into *Communauté d'agglomeration* and *Communauté de communes* is recent [...]. The inter-municipal cooperation learning process moves gradually, step by step' (Syndicat Mixte 2010d, p. 7, authors' own translation).

This 'fresh' inter-municipality cooperation has sometimes proved to be poorly equipped to be able to participate in the territorial development process. Moreover, this problem affects in general inter-municipal cooperation in France and not only the South Loire case, probably due to the fact that French municipalities have long been in fierce competition to attract enterprises, whose 'business tax' represents the main local financial resource.

Nevertheless it is possible to identify at least a 'reactive capacity' of the process that can be understood as a sort of 'adaptability'. This reactive capacity can be witnessed in many circumstances and in particular during the plan's withdrawal and subsequent re-launch. For this purpose, it is useful to understand what actors had learnt from the withdrawal and how the Syndicat planned to go ahead in the second round.

Most of the policy-makers involved underlined that the withdrawal of the Territorial Cohesion Plan in the first place did not bring into question the main choices of the plan. In particular, the strategies of housing allocation, and those for the housing mix and the territorial balance, survived as fixed points of the territorial organisation and development strategy, as M. Vincent, the Syndicat president, stated in the editorial explaining the Administrative Court decision (Syndicat Mixte SCOT Sud-Loire 2012). An updating on specific issues was nevertheless necessary. In particular, it concerned: new territorial needs (the diagnostic analysis was conducted before the credit crunch, thus in a context of a radically changed global economy); the introduction of the so-called 'Grenelle II Law' that modified some environmental actions; and, finally, problems related to green corridors. During the plan's re-launch, policy-making actors actually engaged in such issues, trying to respond to new territorial scenarios.

Furthermore, the Syndicat identified some critical problems to be addressed and committed itself to finding solutions. In order to face the general criticism that the plan was Saint-Étienne-centred (as will be explained in the next section), the Syndicat conducted an additional analysis of the neglected rural areas. Moreover, in order to improve the participation at a closer level to citizens, the Syndicat involved municipalities through local meetings. Thus, the process proved to be reactive and, somehow, actors were able to learn from their mistakes. Nevertheless, the most important reason for criticism – namely the lack of participation of private economic interests – seemed to be not considered as an object of institutional learning.

Realising place-based/territorial specificities and impacts

In order to analyse the extent to which the territorial governance process was sensitive to the territorial/place-based specificities and impacts of the plan, a reflection on three levels can be conducted: the first level concerns the how the perimeter of action was defined and the general characteristics of the area; the second level concerns the way in which different territorial characteristics were taken into account; the third level regards the way in which territorial knowledge affected the process.

Starting with the first level, the perimeter of action was pre-defined by the Territorial Planning Directive for the Lyon Metropolitan Area and decision-makers' endorsements which extended beyond municipalities' borders. The outcome has been an assembly of very different areas. In every official document, the plan's territory is defined as 'multiple'. It presents, in fact, heterogeneous characteristics: it shows both a metropolitan character (due to the proximity to the metropolitan area of Lyon), and a natural environmental character (23 out of the 117 municipalities within this Territorial Cohesion Plan belong to the Natural Regional Park of Pilat). Furthermore, rural areas and river basins are also included in the area. Differences are wide even among municipalities within the same Inter-Municipal Cooperation Structure.

The second level of reflection concerns the way in which territorial characteristics were taken into account. For this, the plan committed itself to give priority to territorial analysis, which emerged from the planning documents of different areas involved. In this sense, the plan's main function has been to synthesise existing territorial knowledge. Aiming at organising spatial planning for this wider area within a systematic shared framework, the territorial governance process took into account the sub-regional existing planning documents presuming that in this way different territorial characteristics and needs could be adequately considered. The first sub-regional area is that of Saint-Étienne, whose development strategy was organised in relation to three main themes: economic repositioning and competitive reinforcement, urban regeneration, and social and environmental sustainable development. The second sub-regional area is that of Pays du Forez, whose strategy was planned on three main axes to be improved: the residential function, the enterprise attraction, and tourism and leisure supply. The last sub-regional area, the Mount of Pilat, whose spatial development is obviously connected to the Natural Regional Park of Pilat, was mainly concerned with environmental preservation and economic, agricultural and tourism development.

The territorial governance process covered most of these axes and priority areas. The analysis, conducted at the beginning of the process, highlighted three main objectives that the Territorial Cohesion Plan should deal with: preserving the quality of life, enhancing the South Loire Region's vitality within the metropolitan area of Lyon, and promoting sustainable urban development. Thus, from the strictly formal point of view, the territorial governance process seems to envisage a 'place-based consistency'.

However, moving from declarative statements, a number of objections were raised: some municipalities considered the Territorial Cohesion Plan to be too Saint Étienne-centred and scarcely sensitive to the rest the area. It is important to note that the main frictions on this topic occurred in some of the more 'problematic' fields, where the plan tried to be more prescriptive, namely in particular in the housing supply and in commercial settlement policies. Criticism came also from delegates of rural areas, who claimed wider room for their voices to be heard. They felt rural areas were not adequately represented and local needs (nature preservation, the improvement of the quality of life and economic well-being of people living in relatively isolated and sparsely populated areas, etc.) were considered only marginally in the plan's development strategy, as admitted by the Syndicat (personal communication 2013). It is for this reason that the re-launched Territorial Cohesion Plan dealt with these areas more thoroughly.

The last level of reflection concerns the link between the territorial governance process and the utilisation of territorial knowledge. It is worth asking whether the latter affects the former. Actually, in this case the mutual generation of territorial knowledge was an outcome of the territorial governance process rather than its guiding principle. As one respondent stated: 'One of the most important outputs of this territorial governance process was the increased territorial knowledge. Now, everyone knows what is happening elsewhere' (personal communication 2013). Still another respondent argued: 'A shared territorial knowledge was an important output but the attained level is still inadequate for further collaboration' (personal communication 2013). It was felt that the lack of common and shared territorial knowledge in the beginning held up the process and made the initial phases more difficult. At the same time, its general increase can be considered as one of the most important outputs of the process.

Conclusions

The territorial governance process within the making of the South Loire Plan for Territorial Cohesion has shed light on some of the main aspects that characterise the development of the regional driving city, Saint-Étienne, where the structure of social, political and above all economic relations has not been able to develop a capacity for collective action and shared projects. In particular, the fact that the involvement of private economic actors was only marginal played a crucial role and impacted on the process negatively.

Concerning the first dimension, the coordination of actions of different actors and institutions, this process was entrusted to the Syndicat. Its leadership as project manager in collaboration with the local Urban Planning Agency was recognised and accepted by all actors. On the other hand, political leadership was exercised through a representation system of interests that sometimes proved to be inadequate. Conflicting interests, especially arising from municipalities, threatened the process and, in some cases, compromised it. Previous experiences of shared planning were inadequate; recent forms of cooperation were too new and few shared projects existed, and this hindered the territorial governance process. This inadequacy worsened because of the absence of private economic and commercial actors and stakeholders. Public meetings, forums, workshops and conferences were held in the attempt to address these problems and in some cases managed to mitigate them. When the plan was re-launched most of these problems were tackled and solved.

The second dimension concerns the integration of policy sectors. Here the Territorial Cohesion Plan proved to be attentive to public policy packaging since it is formally compatible with higher-level laws and documents (in particular, the 'Solidarity and Urban Renovation Law', the French Urban Code and the Territorial Planning Directive for Lyon Metropolitan Area). Actually, this fine-tuning is a mandatory feature, since it is a prerequisite prescribed by law, and thus it can be understood as a formal characteristic more than as a positive feature of the process. Some structures were useful arenas to gather information and knowledge thus facilitating the synergy among decision-makers, policy-makers and practitioners and dealing with conflict (in particular the technical committee and the working groups).

The third dimension deals with stakeholder participation. Formally it was well planned and performed. The working groups coordinated by the local Urban Planning Agency seemed to be a useful platform and the media tools (regional news, local newsletter, dossiers, publications, temporary expositions, web site, etc.) were quite informative, accessible and comprehensive. However, the (political) decision to exclude economic stakeholders in the first stages of the process remains a thorny issue.

The fourth dimension is the adaptation to changing contexts: the well-established procedure facilitated possible adaptabilities but also implied some rigidity. On one hand, the process proved to be 'reactive' to some internal and external inputs. On the other hand, the Syndicat seems to have learnt from its failure and in 2012–2013 it was looking for a more careful analysis of territorial needs and for a wider involvement of municipalities.

Concerning the last dimension, taking into account place-based territorial specificities and impacts, it seems that territorial characteristics have been considered sufficiently because the shared territorial knowledge increased and improved, although quite feeble at the beginning. This could be considered as a result of the territorial governance process.

If we take into account the distinction between the 'governance of territories' and territorial governance dealt with in Part I of this book, we can acknowledge that the South Loire Territorial Cohesion Plan was perhaps initially more characteristic of 'governance of territories', supported by many effective operative tools. However, many efforts have been undertaken over time to improve territorial sensitivity with regard to needs and characteristics of the whole region. One clear example is how some problematic relationships among institutions were dealt with and overcome and how a common territorial knowledge grew as an output of the process itself. Taking into account all these elements, the Territorial Cohesion Plan elaboration can be seen as an initial and important milestone towards effective territorial governance to achieve shared development in the South Loire Region.

References

Béal, V., Dormois, R. and Pinson, G., 2010. Relancer Saint-Étienne. Conditions institutionnelles et capacité d'action collective dans une ville en déclin. *Métropoles*, 8, 1–25.

SCOT Sud Loire, 2015. *Bienvenue sur le site du SCOT Sud Loire.* http://www.scot-sudloire.fr/ [Accessed 16 March 2015].

Syndicat Mixte SCOT Sud-Loire, 2005. *La concertation: pourquoi, avec qui, comment?* Saint-Étienne.

Syndicat Mixte SCOT Sud-Loire, 2010a. *Document d'Aménagement Commercial.* Saint-Étienne.

Syndicat Mixte SCOT Sud-Loire, 2010b. *Document d'Orientations Générales.* Saint-Étienne.

Syndicat Mixte SCOT Sud-Loire, 2010c. *Project d'Aménagement et de Development Durable.* Saint-Étienne.

Syndicat Mixte SCOT Sud-Loire, 2010d. *Rapport de présentation.* Saint-Étienne.

Syndicat Mixte SCOT Sud-Loire, 2010e. *Rapport de Présentation SCOT Sud Loire. Synthèse.* Saint-Étienne.

Syndicat Mixte SCOT Sud-Loire, 2012. *Réunion publique* (15 octobre 2012). Available from: http://www.scot-sudloire.fr/sites/default/files/documents/2013/Concertation/121015-reunion%20publique%20ptx%20Version%20FinaleV3.pdf [Accessed 10 February 2015].

Vant, A. and Gay, G., 1997. Saint-Étienne Métropole ou le découpage du territoire minime *Revue de géographie de Lyon* 72 (3), 177–190.

Wilker, A., 2007. *Saint-Étienne City Report, Report 40.* London: Centre for Analyses of Social Exclusion. Available from: http://sticerd.lse.ac.uk/dps/case/cr/CASEreport40.pdf [Accessed 19 January 2015].

10 Integrating public transport and urban development in the southern Randstad

Marjolein Spaans and Dominic Stead

Introduction

Increasingly functionally interconnected urban regions necessitate integrated metropolitan transport systems. In the Netherlands, and especially in the Randstad (the most urbanised part of the Netherlands in the west of the country), an integrated high-frequency public transport network is seen as an important prerequisite for increasing the competitiveness of the country in terms of business investment and new development. In the southern part of the Randstad, the Stedenbaan ('Cities Line') initiative aims to promote greater integration between public transport and urban development. The initiative combines the creation of a high-frequency light-rail transport system on the existing railway network with a regionally coordinated programme of urbanisation in the proximity of railway stations (labelled as 'influence area of Stedenbaan stations' in Figure 10.1). It aims to increase the development density of around nearly 60 railway stations and to improve the accessibility of station areas to increase rail usership to a level which allows the national rail operator to increase local train frequencies. These strategies are strongly influenced by the concept of transit-oriented development. Common transit-oriented development features include urban compactness, pedestrian and cycle-friendly facilities, and public spaces adjacent to stations (Transit Cooperative Research Program 2002). Transit-oriented development is often seen as offering the potential to boost public transport usership, increase walking, mitigate sprawl, accommodate economic growth, and improve urban spaces (Cervero *et al.* 2004, Evans *et al.* 2007, Geurs *et al.* 2012).

The origins of the Stedenbaan initiative can be traced back to 2002, when the Dutch national government announced its intention to focus on the improvement of public transport at the sub-regional level. Initially, the focus of the initiative was only on infrastructure. The aim was to provide a frequent local train service (in addition to the regional and national train services) on a section of the railway network between Leiden and Dordrecht (see Figure 10.2). Soon afterwards however, the scope of Stedenbaan was broadened to include a spatial dimension: urban development around stations (Balz and Zonneveld 2015). The rationale was that improvements in the quality of public transport

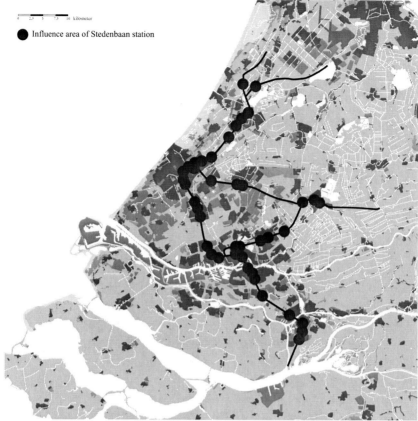

Figure 10.1 Relation between regional rail stations and urban development
Source: Own adaptation based on Atelier Zuidvleugel (2006)

nodes increase the attractiveness of housing, offices and facilities. Moreover, increasing urban development near public transport nodes was seen as a means of promoting the use of public transport and improving accessibility.

Territorial governance in relation to regional transport and spatial planning

The Dutch government structure is a three-tiered, decentralised unitary model, based on the self-government of provinces and municipalities. Co-government is an underlying principle: national government involves the provinces, the municipalities, or both in the formulation and implementation of its policies. Compared to many other European countries, the sub-national levels of government in the Netherlands have considerable responsibility (OECD 2007, p. 157). The responsibilities of the municipalities are more substantial than those of the provinces although the responsibilities of the

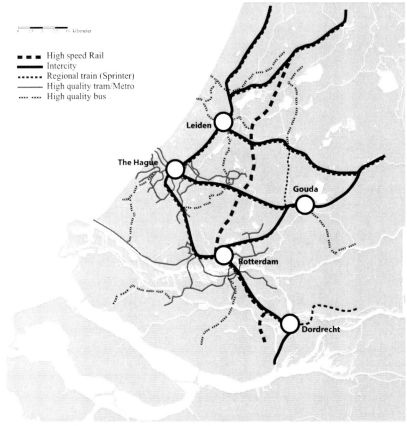

Figure 10.2 Public transport network in the southern Randstad

Source: Own adaptation based on Programmabureau Stedenbaan (n.d.)

provinces have increased over recent years as a result of the decentralisation of certain planning roles (see below). Municipalities are responsible for a wide range of policy sectors including roads, public transport, housing, spatial planning, environment, social services, economic development, education and healthcare. Although municipalities share many of their responsibilities with national government they are nevertheless relatively independent. Cooperation between Dutch municipalities is very common: a typical local authority will have close to 30 cooperative arrangements (OECD 2007, p. 170). Many of these arrangements are task specific and related to a single issue, where each agreement involves a different set of municipalities and/or different timescales.

Around the turn of the millennium, two regional administrative platforms were created in the Randstad: one in the north and the other in the south. The administrative platform for the southern part of the Randstad (the 'South Wing'), *Bestuurlijk Platform Zuidvleugel* or *BPZ*, covers the area surrounding the Hague and Rotterdam (Figure 10.3) and comprises eight

Public transport and development 129

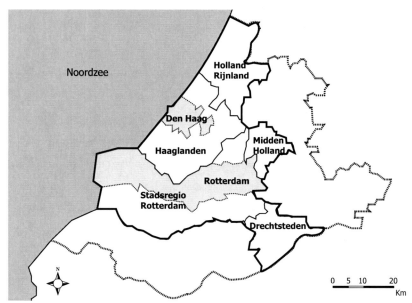

Figure 10.3 Boundaries of the administrative platform for the South Wing
Source: Own adaptation based on information from Provincie Zuid-Holland

partners: the Province of Zuid-Holland, five regional cooperation bodies including the city regions of Rotterdam (*Stadsregio Rotterdam*) and The Hague (*Haaglanden*), the regions of Holland Rijnland (the northern part of the province with Leiden as the largest city), Drecht Cities (Dordrecht and surrounding municipalities) and Midden-Holland (Gouda and its environs) and the municipalities of Rotterdam and The Hague. The Administrative Platform for the South Wing was not meant to become a new decision-making layer of government, but rather a partnership arrangement which is used to secure agreements about projects and investments without a transfer of competences. Cooperation at the city-region level is often hampered by the lack of implementation power: every municipality that is part of these cooperative arrangements can veto decisions (OECD 2007, p. 160).

In 2003, eight city regions (*stadsregios*) in the Netherlands were created, each of which consist of a large city with the surrounding municipalities that form part of the same daily urban system (Figure 10.4). These city regions were given responsibilities for transport, housing, the environment and regional economic development, and they have become particularly important actors in transport policy. However, these city regions have limited influence on regional rail transport services provided by the national rail operator (NS). Despite a contract between the NS and the national government, requiring NS to consult with decentralised governments about the services it provides, NS generally prioritises services for long-distance travellers rather than local or regional services. It is therefore difficult for individual regions to negotiate

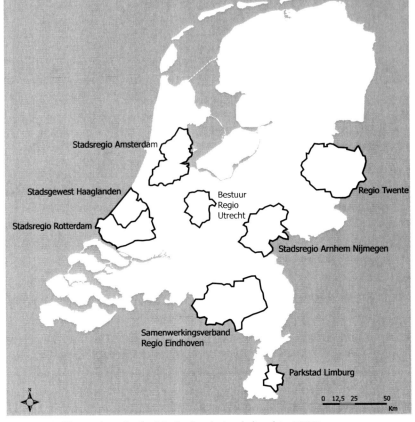

Figure 10.4 City regions in the Netherlands (as defined in 2003)

Source: Own adaptation based on Ministerie van Binnenlandse Zaken en Koninkrijksrelaties (2010, p. 22)

with the national rail operator (NS) for the use of the main railway network to improve regional public transport, as is the case in the southern Randstad. This is an issue that the Stedenbaan initiative attempts to address.

Territorial governance arrangements in Stedenbaan

The governance arrangements in the southern Randstad fit with the observation that polycentric metropolitan regions are particularly keen on 'soft governance arrangements' (OECD 2007, p. 175) and that many governance partnerships for polycentric regions are bottom-up initiatives coming from municipalities themselves, rather than driven by the national government, often with partners from private and voluntary sectors and other public and private agencies. These partnerships do not have decision-making powers but can influence decision-making processes and seek implementation by making recommendations to the decision-making bodies. These partnerships can best be described in terms of strategic positioning, project orientation, actor networking, agenda-setting and advocacy.

The arrangements are also in line with the trend that many metropolitan regions across the world are placing greater emphasis on voluntary instruments for coordination and cooperation. In terms of efficiency, it may not be optimal to rely on cooperative mechanisms to implement their policy, but they have their own merits such as fostering communication and limiting bureaucratic mission creep (i.e. the tendency of bureaucracies to try to claim more powers and resources). On the other hand, experiences of voluntary cooperation arrangements are most often difficult if not impossible to implement in the context of conflicting relationships between different territorial layers or when there are high intra-metropolitan disparities (OECD 2007, p. 191).

Coordinating the actions of actors and institutions

Over the last decade, a more bottom-up cooperation structure has emerged in the South Wing in the form of the Metropolitan region of Rotterdam and The Hague. Under this arrangement, the two main cities (Rotterdam and The Hague) play a major role, which is in contrast to the South Wing Cooperation where no single body has a leading role. The status of the metropolitan region gained momentum in 2010 when the national government announced the abolition of city regions by January 2015. Since the city regions act as transport authorities and receive funding from national government, new arrangements were sought. One option was that the responsibilities for infrastructure – and the related budget of roughly €0.5 billion per annum – would be transferred to the province. Another option was to place the Metropolitan region at the forefront and give the responsibilities for infrastructure to the Metropolitan region, which the mayors of Rotterdam and The Hague favoured (Spaans and Zonneveld 2015). Ultimately it was decided that responsibilities should be given to the Metropolitan region, according to the second option.

As a result of the above changes in responsibilities for infrastructure, the Stedenbaan initiative now covers the same territory as the Metropolitan region of Rotterdam and The Hague, which is responsible for managing the infrastructure budget. Because the Metropolitan region is still under development, it does not have legal powers (at the moment at least), with the exception of the powers and responsibilities of the two city regions. Consequently, the Stedenbaan initiative is essentially a partnership arrangement between various public and private parties that operates with very few statutory powers or instruments at its disposal. As such, it is reliant on 'soft' processes of governance, primarily taking a coordinating and information-provision role and using powers of argument and persuasion to reach agreements between the various actors involved. A deliberate choice was made in the Stedenbaan initiative not to develop new instruments but

132 Marjolein Spaans and Dominic Stead

to closely link to planning instruments of participating government tiers, such as the provincial structural vision (*provinciale structuurvisie*) and the provincial legally binding land-use regulations (*provinciale verordening*) (personal communication 2012).

Actors and institutions in Stedenbaan

The Stedenbaan initiative was originally initiated by the Province of Zuid-Holland and the city of Dordrecht together with the national rail operator (NS). Alongside these, key actors include the rail infrastructure manager (ProRail) and the other partners of the Administrative Platform for the South Wing (BPZ). Although property developers are centrally involved in the development process, and are crucial for the success of Stedenbaan, they were not involved as a formal actor in the Stedenbaan initiative. The actors were limited to governmental (or semi-governmental) bodies. Moreover, a deliberate choice was made to form a small group of key actors in order to simplify its management. From the beginning of the initiative, a key management principle has been 'one organisation, one vote' (personal communication 2012).

Alongside the Steering Group, there is the Administrative Committee (*Bestuurlijke Commissie*), in which both the transport and spatial planning sectors are represented. Only elected (rather than appointed) representatives are members of the Administrative Committee. In the past, there has been tension between the mayors of the cities of Rotterdam and The Hague and the Commissioner of the Province of Zuid-Holland, all three of whom are appointed rather than elected. More recently however, the mayors of the two cities have cooperated together on the development of the Metropolitan region of Rotterdam and The Hague. Formally the two major cities may be represented separately, but as the city region is a bottom-up representation, the Alderman of the city of Rotterdam is also the political representative on traffic and transport for the city region of Rotterdam. The presence of Rotterdam and The Hague is an issue in the composition of platform meetings as the two major cities do not feel equally represented by their city region. All working groups meet annually to formulate an action plan for the year, which is approved by the Administrative Commission. The implementation of the action plan is primarily in the hands of the municipalities (personal communication 2012).

The Stedenbaan initiative is not binding for local or provincial authorities. Instead, it acts as a platform for dialogue on spatial planning, housing, employment, transport and accessibility among local governments. Therefore, its influence over national policies is limited: other bodies such as the association of municipalities (VNG) and the association of provinces (IPO) have more influence. However, the cities of Rotterdam and The Hague are powerful sub-national institutions and have direct connections to the national government. Like Amsterdam and Utrecht – the other two largest cities in the Netherlands – they are more powerful than other municipalities. Relations between the four biggest cities have always been competitive since no city has ever become clearly dominant (OECD 2007, p. 142). Thus, the creation of the Metropolitan region of Rotterdam and The Hague potentially concentrates power/influence into the metropolitan region of these two cities (i.e. Rotterdam and The Hague).

The Stedenbaan initiative has an additional role of helping to bring regional policy issues to the attention of the national government. Thus, the added value of the Stedenbaan initiative is in agenda-setting, particularly in terms of issues related to the improvement of regional public rail transport and the close relationship between regional public rail transport and urban development around stations (personal communications 2012). One issue which Stedenbaan is currently seeking to address is the expansion of railway infrastructure capacity between Delft-South and Schiedam, which connects Rotterdam and The Hague, and is currently considered to be a major bottleneck in the metropolitan region (personal communication 2012).

Integrating policy sectors

Cross-sectoral policy integration

The integration between public transport planning and urban development in the Netherlands takes place at different levels. The 'Randstad 2040 Structural Vision' (*Structuurvisie Randstad 2040*, Ministerie VROM 2008) and the Randstad Urgent Programme addressed social, cultural, ecological and economic trends and challenges and the spatial implications related to the spatial structure of the Randstad. A close relation between mobility and urban development was given high priority. The first document – the Randstad 2040 Structural Vision – is part of the government-wide programme, in which the national and provincial governments, municipalities and metropolitan regions aim to tackle a range of policy challenges in the Randstad. The overall aim of the programme is to strengthen the economy of the Randstad. The Structural Vision sets out a long-term spatial development vision in terms of building and planning. One of the ambitions is to closely relate development and accessibility in both the northern and southern Randstad. Stedenbaan is introduced as a good example how to deal with this issue. The second document – the Randstad Urgent Programme – contains a set of projects that require decisions in the short term. The document does not relate development and accessibility directly and Stedenbaan is not mentioned explicitly in the list of projects. Not only is the Stedenbaan initiative embedded in national and local policy, it is also closely aligned with regional policy within the South Wing. It is for example one of the five South Wing programmes (the other four comprise the Economic Agenda, the Accessibility Package for road infrastructure, the Urbanisation Programme and the Metropolitan Landscape).

134   *Marjolein Spaans and Dominic Stead*

The statutory spatial planning documents to which the Stedenbaan initiative is aligned are the national, provincial and local structure visions. City regions can also formulate structural visions, although these are not mandatory. The statutory provincial structure vision – approved in 2010 – emphasises the relation between urban development and mobility. It mentions Stedenbaan as an accelerator for spatial differentiation in living and working environments and is considered essential in the region's continued urbanisation. In provincial documents, the Stedenbaan initiative is presented as an integrated concept and not as separate sectors only coming together in the programme itself.

In terms of national policy documents and programmes, the Stedenbaan initiative is closely aligned to the National Policy Strategy for Infrastructure and Spatial Planning (SVIR: *Structuurvisie Infrastructuur en Ruimte*, Ministerie van Infrastructuur en Milieu 2012). The strategy presents a vision for spatial planning and mobility. It includes the infrastructure projects in which national government wants to invest in the future. Provinces and municipalities have been given more responsibilities for spatial planning which were previously in the hands of the national government. The state retains responsibility for certain planning issues of national importance. Stedenbaan is also connected to a number of national infrastructure programmes, including the national Programme on High Frequency Rail Transport (*Programma Hoogfrequent Spoorvervoer*) coordinated by the Ministry of Infrastructure and the Environment. The essence of this programme is the construction of new rail infrastructure for the transportation of goods and for regional public transport systems with multimodal connections, enabling shorter journey times and higher frequencies. It also relates to the programme on better utilisation of transport infrastructure (*Programma Beter Benutten*) which is managed by the same ministry.

Barriers to cross-sectoral policy integration

When a new government was formed in 2010, a decision was made to merge the previously separate ministries responsible for spatial planning, mobility, environment and infrastructure. This change was also reflected in the national government's long-term investment programme on infrastructure, land use and transport (*Meerjarenprogramma Infrastructuur, Ruimte en Transport*, or MIRT programme). One of the aims of the new programme was to promote coherence between the policy fields of spatial planning and infrastructure and between central and regional policy. Since this major reorganisation in 2010, the national political interest in spatial planning decreased, both in terms of responsibility and investment. In addition, the economic crisis strongly affected the property market, and urban development came close to a standstill. Moreover, the South Wing of the Randstad was facing a governance challenge as central government threatened to transfer responsibilities back to the eight city regions. One consequence of these changes was that the two regional government bodies were in closer competition for power: (i) the Administrative Body of the South Wing in which the emphasis is on the province and the two city regions; and (ii) the Metropolitan region of Rotterdam and The Hague in which the emphasis is on the two major cities and which covers a smaller territory than the South Wing.

Administratively, the two sectors of transport and spatial planning are not always equally represented in decision-making processes, and consequently that issues are not fully discussed in the Administrative Commission. While the transport sector is usually represented by provincial and local politicians, the spatial planning sector is often represented by senior policy officials instead. Consequently some issues regarding development and transport are not fully or equally discussed at meetings as they are agreed in advance before the meetings (personal communication 2012).

Perceived synergies of the cross-sectoral approach

The assumption underlying the Stedenbaan initiative is that by providing high-quality public rail transport, specific hubs can be turned into attractive places to build homes, offices and facilities. Achieving urban development around public transport nodes is also expected to result in more passengers using public transport and better accessibility. The outcomes of the programme are dependent on negotiation and compromise between the partners involved. To date, the focus has been on public transportation and urban development and less on the synergy for the economic output (personal communication 2012).

Mobilising stakeholder participation

Since the Stedenbaan initiative is predominantly a platform for provincial and local politicians, direct involvement with the general public is limited. Issues of public involvement and participation are generally considered to be a task for municipalities at specific nodes. Since 2011 however, there has been more attention on implementation, and this has led to greater involvement of the property development sector in discussions, conferences and meetings (personal communications 2012). Thus, the views and inputs of the development sector have been increasingly taken into account in the Stedenbaan initiative, even though the sector is not formally part of the initiative. Stronger links with the development sector are also a consequence of the economic crisis and the necessary reorientation in urban development. In some nodes, where for example the national rail network adjoins regional light-rail systems (e.g. the stations of Gouda and Den Haag Laan van NOI), attempts were made as part of the Stedenbaan initiative to form strategic alliances between major office users, the national rail operator (NS) and the public transport operator in order to try to steer new development at these specific locations (personal communications 2012).

Being adaptive to changing contexts

Property development has been severely affected by the economic crisis over recent years. As mortgages became more difficult to secure, housing sales decreased substantially and the supply of new housing practically came to a standstill. At the same time it became more difficult to develop brownfield areas as they are more expensive to develop in existing urban areas. This either requires public subsidies or results in higher housing prices. Alternative or experimental forms of residential or employment development are generally considered with extreme caution by property developers and investors.

At the same time as the property crisis, major financial cuts in public expenditure have affected public transport. Power shifts have taken place (which began long before the current property development crisis) in which certain powers have been transferred from formal to informal bodies. The recent debate about the transfer of responsibilities for the transport authority is likely to affect the way in which the Stedenbaan initiative is organised in the future. The current proposal to transfer the transport authority from the two city regions to an authority covering the Metropolitan region of Rotterdam and The Hague will effectively decrease the number of partners in the Stedenbaan initiative, which may have efficiency benefits.

Safety regulations may pose barriers to urban development around stations, or the rail network more generally. This is primarily related to risks that the use of railway infrastructure poses to the surroundings (e.g. accidents during the transport of hazardous goods by rail) by goods transport. This is an important issue south of Rotterdam where goods from the harbour are transported through built-up areas. Safety regulations specifically apply to hazardous substances and influence housing and working locations. If the transport of goods by rail was diverted away from inner-city railway sections, this could increase the development opportunities in certain parts of the Randstad. The Stedenbaan initiative has helped to put this issue on the national and international agendas (personal communication 2012).

Partly as a consequence of the changing political and economic context (e.g. the property market crisis and national budget cuts), the need for changes to the Stedenbaan initiative is closely monitored. The annual monitoring reports assess progress of the overall programme and consider the extent to which objectives and planned activities have been met (personal communications 2012). As such, the Stedenbaan initiative is a flexible and cooperative platform that is being adapted to new economic and political circumstances. Both institutionally and individually, learning is taking place as the context of the Stedenbaan initiative evolves.

Realising place-based/territorial specificities and impacts

Because the southern Randstad is one of the most densely populated regions in the world, the efficient use of land is particularly crucial. However, compared to other densely populated areas in the world, the Randstad is characterised by relatively low-rise development. Without a coherent approach to the management of mobility, economic development could easily suffer. Public transport policy is primarily made and implemented at the national and local levels, while few powers rest with the regional level even though the South Wing of the Randstad is a polycentric urban region in terms of passenger transport. In order to provide greater accessibility to an efficient public rail transport system, new residential and employment developments need to be located close to public transport nodes. Some of these nodes require development on brownfield sites which are often more expensive than greenfield development (personal communication 2012).

Analysis by Meurs and Zandee (2012) has pinpointed a number of key factors that can help to achieve more coordinated urban development around railway stations. Their analysis underlines the importance of regional selectivity and the identification of clear profiles for development. With respect to regional selectivity, the Province of Zuid-Holland has taken the lead in trying to reduce the number of potential new housing, office and retail locations in its planning activities and promoting a small number of key development locations (personal communications 2012). To date, this has not been done in the context of Stedenbaan. Meurs and Zandee (2012) also suggest that each node needs a clear profile that distinguishes it from other nodes since issues of quality of place and spatial identity are important for the success of development.

In further analysing the Stedenbaan case, two levels are key: the regional infrastructure network and the individual stations or nodes. The Stedenbaan initiative addresses both levels. In terms of development opportunities around individual stations, various studies have been undertaken to identify potential areas for residential and employment development. Morphological and market analyses have been performed to assess the potential and addressing the specificities of each node. This reflects a place-based approach in which different types of nodes are distinguished in terms of accessibility to employment. The links between the rail network and territory provide opportunities for different types of development. The position of each station within the Stedenbaan network, as well as its territorial characteristics, were identified as part of this exercise (personal communications 2012).

Conclusions

The Stedenbaan initiative aims to promote greater integration between public transport and urban development in the South Wing of the Randstad. It combines two main strategies: (1) the creation of a high-frequency light-

138 *Marjolein Spaans and Dominic Stead*

rail transport system on the existing railway network; and (2) a regionally coordinated urbanisation programme based on the development of areas around the railway stations. It has also helped to bring policy issues from the region to the attention of national government.

The Stedenbaan initiative primarily has a platform function where coordination and promotion activities are central. As such, it illustrates a partnership arrangement between various public and private parties. There are few statutory powers available for the implementation of the Stedenbaan initiative and thus a lack of hard powers and instruments to steer private development. It chiefly employs soft instruments and a soft mode of governance, primarily taking a coordinating and information-provision role and using argument and persuasion to reach agreements between the various actors involved. Implementation of its objectives often occurs at a local level (e.g. individual railway nodes). It is also at this local scale that the mobilisation of stakeholder participation often takes place. Because of the platform function and the fact that it is less concerned with policy implementation, it may also be more adaptive to changing contexts. The Stedenbaan initiative relates to both vertical and horizontal policy coordination. Vertical coordination mainly links municipalities with both formal and informal regional government bodies and less directly with national government. Horizontal coordination relates urban development with public rail transportation. The aspect of public policy packaging is intrinsic in the Dutch spatial planning system which can be typified as consensus seeking. The Stedenbaan initiative provides a means of vertical and horizontal alignment of government policy.

The issue of governing capacity was one of the leading principles in putting the platform in place: a deliberately small group of participants, no property development representation, no appointed politicians, and decisions on the basis of 'one organisation one vote'. The Stedenbaan initiative was set up as a strategic platform and not one with responsibilities for implementation. It was a deliberate choice to link to statutory planning documents at the provincial and local levels.

Involvement of the general public in the Stedenbaan initiative is quite limited because it is predominantly a platform for provincial and local politicians. Public involvement is generally seen to be a task for municipalities at individual nodes. Representation by the province, city regions and cities in the Stedenbaan initiative means that democratic legitimacy and public accountability is indirect. While economic changes (e.g. the property market crisis) have meant that more attention has been given to implementation, the involvement of new formal partners or the general public has not changed.

Confronted with various economic and political changes, the Stedenbaan initiative has responded by adapting its focus and using evaluation instruments and a yearly monitoring exercise. The results of the latter are used in a reflexive way by the participants in the platform. The adaptability of the Stedenbaan initiative is reflected in its structure: a platform without instruments of its own but closely linked to instruments by the participants and a flexible structure by organising related *ad hoc* debates if changes in the context require.

Involvement of different levels of government (provincial, sub-regional, local) are represented in the Stedenbaan initiative has provided a mechanism of vertical policy coordination. The territoriality of the network and the nodes within it have been addressed extensively in the Stedenbaan initiative. This has included work to identify the specific development potentials according to the territorial specificities of each node on the network. In order to promote a diversity of development, maximise synergies between nodes and avoid unnecessary competition between them, the province has actively promoted complementary types of development across the network. This can be seen as one of the successes of the Stedenbaan initiative.

References

Atelier Zuidvleugel, 2006. *Ruimte en Lijn Atelier Zuidvleugel: Ruimtelijke Verkenning Stedenbaan 2010–2020, Zuidvleugel van de Randstad.* Commissioned by Commissie Stedenbaan RO. Den Haag: Atelier Zuidvleugel.

Balz, V. and Zonneveld, W., 2015. Regional Design in the Context of Fragmented Territorial Governance: South Wing Studio. *European Planning Studies*, 23 (5), 871–891.

Cervero, R., Murphy, S., Ferrell, C., Goguts, N. and Tsai, Y.-H., 2004. *Transit-Oriented Development in America: Experiences, Challenges and Prospects.* Washington DC: Transportation Research Board, National Research Council.

Evans, J.E., Pratt, R.H., Stryker, A. and Kuzmyak, J.R., 2007. *Transit Oriented Development. Traveler Response to Transportation System Changes.* TCRP report 95. Washington: Transportation Research Board.

Geurs, K., Maat, K., Rietveld P., and de Visser, G., 2012. Transit Oriented Development in the Randstad South Wing: Goals, Issues and Research. Paper presented at the conference '*Building the Urban Future and Transit Oriented Development*', Paris, April 16–17.

Meurs, H. and Zandee, R., 2012. *Visie: Voorkom suboptimale multimodale knooppunten, Verkeerskunde.* Available from: http://www.verkeerskunde.nl/visie-voorkom-suboptimale-multimodale-knooppunten.28039.lynkx [Accessed 26 May 2014].

Ministerie van Binnenlandse Zaken en Koninkrijksrelaties, 2010. *Plussen en minnen; Evaluatie van de WGR-plus.* Den Haag: Ministerie van Binnenlandse Zaken en Koninkrijksrelaties.

Ministerie van Infrastructuur en Milieu, 2012. *Structuurvisie Infrastructuur en Ruimte.* Den Haag: Ministerie van Infrastructuur en Milieu.

Ministerie VROM (Volkshuisvesting, Ruimtelijke Ordening en Milieubeheer), 2008. Structuurvisie Randstad 2040. Den Haag: Ministerie VROM.

OECD – Organisation for Economic Co-operation and Development, 2007. *OECD Territorial Reviews: Randstad Holland, The Netherlands.* Paris: OECD.

140 *Marjolein Spaans and Dominic Stead*

Programmabureau StedenbaanPlus, [n.d.]. *Stedenbaan Plus Transit Oriented Development in the South Wing of the Randstad*. Den Haag: Programmabureau StedenbaanPlus.

Spaans, M. and Zonneveld, W., 2015. Evolving Regional Spaces: Shifting Levels in the Southern part of the Randstad. In: P. Allmendinger, G. Haughton, J. Knieling and F. Othengrafen, eds. *Soft Spaces in Europe. Re-Negotiating Governance, Boundaries and Borders*. Abingdon: Routledge, 95–128.

Transit Cooperative Research Program, 2002. *Transit-Oriented Development and Joint Development in the United States: A Literature Review*. Research Results Digest 52. Washington DC: Transportation Research Board of the National Academies.

11 Maintaining stable regional territorial governance institutions in times of change

Greater Manchester Combined Authority

Paul Cowie, Ali Madanipour, Simin Davoudi and Geoff Vigar

Introduction

There has been almost continuous change in regional governance structures in the UK since the 1970s. A whole variety of regional governance institutions has come and gone since the introduction of metropolitan county councils in 1974. The waxing and waning of regional governance in the UK is largely related to the relative strength of the various political powers at any one time, but is also affected by political influences at the EU level (Tewdwr-Jones 2012). Very broadly the devolution of financial and political power to the regions has been at its height during periods of left of centre national government. Conversely the tendency to retain power at the centre tends to be stronger during periods of right-of-centre national governments.

Both of these trends, however, should be placed in the context of a highly centralised structure of government in the UK, whereby the political and economic power rests primarily within the national government. In this context, changes in local governance may take the form of decentralisation or recentralisation, namely fluctuations in the distribution of political power between central government and regional governance. Furthermore, the ideological differences that revolve around the desired size of the state influence this relationship. The abolition of the regional tier of government by the current government in 2010 is seen as an example of this move towards the reduction of the state. Meanwhile, the role of the market has been the other side of the coin from this vision, hoping that a reduction in the size of the state would bring about an expansion in the role of the market. Decentralisation, which has been manifested in regional devolution and the policy of localism, introduced by the Coalition government in 2011, has been in line with this shifting balance between the state and the market (Davoudi and Madanipour 2015).

In the UK there is currently a shift back towards greater regional devolution. This is partly due to the relative success, both politically in the case of Scotland and economically in the case of Greater London, of those areas which currently enjoy a degree of political and financial autonomy. The phenomenal move towards devolution in Scotland, and its success in securing new powers away from the centre, has encouraged the English regions to demand higher levels of autonomy. At the same time, the noticeable popularity and visibility of the directly-elected mayor in Greater London and his capacity for coordinating strategic policy making for the capital region have been seen as the way forward for the other English regions.

The second driver for greater regional governance in the UK revolves around economic growth and ideas of smart specialisation (Rodríguez-Pose *et al.* 2009). Smart specialisation accords with the Europe 2020 strategy and an understanding that regions need to concentrate on their relative strengths to compete in a globalised economy (European Commission 2010). Smart specialisation is a response to processes of Europeanisation and globalisation, which result in local authorities competing with each other in the global marketplace to attract inward investment. This shift to greater devolution is enhanced by a perceived need to rebalance the national economy away from London and the South East. A number of reports have highlighted the productivity and wealth gap between the UK's secondary cities and London when compared to other developed countries (Heseltine 2012, RSA 2014). One of the ways for the secondary cities to regain some of their competitive advantage, it is argued, is to have greater control over long-term strategic planning and investment. This requires a degree of political and financial autonomy. While the pressure for globalisation and the pressure for decentralisation and localism have gone hand in hand for some time, what brought them into sharper focus was the global economic crash of 2007/2008, which has challenged the existing political and economic arrangements, forcing a search for new alternatives.

Greater Manchester is seen as one of the leading regions in relation to a new drive to devolve greater powers to the regions. This is in part due to its history of regional partnership and strategic thinking developed over the past 40 years. In 2011 it became the first secondary city region to have a statutory metropolitan governance institution: a Combined Authority. The formation of the Combined Authority followed a significant period of informal governance in the region. This case study aims to outline how Greater Manchester has been able to retain a significant element of territorial governance capacity in the face of almost constant change and challenge from the centre.

Background to the case study area

Greater Manchester is situated in the north west of England. It is part of a chain of northern cities which stretches from Liverpool in the west though Greater Manchester and Leeds ending with Hull at the eastern most end of the chain. Manchester makes claims to be the first modern city having

Maintaining regional territorial governance institutions 143

been at the forefront of the industrial revolution. Conversely this also means Greater Manchester was one of the cities to suffer badly as the economy moved into a post-industrial phase. Notwithstanding its recent difficulties Greater Manchester still makes a significant contribution to the wealth and prosperity of the UK being the second city, after London, in terms of Gross value added (AGMA 2010).

The modern history of regional governance in Greater Manchester starts with the formation of the Greater Manchester County Council in 1974. The county council was responsible for strategic planning in the region as well as other public services which were deemed to be best run at this level, e.g. transport, waste management and the fire and rescue service.

During the 1980s the Labour-dominated regional county councils were seen by the right-of-centre central government to present a serious and organised opposition to their power. In 1986 the Conservative Government of Margaret Thatcher, perceiving provincial local government as a hot bed of opposition to her neo-liberal project, abolished metropolitan county councils and replaced them with a series of unitary authorities. Within Greater Manchester these continue to the present day and are shown in Figure 11.1. A key criticism against the abolition of regional government was that it removed the local ability to make strategic decisions and set neighbouring authorities against each other in competition for resources.

Following the change of government in 1997 a new wave of regionalism was started. The 'New Labour' government of Tony Blair introduced a whole suite of new regional bodies, Regional Development Agencies and Regional Assemblies, and strengthened the Government Offices for the Regions created by the preceding (Conservative) Major government throughout England and Wales. All three new regional institutions were constituted with the same geographical boundary which corresponded to the EU NUTS 1 level. Around this time, in addition to the English Regional Development Agencies, Scotland, Wales and Northern Ireland were granted their own devolved powers. In Scotland this was via the regional parliament with Wales and Northern Ireland being granted a regional assembly. This period is seen as the high point for modern regionalism in the UK (Tewdwr-Jones 2012).

The Regional Development Agencies had responsibility for spatial planning and economic development and were tasked to work with the regional unitary authorities whose influence was channelled through the Regional Assemblies. The introduction of the Greater London Authority and a directly-elected mayor for London had seemed a positive development that needed to be extended to the English regions. On top of this, the Government Offices for the Regions were designed to bring central government closer to the regions. The turning point for the shift to ever greater regional devolution came in 2004 when the North East of England was offered the option of having an elected regional assembly. This move to a more democratic regional governance institution was in response to growing criticism of the regional governance structure as being undemocratic and unaccountable to its population. The proposal

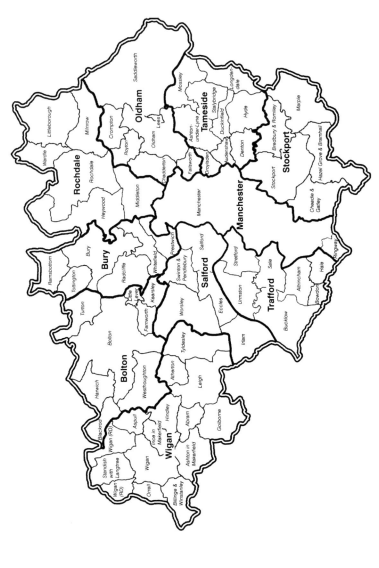

Figure 11.1 The territorial scope of the Greater Manchester Combined Authority

Source: Own elaboration

Maintaining regional territorial governance institutions   145

was resoundingly defeated in a referendum (79 per cent voted against) and therefore the idea of a democratically elected regional tier of government was dropped as government policy. Those who voted against the policy in the North East saw it as adding an expensive but ineffective new layer of bureaucracy which lacked the necessary devolved powers.

The various regional governance institutions that remained were one of the first casualties after the current Coalition government came to power in 2010. Spatial planning was passed back to the local authorities with the introduction of a streamlined national planning policy aimed at freeing up the market to deliver greater economic growth. The Localism Act of 2011 introduced the power of planning at the neighbourhood level (see Chapter 6). This left something of a vacuum in regional governance. The exceptions to this loss of regional governance capacity were the devolved governments in Scotland, Wales and Northern Ireland and Greater London which retained its directly-elected mayor and regional assembly. To fill the strategic regional gap, Local Enterprise Partnerships were introduced as local networks of collaboration between the municipalities and the businesses.

What is perhaps unique about Greater Manchester is that throughout this period of change it retained a degree of continuity in terms of territorial governance capacity. The primary way this was achieved was through the Association of Greater Manchester Authorities, which was formed in 1986 following the abolition of the Greater Manchester County Council. It was felt by the various authorities that there needed to be a continuing coordination of policy and strategic planning at the regional scale. The Association of Greater Manchester Authorities was formed as a joint committee of the ten unitary authorities and took on responsibility for some of the functions of the old county council which were not passed to the unitary authorities such as transport and waste management. It also retained a commitment to coordinating other policy such as economic development, health and housing, primary responsibility which was passed to the individual local authorities.

This continued regional territorial governance capacity was retained throughout the period of the Regional Development Agencies and up to the current Coalition government's changes to regional governance. As it became apparent that there was a need for some form of regional governance, Greater Manchester was able to mobilise and be at the forefront of these changes. Greater Manchester was able to take advantage of initiatives such as City Deals and Local Enterprise Partnerships. These policy programmes had a narrow economic development focus and were seen as a response to the post-2008 crash economic difficulty faced by the country (e.g. Ward and Hardy 2013). The need for a broader based approach to territorial governance was acknowledged with the creation of Combined Authorities. These were in essence a statutory version of the structure put in place in Greater Manchester through the Association of Greater Manchester Authorities. Not surprisingly therefore Greater Manchester became the first Combined Authority on 1 April 2011.

Coordinating actions of actors and institutions: doing the same things differently

Within the story of Greater Manchester the coordination of actors and institutions has been closely linked with the aim of integrating policy sectors. The formation of the Association of Greater Manchester Authorities was in part born out of a need to continue managing certain public services at the regional level. To begin with, strategic planning at a regional level for policy sectors such as health, economic development and housing were delegated to the Association of Greater Manchester Authorities. This association and the subsequent Greater Manchester Combined Authority share similar governance structures, in which the leaders of the component unitary authorities make up the membership of the Combined Authority. In addition to their governance roles the individual local authorities also had a significant role in developing policy. Each of the constituent authorities also led on a particular policy area with a member from that authority taking the lead.

In addition to the formal governance structure, a whole series of other institutions have been formed as a way of coordinating as wide a range of stakeholders as possible. Figure 11.2 shows the various institutions formed as part of the territorial governance structure in Greater Manchester. This family of governance institutions has a variety of structures; some are partnerships while others are sub-committees of the main board of the Association of Greater Manchester Authorities. A number of the institutions, for example the Manchester Investment Delivery Agency Service and Marketing Manchester, are limited companies wholly owned by the Association of Greater Manchester Authorities but operating independently. This is a flexible way of finding a suitable governance institution for a particular policy issue.

At the core of the structure are the Greater Manchester Combined Authority and the Association of Greater Manchester Authorities. The association has continued to have relevance to lead on certain policy sectors which the Combined Authority does not have statutory authority to cover, e.g. health and culture. This flexible structure also allowed non-governmental organisations to play a role in the development and coordination of policy. One of the earliest examples of this was the Business Leaders Council. This council was comprised of representatives from the major businesses in the region. The role of the Business Leaders Council is to act as a critical friend to the Association of Greater Manchester Authorities and the Greater Manchester Combined Authority and provide a business perspective on strategic policy issues. Having this close working relationship with business stakeholders proved to be beneficial when seeking to take advantage of national government policy initiatives. A good example of this was the City Deal programme, which was introduced by the Coalition government as agreements between the central government

Maintaining regional territorial governance institutions   147

and local authorities in major city-regions, giving them more powers in exchange for accepting more responsibility for local economic growth. The stakeholders interviewed pointed out Greater Manchester was one of the first city-regions to sign such a deal and they felt the relationship and trust developed between the public and private sector stakeholders was vital to their success. As a private sector member of the Local Enterprise Partnership put it: 'We recognise how beneficial it is to have such a strong, cohesive and mature leadership in the public sector' (personal communication 2012).

What is perhaps lacking within the territorial governance structure is representation from civic society; for example charities and community groups. When asked about this the key stakeholders made it clear this was the responsibility for the individual authorities rather than the Greater Manchester Combined Authority. This does raise the question as to why only certain issues are deemed best tackled at the regional level. One could argue this is down to the dominant discourse of functional economic areas which is driving the current regional devolution debate (Cooke and Clifton 2005). As the name suggests, economic issues are at the core of this debate, as a result of which they may be crowding out legitimate calls for the response to societal issues to be coordinated at the regional scale.

Recently questions have been raised which link greater regional devolution and democratic legitimacy. In November 2014 the so called 'Devo Manc' proposal was outlined by the Chancellor, George Osborne. The proposals devolve long-term budgets for housing, transport, welfare and economic development to the Combined Authority as well as granting it greater planning powers (Manchester City Council 2014). In the case of Greater Manchester more devolution has been accompanied by the requirement to have an elected mayor as the democratically accountable leader of the Combined Authority. Interestingly this was the last thing current regional leaders wanted when the issue was raised during the case study.

Integrating policy sectors

As has been outlined above, one of the main motivations for retaining governance capacity at the regional level in Greater Manchester is to integrate policy sectors. There has been much debate in the regional development literature about the optimal level for territorial governance with functional economic areas being the method chosen in relation to Greater Manchester. Functional economic areas are based on daily commuting patterns and economic activity (Davoudi 2009). The stakeholders interviewed for the case study agreed that for Greater Manchester this is an appropriate model to use to define the boundaries of the territory. They also confirmed this coincides with a more culturally based definition of the region, that is, people who would probably define themselves as 'Mancunian' or else have a strong regional affinity.

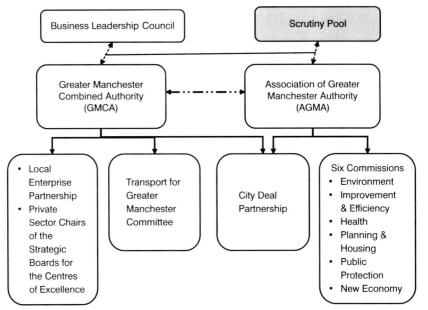

Figure 11.2 The 'institutional embeddedness' of the Greater Manchester Combined Authority

Source: Own elaboration

As can be seen from Figure 11.2, the integration of policy sectors was undertaken by a variety of mechanisms:

- a portfolio structure which designated a lead member from each constituent authority to a particular policy portfolio;
- a series of commissions established to review a particular issue facing Greater Manchester; and
- finally sub-committees of the Combined Authority dealing with the delivery of particular services.

This adaptability was essential to allow as many stakeholders as possible to participate in the governance structure whilst at the same time complying with the various statutory requirements set down by the national government. The organisational structure includes formally constituted committees and informal partnership bodies. This permits a range of institutional stakeholders to collaborate and work together. For example in the area of health and wellbeing, organisations such as the National Health Service, educational establishments and the local authorities develop policy to tackle issues such as obesity which requires both preventative and reactive policy prescriptions.

Figure 11.2 also shows how the governance structure within Greater Manchester has been coordinated around two key themes; reform and growth. By organising the governance around two broad themes it has been

Maintaining regional territorial governance institutions 149

possible for the Combined Authority to bring together different stakeholders with interest in different policy sectors with a view to tackling broad based local socio-economic problems.

To do this, a structured approach was taken to developing policy and to seeking the resources to carry through the policy to completion. The first stage was to establish a series of commissions to review policy for a particular problem. There were initially seven commissions formed by the Association of Greater Manchester Authorities to review: health and wellbeing; environment; planning and housing; transport; economy; public protection and improvement and efficiency. In reality the transport commission was subsumed by the Transport for Greater Manchester committee and did not actually come into effect. Each of the commissions had a remit to understand the situation as it was and advise on what steps would be needed in the future.

Once the Combined Authority came into being and as a number of the commissions had reached a conclusion in relation to their original remit, some of the institutions changed to take on more of a role in the delivery of policy. This was particularly the case in relation to economic growth following the publication of the economic commission's Manchester Independent Economic Review (2009). The review identified a number of economic priorities for the region. New institutions such as 'New Economy' and the 'Manchester Investment Delivery Agency Service' were formed to produce programmes and secure investment to produce the growth needed. These bodies are independent companies but owned by and answerable to the Combined Authority and the Local Enterprise Partnership. This evidence-based systematic approach to policy development has allowed the region to be a frontrunner in a number of national policy initiatives, such as City Deals and Local Enterprise Partnerships. The approach taken by Greater Manchester has allowed it to hold a strong position in terms of evidence and track-record when it comes to delivering new policy programmes.

In Greater Manchester therefore almost an ecosystem of institutions and organisations has been developed to deliver different aspects of territorial governance. This is a reflection of the fact that no body or institution can be effective in bringing together various policy sectors to address specific issues. A combination of statutory authorities, partnerships and independent bodies all play a role in both ensuring strong policy integration and wide stakeholder engagement as will be discussed in the next section. There are a number of possible reasons for the success Greater Manchester has had in retaining a regional governance capacity. It can partly be explained by the continuity offered by key political leaders in the various local authorities and the dominance of left of centre parties. However the same could be said for other regions such as the North East which have failed to retain a similar regional capacity. It may also be serendipity that the Combined Authority was abolished at a time when the need for economic redevelopment of the region was most pressing in the face of increased globalisation of trade (Barlow 1995). It was recognised that the challenge posed by globalisation

150 *Cowie, Madanipour, Davoudi and Vigar*

needed to be tackled at the regional level and the Association of Greater Manchester Authorities was able to fulfil that strategic governance role.

Mobilising stakeholder participation

As outlined in the previous section, one thing that the Association of Greater Manchester Authorities and the Combined Authority have been successful in has been the ability to mobilise stakeholders within the territorial governance structure. The structure has a balance between democratically elected officials and representatives of various policy sectors. The stakeholders interviewed as part of the case study felt this approach was sufficiently accountable and open whilst at the same time avoided some of the party political pitfalls that sometimes affect governance institutions which are wholly democratic. This raises fundamental questions as to the role of democracy within territorial governance institutions. The general feeling amongst the stakeholders interviewed for the case study was that the technical and strategic decisions which needed to be made for the region were too abstract and difficult for the general public to engage with.

There is a risk for territorial governance institutions in taking this somewhat relaxed approach to democratic legitimacy. The perceived lack of democratic legitimacy was one of the major reasons for the demise of Regional Development Agencies. In the case of both, the Association of Greater Manchester Authorities and the Combined Authority, democratic legitimacy is attained by virtue of the presence of elected politicians drawn from the constituent authority. This is a form of a delegated democratic legitimacy. During the case study it was acknowledged by stakeholders that this method of demonstrating democratic legitimacy was not ideal. However it was felt that the cooperative nature of both organisations and the strategic focus of decision-making would make it difficult to achieve democratic consensus across the whole region. It was also felt by stakeholders that the present partnership approach to governance allowed the decision-making process to rise above party politics. The Greater Manchester regional territorial governance institutions (i.e. the Association of Greater Manchester Authorities and the Combined Authority) are very much within the definition of a neo-liberal managerial governance system as outlined by Peck and Tickell (2002). The stakeholders also relied on a form of substantive legitimacy (Cowie and Davoudi 2015) in that as both institutions were perceived to be successful in their outcomes, the process by which those outcomes had been achieved would not be questioned.

On the one hand, as was outlined previously in the case of the North East of England (cf. Chapter 6), the public are generally sceptical of additional levels of bureaucracy. On the other hand national governments seem to be reluctant to devolve more powers to the regional level without some form of democratic accountability. Further research is needed to examine how this balance is managed in practice.

Maintaining regional territorial governance institutions   151

There was also evidence from the stakeholders interviewed for the case study that this long- term, balanced approach to stakeholder engagement also avoided fights over significant investment decisions. This was perceived to be one of the benefits of not having a direct democratic element to the governance structure. Decision-making was seen to be above party politics and even able to balance spatial differences in the allocation of investments.

It was clear from speaking to individual stakeholders that some of the infrastructure investments made had benefited particular areas within Greater Manchester. This could have resulted in 'turf wars' over which areas were being missed out. This was avoided by an understanding that the economic benefit to Greater Manchester as a whole outweighed the lost opportunities for individual areas. This is particularly the case for the larger inward investment programmes such as the City Deal. One of the reasons Greater Manchester was able to be one of the first areas to benefit from the new City Deal programme was its history of collaborative working.

In addition to directly involving stakeholders in the decision-making process, territorial governance requires levels of transparency and accountability. On these measures the two Greater Manchester regional territorial governance institutions present a somewhat more balanced picture. Whilst all the decisions are made by publicly accountable bodies and the notices of meetings are published, in reality there is very little public scrutiny of the institutions. It should be noted that there is a formal overview and scrutiny infrastructure. The Scrutiny Pool is a committee of elected representatives from the ten local authorities. The terms of reference for this committee include oversight of budgets and key decisions made by the main territorial governance institutions and the various associated committees and independent bodies.

As with the meetings of the main institutions, the meetings of the Scrutiny Pool are open to the public. One of the arguments put forward by the stakeholders is that this system of partnership and collaboration avoids the tendency to have decisions made on a party political basis. All the stakeholders interviewed for the case study stated that in their experience the current governance structure did operate on a non-party political basis and this could be put at risk if a more directly democratic process was put into effect.

Another aspect of scrutiny and accountability is the role other civic institutions have in relation to territorial governance. The media, in particular local newspapers, are one civic institution that plays a significant role in relation to providing the general public with information about the conduct and results of territorial governance institutions. This is not a role they currently fulfil as the lead reporter on the local paper admitted they tended to accept at face value the information provided by the press office of the Association of Greater Manchester Authorities and the Combined Authority. He conceded that as these institutions gained greater powers and financial autonomy it may be the case that greater scrutiny would be needed (personal communication 2012).

Being adaptive to changing contexts

The governance structure established within Greater Manchester has had significant benefits in terms of adaptability. During the low points of regionalism in the UK it was often difficult for stakeholders at a city region level to achieve any strategic projects. It was also the case, to a lesser extent, during the period in which Regional Development Agencies were the dominant territorial governance institution. The critical decisions were often taken at a higher level and in particular control over spending and finance was tightly controlled.

The partnership working within Greater Manchester allowed the region to take a more strategic approach to these types of negotiations. This was done by having a sound evidence base on which to develop their proposals as well a unified voice across the region when entering into discussions with central government. Over time this developed into an institutional understanding between the region and central government. It also highlighted the capacity within the region to deliver these large-scale collaborative projects. Perhaps the most significant example of this is the Manchester tram system. This project, which did not directly benefit all ten local authorities, was supported by the Association of Greater Manchester Authorities. As one interviewee from a local authority pointed out: "Whilst this area did not directly benefit, we know in the future there are going to be projects which benefit us and we are happy to let things balance out" (personal communication 2013).

This shows a degree of trust and reciprocity within the territorial governance structure, something which proponents of social capital such as Robert Putnam (Putnam *et al*. 1993, Putnam 2000) argue is necessary to ensure strong territorial governance institutions. This institutional capacity is perhaps born out of the political stability within the region. Whilst many of the local authorities are controlled by the Labour Party there are a number of local authorities controlled by other parties. What many of the authorities do have however is stability and continuity of leadership. This is particularly the case with Manchester itself whose Leader, Sir Richard Leese and its Chief Executive, Sir Howard Berstein, have been with the council since the late 1990s.

This institutional capacity has also been of great benefit when negotiating with national government. As the stakeholders pointed out in the case study, it is not just about having a powerful voice at a national and supra-national level; it is about knowing what works and when. The ability to build capacity over time can be seen in the way the region bid for a number of major sporting events. The initial ambitious aim was to secure the summer Olympics. Ultimately this bid failed but the knowledge and experience developed during the course of that process was utilised successfully in the bid for the 2002 Commonwealth Games.

This flexibility and capacity is also relevant when considering efforts that have been made to capitalise on the various strengths and opportunities available to Greater Manchester. An example of how a new opportunity has presented itself and been included into the strategic planning for the region is the example of grapheme. This novel material was discovered by researchers at the University of Manchester and has resulted in a concerted effort of a number of partner organisations to seek commercial applications for it (personal communication 2013).

Realising place-based/territorial specificities and impacts

The current boundary for the Combined Authority is largely a result of history. As outlined in the first section it corresponds to the ten unitary authorities that made up the old Greater Manchester County Council. However it has found relevance in modern economic geography, in particular in relation to the idea of functional economic areas (Coombes and Champion 2011). The retention of a coherent regional identity within Greater Manchester has been in the face of considerable external pressure to reform territorial governance, either down to the local authority level or up to the NUTS 1 determined Regional Development Agencies. The stakeholders interviewed in this case study all made the point that functional economic areas are the natural way to determine the extent of any territorial governance institution. In the Greater Manchester case this is perhaps because of a strong cultural identity within the region.

This cultural and socio-economic sense of place is then consolidated through the actions of the governance institutions. Major projects such as the tram network or events such as the Commonwealth Games help develop a shared sense of purpose. This is not without some tension in the Greater Manchester case. At the heart of the region is Manchester itself. Manchester is the main businesses and cultural centre of the region. This does risk Manchester dominating the other local authorities. However the stakeholders within the region were aware of this and took this into account when taking strategic decisions. Some also point to the example of Salford that is developing its own economic niche built around its new BBC media centre on Salford Quays. This was in part facilitated by an extension to the tram network to link the area with the rest of Greater Manchester.

Another aspect of developing a sense of place is the focus placed on knowledge and evidence within the Greater Manchester governance structure. One key example of this evidence-based approach is the Manchester Independent Economic Review (Manchester Independent Economic Review 2009). This extensive piece of work sought to inform the debate about the future of the region and the particular challenges and opportunities it faced. It was seen to be a particularly useful tool to engage in debate with central government, particularly the treasurer, who now demand evidence-based policy arguments.

This commitment to informed and evidence-based policy making has continued through the use of the various policy commissions. This has been

154 *Cowie, Madanipour, Davoudi and Vigar*

particularly useful where policy initiatives span a number of sectors and often have spatially and temporally differentiated outcomes. The Health and Wellbeing Commission is a good example of how this works in practice. This commission is a partnership between local authorities, the National Health Service representatives and the higher education sector. It seeks to tackle issues around health and social care in the region. Often these issues are tackled in isolation and on a reactive rather than proactive basis. This joined-up approach can overcome some of the practical policy difficulties encountered when this large-scale strategic approach is taken. In most cases it is perhaps better to spend scarce public resources to prevent health issues arising in the first place. However this can present institutional difficulties if, for example, the National Health Service money is spent on healthy eating in schools or on improving community social care. The effect of the policy on long-term National Health Service spending may be difficult to prove. Having a clear place-based approach to tackling some of the social issues and a common pool of resources can help overcome these problems.

Conclusions

Regional territorial governance has been undergoing yet another period of change in the UK since the Coalition government came to power in 2010. One of its first tasks was to abolish existing regional governance institutions. As it became apparent that the financial crisis would have a lasting impact on growth it was recognised that some form of regional institutional capacity was needed to deliver the government's growth agenda. This resulted in a number of new initiatives targeted at city-regions. The case of Greater Manchester is considered to be a success in engaging with these various, *ad hoc*, programmes, making it important to examine why Greater Manchester was able to adapt to the new institutional landscape whilst at the same time retaining a core stability and capacity in terms of territorial governance. The history of the metropolitan region's governance dates back to the 1970s when the Manchester County Council was formed. Since that time governance at the city region level has gone through a period of being on an informal partnership basis and has now returned to a statutory governance structure. Despite, or even because, of these changes Greater Manchester has developed a series of governance institutions and institutional practices that have allowed it to tackle cross-sectoral issues, engage with policy networks at various scales and maintain a strong sense of territoriality that can offer a number of lessons to other city-regions.

The success of Greater Manchester in the creation of a strategic level of regional governance could be explained through a number of theoretical perspectives. It shows the extent of path-dependency in how different regions respond differently to new circumstances. The long history of coordination among the different authorities, the political and economic primacy of the city of Manchester, and its strong historical identity, have all played a major role

Maintaining regional territorial governance institutions 155

in paving the way for the emergence of a new form of regional partnership. Greater Manchester has enjoyed a degree of institutional continuity, which has enabled it to act quickly when the circumstances have changed. In the regions where social capital and identity have not been as strongly shared, the result has been very different. In Greater Manchester, a fairly clear sense of place, the ability to bring together different stakeholders and integrate policy areas was made possible through this institutional continuity. At the same time, it shows that the prevalence of a technocratic arrangement and an economic growth direction may be accompanied by relatively weak mechanisms for democratic participation and accountability.

References

AGMA – Association of Greater Manchester Authorities, 2010. *Greater Manchester Local Enterprise Partnership: A Proposal to the Government.* Manchester: Association of Greater Manchester Authorities.

Barlow, M., 1995. Greater Manchester: conurbation complexity and local governance structure. *Political Geography,* 14 (4), 379–400.

Cooke, P. and Clifton, N., 2005. Visionary, precautionary and constrained 'varieties of devolution' in the economic governance of the devolved UK territories. *Regional Studies,* 39 (4), 437–451.

Coombes, M. and Champion, T., 2011. Migration and commuting: local and regional development links. In: A. Pike, A. Rodríguez-Pose and J. Tomaney, eds. *A Handbook of Local and Regional Development.* London: Routledge, 182–192.

Cowie, P. and Davoudi, S., 2015. Is small really beautiful? The legitimacy of neighbourhood planning. In: S. Davoudi and A. Madanipour, eds. *Reconsidering Localism.* London: Routledge, 168–191.

Davoudi, S. and Madanipour, A., eds., 2015. *Reconsidering Localism.* London: Routledge.

European Commission, 2010. *Europe 2020: A Strategy for Smart, Sustainable and Inclusive Growth.* COM(2010) 2020 final.

Heseltine M., 2012. *No Stone Unturned in Pursuit of Growth.* London: Department for Business Innovation and Skills.

Manchester City Council, 2014. *Devo Manc: Greater Manchester and Government Teach Trailblazing Agreement.* Available from: http://www.manchester.gov.uk/news/article/7015/devo_manc_greater_manchester_and_govt_reach_trailblazing_agreement [Accessed 20 December 2014].

Manchester Independent Economic Review – MIER, 2009. *Independent Review ,* Available from: http://www.manchester-review.org.uk/projects/view/?id=720 [Accessed 19 June 2012].

Peck, J. and Tickell, A., 2002. Neoliberalising space. *Antipode,* 34 (3), 380–404.

Putnam, R., 2000 *Bowling Alone: The Collapse and Revival of American Community.* New York: Simon & Schuster.

Putnam, R., Leonardi, R. and Nanetti, R., 1993. *Making Democracy Work: Civic Traditions in Modern Italy.* Princeton, NJ: Princeton University Press.

Rodriguez-Pose, A., Tijmstra, S. and Bwire, A., 2009. Fiscal decentralisation, efficiency and growth. *Environment & Planning A,* .41 (9), 2041–2062.

RSA – Royal Society for the Encouragement of Arts, Manufactures and Commerce 2014. *Unleashing Metro Growth: Final recommendations of the City Growth Commission.* Available from: http://www.citygrowthcommission.com/wp-content/uploads/2014/10/City-Growth-Commission-Final-Report.pdf [Accessed 12 December 2014].

Tewdwr-Jones, M., 2012. *Spatial Planning and Governance: Understanding UK Planning.* Basingstoke: Palgrave Macmillan.

Ward, M. and Hardy, S., 2013. *Where Next for Local Enterprise Partnerships?* London: The Smith Institute.

Wikimedia commons, 2015. File: Greater Manchester County – no key – greyscale.png Available from: http://commons.wikimedia.org/wiki/File:Greater_Manchester_County_-_no_key_-_greyscale.png [Accessed 12 May 2015].

12 Limited involvement

The role of local and regional actors in the Hungarian Structural Fund management

Cecília Mezei

Introduction

This chapter investigates the impacts of the European Cohesion Policy in Hungary. It analyses the planning, implementation and institution building processes related to the management of Structural Funds in Hungary in the 2007 to 2013 programme period. A specific focus is laid on the related activities and the local and regional stakeholders' roles therein. As a part of the National Strategic Reference Framework, Hungary elaborated eight 'Sectoral' and seven 'Regional' Operational Programmes, such as the one for the South Transdanubian Region, which will serve here as a concrete example, specifically with regard to the involvement of local partners.

South Transdanubia (see Figure 12.1) is one of the least developed NUTS 2 Hungarian regions, ranked number 219 out of the 262 European regions in the Regional Competitiveness Index 2013 (Annoni and Dijkstra 2013). The region's main problems are a high unemployment rate, the lack of enterprise creation and jobs, increasing poverty as well as a number of isolated 'cul-de-sac' settlements, due to the lack of functioning road infrastructure and public transport (OFTK 2014). It was no coincidence that the main strategic objective of the region's Operational Programme for 2007–2013 was to respond to these fundamental problems (cf. Government of Hungarian Republic 2007).

Structural Funds have a significant impact on public administration, especially in the Central and Eastern European countries where the absorption of EU subsidies was the highest motivation of national and local policies (Pálné Kovács 2011). In the absence of possessing sufficient resources for development, the proper utilisation of EU resources has been one of the most crucial political objectives in these countries. After the global financial crisis the proportion of EU subsidies in public investments had increased and the impact of Cohesion Policy became even more profound in Central and Eastern European countries (CEC 2014). Due to this, the preparation of the implementation of the Structural Funds resulted in fundamental administrative reforms in the new member states with the aim of managing and utilising the Structural Funds as efficiently as possible. In the course of shaping the institutional system, the EU regulations had to be respected. These, however, were changing over time together with the aims and tools of the European Union's Cohesion Policy. As a consequence, from the very beginning Central and Eastern European countries were 'shooting at moving targets' as regards both the national and regional objectives of Cohesion Policy and the national Structural Fund management structures established to effectively allocate the resources (Mezei 2015).

While in general the European Union considers the structure and functioning of public administration as a national internal affair, it has established a fairly strong adaptation pressure by regulating the rules of the utilisation of the Structural Funds (Pálné Kovács 2011). This pressure on administrative reforms – beginning with the EU-accession process – was simultaneous with the building of Structural Fund management in all of the Central and Eastern European countries. However, the emerging governance regimes dealing with the management of Structural Funds had to face a

Figure 12.1 The territorial scope of the South Transdanubia Region in Hungary

Legend: 1) country boundary, 2) boundary of NUTS 2 regions, 3) boundary of NUTS 3 self-governing regions

Source: Own elaboration

considerable challenge, since traditional government structures and practices in the Central and Eastern European countries do not harmonise with the principles of decentralisation, partnership, efficiency, transparency and strategic integrative planning (Pálné Kovács 2013). Thus, the Central and Eastern European countries have chosen different trajectories for shaping their Structural Fund institutional system (Bachtler and McMaster 2007). The EU regulations relating to Structural Fund management contained several elements which could easily be 'fulfilled' ostensibly. Some countries chose this way, while others launched more fundamental changes. The former ones were the so-called 'imitating countries', and Hungary was one of them, since Hungary was proficient at building 'unfamiliar' institutions and in introducing rather cosmetic governance reforms (Pálné Kovács 2013).

For the Central and Eastern European countries, 'partnership' was regarded as one of the key principles in this regard. However, they have encountered serious difficulties during its implementation due to the legacy of centralism, the lack of traditions of working in partnership, and the weakly institutionalised subnational authorities (Dąbrowski 2011). The system of multi-level governance, the degree of decentralisation and participation in decision-making and power, however, varies among the Central and Eastern European countries (Bruszt 2008). In the following section, our case study of South Transdanubia will focus on the five dimensions of territorial governance in order to analyse the planning and implementation of the South Transdanubia Operational Programme for the 2007–2013 programming period.

Coordinating actions of actors and institutions

At the regional level of the Hungarian public administration system there are no self-governments with elected representatives. Self-governments operate solely in settlements and counties. South Transdanubia consists of three of such counties (Baranya, Somogy and Tolna) and a total of 656 settlements. In addition each Hungarian NUTS 2 region previously had a Regional Development Council and a Regional Development Agency. The latter has been founded and supervised by Regional Development Councils and operated as the councils' executive bodies. The Regional Councils operated from 1996 to 2011 and consisted of the representatives of dominant self-governments and micro-regional councils and the delegates of certain ministries, whereas the civil partners had only consultation status. However, the councils had a limited role regarding financial aspects because of the limited decentralised regional development resources. At the end of 2011, the Hungarian Government abolished the Regional Councils and assigned the responsibility for regional development to the county governments.

Be this as it may, during the programming period 2007–2013, these regional development actors played only a secondary role in the planning and implementation processes related to the management of the Structural Funds (Pálné Kovács and Varjú 2009). The main reason is that the steering

160 Cecília Mezei

competencies of the National Strategic Reference Framework and the Operational Programmes have been concentrated in one single mega-organisation, namely the so-called National Development Agency. This national institution – which was organisationally independent from the ministries and the public administration – had been established for the preparation and implementation of the National Strategic Reference Framework for the 2007–2013 programming period. The agency conducted the bi- or multi-lateral consultations and the numerous Working Group discussions during the planning phase of the Regional Operational Programmes. The Regional Development Agencies and other regional actors were usually invited to these forums. While independent Regional Operational Programmes were elaborated for all of the NUTS 2 regions, the role of the managing authority was not fulfilled by a 'regional' organisation since this task had been integrated into a central organisation, the so-called Regional Operational Programmes Managing Authority of the National Development Agency.

During the planning phase for the 2007–2013 programming period, certain programmes were passed on from the drafts of sectoral programmes to regional programmes, so the decisions were always taken by the sectoral ministries (personal communications 2012 and 2013). As a consequence, the Regional Operational Programmes contained the residual parts of the National Strategic Reference Framework. The seven Regional Operational Programmes were not representative of the specific regional characteristics, as only the powerful regional political actors (city mayors or Members of Parliament) could fight for regional interests against the much stronger sectoral ministries (personal communication 2012). The lack of a ministry responsible for regional development in the Hungarian governmental system further weakened the possibility to incorporate a territorial approach into Structural Fund management. The only 'quasi' regional stakeholders involved in the implementation of the Regional Operational Programmes were the Regional Development Agencies. However, as its intermediate bodies they were dependent on the centralised National Development Agency and thus were rather limited in representing regional interests (Pálné Kovács and Varjú 2009).

With regard to the planning process of the South Transdanubia Operational Programme, Pálné Kovács and Varjú (2009) further argue that a number of policy makers working for the National and Regional Development Agencies were able to acquire a dominant role because they were familiar with the procedural, organisational and institutional requirements, the specific terminology in relation to EU Cohesion Policy, the logic of stakeholder consultation mechanisms and the competencies of the different administrative and political tiers. This specific knowledge was at least at that time the privilege of a narrow group of experts in Hungary. A paradox is that the employees of the National Development Agency were new and young technocrats with otherwise relatively poor knowledge of public administration (ibid.).

A rather peculiar situation occurred when the Regional Development Agencies were given the role as 'intermediate bodies' within the Structural

Fund management, while the Regional Development Councils, which had contractual relationships (regarding ownership, budget etc.) with the Regional Development Agencies, were excluded from this process (personal communication 2012). The Regional Development Councils' only role was restricted to their membership in the Monitoring Committee. In addition to Regional Development Agencies, one further organisation called VÁTI Hungarian Nonprofit Ltd. for Regional Development and Town Planning – with regional departments – was also involved as an intermediate body in the Regional Operational Programmes. It was felt that the involvement of VÁTI was not justifiable since the Regional Development Agencies alone would have been capable of handling this task (personal communication 2012). However the Regional Development Agencies' planning competencies concerning their own regions and their functioning in the preparation of calls for projects caused difficulties, because these activities affected VÁTI's scope of action. As a response to this, from 2008 onwards, an intensified centralisation of Structural Fund management resolved this problem (personal communications 2012 and 2013).

During the phase of preparation for the 2007–2013 Cohesion Policy period in Hungary, the Regional Operational Programme's Managing Authority of National Development Agency handed in concrete templates concerning the structure and the potential development directions of the Regional Operational Programmes to the Regional Development Agencies. It turned out that these templates were a powerful means to guide the implementation of the funds rather than facilitating 'bottom-up' ideas or needs articulated by local and regional actors in the South Transdanubian Region for instance. In addition, from 2008 onwards until their abolition in 2011, the Regional Development Agencies and Councils had been totally excluded from the tendering processes of the Regional Operational Programmes (personal communication 2012).

The Regional Operational Programme's Managing Authority had its own internal procedures, which regulated all of the intermediate bodies' contracts, relations and communications. Until 2010, this national authority for regional affairs and the Regional Development Agency of South Transdanubia had been in a close contact. But later on, even this attempt at vertical coordination became centralised, since all local and regional demands had to be channelled through the National Development Agency. This agency enforced its own ideas through standardised positions, regulations, control and supervision of the selected intermediate bodies. Particularly after the parliamentary elections in 2010 a radical institutional transformation occurred within the complex Structural Fund management system, which involved the appointment of new intermediate bodies and organisational leaders.

However, in the background there was a continuous tendency towards centralisation. There was an attempt to incorporate the statements of the ex-ante evaluation into the National Strategic Reference Framework. During the programming period, a mid-term evaluation was also prepared (KPMG 2011) without any direct impacts on the further planning processes. Before the publication of the mid-term evaluation report, the new government in place initiated financial reallocations between the Sectoral Operational Programmes (in favour of economic development, enterprise development and job creation priorities), which were subsequently approved by the European Union.

Further changes have occurred since 2012 as a consequence of the abolition of the Regional Development Councils. The county governments remained the only actors concerned with local and regional development, even though they lacked sufficient strategy-making competence (Pálné Kovács 2014). The hitherto centralised control of the Regional Development Agencies had limited their functions related to the generation of projects or assisting and improving the position of local applicants and this has had a highly negative impact on the quality of the project proposals. In addition, there was no other regional stakeholder who would have been able to fulfil the Regional Development Agencies' functions in terms of project generation and regional knowledge.

Integrating policy sectors

During the planning phase of the National Strategic Reference Framework, the sectoral ministries' priorities dominated the debate. However, sectoral interests were often overruled by political interests, for example during the formation of the overall Structural Fund management system and the involvement or omission of other actors or partners. These decisions were influenced neither by sectoral nor by regional interests.

The Government Commission for Development Policy was established in order to strengthen the governmental coordination of developmental policy during the planning phase of the National Strategic Reference Framework. It only operated until 2008. Its task was to coordinate the various national (sectoral, regional and other horizontal) strategies. In addition in 2006, a government advisory body responsible for regional development was formed in order to represent local interests more efficiently. However, it was rather the National Development Council that made efforts to include experts, governmental actors and Regional Development Agencies.

Nonetheless, since there was no ministry responsible for the coordination of sectoral and regional interest, conflicts emerged mainly during the harmonisation of operational programmes coordinated by the National Development Agency. On the other hand, regional interests were under-represented in general in the development of the operational programmes. Furthermore, it was felt that the operational programmes were filled with broad objectives in which everything and anything could be included later on (personal communication 2012). Due to the dominance of sectoral interests, bottom-up regional concepts were hardly included in the Regional Operational Programmes. Further evidence of the modest integration of local and regional interests and territorial specificities is the fact that the strongly filtered Regional Operational Programmes of the seven NUTS 2 regions were hardly distinguishable from each other.

The central governmental decision-makers also influenced the tendering phase for project proposals. Calls could be announced only on the approval of the relevant ministry. Initially, Regional Development Agencies as intermediate bodies were involved in calls for proposals and action plans but their functions had been gradually reduced since 2008 and terminated in 2011 (personal communication 2012). From the point of view of the National Development Agency, the reasons for the centralisation were the homogeneous regional visions and the almost identical operational programmes and priorities and the questionable success of the launched initiatives of the Regional Development Agencies (personal communications 2012 and 2013). There were also problems identified regarding the centralised project selection procedures, which resulted in low project quality and lengthy bureaucratic procedures (Bachtler *et al.* 2014).

The planning phase of the South Transdanubia Operational Programme was launched at the end of 2004 and also took place in a rather centralised scheme. The elaboration of this regional programme strictly followed the continuously changing requirements of the European Union and the central governmental expectations (Pálné Kovács and Varjú 2009). Following the decision on the main targets, the planning team determined the so-called strategic development programmes which were elaborated for each major sector with the exception of rural development. Then the National Development Agency defined priority frames for the South Transdanubia Operational Programme (and the other Regional Operational Programmes as well) in which the prepared strategy had to be placed.

Mobilising stakeholder participation

Similar to other Central and Eastern European countries, Hungary has neither traditions nor national rules for partnership-building and civil society self-organisation has been weak. Consequently, when central authorities within the Structural Fund institutional system were looking for partners whose involvement would match the European Union's requirements they tended to select partners in an arbitrary manner. The result was that the more active and less 'disciplined' civil organisations were often excluded. The opportunity for partnership building resulted in a competitive situation where a number of civil organisations took the opportunity to consolidate their positions. Smaller civil organisations did not dispose of the sufficient capacities to enable them to participate as a partner in the public consultations. From the point of view of Structural Fund institutions, partnership building was seen as a compulsory extra task, as they primarily only wanted to only imitate its performance rather than adapt to the performance requirements (Perger 2009).

164   *Cecília Mezei*

Another facet to the 'making of partnerships' was the public consultation process within the planning phase of the Regional Operational Programmes. Professional groups and civil society organisations were in many cases only involved in an indirect way in these public consultations, which meant that they could take part in the consultations, but some of their proposals were ignored or were only partially incorporated into the planning process (KPMG 2011).

The tools for public information dissemination to stakeholders were websites, reconciliation and consultation boards, questionnaires, strategic background surveys and thematic and regional working groups (Molnárné Hegymegi 2009). Formal legitimacy was provided during the preparation and implementation of the National Strategic Reference Framework, which was guaranteed by the National Development Agency through the obligatory procedures of publicity provision, societal consultation, assessment and the inclusion of partners (e.g. Monitoring Committees).

The public consultation of the National Strategic Reference Framework was a two-month procedure involving almost 400 organisations. The National Development Agency sent letters or emails to the partner organisations registered during the former consultation process or those that were found in the ministerial databases. The participants however complained about the one-way communication: in the majority of the forums the intentions of the central government were introduced and the partners' comments were recorded on why the recommendations could not be accepted (Pálné Kovács and Varjú 2009). During the programming period the stakeholders were able to deliver their own opinions via on-line forums. However, the time devoted to requesting comments was short and the involved bureaucrats faced a number of regulations which prevented other stakeholders from engaging accordingly, so that only smaller modifications were made to the National Strategic Reference Framework based on these consultations (personal communication 2012).

The South Transdanubia Operational Programme preparation was led by a 'Regional Working Group' following the EU Community Strategic Guidelines on the principles and priorities of Cohesion Policy 2007–2013 (CEC 2006). The Working Group of this region had in total 47 members. It represented elected members from 25 micro-regions (i.e. settlements of the state-delimited micro-regions) and the representatives of big cities with special status as well as delegated members from the development councils of three counties (Somogy, Tolna, Baranya). But there were no civil partners involved at all (Pálné Kovács and Varjú 2009). This Working Group had seven sectoral sub-groups to which other experts were also invited. Although the Working Group was in principle open for further members, no one applied for membership. Members who entered through invitation were highly active (personal communication 2012).

Certain members, for example from the agricultural and higher educational sectors were absent from the sessions because during ministerial reconciliations entire sectors were removed from the 'Regional' South Transdanubia Operational Programme to a 'Sectoral' Programme (personal communication 2012). The regional stakeholders had varying opportunities to participate in the negotiations about the priorities of the programme. Here previous cooperation experiences with the Regional Development Agency and the Regional Development Council can be considered as an advantage, yet there were certain groups which were excluded from the negotiation, since the involvement of a number of stakeholders functioned only in an *ad hoc* manner (personal communication 2013). While the central actors of Structural Fund management mostly only 'imitated' the process of partnership building as specified by the EU, the Regional Operational Programmes, such as the South Transdanubia Operational Programme, were comparatively more successful since they were able to engage a wider circle of stakeholders.

Actors from the business sector within the region were almost completely absent from the planning process of the South Transdanubia Operational Programme (Pálné Kovács and Varjú 2009). Instead, various entrepreneurial organisations were responsible for representing their interests. Nonetheless, the South Transdanubia Operational Programme has been concentrated on community-type developments and was less focused on project opportunities for the private sector.

Being adaptive to changing contexts

Due to political elections a number of personal and institutional changes within the sectoral ministries occurred. This in addition to the unclear division of labour between ministries inhibited the development of bureaucratic routines throughout the management of the Structural Funds (KPMG 2011). After 2008, the changing intermediate bodies caused problems in communication with stakeholders and beneficiaries. The resulting erratic communication was also caused by the fluctuation of staff in the Structural Fund management organisations at almost each level and hindered the accumulation of organisational knowledge in general. The impacts of the governmental change also reached the National Development Agency. From 2010 onwards, serious personal and organisational changes were undertaken precisely when the preparation for the new programming period, the elaboration of mid-term evaluation reports and the rethinking of rules for using the funds in light of the financial crisis were on the agenda.

A continuous system of feedback served as the basis of the accumulation of knowledge within the National Development Agency during the management and coordination of the Sectoral and Regional Operational Programmes. External expert views were prepared, internal institutional investigations performed, opinions submitted by intermediate bodies and applicants, and each call was considered within a public debate (personal communications 2012 and 2013). As a result, a continuous modification of detailed procedural guidelines took place within the intermediate bodies and the managing authorities of the Regional and Sectoral Operational Programmes. This modification included communication practices, the methods of implementation, authorisation and control, the calls as such, and practically the entire operation of coordination.

While personal and institutional learning generally encountered obstacles due to the fluctuation of staff and the changing cooperating and implementing bodies, positive processes did also occur in this respect. For instance, experience showed that the institutional changes within the institutional system were often accompanied by bringing in experienced and knowledgeable personnel (personal communications 2012 and 2013).

In general, a wide circle of regional stakeholders acquired knowledge in the preparation and formulation of potential projects. For example many consulting companies were established which 'filtered' the tenders in advance in order to select the 'good' ones. The consultants involved during the planning phase of Regional Operational Programme also acquired a lot of knowledge of their region and established corresponding local networks (personal communication 2012).

In the South Transdanubia Region the Regional Development Agency had accumulated regional and programming knowledge from the regional actors on the basis of their previous planning and project experiences. The involvement of the Regional Development Agency into the planning and implementation of South Transdanubia Operational Programme thus strengthened the utilisation of regional knowledge. The lack of other involved regional stakeholders with sectoral knowledge or knowledge about territorial development had, unsurprisingly, a negative impact on the utilisation of potential regional knowledge.

The interviewees expressed different opinions about risk-taking possibilities and experimentation during the planning and implementation phase of the South Transdanubia Operational Programme. Some have argued that the entire Regional Operational Programme making was in fact an experiment as there had not been such a programme earlier in Hungary. Others mentioned that because of the economic crisis, the Hungarian regions experienced more opportunities for experimentation since 2009 as the whole government was engaged in seeking a way out of the crisis (personal communications 2012 and 2013).

There was no evidence of taking contingencies into account or consideration of a possible 'plan B'. All actors adapted to higher-level political decisions and frameworks, i.e. at the governmental level as well as at the EU level. That is why the actors involved rather tried to amend the given 'plan A' version for the management of the South Transdanubia Operational Programme within the feasible scope of possibilities. They made efforts to adjust to rules and the pre-defined processes in lieu of being proactive or being prepared for different scenarios (personal communications 2012 and 2013). This behaviour can eventually also be explained by the lack of time, since available time and resources of South Transdanubia Operational

Programme management were spent on just following procedures, becoming familiar with the current rules and being prepared for the next step of the process (personal communications 2012 and 2013).

Realising place-based/territorial specificities

The 2007–2013 programming period was the period when the Hungarian NUTS 2 regions had separate Regional Operational Programmes. During the programme period 2004–2006, immediately following the accession to the EU, only one integrated Regional Operational Programme was made for all of the regions. For the 2014–2020 programming period none of the Hungarian NUTS 2 regions (except for the capital city's NUTS 2 region), have individual regional operational development programmes. However, it should be noted that Hungarian regions lack administrative traditions, regional identity and corresponding regional actors and institutions to facilitate these programmes.

That said and turning back to the South Transdanubian Region one can assert that the administrative boundaries hindered the planning and implementation of this Regional Operational Programme in the 2007–2013 period in several respects. During the planning of the Regional Operational Programme, the three counties of the South Transdanubia Region strived to attain 'harmonisation' in respect of development resources (i.e. the same amount of money) and the development directions (i.e. similar investments). The regional interests could not be channelled into the programme, as there was no stakeholder who could have represented them. The Regional Development Council was comprised of county and local self-governmental politicians, which represented only the local interests. The Regional Development Agency was dependent on the Council, which meant that the possibilities of regional cooperation could not be exploited. Each stakeholder tended to think in terms of projects the realisation of which were located within administrative borders (county, settlement) (personal communications 2012 and 2013). That is why no complex and more territorial sensitive programmes were realised on the basis of the South Transdanubia Operational Programme.

Conclusions

This chapter investigated the practices of territorial governance related to the planning and implementation of the Structural Funds in Hungary in general and in the South Transdanubian Region more specifically in the 2007 to 2013 programme period. One main finding is that regional stakeholders were insufficiently involved in the processes and that, mainly as a consequence of this, regional knowledge could not be utilised in an optimal manner. Another key issue is that the strong tendency towards centralisation of different governance areas (public administration, development institutions, Structural Fund management institutions, etc.), has limited the potential

168 *Cecília Mezei*

and efficiency of a number of features of 'good' territorial governance in particular regarding the coordination of actions of actors and institutions and the integration of policy sectors.

In the Hungarian Structural Fund management system the central actors (government, ministries, and a separate Structural Fund management institution, namely the National Development Agency) played a dominant role in the preparation of the National Strategic Reference Framework. Although in the South Transdanubia region there was a long preparation phase for the Regional Operational Programme, with a lot of consultation forums for the 'well-known' regional stakeholders (former partner organisations) and a number of external experts and central ministerial representatives, a distinct Regional Operational Programme reflecting South Transdanubia's territorial specificities could not be realised. Ultimately, the South Transdanubia Operational Programme contained all of the priorities passed on from the Sectoral Operational Programmes and was similar to the other six Hungarian Regional Operational Programmes. Although the specific problems of the South Transdanubian Region were well identified (lagging economy, problems of accessibility, fragmented settlement structure, demographic decline, increasing poverty, etc.) the approved Regional Operational Programme contained no far-reaching response for tackling these disadvantages in the end.

The enforcement of the regional approach was hindered within the implementation phase of the South Transdanubia Operational Programme, where instead of sound regional development investments, many fragmented projects were realised. The Operational Programme management was overly centralised from the start, and became even more in the meantime, although other examples, such as in Poland, show that local and regional stakeholders may participate in the Structural Fund management in different roles and to a greater degree.

The planning, coordination and implementation of the South Transdanubia Operational Programme took place in a centralised scheme (Pálné Kovács and Varjú 2009), and had become even more centralised during the investigated period (personal communications 2012 and 2013). In addition, little emphasis was given to the alignment of Regional Operational Programmes and the spatial aspects with sectoral policies in Hungary. The lagging regions' failure to channel the regional needs and local actors into the development processes can be seen in the resulting lack of economic and social convergence, problems of territorial cohesion and the growth of social inequality (OFTK 2014). The South Transdanubia Operational Programme is a typical representation of the problems stemming from the neglected territorial aspects and the deficiencies of partnership building in Hungary.

As a positive note, one can say that the preparation of the Regional Operational Programme for the South Transdanubian Region has helped to build up institutional capacities in regards to 'partnership', 'territorial knowledgeability' and 'regional development management'. However, due to the fact that the 2014–2020 programming period has not included individual Regional Operation Programmes (except for the capital city's NUTS 2 region), these capacities will not be activated anymore and will most likely just wither away.

References

Annoni, P. and Dijkstra, L., 2013. *EU Regional Competitiveness Index RCI 2013*. Luxembourg: European Commission Joint Research Centre Institute for Security and Protection of the Citizens. Available from: http://ec.europa.eu/regional_policy/sources/docgener/studies/pdf/6th_report/rci_2013_report_final.pdf [Accessed 14 March 2015].

Bachtler, J. and McMaster, I., 2007. EU Cohesion Policy and the role of the regions: investigating the influence of Structural Funds in the new member states. *Environment and Planning C: Government and Policy* 26 (2), 398–427.

Bachtler, J., Mendez, C. and Oraže, H., 2014. From conditionality to Europeanization in Central and Eastern Europe: administrative performance and capacity in Cohesion Policy. *European Planning Studies* 22 (4), 735–757.

Bruszt, L., 2008. Multi-level governance – the eastern versions: emerging patterns of regional developmental governance in the new member states. *Regional & Federal Studies* 18 (5), 607–627.

CEC (Commission of the European Communities), 2006. *Community Strategic Guidelines on Cohesion (2006/702/EC)*. Brussels: European Commission. Available from: http://ec.europa.eu/regional_policy/sources/docoffic/2007/osc/l_29120061021en00110032.pdf [Accessed 12 January 2015].

CEC (Commission of the European Communities), 2014. *Investment for Jobs and Growth. Promoting Development and Good Governance in EU Regions and Cities. Sixth Report on Economic, Social and Territorial Cohesion*. Brussels: European Commission. Available from: http://ec.europa.eu/regional_policy/sources/docoffic/official/reports/cohesion6/6cr_en.pdf [Accessed 26 February 2015].

Dąbrowski, M., 2011. *Partnership in Implementation of the Structural Funds in Poland: 'Shallow' Adjustment or Internalization of the European Mode of Cooperative Governance?* Working Paper Series. Working Paper No. 05/2011. Vienna: Institute for European Integration Research. Available from: https://eif.univie.ac.at/downloads/workingpapers/wp2011-05.pdf [Accessed 12 January 2015].

Government of Hungarian Republic, 2007. *South Transdanubia Operational Programme 2007–2013*. CCI number: 2007HU161PO011, Budapest: Government of Hungarian Republic.

KPMG, 2011. *Az Operatív Programok félidei értékeléseinek szintézise*. Budapest: KPMG. Available from: palyazat.gov.hu/download/34356/Félidei_szintézis_riport_110531.pdf [Accessed 13 May 2015].

Mezei, C., 2015. Building institutions for the structural funds in the Visegrad countries. In: A. Bodor and Z. Grünhut, eds. *Cohesion and Development Policy in Europe*. Pécs: Institute for Regional Studies Centre for Economic and Regional Studies Hungarian Academy of Sciences. 60–71.

Molnárné Hegymegi, K., 2009. *A magyar civil szerveztek részvétele az európai uniós Strukturális Alapokra vonatkozó operatív programok tervezésében és*

170   *Cecília Mezei*

végrehajtásában. Zárótanulmány a kérdőívek és az interjúk feldolgozása alapján. Budapest: Magyar Természetvédők Szövetsége. Available from: www.mtvsz.hu/dynamic/SFteam_tanulmany2009_magyar_HU.pdf [Accessed 13 May 2015].

OFTK, 2014. *Az Országgyűlés 1/2014. (I. 3.)* OGY határozata a Nemzeti Fejlesztés 2030 – Országos Fejlesztési és Területfejlesztési Koncepcióról. *Magyar Közlöny,* 1, 7–298.

Pálné Kovács, I., 2009. Europeanisation of territorial governance in three Eastern/Central European countries. *Halduskultuur,* 10, 40–57.

Pálné Kovács, I., 2011. Top down regionalism – EU adaptation and legitimacy in Hungary. In: S.A. Lütgenau, ed. *Regionalization and Minority Policies in Central Europe: Case Studies from Poland, Slovakia, Hungary and Romania*. Innsbruck: StudienVerlag, 113–127.

Pálné Kovács, I., 2013. Miért hagytuk, hogy így legyen? A területi decentralizációs reformok természetrajza Magyarországon. *Politikatudományi Szemle,* 22 (4), 7–34.

Pálné Kovács, I., 2014. *Az önkormányzati rendszer és a területi közigazgatás átalakulása 2010–2013*. MTA Law Working Papers 2014/02. Budapest: Hungarian Academy of Sciences. Available from: http://jog.tk.mta.hu/uploads/files/mtalwp/2014_02_Palne_Kovacs_Ilona.pdf [Accessed 17 May 2015].

Pálné Kovács, I. and Varjú, V., eds., 2009. *Governance for Sustainability – Two Case Studies from Hungary*. Discussion Papers. No. 73. Pécs: Centre for Regional Studies of the Hungarian Academy of Sciences. Available from: http://discussionpapers.rkk.hu/index.php/DP/article/view/2332/4359 [Accessed 13 May 2015]

Perger, É., 2009. *EU kohéziós támogatások felhasználásának intézményrendszere és a forrásfelhasználás hatékonysága, eredményessége*. Budapest: ECOSTAT Kormányzati Gazdaság– és Társadalom-stratégiai Kutató Intézet. Available from: http://www.kozigkut.hu/doc/perger_09szept.pdf [Accessed 13 May 2015].

13 The rise of a new territorial governance domain

Flood management in the Rhine river basin

Wil Zonneveld and Alexander Wandl

Introduction

The idea of the river basin as a kind of archetypal, natural 'planning region' goes back to Patrick Geddes and his concept of the 'valley section', developed in the early twentieth century (Hall 1988, p. 140). Although a river basin may form a natural region with clear perimeters, from the perspective of territorial governance, it does not automatically form an integrated region. This is largely because almost every river basin cuts through administrative borders. Large rivers such as the Rhine often cut across international borders, which remain the most entrenched administrative boundaries, even within the European Union (EU). Nevertheless, cooperation between the countries bordering the Rhine predated the 1958 establishment of the European Economic Community by no less than eight years. The International Commission for the Protection of the Rhine (ICPR) was created as early as 1950, only a few years after the Second World War, and remains active today. Its establishment was prompted by major concerns about water quality. Decades later, the International Commission for the Protection of the Rhine also became a main channel for addressing water quantity issues, a development that was directly related to the so-called EU Floods Directive of 2007 (EC 2007). As a separate institutional entity, the International Commission for the Protection of the Rhine has become embedded in EU policies, although one of the participating countries (Switzerland) is not a member of the EU.

Addressing water quality issues has an obvious, although often indirect, territorial impact, as it mainly involves limitations on the performance of functions and activities, such as industry or agriculture. Water quantity management often affects the location of these functions and activities as well, so it tends to have a more profound territorial impact. Whether we are concerned with water quality or quantity, however, there are relationships between water management and territorial development, as well as between the places, areas and regions along a river. We can describe these as 'horizontal' relationships. The Rhine river basin, for example, forms a mega-region that could never be managed from a single point (overlooking the fact, for the sake of argument, that international borders would in any case prevent this). For governance reasons, the Rhine river basin area is thus horizontally divided into several sub-areas in which practical actions and projects are planned and implemented (Gilissen, 2009, Van Rijswick *et al.* 2010). One of these covers more than half of the Netherlands and includes the watershed of the cross-border River Vecht, and therefore parts of North-Rhine Westphalia: the Rhine delta.

There are also clear vertical relationships, as managing water and territorial development connects governments and other actors at different levels of scale. For example, in this chapter we refer to what is known as the German–Dutch Working Group on High Water, in which the Dutch Province of Gelderland and the German State of North-Rhine-Westphalia (NRW) cooperate, amongst others. The point is not only that these administrative areas are of different sizes and have different competences, but also that this working group can only function thanks to a declaration signed by the responsible ministers in the Netherlands (i.e. at the national level) and the State of North-Rhine Westphalia. This example reveals how the horizontal and vertical dimensions are intertwined.

Clearly the subject at hand requires a certain focus, given the space limitations of a book chapter. We will pay particular attention to the management of water quantity: the fact that strong links are emerging between water quantity management and spatial planning makes this an interesting case from the perspective of 'territorial' governance. Geographically, we focus primarily on the area covered by the Working Group. The activities of this group take place within larger spatial frameworks, however, which we will also cover in this chapter.

Coordinating actions of actors and institutions

Cross-border cooperation on water quantity management takes place within a multi-faceted framework that includes international treaties, conventions and political agreements, EU law as well as national law and, in the case of Germany, also state law. Underlying this framework is the political-normative principle of solidarity, which is in essence a territorial principle: countries and regions are not supposed to transfer the burden of flood risk downstream to other countries and regions. This principle is engraved in European law, but it is also a norm in transnational and cross-border politics.

Transnational Rhine river cooperation: the necessity of having a formal basis

Cooperation in the Rhine basin has required the establishment of cooperative bodies. In general, such bodies – although they are sometimes set up informally – have a formal basis, either in terms of treaties or

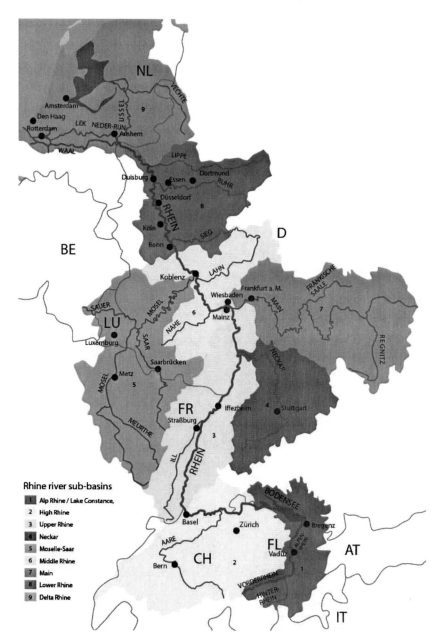

Figure 13.1 The Rhine river basin and its sub-basins
Source: Own adaptation based on ICPR 2015

174 *Wil Zonneveld and Alexander Wandl*

conventions or in terms of some kind of political agreement. In our case, Table 13.1 identifies the most important treaties or conventions and political agreements and the relationship with the relevant organisations, the bodies that are responsible for cooperation. The most important frameworks for cross-border cooperation in this case were mentioned in the introduction: the International Commission for the Protection of the Rhine and the German–Dutch Working Group on High Water, or 'the Working Group' in short.

As explained above, whilst the International Commission for the Protection of the Rhine was established in 1950, it gained a legal status under the so-called Bern Convention (in full: the Convention on the Protection of the River Rhine), signed in 1963 (Van Rijswick and Havekes 2012, p. 229). Other treaties followed, including the 1976 International Convention on the Prevention of Chemical Pollution of the Rhine. Among other things, this convention resulted in action plans for the Rhine and (at a later stage) the North Sea (Van Rijswick and Havekes, 2012, p. 22). The Bern Convention was renewed in 1999, this time with the EU being included as one of its signatories. In fact, this convention was a follow-up to the 1992 Helsinki Water Convention, generally considered to be of great importance for Europe, as it forms the basis for two key EU water directives: the Water Framework Directive (EC 2000) and the Floods Directive (see below):

> It requires riparian states of transboundary waters to cooperate on the basis of agreements aimed at the prevention, control and reduction of transboundary impact. Among other things, the agreements must provide for the establishment of joint bodies to achieve these aims for each catchment area. International law is thus […] based on a river-basin approach.
>
> (Van Rijswick and Havekes 2012, p. 229)

The International Commission for the Protection of the Rhine is responsible for developing strategic goals at the international level and the integration of its core policy fields: flood management, water quality and water ecology. It is responsible for international agreements and reports in relation to both EU water directives. The International Commission for the Protection of the Rhine has a relatively elaborate structure, stretching from a Plenary Assembly and a Coordinating Committee at the top to working groups and expert groups that deal with 'technical' issues (an administrative term for issues on the ground, where the practicalities of spatial and water management become tangible; more details of the organisation's structure can be found on the International Commission for the Protection of the Rhine website). As one might imagine, the International Commission for the Protection of the Rhine works on the principle of consensus, as, unlike the EU, none of its organisational components or the organisation as a whole has the competence to enforce and monitor the policies in the directives.

A new territorial governance domain 175

Table 13.1 International conventions, declarations and relevant organisations

Treaties, conventions and declarations	Organisations/operational practice
Multilateral	
1963: Convention on the Protection of the River Rhine: 'Bern convention"	1950: International Commission for the Protection of the Rhine against Pollution (original name; formal status from 1963 onwards)
1992: Convention on the Protection and Use of Transboundary Watercourses and International Lakes: 'Helsinki Convention' (in force: 1996)	EU 2000 Water Framework Directive (WFD) and 2007 Floods Directive leading to river (sub) basin cooperation bodies (Rhine, Meuse, Scheldt, Danube, etc.)
1999: Convention on the Protection of the Rhine (NL, D, F, L, CH and EU)	ICPR: International Commission for the Protection of the Rhine (working domain: WFD and Floods Directive) • Ministerial Meetings (including the EU Environment Commissioner) and Plenary Assembly • Working groups
Bilateral	
1960: Border Convention (D, NL; mostly dealing with exact location of country border and cross-border road infrastructure); revised in 2002	1963: Permanent German–Dutch Border Water Commission including sub-committees on 7 sub-basins (Commission and sub-committees dormant since about 2000; role taken over by German–Dutch Working Group on High Water)
Cross-border	
2007: Common Agreement ('Gemeinsame Erklärung') on Flood Protection (Province of Gelderland, Ministry of Transport, Public Works and Water Management (NL), Ministry of Environment, Conservation, Agriculture and Consumer Protection in North Rhine-Westphalia); time frame: 2007–2012 (renewed in 2013)	German–Dutch Working Group on High Water (founded in mid-1990s)

Source: Authors' own elaboration

176 *Wil Zonneveld and Alexander Wandl*

Regulative power: the two European water directives

Apart from treaties, the EU has three types of legally-binding tools, directives being one of these. These oblige EU member states to achieve results, but *how* they achieve these, in a legal sense, is up to the member states themselves. In October 2000 the European Water Framework Directive (WFD) came into force. In short, the main objective of the directive is that the quality of surface water and groundwater throughout the EU should be of a good quality by the year 2015; or, in the words of the directive, it should achieve a 'good status'.

With regard to surface water, the directive is based upon a distinction between river basins and river-basin districts, the latter forming the main unit for the management of water quality. Such a district is described as 'the area of land and sea, made up of one or more neighbouring river basins together with their associated ground waters and coastal waters' (EC 2000, p. 6). EU member states had until December 2003 to define the perimeters of the river-basin districts and the river basins within them. In doing so, they were also obliged to identify the 'competent authority for the purposes of [the] Directive' (EC 2000, p. 8). Thus like the Bird and Habitat Directives – for which the special protection areas are the main territorial unit – the Water Framework Directive implies a kind of indirect territorial governance policy along a sectoral line, namely water, because it prescribes – albeit in general terms – territorial units and the objectives of policies, plans and actions that have territorial impacts.

The Water Framework Directive is primarily concerned with improving water quality; when the directive was adopted, 'the time was not ripe for a truly integrated directive that would also regulate flood protection and water scarcity' (Van Rijswick and Havekes, 2012, p. 254). The serious floods that occurred during the 1990s, together with growing awareness that the necessary measures could best be coordinated and taken at river-basin level, eventually led in 2007 to the adoption of the Directive on the Assessment and Management of Flood Risks (the Floods Directive). Like the Water Framework Directive, the Floods Directive is based on the river basin approach. In fact, both directives are to be applied and implemented as far as possible in a coordinated and integral manner. As suggested above, the basic principle is that of solidarity: countries and regions are not supposed to transfer the burden of flood risk (and threats to water quality, for that matter) downstream to other countries and regions. Transnational and cross-border water management is therefore grounded in a clear legal and political-normative principle.

Building governance capacity in a cross-border region

A country's border is not a natural border when it comes to river basins or sub-basins. Even when a river does form a border, the watershed is located on

A new territorial governance domain   177

Table 13.2 Structure of the water management administration in Germany (here NRW) and the Netherlands

North Rhine-Westphalia (NRW)	The Netherlands
Federal State: concurrent legislative power (not used)	
NRW: Ministry for Climate Protection, Environment, Agriculture, Nature Conservation and Consumer Protection (MUNLV); within this ministry: Agency for Nature, Environment and Consumer Protection (LANUV)	Ministry of Infrastructure and the Environment; Ministry of Economic Affairs: legislation
District (*Bezirk*)	Province
Sub-district (*Kreis*)	
Dike associations (*Deichverbände*) and municipalities	Water boards and municipalities

Source: Authors' own adaptation based on Van der Molen (2011)

both sides of the border. A country's border does form a clear demarcation line, however, when it comes to the planning and implementation of policies and strategies. Table 13.2 shows the formal structure of water management in Germany and the Netherlands.

This raises the question as to how action should be coordinated, given that the governmental structures in the two countries do not match (as shown by Table 13.2) and, moreover, competences are distributed differently across the various levels. The German–Dutch Working Group on High Water has become an important agent in this respect. The initiative to found the Working Group in the mid-1990s, after the main flood incidents in 1993 and 1995, came from the Dutch Province of Gelderland in the east of the Netherlands. The province had several reasons for wanting to extend cooperation (Wiering *et al.* 2010). First, the existing cooperation in the Rhine basin was at that time overly focused on water quality, and insufficient attention was being paid to implementation. Second, existing initiatives were located at national level, and cooperation between regional bodies was lacking.

The Province of Gelderland contacted the State of North-Rhine Westphalia in order to establish some form of cooperation on flooding policies in the border area. Together with the Dutch eastern regional office of the national Directorate General for Public Works and Water Management and the Rivierenland water board, they became the lead participants in the Working Group, which was set up in 1997. From 2007, the activities of the Working Group were politically embedded in a so-called Common Declaration (*Gemeinsame Erklärung*), which lasted until 2012. The signing of a follow-up declaration was delayed for some time due to elections on both sides of the border. Although the Working Group remained active, the delay hindered the implementation of concrete projects (personal

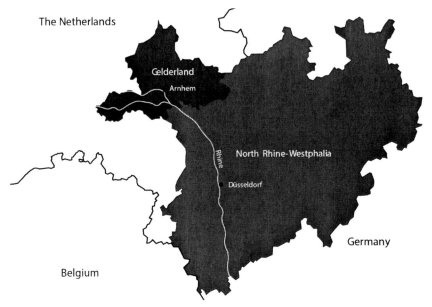

Figure 13.2 The area of the main partners in the German–Dutch Working Group on High Water

Source: Own elaboration

communication 2012). This again demonstrates the importance of legal and political frameworks in dealing with cross-border or transnational issues. A new Common Declaration was eventually signed in 2013.

Flooding is a classical asymmetrical 'upstream-downstream' problem (Wiering *et al.* 2010). The Rhine case also features some symmetrical elements, however, because taking flood measures downstream can have a limited, but sometimes substantial, impact upstream (slowing down or speeding up the water flow) or can be of importance for the region as a whole. Moreover, protecting polders from flooding and regulating the water situation in the entire region are both activities that are clearly affected by cross-border mutual interdependencies (Wiering *et al.* 2010, p. 2664). In fact, in the Gelderland- North-Rhine Westphalia border area there are two shared 'dike rings', areas of land that are protected from flooding by an individual dike. This means that if a dike breaks on one side of the border, land on the other side of the border is also flooded. The so-called 'dike ring 48' (the use of prosaic numbers instead of names is a clear indication of how technological issues continue to dominate water management) is the most important reason why this dike is referred to as a 'system dike' (Waterschap Rijn en IJssel 2014).

Integrating policy sectors

From a new Dutch approach to joint practice along the Rhine

Before we address the activities of the German–Dutch Working Group, we will take a closer look at how water quantity issues are *framed*, starting with the Netherlands, and how this framing has led to a series of interventions along the entire Rhine. Until the 1980s, water quantity management in the Netherlands was strongly focused on meeting the territorial needs arising from spatial planning, as well as society at large. Water management ensured 'dry feet' and good conditions for the use of land through an elaborate system of dikes, canals, sluices and pumps (or windmills, before the age of steam); in other words, a hard engineering system intended to push out as much water as possible. Critical periods of near-flooding in 1993 and 1995 and regular problems resulting from excessive local rainfall created momentum for a new approach, based on the notion of resilient and adaptive water management and known as 'Room for Water' (*ruimte voor water*).

Historically, and especially since the mid-nineteenth century, the amount of land available for water in the Netherlands has sharply decreased over time, due to land reclamation and factors such as the building of urban areas in the forelands of rivers (Van Stokkoma *et al.* 2005). As a general approach, 'Room for Water' has also led to a major revision of policies on the management of the Dutch river system. This became known as 'Room for the River', an approach that started with a directive in 1996 in response to the near-floods and mass evacuation of people in the preceding year. This directive contains regulations on the use of riverbeds and has the objective of eliminating vulnerable land uses from flood plains (Wolsink 2006, p. 477, Silva *et al.* 2004). The main components of this directive – which in themselves can be seen as an integration of the 'sectors' of water management and spatial planning/development – are (Silva *et al.* 2004):

- New developments such as housing, buildings or flow-obstructing infrastructure in the floodplains are no longer allowed; this also holds for the expansion of existing buildings.
- Water embankments and the zones they protect will be assigned a land use. Land that is part of a winter bed will be assigned to 'public works'. In the case of more than one land-use assignment, the principal land use is to protect against high water, so this is given priority.
- A system of construction permits is needed for all activities that may hinder the draining of water or that may cause a decrease in water storage capacity.

The fact that it was possible to gain political acceptance for such an approach, and moreover in a binding form, can only be explained in view of the window of opportunity opened by the events of 1993 and 1995 (Wolsink 2006, see also Woltjer and Al 2007). The components of the 'Room for the River' directive were included in several statutory national planning documents, as well as a policy programme that is supposed to be finalised in 2015. In 39 locations, measures have been or will be taken that give the river space to flood safely. Such measures include depoldering, the lowering of groynes, the creation of (temporary) water storage areas, dike relocation to enlarge the riverbed and the construction of secondary channels to lower high water tables in the main river.

The Room for the River programme is not just a sectoral water management strategy, however; the aim is to design measures in such a way that they improve the spatial quality of the immediate surroundings. The link with urban development objectives is especially important here: the enlargement of riverbeds near urban areas is expected to contribute to the renewal of urban water fronts and the creation of new recreational areas (Redeker 2013). More room for nature can be created as well, although nature development and water safety can sometimes conflict. There are examples of Natura 2000 projects leading to overgrown areas in flood plains, thereby obstructing the free flow of water. If such cases prove to be serious, the general rule – as laid down, for instance, in the EU Habitat directive – is that safety should weigh more heavily than nature. Dike relocation can compensate for the blocking effects of overgrown flood plains, but such solutions are prohibitively expensive and can also destroy spatial qualities: a century old dike can have important cultural heritage values (personal communication 2012).

Nevertheless, on the whole, the 'Room for the River' programme can be seen as an integrative strategy that attempts to link water management goals with policy objectives relating to urban, nature and recreational development. Although it is a Dutch policy, it is drawing increasing international attention, as there is a global interest in approaches that are not (entirely) based on classic hard engineering interventions. As such, there is also a great interest from Germany and Switzerland, where the approach is called *Raum für die Flüsse* (an almost literal translation from the Dutch) (personal communication 2012).

These countries already are putting this approach into practice: projects comparable with those implemented in the Netherlands have been and will be carried out upstream as part of the 'Action Plan on Floods' for the Rhine, adopted by the International Commission for the Protection of the Rhine on the occasion of the twelfth conference of Rhine Ministers on 22 January 1998 in Rotterdam (the reader is referred to the International Commission for the Protection of the Rhine website for more information about this plan). The time horizon of the plan is 2020 and progress is monitored through interim plans with progressive five-year time horizons (i.e. 2005, 2010 and 2015). It is expected that by 2020, approximately 12 billion euros will have been spent by the Rhine states.

This development reinforces the observation that we emphasised above: there is no management authority at the level of the Rhine river basin.

A *new territorial governance domain*   181

No competences are shared or have been handed over to a transnational organisation. Instead, policies are aligned and their implementation is monitored though high-level political meetings. One should not underestimate the extent to which such meetings require long preparation, including overviews and progress reports that in themselves serve to stimulate the implementation of political agreements. As governments and the politicians in charge of the implementation of the International Commission for the Protection of the Rhine Action Plan tend to change, it is standard practice to re-state the political will to proceed along the lines of the Action Plan. On the Dutch side of the border, a new policy programme was presented by the government in 2014, called the Delta Programme. Rather than addressing urgent issues of water safety, this programme looks far into the future, as it seeks to prepare the country for the long-range effects of climate change on the water system. Unlike the 'Room for the River' programme, it covers the entire country, including the coast. A discussion of this programme would be beyond the scope of this chapter, as it is relatively new and only covers the Netherlands; however, we can expect that international coordination will take place via the International Commission for the Protection of the Rhine.

Soft cooperation: the German–Dutch Working Group on High Water

Within the framework of the International Commission for the Protection of the Rhine, there are no bodies with the competence to implement physical projects. The same is true of the cross-border German–Dutch Working Group on High Water. The group studies the functioning of the Rhine river system, and how this knowledge can be used in the coordinated policies and projects carried out by the competent authorities on each side of the border. According to eye witnesses, whilst the initial activities might appear modest to most outsiders, their importance should not be underestimated: the development of a shared understanding of flood control in the context of the entire cross-border water system (personal communication 2012). The first period of activities was dominated by joint research projects, mostly modelling of flood risks. The techniques used included those developed for the preparation of the Dutch 'Room for the River' policy document. One important highlight so far was the finalisation of the so-called Lower Rhine Study (*Niederrheinstudie*) in 2004. Thus although the relationship between the two sides of the border may be regarded as asymmetrical, as we suggested above, the Dutch participants in the Working Group have had something to offer to their German counterparts, namely knowledge and expertise (personal communication 2012).

The Working Group consists of civil servants and researchers. Politicians are not closely involved in the activities. In fact, members of the Working Group regard this as an asset, as political involvement might lead to pressure to achieve (rapid) results. In addition, because they are rooted in concrete areas and locations, regional policy actors tend to have a greater sense of the urgency of problems and more local and regional knowledge than national state actors (personal communication 2012, see also Wiering *et al.* 2010, p. 2665).

One key issue that has been discussed in the Working Group is the level of flood risk. Although this has obvious physical connotations, the issue has been approached on a purely conceptual level. The discussions have revealed differences in terms of attitudes towards possible long-term developments (personal communication 2012). The Dutch respondents generally consider the German attitude to be somewhat laid back in contrast to that of the Netherlands, where a policy culture has developed in recent years that pays more attention to the likelihood of developments such as climate change and their possible effects and scenarios. How much water might pass through the Rhine at the town of Lobith – which is located directly on the border – at times of high water is the key issue here. The Dutch policy document 'Room for the River' assumes 16,000 m^3 per second, while the expectation for the more distant future is that this could rise to 18,000 m^3 per second, or even more. The Lower Rhine Study accepts 16,500 m^3 per second. In Germany, it is thought that such a high figure will not be reached at Lobith, because so many areas will already be flooded upstream (in Germany). This figure was used by groups opposing the plan to create an emergency retention area in the Ooij Polder, an area of ecological value near the German–Dutch border (personal communication 2012, see also Wiering 2010); a campaign that was ultimately successful.

One key area in which the Dutch respondents think Germany is clearly ahead of the Netherlands is that of so-called object protection (*Objektschutz*). First, areas and objects that could be affected by flooding are mapped in detail in the context of regional plans (*Regionalpläne*). Second, in Germany, responsibility for the effects of building in a flood-prone area lies with the initiator. The feeling amongst Dutch respondents is that in terms of this aspect, at least, German policies are more sophisticated (personal communication 2012).

Mobilising stakeholder participation

Mobilising stakeholder participation entails giving stakeholders an insight into the design of territorial governance processes and/or the opportunity to shape them. In this case, water management meets spatial planning at different levels of scale. As a 'new-generation' directive, the EU's Water Framework Directive and the Floods Directive require public involvement in the implementation process. This is generally interpreted as the involvement of key stakeholders and the broader public in formulating river-basin management plans. The implementation of both directives was a challenge on both sides of the border, as both countries lack a tradition of stakeholder involvement in water management (as compared to spatial planning, where there is an extensive tradition of such involvement); the organisation of participation in what used to be a very technical domain is by no means self-evident. We will now look how stakeholder participation has been organised at different levels of scale.

The involvement of civil society within the International Commission for the Protection of the Rhine takes place at the level of what are known as working groups. Working group and plenary meetings are open to non-governmental organisations (NGOs) and intergovernmental organisations. NGOs play a crucial role in integrating the different working groups, as they often have less compartmentalised interests and ways of working. Other instruments used by the International Commission for the Protection of the Rhine to involve and inform a broader public include the organisation of expert workshops and information provision, both in form of brochures and interactive online content.

The Working Group focuses primarily on the technical and administrative aspects of cooperation, but it also plays an important role in providing information to the wider public. It used to publish a bilingual 'High Water' magazine each year (the *Hoogwatermagazine/Hochwassermagazin*). Time is needed to reach a shared understanding on an issue as complex as flood control. As much emphasis has been put on technical issues to date, there has been less need, and also less interest from outside, to involve societal stakeholders such as NGOs that are active in landscape ecology, for instance, in the activities of the Working Group. NGOs such as these participate in the biannual High Water Conference (*Hoogwaterconferentie Stroomgebied van de Rijn/Hochwasserkonferenz Rheineinzugsgebiet*), however, which is organised within the framework of the Shared Agreement. The conference of October 2014 drew considerable attention, as it focused on the sensitive issue of cross-border dikes, and in particular dike ring 48, mentioned above. Municipalities and other local actors often send representatives to the Working Group. This means that when concrete projects are planned at the local level, local representatives are involved from the beginning and also play a crucial role in the integration of these projects into local planning documents and processes (personal communication 2012).

Evidence is emerging that suggests that a crucial role is played by the discursive headings under which concrete measures are proposed. High water protection measures tend to be accepted and lead to a constructive collaboration between government, the private sector and civil society at large (similar experiences in other countries have been reported). If concrete projects are put forward under the heading of river ecology or improving environmental qualities, however, they can garner strong opposition, especially from agricultural lobbies. In some cases, the topic of high water protection is used as the prime project aim so that other, more controversial topics can be implemented in the shadow of the flood protection measures (personal communication 2012).

Being adaptive to changing contexts

In this section, we look at how territorial governance responds to changing contexts by means of various learning and feedback mechanisms. The management of the Rhine in the cross-border region of Germany and the Netherlands has had to deal with several changing contexts, one of these being how the water system behaves (or is expected to behave). We have already discussed at length the emergence of the 'Room for the River' approach, which is basically an adaptation strategy: adapting water defence works and the spatial layout of entire areas to the increasingly capricious nature of rivers.

Changes in the legal context also call for adaptation, and here we refer to the implementation of the two EU directives. Both directives are themselves the result of societal and political changes, partly in relation to changing risks: 1) the increasing flood risk, both in terms of frequency and intensity; 2) increasing ecological awareness on the part of the population, and therefore greater public demand concerning the ecological and landscape quality of flood protection measures; and 3) a paradigmatic shift concerning flood management, away from a hard engineering approach and towards adaptive flood protection. As a result of these changes, integrated approaches towards river management have been put in place. Two aspects have played a crucial role in this process: institutional learning and flexibility.

Both the International Commission for the Protection of the Rhine and the German–Dutch Working Group are 'learning machines', a term we borrow from Faludi's (2008) analysis of European integration. We described the working of the two organisations above. One interesting issue that we have not yet mentioned, however, is at play in the Working Group and relates to differences in physical geography. In Germany, the Rhine has cut much more deeply into the landscape than on the Dutch side of the border. Due to changes in relief, the areas that might flood in Germany are smaller, whereas higher ground is on the whole much closer by than in the Netherlands. When areas are flooded or threatened with flooding in the Netherlands, higher ground tends to be much further away and much more difficult for large numbers of people to reach (personal communication 2012, see also Verwijmeren 2007). This has an obvious impact on attitudes towards risk. In other words, here we are dealing with place-based perceptions of flood risks.

There is also the general issue of how a water system behaves and what long-term adaptive strategies might be adopted to deal with this. To arrive at a common understanding of these issues, commissioning research into the water capacity of the rivers, expected rain and flood amounts and the capacity of technical and other measures to manage risk and damage has proved essential. The results of this research have provided the basis on which to work towards common tools, methods and norms. In addition, of course, the establishment of the German–Dutch Working Group can itself be regarded as an indication of the flexibility and adaptability of local and regional institutions. These institutions were not entirely satisfied with a situation in which water management was primarily focused on water quality issues while at the same time ignoring local and regional levels of government. At least, this was how the situation was perceived (personal communication 2012).

Realising place-based specificities and impacts

We began this chapter by suggesting that a river basin can be regarded as a natural region, but one whose perimeters by no means match administrative boundaries. The establishment of the International Commission for the Protection of the Rhine can be seen as a clear response to this. We also described the German–Dutch Working Group, which, on a different geographical scale, has tried to deal with the border issue by focusing on clearing the ground for decision-making on both sides of the border through joint fact-finding and research. The Working Group is clearly a Dutch-North Rhine-Westphalia affair. Interestingly, though, this cooperation may have a much broader German dimension. Flood risks in the Netherlands are influenced by events upstream in Germany and the projects that lower these risks. The same is true for North Rhine-Westphalia, however, in relation to other German states upstream. The availability and accessibility of Dutch knowledge through the Working Group could influence the position of North Rhine-Westphalia vis-à-vis other German states, because there is relevant knowledge to be shared (Wiering *et al.* 2010, p. 2666).

There is also an important discursive dimension here: the notion of cross-border cooperation *per se*. North Rhine-Westphalia is itself largely dependent on measures taken in upstream German states. As a result, it is greatly in the interest of North Rhine-Westphalia to stress the notion (or discourse) of 'solidarity between people upstream and downstream'. This notion is enshrined in the two EU water directives, but it nevertheless requires constant political affirmation. The consequence of stressing this approach is that cooperation with actors in the area downstream of North Rhine-Westphalia, namely actors in the Netherlands, becomes an important, and in a sense even inevitable, aspect of motivating actors upstream in the Rhine river basin (Verwijmeren 2007, pp. 110–111, Wiering 2010, Wiering *et al.* 2010, p. 2666). From this perspective, cross-border cooperation shows (or might show) a spill-over pattern: what is demanded from others upstream cannot be denied to people and government agencies downstream.

We can conclude that the 2007 EU Floods Directive, preceded by the 2000 Water Framework Directive, landed in a context of well-functioning governing organisational structures, with sufficient personnel and funding. Or, as one respondent put it, 'we are doing what we've been doing for decades, but now with a stronger legal framework that puts us in a better position to take initiatives' (personal communication 2012). National and regional government structures are supported by well-established transnational and cross-border governance bodies, which have played an instrumental role in the establishment of the two EU directives.

Clearly, the Working Group (politically embedded via an agreement and a steering group) and the International Commission for the Protection of the Rhine (politically embedded via a transnational treaty) have both developed institutional capacity in relation to water management. It should be emphasised, though, that their actions are not directed towards actual spatial interventions. So far, the Working Group has carried out preparatory technical projects, mainly at the level of research. As of yet, there has been no shift towards joint policy and implementation projects (Wiering *et al.* 2010, p. 2666). These remain the responsibility of the present territorial administrative units, including the province, water boards and the Directorate General for Public Works and Water Management (*Rijkswaterstaat*) on the Dutch side, and the dike associations, municipalities and districts on the German side.

Conclusion

Due to the hydrological and ecological conditions, there are many intrinsic relationships within the catchment area of rivers. For this reason, river basins are conceived as the most important units for water planning and management. This is reflected in the two EU water directives, but also in the International Commission for the Protection of the Rhine, one of the earliest intergovernmental bodies created in Europe after the Second World War.

The nature and focus of cooperation in the Rhine river basin changed drastically as a result of the near-floods of 1993 and 1995. These led to a sudden awareness of the limitations of a technical approach to flood control based solely on hard engineering. Dikes, dams and other civil engineering works cannot fully exclude the risk of flooding, especially as over a period of many decades, such works have made the overall territory available for water flows ever smaller, while pumping installations and land use have increased the speed with which surface water enters into these flows. A new 'discourse' thus emerged that basically implied that water would need to be accommodated.

In 1999 a new Rhine convention came into force, and at a lower level of scale – between the Netherlands and North Rhine-Westphalia – a political agreement was signed in 2007 that formed the framework for a productive process of cross-border cooperation in the German–Dutch Working Group on High Water. 'Productive' does not imply actual joint territorial interventions or joint water management works, but the necessary preparatory activities. These activities have focused on research into risks and how to measure these. The years following the agreement saw the co-production of knowledge and knowledge transfer across the border.

The 'Room for the River' approach in the Netherlands and similar approaches in Germany have resulted in a territorialisation of water management: water management is still reliant on technical tools and solutions, but it also needs a territorial strategy. The picture now includes clear linkages with urban development, agriculture, ecology and cultural heritage, and vice versa: there is a need, for instance, to incorporate water management into spatial planning. In our view, this entails a clear tendency towards what in this volume is regarded as policy packing; in fact, a novel form of territorial governance.

One specific feature of water management at the level of river basins is its cross-border and transnational nature, the latter being the level at which the International Commission for the Protection of the Rhine operates. It is at these levels that we have encountered the importance of norms and the need to codify them. The most important norm is that the burden of flood risk should not be transferred downstream. Such a norm needs codification, however, to become operational at higher levels of scale across administrative borders. We have seen that this can take place through conventions, 'common declarations' and ultimately directives, at the national or European level. In this way, norms eventually become part of the rule of law. From the perspective of territorial governance, such norms need to be left open and not prescriptive in relation to practical actions; actors need to retain the possibility of adapting such norms to place-specific circumstances.

References

EC – European Commission, 2000. Directive 2000/60/EC of the European Parliament and of the Council of 23 October 2000 establishing a framework for community action in the field of water policy. *Official Journal of the European Communities*, L327, 1–72.

EC – European Commission, 2007. Directive 2007/60/EC of the European Parliament and of the Council of 23 October 2007 on the assessment and management of flood risks. *Official Journal of the European Union*, L288, 27–34 [Floods Directive].

Faludi, A., 2008. The learning machine: European integration in the planning mirror. *Environment and Planning A,* 40 (6), 1470–1484.

Gilissen, H.K., 2009. *Internationale en regionaal grensoverschrijdende samenwerking in het waterbeheer.* The Hague: Sdu publishers.

Hall, P., 1988. *Cities of Tomorrow.* Oxford: Blackwell.

ICPR – International Commission for the Protection of the Rhine, 2015. *Maps International Rhine River Basin District.* Available from: http://www.iksr.org/en/rhine/maps-of-the-river-basin/index.html [Accessed 10 April 2015].

Redeker, C., 2013. *Rhine Cities/Urban Flood Integration (UFI).* PhD diss., Delft University of Technology. Available from: http:// http://repository.tudelft.nl/view/ir/uuid:3a565b44-8150-4717-95e7-ee2393c42053/ [Accessed 25 February 2015].

Silva, W., Dijkman, J.P.M. and Loucks, D.P., 2004. Flood management options for the Netherlands. *International Journal of River Basin Management* 2 (2), 101–112.

Van der Molen, J., 2011. *Crossing Borders: Een kader voor het tot ontwikkeling brengen van grensoverschrijdende samenwerking in watermanagement* [Crossing Borders: A framework for cross-border cooperation in water management].

PhD Diss., University of Twente. Available from: http://doc.utwente.nl/78080/ [Accessed 26 February 2015].

Van Rijswick, H.F.M.W., Gilissen, H.K. and Van Kempen, J.J.H., 2010. The need for international and regional transboundary cooperation in European river basin management as a result of new approaches in EC water law. *ERA Forum* 11 (1), 129–157.

Van Rijswick, H.F.M.W. and Havekes, H.J.M., 2012. *European and Dutch Water Law*. Groningen: European Law Publishing.

Van Stokkoma, H.T.C., Smits, A.J.M. and Leuven, R.S.E.W., 2005. Flood defense in the Netherlands: a new era, a new approach. *Water International* 30 (1), 76–87.

Verwijmeren, J. 2007. Cross border co-operation and the Dutch-German Working Group on High Water. In: J. Verwijmeren and M. Wiering, eds. *Many Rivers to Cross: Cross Border Co-operation in River Management*. Delft: Eburon Academic Publications, 93–118.

Waterschap Rijn en IJssel, 2014. *Voorstel aan het algemeen bestuur* [Proposal to the general board]. Available from: http://www.wrij.nl/publish/pages/994/vst_consultatie_deltaprogramma_2015_110314.pdf [Accessed 26 February 2015].

Wiering, M., 2010. Grenzen aan de samenwerking in het Rijnstroomgebied; Duits-Nederlandse werkgroep Hoogwater. *Geografie* 19 (6), 34–37.

Wiering, M., Verwijmeren, J., Lulofs, K. and Feld, C., 2010. Experiences in regional cross border co-operation in river management: comparing three cases at the German–Dutch Border. *Water Resources Management* 24 (11), 2647–2672.

Wolsink, M., 2006. River basin approach and integrated water management: Governance pitfalls for the Dutch Space-Water-Adjustment Management Principle. *Geoforum* 37 (4), 473–487.

Woltjer, J. and Al, N., 2007. Integrating Water Management and Spatial Planning. *Journal of the American Planning Association* 73 (2), 211–222.

14 The trilateral nature park Goričko-Raab-Őrség

A project-based mode of territorial governance

Marko Peterlin and Maja Simoneti

Introduction: the evolution of cross-border cooperation in the trilateral nature park

Natural areas form an intrinsic component of the territory, crossing all kinds of administrative borders, from municipal to regional and national borders. This relates particularly to mountain regions and the fact that while their highest ridges often form administrative boundaries between both nations and sub-national administrative entities, such boundaries also divide ecosystems (Price 1999). This chapter investigates the evolution of the efforts for a coordinated protection and management of natural areas in such a cross-border context. It does so based on the analysis of the Goričko-Raab-Őrség trilateral nature park, connecting natural areas in Slovenia, Hungary and Austria.

The need for a coordinated approach to the protection and management of natural areas began to gain ground in the Alps, most notably with the founding of the International Commission for the Protection of the Alpine Regions (CIPRA) in 1952. In its founding document, the International Commission for the Protection of the Alpine Regions called for a convention to protect the Alpine environment and its natural resources. The process took a considerable length of time (CIPRA 1992) and 'The Alpine Convention' was finally signed in November 1991. The convention has led to the recognition that many issues cannot be solved only through national legislation, but rather that coordinated regional cross-border approaches and initiatives are essential to solve common problems (Price 1999).

The trilateral nature park Goričko-Raab-Őrség is situated in the eastern part of the Alps, where transnational and cross-border cooperation evolved mostly within the Alps-Adriatic Working Community. In the mid-1960s intense diplomatic contacts between heads of regional governments of Carinthia in Austria, Slovenia (initially a federal unit within Yugoslavia), and Friuli-Venezia Giulia in Italy, started to develop (Valentin 2006). Later on, when Croatia, the Austrian region of Styria, and the Italian region of Veneto also joined the cooperation during the mid-1970s, the Working Community of the Eastern Alpine Regions, which soon became known as the Alps-

190 *Marko Peterlin and Maja Simoneti*

Adriatic Working Community (AAWC), was formally founded at a meeting in Venice in November of 1978. Its membership changed quite often, but most of the time it also included other regions in the north of Italy, in eastern Austria as well as regions in the south-western part of Hungary. Although protection and management of the natural areas have not been at the core of the Alps-Adriatic Working Community cooperation, it has nevertheless formed an important part of the cooperation since its inception (Price 1999).

The fall of the Iron Curtain in 1989 and major political, social and economic changes in Central and Eastern Europe, as well as the emergence of new independent states and the war in Yugoslavia thoroughly transformed the context for cooperation in the area during the early 1990s. The role of the EU also began to grow during that period, in particular after 1995, when Austria became an EU member state, and Slovenia and Hungary began the accession processes. Through the EU INTERREG initiative and various pre-accession programmes, external funding for cooperation was also available for the first time, which gave a boost to cooperation initiatives. Price (1999) thus notes that a number of what he calls 'INTERREG regions' have been designated along the boundaries between EU member states and the non-member states.

The trilateral nature park Goričko-Raab-Őrség is one of these cooperation structures that emerged in the last two decades with the aim of coordinating protection and management of natural areas across borders. As Dešnik and Domanjko (2011) explain, the idea of establishing the park emerged in the early 1990s at one of the workshops aimed at developing a vision for the area after the fall of the Iron Curtain. An interviewee recalls that the workshop, organised in Austria, was also built on informal personal contacts, established through decades of cooperation within the Alps-Adriatic Working Community, like many other projects funded by INTERREG and other EU cross-border cooperation programmes (personal communication 2013). INTERREG here refers mainly to the INTERREG IIA (1994–1999) and INTERREG IIIA (2000–2006) programmes. Other cross-border cooperation programmes have been 'the programme of Community aid to the countries of Central and Eastern Europe' (PHARE), which was launched in 1994 and replaced in 2007 by the 'Instrument for Pre-Accession Assistance' (IPA). In contrast to the cooperation within the Alps-Adriatic Working Community, which was limited to the officials mandated from the administrations of member regions (Price 1999), initiatives funded by INTERREG and the other mentioned cross-border cooperation programmes involved also private and independent non-governmental actors.

Three parks from the beginning

Despite the vision to establish a joint nature park, the three parks constituting the trilateral nature park Goričko-Raab-Őrség were established in their present form separately, following national legislative frameworks in the

Nature park Goričko-Raab-Őrség   191

Table 14.1 Facts and figures of the three parks

	Goričko Nature Park	Raab Nature Park	Őrség National Park
State	Slovenia	Austria	Hungary
Established	2003	1998	2002
Place of park Authority	Grad	Jennersdorf	Őriszentpéter
Area (ha)	46,200	15,000	44,000
Natura 2000 area	96%	None	100%
Inhabitants	25,000	10,000	16,000

Source: Authors' own adaptation based on Dešnik and Domanjko (2011)

years between 1998 and 2003. The Raab nature park (*Naturpark Raab*) in Austria was established as a landscape protection area that is designated by the State Government of Burgenland. Its aim was to fulfil four functions: nature protection, tourism, education and regional development (personal communication 2013). It was established in 1998 on a territory encompassing seven municipalities. The Őrség national park (Őrsegi Némzeti Park) in Hungary was established in its present form in 2002, following the reform and expansion of several protected areas. The park authority also effectively serves as a nature protection authority on the county level, overseeing an area substantially larger than the park itself (personal communication 2013). The Goričko nature park (*Krajinski park Goričko*) in Slovenia is protected under the 'Slovenian Act on Nature Protection' (Republic of Slovenia 1999) as a landscape park. Its main concern and focus of work is nature conservation. It was established in 2003 by the national government after gaining support of local authorities.

Although numerous documents and projects have mentioned the trilateral park since late 1990s, no common formal document defining the trilateral nature park as such existed until 2006, when the first Partnership Agreement was adopted by the heads of park authorities.

Coordinating actions of actors and institutions: a major challenge when crossing borders

Governing capacity: the role of the park authorities

Despite the ambition for a joint trilateral park authority, the trilateral nature park Goričko-Raab-Őrség currently does not operate like one park entity but rather as three separate ones, each following its own national policy system and governance culture. In this respect, park authorities are key institutions coordinating actions of actors and institutions in all three countries. But their roles and competences in relation to the different governance levels, as well as their organisation and capacity differ considerably between the countries. While in Austria their role is primarily a platform for coordination between local actors and institutions, in Hungary the park authorities serve primarily as an authority at the county level, and in Slovenia they are a mixture of both.

The park authority of the Raab national park in Austria was established as an association by the participating municipalities with the intention to manage the protected area in a way that would give added value to the local community (personal communication 2013). As an association, the park authority is managed directly by the municipalities through monthly meetings of its board, consisting of mayors of all municipalities. The board defines the work plan and takes care of its implementation. Also, the park authority is funded mostly by the participating municipalities. The staff is small with only three part-time employees and a few full-time employees. The park authority is a firmly local institution, having regular contacts with the regional level in the field of tourism and somewhat fewer contacts with nature protection. There is practically no connection at all to the national level (personal communication 2013). Although limited in resources, it seems to function very effectively as a platform for coordinating local actors in order to contribute to the protection of natural areas by focusing primarily on sustainable agriculture and other specific projects.

In Hungary, as already mentioned, the park authority of the Őrség national park is legally responsible for nature protection and management of the park area, for overseeing the protected area in a wider region and for issuing permissions for all interventions and land use changes in protected areas of the county. Effectively, it also has the role of the county authority in relation to nature protection (personal communication 2013). It has a staff of 32 permanent employees, around 50 project-based staff and 50 to 60 more people with park operations (personal communication 2013). It is primarily a county (sub-regional) level institution, but includes municipalities as partners in many projects. The cooperation with the national level, on the other hand, is mostly limited to the formal procedures.

In Slovenia, the park authority also can be seen as a platform, connecting the national with the local level. Formally, the park has been established by a governmental decree based on national law, giving it competences mostly in relation to nature protection, with some tasks also related to tourism as well as local and regional planning (Goričko Nature Park 2005). The board of the park consists of five representatives from the national level, five representatives from the municipalities and one representative from the general public (personal communication 2013). But there are also inconsistencies with regard to this mediating role. The park authority is, for instance, not recognised as a stakeholder in the planning processes for infrastructure of national importance (personal communication 2013). This is seen as a problem also from the point of view of one municipality, which would prefer a stronger role of the park authority in the national programming and planning processes and thus take

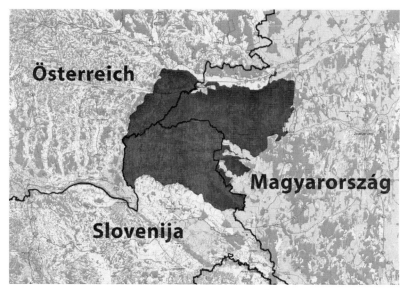

Figure 14.1 The Trilateral nature park Goričko-Raab-Őrség
Source: Own elaboration

on the role as the voice of the people living there at the national level (personal communication 2013).

A 'soft' leadership model

The trilateral park has slowly taken shape in the last two decades, with slow but decisive steps in the same direction in all three countries. This is a clear sign of a shared vision and the ability to secure its implementation. There is no clear evidence though that this shared vision and the steps towards its implementation were formulated from the beginning. It is more likely that they emerged as a result of a continuous cooperation between the actors in the area with the commonly shared vision to address nature and landscape protection in the three countries. If this decentralised visioning process can be considered in terms of leadership, we might refer to a 'soft' and decentralised leadership model.

Towards a partnership agreement

Despite the widely perceived importance of informal cooperation across borders, the need for a more formalised cooperation platform has also been clearly expressed. The Environmental Audit Report on the tri-border area of Hungary, Slovenia and Austria, prepared jointly by the Supreme Audit Institutions of the Republic of Hungary, the Republic of Slovenia and the Republic of Austria in 2006, for instance, recommended to intensify trilateral cooperation for the joint nature park Raab-Őrség-Goričko and suggested the elaboration of a joint trilateral management plan to provide an effective use of resources and the efficient development of the natural habitats.

(State Audit Office of Hungary *et al.*, p. 8)

Dešnik and Domanjko (2011) argue that a common cross-border management plan of the trilateral park would be important due to the varying status and capacities of the protected areas and the need to comply with the requirements of the Natura 2000 network and other EU policies. Such a plan could integrate nature and landscape protection goals with the sustainable development objectives of the region and the wellbeing of local communities. This need was a starting point for a Partnership Agreement in 2006, which was developed as a first step towards a more institutionalised cooperation within the trilateral park. The document was written in all three languages and the first version was publicly signed in May 2006 in Windisch-Minihof (Austria) at the celebration of the European Parks Day. Three years later, the renewed Partnership Agreement was signed in Őriszentpéter (Hungary). The initial version of the agreement declared the intention for cooperation in the fields of nature protection, tourism, culture, education and regional development (Raab nature park *et al.*, 2006). Cooperation should take place through:

- raising public awareness in the fields of nature protection and environment, through raising awareness of youth, adults and employees in the fields of industry and crafts, in particular in agriculture and forestry,
- planning of joint events, emphasising diversity in cultural heritage and cultural activities,
- joint design of promotion and communication material, which will present the area to the tourism and agricultural markets as suitable for healthy living and recreation,
- the formulation of a common management plan, in which the aspects of heritage protection and restructuring of natural habitats will be emphasised,
- joint search for funding from the European Union,
- joint cooperation within the European Green Belt Initiative.

Based on the Partnership Agreement, half-yearly meetings of park authorities were also envisaged. Even more intense formal cooperation between the park authorities began in November 2012 (personal communications 2013). It was then planned that the heads of the park authorities would meet each month.

Integrating policy sectors

Public policy packaging: between informal coordination and conformance to higher levels

Relevant policy sectors in the case of the trilateral park include nature conservation and biodiversity, agriculture, tourism, forestry as well as rural development. The main actors in relation to cross-sectoral integration are again the managing authorities of all three parks, which hold a key role in relation to the mentioned policies in the trilateral park. As they operate in the framework of national policies, other key actors are national administrations, mostly the ministries responsible for the above-mentioned policy sectors in the three countries involved (in Austria and Hungary also regional administrations). Other actors include for instance municipalities, non-governmental organisations, farmers and the agricultural industry as well as tourism organisations.

There are considerable differences in the way cross-sectoral coordination works across the three countries. In *Slovenia*, some formal procedures exist both for coordination between policy sectors as well as for coordination across governance levels. Nevertheless, all interviewees in Slovenia noted that for various reasons formal procedures do not always work well. The director of the park authority even argued that from their point of view informal ties between responsible officials are more important for effective coordination, since mutual trust seems to be crucial for collaboration across borders (personal communication 2013). This was confirmed also by the director of the regional development agency (personal communication 2013) as well as by the official from the Ministry of the Agriculture and Environment, who noted that formal and informal procedures overlap and complement each other (personal communication 2013).

Policy packaging across governance levels works mostly through conformance to higher levels, since a number of policies relevant for the park must conform to the national regulations with regard to e.g. Natura 2000, which in turn has to comply with the EU Habitat and Birds directives. The same goes for municipalities, which must conform to national regulations when they are preparing their spatial plans. Both representatives of municipalities, a mayor and an official, noted that a lot of negotiations are needed during these processes (personal communication 2013) that often result in conflicts between different sectors (such as between nature protection and agriculture) at the national level (personal communication 2013). Both also brought up the issue that informal channels through personal contacts between officials at local and national level, and sometimes also with the political level, are crucial and much more efficient than formal channels for effective coordination.

In *Austria* the park authority is in continuous formal and informal contacts with the municipalities. Continuous but less intense contacts also exist with the regional level, especially in relation to tourism, while there are almost no contacts with the national level. As a general rule, the manager of the park authority noted that informal contacts work better when dealing with issues in general, but formal procedures are necessary for precise agreements on all levels (personal communication 2013).

In *Hungary* the park authority has a strong role in formal procedures and decision-making, serving also as a responsible national institution for nature protection at the county level. It is thus involved in formal policy-making at the national level through procedures in which the county level is involved (i.e. in the fields of nature protection, forestry, agriculture, and water management). Some informal contacts with officials at the national level are nevertheless helpful (personal communication 2013). Formal procedures are also more important at the county level, where the park authority is preparing mandatory guidelines for the ten-year plans in the fields of forestry, agriculture and water management. Less formal contacts are at work in relation to tourism, where the park authority has no formal role and cooperation is mostly project-based.

Despite the differences, similarities also exist in terms of mechanisms for coordination of public policies in all three countries. In Slovenia and Hungary, and to some extent also in Austria, participation of actors in the formulation of some sort of plans was considered beneficial for coordination between public policy sectors. The director of the Mura regional development agency in Slovenia saw the planning process through which the National Spatial Plans for infrastructures of national importance are formulated as a tool to discuss the plans with the sub-regional level partnerships and municipalities (personal communication 2013) and align them with the regional development point of view.

Other kinds of planning processes were also mentioned as useful tools in this respect. The official from the Ministry of the Agriculture and Environment in Slovenia saw an opportunity for aligning agriculture and biodiversity polices through the Natura 2000 management plans (personal communication 2013), and this was reiterated also by the official of the Őrség national park (personal communication 2013). Both also noted that funding could help in this respect. In Austria the act, establishing the park served a similar role. A number of negotiations with different sectors, mostly at the level of the Austrian state of Burgenland, took place at the time when the act was being prepared. Much of the informal communication with various actors, such as agriculture chambers, farmers and the general public was carried out personally by the mayor of Mogersdorf at that time (personal communication 2013).

Cross-sector synergy: barriers and solutions

Most evident barriers for cross-sectoral integration were identified between policy sectors at the national level. In *Hungary*, very few management plans for Natura 2000 areas are actually implemented, because they cannot pass the inter-sectoral negotiations at the national level (personal communication 2013). In *Slovenia*, several interviewees stressed that there is no systematic cross-sectoral coordination (personal communications 2013) and that coordination at the regional and local level is sought for each project separately (personal communication 2013). It was emphasised that barriers to cross-sectoral integration typically do not appear at the level of practitioners and policy-makers, but rather at the level of politicians (personal communication 2013). Interestingly, Strategic Environmental Assessments (SEA) of municipal spatial plans was mentioned as a means to deal with the conflicts between nature protection and agriculture at the national level. The external expert, preparing the main part of the environmental report, was identified as an efficient mediator between both policy sectors (personal communication 2013). In *Austria*, synergies between tourism, agriculture and nature protection are sought by the park authority through development of regional products. These include for example local food products or tourist destinations based on nature protection (personal communication 2013).

Mobilising stakeholder participation

Democratic legitimacy: different democratic cultures

As park authorities are key institutions in all three parks, other stakeholders can be considered in relation to them. In *Hungary* the park authority has a very strong formal position in relation to other stakeholders. At the local level these include mainly municipalities, but also tourism and agriculture organisations, farmers and other residents of the park. Established on a strong legal basis by the national law, the need to secure democratic legitimacy among these stakeholders was not so evident at the beginning. This resulted in conflicts with local residents after the park was granted its current protection status in 2002, despite the fact that the local residents were previously in favour of establishing the park (personal communication 2013). These conflicts are slowly ebbing, as the park is offering more and more services for farmers and local residents.

In *Austria* the starting position was different. In the preparatory phase the agreement between local stakeholders was gained by involving municipalities, farmer and tourist organisations to establish the association that is managing the park authority (personal communication 2013). Securing democratic legitimacy in this context is rather self-evident, as the elected representatives of all municipalities within the park effectively manage the park authority. It thus works through a combination of representative and participative democracy and it seems to function rather well.

In *Slovenia* the park was established by the national government, but with the formal agreement of the municipalities within the park. Some of the stakeholders, mostly regional or local representatives of different sectoral administrations, were also involved in the preparatory processes.

198 *Marko Peterlin and Maja Simoneti*

Nevertheless, the park is now commonly perceived among local residents, especially farmers, as being imposed by the state and thus an obstacle to development (personal communication 2013). The director of the park authority considers this is also a problem of communication at the level of the municipalities and the flow of information at the local level (personal communication 2013).

Interestingly, the lack of public support for the park in Slovenia may also be the consequence of the inclusion of the vast majority of the Goričko nature park into the Natura 2000 network, as mentioned by the representative of the Slovenian Ministry of the Agriculture and Environment. He pointed out that due to time pressure during the EU accession the process of designation of Natura 2000 areas in Slovenia lacked public debate, and the residents of the designated areas were not included as stakeholders. This resulted into a wide-spread opposition against Natura 2000 in general (personal communication 2013).

These differences in democratic legitimacy processes do not seem to have much of an impact on the coordination of the three parks so far, perhaps also due to the prevailing mode of informal cooperation across borders. But this may change if a more institutionalised cooperation prevails in the future.

Being adaptive to changing contexts

Despite the fact that the trilateral park is a relatively recent structure, as previously mentioned, it seems to follow a rather stable course of development towards territorial governance of a cross-border natural area. The interviewees mostly confirmed the observation that the economic crisis does not have much of an impact on the trilateral park, which seems to be a sign of adaptability to changing contexts.

Institutional learning through joint projects

Institutional learning can be considered here as a mechanism for the construction of collective knowledge needed for effective coordination of joint projects across borders. One representative of the Őrség national park mentioned that joint projects, in which both the nature park Goričko and the Őrség national park take part, are the most important mechanisms of coordination. They contribute both to strengthening of informal ties between actors on both sides of the border and also to expanding common knowledge (personal communication 2013). Dešnik and Domanjko (2011) explain that there was no previous research conducted on the environmental quality in the Goričko area. Cross-border cooperation enabled the exchange of data as well as knowledge about the area. As an example the project 'Landscape in harmony' was mentioned, funded by the cross-border cooperation programme Slovenia-Hungary, promoting sustainable use of Natura 2000 habitats in Őrség and Goričko. The natural, economic and social potentials of the three Natura 2000 sites were surveyed and the results were recorded in a sustainable land use strategy. In this way the project contributed both to formal knowledge and to individual learning.

Although no common park institution has been formed so far, the three park administrations informally coordinate applications for new joint projects in such a way that builds on the formal knowledge and experiences of previous cross-border projects (personal communications 2013). The lessons learned previously in these projects are then integrated in the identification of new goals for the parks and their implementation, as an important aspect of institutional learning.

Coping with changing contexts

Since different approaches of governing exist in each part of the trilateral nature park, its future is eventually at risk, due to changing political and/ or other conditions. The representative of the Raab nature park in Austria stressed that on the Austrian side the park is considered more of a project than an institution. The association managing the park was founded with a clear mission, which is to give added value to the local communities in terms of tourism and rural development. If the municipalities would cease to recognise the need for the existence of the park, it would be closed down (personal communication 2013). In Hungary and Slovenia, on the other hand, the parks are largely dependent on the decisions made by the national level. The director of the Goričko nature park (personal communication 2013) pointed out that the park still does not have a permanent management plan, because it has been awaiting approval at the national level for several years now. Although any of these aspects can change the structure of the trilateral nature park in the future, any contingency plan or other mechanisms to react on such potential changes are not in place.

Realising place-based/territorial specificities and impacts

The trilateral park is part of the European Green Belt Initiative spanning 13,000 km of land behind the former Iron Curtain, from the Barents Sea in the north to the Adriatic and Black Seas in the south. With the vision of becoming the backbone of an ecological network, the European Green Belt Initiative is a symbol of cross-border cooperation in nature conservation and sustainable development (Strauss and Diehl 2011). However, the defining element of the trilateral park is the national borders, which have divided the area for decades. As the director of the regional development agency noted, it was the parks' peripheral situation in all three countries, which directly or indirectly contributed to the well-preserved natural areas (personal communication 2013). All three border regions faced virtually the same problems: an ageing and under-educated population, small farms with few development prospects in traditional farming, abandoned fields,

200 *Marko Peterlin and Maja Simoneti*

no industries or large infrastructure, long distances from national centres, a high degree of out-commuting and a large number of abandoned houses (Dešnik and Domanjko 2011).

Project-based territorial governance: the role of territorial cooperation

Due to the decentralised leadership model and different governance contexts in which the parks operate, the main challenge of the trilateral park remains its coordination. The capacity to coordinate related issues and projects across borders is thus of crucial importance for the effective territorial governance in the trilateral nature park Goričko-Raab-Őrség. As Dešnik and Domanjko (2011) argue, cross-border cooperation that encompasses all three countries and the possibility to apply for EU funds were important from the very beginning. As verified by all interviewees, through cross-border cooperation the exchange of experiences, place-based knowledge and ideas between actors across borders have been facilitated; trust and social capital have been built up, both at formal and informal levels. Within this specific mode of cross-border governance, a common understanding of the territorial challenges could be developed (personal communications 2013). This was realised by establishing partnerships beyond the managing authorities of all three parks and the municipalities within the three parks, namely through integrating other levels and partners from all relevant sectors (i.e. political and administrative bodies, research institutions, foundations, schools, universities and NGOs) (Dešnik and Domanjko 2011).

In this vein, the two aforementioned authors also point to the importance of territorial cooperation projects for overcoming language and cultural barriers, which were a problem at the beginning. Communication barriers have been overcome by training, especially in English, on the one hand, as well as through regular visits, workshops and assistance received from experts from other countries, on the other.

A few problems were mentioned in relation to territorial cooperation as well. One representative of the Őrség national park mentioned that large differences in the availability of human resources of the park authorities make cooperation with the Raab nature park difficult (personal communication 2013). Another Őrség National Park representative pointed out that cooperation of all three parks was much easier before 2007, when all three parks were still part of one PHARE CBC programme ('the programme of Community aid to the countries of Central and Eastern Europe'). This has later changed when separate cross-border cooperation programmes were formed for bilateral cooperation across borders (personal communication 2013). A representative of the Raab nature park emphasised, however, that cross-border cooperation does not need to be funded by the European Union. Cooperation between Raab and Goričko nature parks is mainly based on informal coordination of their own projects, funded by various other

Nature park Goričko-Raab-Őrség 201

sources, such as national, municipal or private (personal communication 2013). Hence, the human resources needed for coordination and the required territorial knowledge are thus either included in their own projects or funded indirectly by other projects.

Conclusions: a project-based mode of territorial governance

Currently the trilateral park does not function as one entity, but rather as three separate parks. Each park conforms to its own national policy system and governance culture. Key institutions coordinating actions of actors and institutions are park authorities in all three countries, but their roles and competences in relation to the different governance levels, as well as their organisation and capacity differ considerably between the countries. In Austria the park authority is primarily a platform for coordination between local actors and institutions; in Hungary it serves primarily as an authority at the county level, and in Slovenia it is a mixture of both roles.

Similarly, considerable differences between the countries can be observed in relation to cross-sectoral coordination and participatory practices. They both tend to be rather formalised in Hungary, more informal in Austria, and a combination of both in Slovenia. Most pressing conflicts between policy sectors are between nature protection and agriculture, typically at the national level, but they are often felt most drastically at the local level.

Lacking a common cross-border institution, the main challenge of the trilateral park remains its coordinated management. Effective territorial governance of cross-border natural areas relies strongly on the capacity to develop cooperative structures and practices. Connections and trust, needed for cooperation, are mostly the legacy of collaborating through joint projects, either trilateral or bilateral.

Through these cross-border cooperation projects the exchange of experiences, place-based knowledge and ideas between actors across borders are being realised, both at formal and informal levels. A crucial issue seems to be the capacity and flexibility to integrate other actors and institutions and their respective knowledge based on the issue at hand, as well as to cross language, cultural and administrative barriers.

Park administrations also informally coordinate applications for new joint projects in a way to further build up knowledge and experiences gained from previous projects. These are thus integrated in the identification of new goals and their implementation, which is an important aspect of organisational learning, being a central issue in relation to the 'soft' and decentralised leadership model exercised in the trilateral park.

Despite the very slow progress of a more institutionalised cooperation, the lack of a joint management plan and the absence of a trilateral park authority, the trilateral park seems to follow a rather stable course of development towards territorial governance of a trans-border natural area. However, this example of cross-border territorial governance follows almost solely a project-based mode, which bears the risk that once ideas and opportunities for such projects decline, this type of cooperation and coordination across borders might wither away.

In addition one needs to mention here the unequal capacity of the park authorities to carry out territorial cooperation projects, which cause imbalances in the intensity of cooperation between the parks. Together with the strong reliance of the park authorities on national policy these factors may present considerable risks for effective territorial governance across borders in the longer term.

References

CIPRA – International Commission for the Protection of the Alpine Regions, 1992. *Dokumente, Initiativen, Perspektiven: Für eine bessere Zukunft der Alpen*. Vaduz: CIPRA.

Dešnik, S. and Domanjko, G., 2011. Goričko-Raab-Őrség – Developing with Nature in a Trilateral Park. In: M. Vasilijević and T. Pezold, eds. *Crossing Borders for Nature. European Examples of Transboundary Conservation*. Gland, Switzerland: IUCN Programme Office for South-Eastern Europe, 39-41. Available from: https://portals.iucn.org/library/efiles/documents/2011-025.pdf [Accessed 15 November 2014].

Goričko Nature Park, 2005. *Začasne upravljavske smernice v Krajinskem parku Goričko*. Available from: http://www.park-goricko.org/sl/informacija.asp?id_meta_type=59&id_jezik=0&id_language=0&id_informacija=269 [Accessed 15 April 2014].

Kiss, Z. and Szoboszlai, M., 2005. *Public Participation in Settlement Development Procedure in Hungary*. Available from: http://econference.pict.hu/papers/11/Practice_of_public_participation_in_Hungary_v07_English_only.pdf [Accessed 4 March 2015].

Price, M.F., 1999. *Co-operation in the European Mountains 1: The Alps*. Gland, Switzerland: Gland, IUCN Programme Office for South-Eastern Europe. Available from: http://data.iucn.org/dbtw-wpd/edocs/EEP-ER-012.pdf [Accessed 22 January 2013].

Raab Nature Park, Goričko Nature Park and Őrség National Park, 2006. *Partnerstvo o sodelovanju, krepitvi in oblikovanju skupnega razvoja ob tromeji med Madžarsko, Avstrijo in Slovenijo na področju varstva narave, turizma, kulture, izobraževanja in regionalnega razvoja*. Available from: http://www.park-goricko.org/download/1/2006/5/2401_2929_2006_listinaslo.pdf [Accessed 5 January 2015].

Republic of Slovenia, 1999. *Nature Conservation Act*. Official Journal of the Republic of Slovenia, No. 56/99, Available from: http://www.arhiv.mop.gov.si/fileadmin/mop.gov.si/pageuploads/zakonodaja/okolje/en/ohranjanje_narave.pdf [Accessed 22 January 2014].

State Audit Office of Hungary, Court of Audit of Slovenia and Austrian Court of Audit, 2006. *Environmental Audit Report on the Three-border area of Hungary, Slovenia and Austria*, Supreme Audit Institutions of the Republic of Hungary, the Republic of Slovenia and the Republic of Austria. Available from http://www.eurosaiwgea.org/Environmental%20audits/Ecosystems/Documents/2006-

Hungary%20Slovenia%20Austria-Trilateral%20audit.pdf [Accessed 12 January 2015].

Strauss, A. and Diehl, K., 2011. The European Green Belt Initiative – A Retrospective on Crossing Boundaries. In: M. Vasilijević and T. Pezold, eds. *Crossing Borders for Nature. European Examples of Transboundary Conservation*. Gland, Switzerland: IUCN Programme Office for South-Eastern Europe, 8–12. Available from: https://portals.iucn.org/library/efiles/documents/2011-025.pdf [Accessed 15 November 2014].

Unkart, R. and Lausegger, J., 1988. *Arbeitsgemeinschaft Alpen-Adria: Ein Arbeitsbericht*. Millstatt: Provincial Government of Carinthia.

Valentin, H., 2006. *Strategies and Perspectives of the Alps-Adriatic Working Community*. Klagenfurt: General Secretariat of the Alps-Adriatic Working Community.

15 A role for macro-regions
Climate change adaptation in the Baltic Sea Region

Stefanie Lange Scherbenske and Lisa Van Well

Introduction

Adaptation to a changing climate is a territorial governance issue that spans several administrative levels – from the local to the macro-regional and implies the coordination of a range of sectoral interests involving, among others, agriculture, fisheries, integrated coastal zone management, spatial planning and infrastructure, civil preparedness, tourism and water management. In order to align existing policies at different levels, generate knowledge and evidence on possible consequences as well as propose actions and measures, the European Union Strategy for the Baltic Sea Region (EUSBSR), as the first so-called 'macro-regional strategy' within the EU, called for 'a regional adaptation strategy at the level of the Baltic Sea Region' (CEC 2009a, p. 23). The climate change adaptation strategy was expected to 'provide a useful framework for strengthening cooperation and sharing information across the region' (CEC 2009a, p. 23).

Macro-regional strategies represent a still relatively novel approach within the various strands of the EU territorial policy agenda. The EU Strategy for the Baltic Sea Region (adopted in 2009) is the first arrangement of its kind, followed by similar strategies that have been subsequently initiated, including for the Danube Basin (adopted in 2011) and for the Adriatic-Ionian Region (adopted in 2014). A number of other macro-regional strategies are still being debated such as for the North Sea-English Channel Area, Mediterranean Sea and Atlantic Arc, whereas only the EU Strategy for the Alpine Region is currently (status May 2015) under actual preparation.

As a direct response to the summons of the European Union Strategy for the Baltic Sea Region, a project application was submitted to the Baltic Sea Region Programme 2007–2013 with the goal of drafting a climate change adaptation strategy. This transnational cooperation project – Baltadapt – was to work on a national and intergovernmental level and prepare the groundwork for the endorsement of a transnational strategy on climate change adaptation in the Baltic Sea Region. Thus the project intended to set an institutional framework for what policy-makers could consider in developing their climate adaptation strategies and action plans. As a Flagship Project under the European Union Strategy for the Baltic Sea Region running from 2010 to 2013, Baltadapt consisted of 11 partners led by the Danish Meteorological Institute (DMI). The project is also a Lighthouse project under the Council of the Baltic Sea States/Baltic 21 organisation (from now on abbreviated CBSS/ Baltic 21). The initial goals of Baltadapt were to create an umbrella structure for coordinating information on climate change adaptation in the Baltic Sea Region as the 'Baltic Window' hub for decision-makers, to act as a 'knowledge broker' between political decision-makers and research institutions dealing with the question and to embed the project into other existing structures to be able to secure funding without overlapping of institutions (personal communication). As such, the strategy was to: 1) provide goals and visions, 2) clarify links to other strategies and added value in a multi-level governance perspective, 3) identify coordinators and implementers and 4) provide the 'rules of the game' regarding measures to deal with exposure, impact and vulnerabilities to climate change (Baltadapt Third Policy Forum 2013). The Baltadapt project was finalised in 2013 with the publication of the 'Baltadapt Strategy for Adaptation to Climate Change in the Baltic Sea Region' (and an Action Programme). It has prepared the ground for further climate adaptation discussions and actions within the European Union Strategy for the Baltic Sea Region coordination. This chapter chronicles the territorial governance processes around the development of the climate change adaptation strategy at the level of the Baltic Sea 'macro-region' – a process initially coordinated within the Baltadapt project but has continued as a function of the work of the Baltic Sea Region macro-regional cooperation.

Coordinating the actions of actors and institutions: climate adaptation on multi-levels

The call for addressing climate change adaptation at EU level coincided with the efforts towards increasing territorial cohesion by establishing 'macro-regions' within the EU. With regard to climate change adaptation at EU level, both the EU White Paper 'Adapting to Climate Change: Towards a European Framework for Action' (CEC 2009b) and the 'EU Strategy on Adaptation to Climate Change' (CEC, 2013a) proposed improving Europe's resilience to climate change by integrating climate adaptation into all key European policies and enhancing cooperation at all levels of governance. Within these documents, the EU sees its role as a facilitator of coordination and exchange of knowledge among member states in climate adaptation matters (CEC 2009b and CEC 2013a).

As the EU's forerunner 'macro-region' initiated in 2009, the EU Strategy for the Baltic Sea Region is designed to strengthen transnational cooperation among the member states bordering the Baltic Sea. This new and flexible form of territorial management system is linked to the goal of promoting territorial cohesion (Faludi 2010). The strategy provides an Action Plan addressing the priorities Save the Sea, Connect the Region and

206 *Scherbenske and Van Well*

Increase Prosperity (CEC 2013b). The strategy makes no provisions for new institutions, funding instruments or regulations (Dubois *et al.* 2009). Its role is rather as an integrated framework for utilising existing structures, institutions and actions – many of these in the form of projects funded by the 'Baltic Sea Region Programme 2007–2013' and the upcoming programmes. The strategy stresses the need for coordinated joint actions in the Baltic Sea Region on a 'macro-regional' level including discussions with partners external to the process, particularly with Russia (CEC 2009a).

This is facilitated by multi-level governance approaches to implementation, raising awareness and increasing the knowledge base (Baltdapt 2013b). But coordinating these actions within the project was a rather complex undertaking considering the multitude of actors and institutions on all levels which have been involved (First Policy Forum 2012).

Coordination capacity across levels

Project coordination among the Baltadapt actors, both project partners and relevant stakeholders, was addressed through the organisation of meetings, seminars, policy forums and topical workshops. Three policy forums where organised whereby high-level participants from all of the Baltic Sea Region countries were invited to discuss the issues of climate change adaptation. The First Policy Forum in April 2012 in Berlin focused on discussions of what the various stakeholders could expect content-wise from the strategy and how cooperation across administrative levels in each country could be linked. The goals of the Policy Forum were awareness-raising and ensuring high-level political commitment in the region-wide work on climate change adaptation from the transnational to the local level. The Second Policy Forum in December 2012 in Stockholm adopted a more operational focus to understand how a broader range of stakeholders viewed climate change impacts and how they can coordinate their interests. The Second Policy Forum also had the concrete aim of gaining input into the drafting of the strategy. Originally the policy forums were intended as a way to garner support for the strategy from high-level policy- and decision-makers. Although each Policy Forum featured some national and EU-level policy-makers as speakers, it proved to be more difficult than expected to bring them into the workshop discussions as active participants (personal communication 2013). The objective of the policy forums was consequently widened to include many other types of stakeholders from all levels.

Initially there was very little input from the European Commission into the project operation. In their dealings with the Commission, project partners stated that it appeared that two of the concerned Directorates General, for Regional and Urban Policy and for Climate Action, had not previously cooperated around climate change adaptation. Subsequently the Commission followed the project more closely and acknowledged the Baltic Sea Region Climate Change Adaptation Strategy as an important part of the EU Climate adaptation strategy (Third Policy Forum). Thus one of the main goals of the Third Policy Forum in May 2013 in Tallinn was to ensure coherence between the EU-level strategy and the Baltic Sea Region strategy, although it was still unclear how these strategies complemented one another (Glaas and Juhola 2013).

Other transnational and intergovernmental actors were also connected to the project; HELCOM (Helsinki Commission) is a major actor in the Baltic Sea Region and an important stakeholder in the Baltic Sea Region Climate Change Adaptation Strategy, but is not formally involved in the Baltadapt project. HELCOM does not work directly with climate change adaptation issues, as its mandate is intergovernmental work specifically with the marine environment. Nevertheless, many of the issues that Baltadapt dealt with were important HELCOM issues such as biodiversity and fisheries. The Second Policy Forum seemed to unearth some concerns about overlapping responsibilities between HELCOM and the Baltadapt partner, the CBSS/Baltic 21 organisation with regard to the future work on climate change adaptation. However in interviews with both intergovernmental and pan-Baltic actors, each confirmed the desire to work together to bridge the potential areas of conflict by participating in one another's workshops and meetings and striving for 'coherence' in their coordination. Thus the common and very concrete goal of drafting the strategy was a strong uniting element in itself, as well as the chance to make a difference or an impact through the strategy.

Consensual leadership within the project

The leadership roles in the Baltadapt project were dispersed among the partners. The driving forces behind the initiation of the project were the European Commission and the German Federal Ministry for the Environment, Nature Conservation and Nuclear Safety (BMU), although the Danish Meteorological Institute was Lead Partner, according to interviewees, for political reasons. The de facto leadership of the project was diffused among the Work Package Leaders: The Swedish Meteorological and Hydrological Institute (SMHI) was in charge of drafting the strategy. The Ecologic Institute (Subcontractor to BMU) was responsible for the Action Plan, S-Pro, a Berlin-based consulting company for the administration, and CBSS/Baltic 21 for the workshops and policy forums. All formal decisions were taken by the Steering Group consisting of the Work Package Leaders. Interviewees noted that the Swedish team, spearheaded by the Swedish Meteorological and Hydrological Institute (assisted by the University of Linköping) and CBSS/Baltic 21 (an intergovernmental organisation, but located in Stockholm), informally set the tone of the project in their involvement in the strategy and organisation of the workshops and policy forums. This also brought the planning and political aspects of climate adaptation into the discussions and encouraged other partners to think more territorially and strategically. Project partners also seemed to base their decisions on a strong culture of consensus.

Integrating policy sectors

The principles related to climate change adaptation in the BSR mirror aspects of the Europe 2020 Strategy. Adaptation measures in the Baltic Sea Region need to be 'smart' in terms of coordinating actions within sectors integrated through EU policies and the single market; 'sustainable' in the sense of protecting the Baltic Sea as a common resource; as well as 'inclusive' to ensure solidarity for the most exposed and vulnerable territories to increase their adaptive capacity (Baltadapt Third Policy Forum 2013). The macro-regional strategy itself influenced which policy sectors were to be integrated in the climate change adaptation strategy. With its focus on three objectives: (1) Save the Sea, (2) Connect the Region, and (3) Increase Prosperity, the European Union Strategy for the Baltic Sea Region implicitly intersects with a range of climate change issues. The initial Action Plan of the strategy suggested five 'Horizontal Actions': 1) Spatial planning, 2) Cooperating with neighbours, 3) Boosting joint promotion and regional identity, 4) Multi-level governance, and 5) Sustainable development and bioeconomy (CEC 2013b).

A real challenge of the Baltadapt project was to find a 'home' where the strategy could 'reside' in order for the output to transcend the project-level. In February 2013 CBSS/Baltic21 became one of the Horizontal Action Leaders for 'Sustainable development and bioeconomy' in the Action Plan of the European Union Strategy for the Baltic Sea Region. Thereby CBSS/Baltic21 received a mandate from the EU to work with the Baltic Sea Region Climate Change Adaptation Strategy within the Horizontal Action under the broad heading of sustainable development and bioeconomy including three sub-actions, 1) climate change mitigation, 2) climate change adaptation and 3) bioeconomy (CEC 2013b). CBSS/Baltic21 saw itself as very well-placed to be the Horizontal Action Leader of the climate change adaptation sub-action as it represents high-level politicians in all the Baltic Sea Region countries. The Swedish Meteorological and Hydrological Institute is often brought in as expert help in order to ensure that the more technical aspects of climate change adaptation are covered.

In June 2015 the Action Plan was revised and the Horizonal Actions were consolidated to 1) Spatial Planning, 2) Neighbours, 3) Capacity, and 4) Climate. CBSS/Baltic 21 became responsible for the Horizontal Action 'Climate' which links both climate change mitigation and adaptation. The Climate Adaptation Strategy for the Baltic Sea Region as the result of the Baltadapt project has prepared the way for defining the working agenda and the stakeholders involved in this 'new' Horizontal Action.

Policy packaging and focus sectors

Within the Baltadapt project, four focus sectors were chosen for impact assessments: 1) marine biodiversity and habitats, 2) food supply – fishery and agriculture, 3) coastal infrastructure and 4) coastal tourism. In the beginning

A role for macro-regions 209

there was some deliberation around a broader selection of sectors which could be represented in the strategy. In the end the selected sectors within Baltadapt, were those which represented the interests and competencies of the Baltadapt partners. Interviews with project leaders revealed that partners were aware that in choosing the main topics as the basis for the strategy meant explicitly omitting other topics and that this would have ramifications on the sectoral scope of the project.

However much of the work within Baltadapt appeared to be dominated by a clear environmental rationale, largely due to the natural science expertise of many of the partners (personal communication 2013). Partners entered the project with very different expectations as to what would be achieved. The social science or socio-economic aspects of climate change adaptation were only tacitly considered at the beginning of the project. This is perhaps representative of how climate change adaptation is often framed as an 'environmental' issue at odds with economic and social development pathways (Wise *et al.* 2014). One interviewee, however, tempered this observation by saying that each of the four chosen focus sectors deal implicitly with important resource and economic opportunities as well. Nevertheless, the initial stages of the project were marked by dissent on how to bring the various sectors together into one strategic 'package'. Two interviewees alluded to the informal leadership of certain individuals in the project who helped to broaden the focus to get partners to think outside of their 'sectoral silos' with a more 'territorial' focus.

Overcoming barriers to cross-sectoral synergies

Cross-sectoral synergies were realised and evolved as the Baltadapt project progressed. One of the barriers to cross-sectoral integration was that some of the focus sectors in the BSR (such as agriculture or tourism) are thought to have experienced some positive impacts of climate change while other sectors (like fisheries) conceived of climate change as a disturbance to current patterns of resource use. Each topic appears to have established its own 'network' in which climate change adaptation issues were dealt with in respective 'sectoral languages'. During the Second Policy Forum, partners concluded that one way to overcome this 'silo mentality' was to deliberate in terms of issues or problem areas, rather than the sectors or topics (Second Policy Forum 2012). Time pressure to complete the draft of the strategy by September 2013 proved to be a very strong incentive to be open to different ways of linking topics and sectors.

One of the early barriers to cross-sectoral integration was that the territorial scope of the project was under dispute for much of the project life. The Baltadapt project focused mainly on the marine environment ('the Baltic Sea itself') and the coastal areas, but discussions ran from broadening the territorial scope of the climate change adaptation strategy to entire macro-regional territory. This has had far-reaching ramifications for topics

210 Scherbenske and Van Well

or focus sectors which would be included, as well as the actors that would be responsible for the strategy after the completion of the project.

As discussed previously, the climate change adaptation strategy was established as part of one of the Horizontal Actions (previously 'Sustainable development and bioeconomy') of the European Union Strategy for the Baltic Sea Region, which further provides status for the issue as a cross-cutting priority. At the transnational level, there have already been some attempts to create links with other Horizontal Actions specifically the two for multi-level governance and for spatial planning (Third Policy Forum 2013). At the local and regional level the various sectors involved in climate change adaptation are being integrated through personal contacts and close relationships between sectoral actors at local level (personal communications 2012) in light of achieving a specific goal or output. Yet pending a common agreement on the challenge or 'problem' to be solved, cross-sectoral work becomes challenging.

Mobilising stakeholder participation

Stakeholder involvement in formulating the macro-regional strategy

The involvement of stakeholders from all levels and relevant sectors (including business interests and NGOs) is considered to be an essential element of any climate change adaptation strategy and its subsequent implementation (CEC 2013a). Baltadapt partners identified relevant stakeholders on the basis of their networks and employed the snowball-method of gaining further contacts to interested parties in the Baltic Sea Region (including Russia). These contacts were invited to join the three policy forums organised by CBSS/Baltic21. In addition to the policy forums, thematic workshops on agriculture and tourism were organised for stakeholders at regional and local levels. While the project provided for some modest funding of stakeholder participation, many relevant stakeholders were excluded due to the lack of resources, the necessity to travel to a different country, and language barriers. For instance not a single farmer was present at the workshop on agriculture, although the agricultural union representatives from several countries participated. It proved notoriously difficult to attract small enterprises since the costs of participation, in terms of time and money, were prohibitive. To deal with this situation the project was forced to re-allocate some of the budget to finance the participation of certain local/regional level stakeholders. Stakeholders representing the national level authorities were also seen as key stakeholders but their participation was not as extensive as anticipated (personal communications 2013). While relevant stakeholders were informed about the process of how their opinions, comments and ideas would be taken into account, there were a number of unresolved questions concerning the structure, content, geographic scope and legitimacy of the strategy as well as relation to the EU adaptation strategy and national strategies.

Making the strategy relevant 'on the ground'

Climate change adaptation measures are generally performed 'on the ground' at local and regional level, but must be aligned to the existing legal frameworks and national norms of each country (Andersson *et al.* 2015). Several national and regional representatives remarked that a climate change adaptation plan at the level of the Baltic Sea Region would not necessarily aid them with their local climate adaptation work (personal communications 2012). One respondent from a Danish municipality with a strong track record of citizen involvement in preparing a climate adaptation strategy said:

> In the immediate future, a BSR strategy would not mean that we would prepare our climate adaptation plan any differently than we are now, which is in accordance with the national guidelines and norms.
>
> (personal communication 2013)

The few local stakeholders involved in the Baltadapt process remained sceptical about the accountability and utility of a macro-regional climate change adaptation strategy at local levels. It was seen to have very little impact on how they would actually implement climate adaptation measures (personal communication 2012). Baltadapt project partners understood this concern, but maintained that the potential added value of the Baltic Sea Region adaptation strategy was the provision of a framework to facilitate transnational or cross-border cooperation on adaptation to climate change and as a forum for exchanging experiences about local/regional adaptation.

Towards political endorsement

The Baltadapt project formally ended in autumn 2013 with the final conference 'Adaptation to Climate Change in the Baltic Sea Region'. During the conference, the Baltic Sea Region Climate Change Adaptation Strategy and its accompanying Action Plan were presented to policy-makers representing all levels, scientists and other stakeholders dealing with climate change adaptation in the Baltic Sea Region and beyond. In 2014 the 'Baltic Sea Region Climate Change Dialogue Platform' was established under the chairmanship of CBSS/Baltic 21. Since then, four 'CBSS/Baltic 21 – Round tables on Climate Change Adaptation in the Baltic Sea Region' have taken place involving experts from the CBSS member states, national ministries or agencies responsible for climate change (adaptation), representatives from the European Commission and the CBSS/Baltic 21 Secretariat. The platform

212   *Scherbenske and Van Well*

aims to contribute to the implementation of the Council of the Baltic Sea States decisions as well as the EU climate policies and promote cooperation in the area of climate change adaptation, inform policy development, catalyse exchange of information and/or best practices, foster synergies among existing initiatives, explore further cooperation opportunities and contribute to the identification and development of concrete joint initiatives and/or activities (CBSS/Baltic 21 2014, p. 2).

Additionally a CBSS/Baltic21 Pan-Baltic round table on Climate Change was organised in May 2014 for discussions on 'how to address climate change in the Baltic Sea Region in a more coherent and effective manner' and with a focus on pan-Baltic organisations as target group. These meetings function as a platform for the continuous exchange and cooperation of information concerning the state of play in adaptation work on local, regional and national levels, as well as EU policies, potential future activities, projects and funding opportunities.

Being adaptive to changing contexts

Transnational learning on climate change adaptation

Transnational learning within the territorial cooperation projects has been conceptualised as a two-pronged process – ensuring that individual learning becomes institutionalised, and facilitating the transferability of experiences across national borders (Lange Scherbenske and Van Well 2015, forthcoming). In developing the climate change adaptation strategy, individual learning was promoted within the workshops and policy forums. But different challenges and local circumstances (territorial specificities) can be barriers to institutional learning (Lange *et al.* 2012), as the local and regional contexts differ in terms of climate change vulnerabilities, risks and governance arrangements. Individual learning within the Baltadapt project gradually became institutionalised as partners tried methods or approaches developed by the project or as they sought out expert knowledge from each other (personal communications 2013).

During the development of the Baltic Sea Region Climate Change Adaptation Strategy, public authorities, municipalities and regional actors, as well as universities and research institutes, have learned about and transferred 'tools' for dealing with climate change in various contexts. One interviewee stated that methods such as ways of procuring stakeholders' involvement have even been transferred to other institutions at other levels. The Baltadapt project itself has been reflexive of its own governance process through self-evaluations and gathering participant evaluation feedback.

Discussions with interviewees revealed that while the Baltadapt project had ambitions to be a 'knowledge broker' to collect and coordinate studies, scenarios and experiences on climate change adaptation in the BSR, not much learning was gleaned from other transnational or cross-border cooperation projects on climate change adaptation projects, studies and processes with similar elements/features. Since the finalisation of the strategy, it sees its role as a conduit for providing a forum for exchange and learning (Baltadapt 2013b), as one of its main added value aspects.

Adapting to a large, new and 'soft' type of region

Climate change adaptation as such is an ever changing issue as new knowledge on climate impacts, scenarios, models and services is constantly becoming available (EEA 2015). But the topic also implies a certain amount of risk and uncertainty for decision-makers in trying to make sense of the influx of data, scenarios, and forecasts for both today's and tomorrow's climate. At the same time most countries in the BSR have a comparably high adaptation capacity as they enjoy a relatively high standard of territorial development seen from a global or European perspective (EEA 2014).

The act of developing a climate change adaptation strategy for the entire Baltic Sea Region, however, is conditional on adapting to a relatively unknown type of territory. Macro-regions are a fairly new phenomenon in Europe, with the Baltic Sea Region being the pioneer macro-region. While forms of territorial cooperation around the Baltic Sea have been on-going for many years (Sterling 2008, for instance, counts around 40 active pan-Baltic organisations) the European Union Strategy for the Baltic Sea Region brings with it new challenges; mainly working within a 'soft' territory that demands no new institutions, no new regulations and no new funding (Metzger and Schmitt 2012). The actions for climate change adaptation thus need to be coordinated within existing institutions, programmes and projects. The different national governmental contexts and power structures for Baltic Sea states are also factors in the success or failure of the strategy's implementation. National and local authorities do not always have much scope for experimentation or room for manoeuvre within the framework of rules, regulations and norms aiming at goals such as coastal protection (personal communication 2013). Unencumbered as such by the need to implement 'hard' measures within a constrained policy environment, transnational actors may experience more flexibility and can contribute with new perspectives on how to mainstream adaptation into other relevant policies.

Considering the nature of the BSR as an informal grouping of sovereign states (albeit with a long history of cooperation) and as a very large geographical territory, makes the development of the climate change adaptation strategy unwieldy. It is often difficult to integrate sectors, actors, stakeholders and knowledge for such a diverse territory. This is perhaps why the sectoral approach seems to persist. This is also the way that one of the important project stakeholders, HELCOM, approaches climate change. HELCOM does not have a specific strategy or policy for climate change adaptation, but rather looks at how policies need to be adaptive to the changing contexts that climate change brings about (personal communication 2013).

214 Scherbenske and Van Well

Experimentation and flexibility

In developing the climate change adaptation strategy for the Baltic Sea Region there was little guidance from the European Commission and not very concrete expectations of what the strategy should look like. Therefore Baltadapt project leaders were able to try out new ideas. As the strategy would not be binding in character, there was some room for experimentation. Due to the lack of a firm framework, it was not entirely clear to project leaders to whom the strategy should be addressed, which territory it should cover and what would happen to the strategy after the end of the Baltadapt project (personal communications 2013). The finalised strategy addresses a rather broad target group in the sense that 'implementers represent members of governance at all spatial levels (local, regional, national, macro-regional), including also the private and the research communities' (Baltadapt 2013b, p. 36). As the strategy quotes:

> Although the Baltadapt project has had a focus on the Baltic Sea water body and its coastal zones, the proposed BSR-wide Climate Adaptation Strategy is recommended to cover other (land-based) relevant issues within the whole BSR.
>
> (Baltadapt 2013b, p. 8)

Any barriers to flexibility within the project came from the sectoral interests and 'silo mentality' of the stakeholders involved in Baltadapt (personal communication 2013).

Realising territorial specificities and impacts

Territorial relationality and disputed territorial scope

All Baltic Sea Region countries will be affected to some degree by the impacts of climate change. Localities and regions throughout the Baltic Sea Region face common challenges that come with climate change (e.g. flood risk) whereas specific impacts are affected by local circumstances such as geography, surface structure, land use, and instigated protection measures. Yet considering that the Baltic Sea itself represents a common and shared ecosystem, all states bordering the sea have a stake in ensuring that it retains its viable environmental, social and economic capital. Within the member states, 'hard' administrative borders define the local and regional areas of intervention in which public authorities implement respective policies and laws within their jurisdictions. Interviews with project partners confirmed that the 'governmental perspective' (see also Chapters 2 and 3) can be considered a barrier to territorial governance as these jurisdictional boundaries could hamper individual and institutional learning and cross-border and transnational cooperation. As discussed earlier, the territorial scope of the Baltadapt project itself was originally disputed. The Baltadapt project initially focused only on the marine environment ('the Baltic Sea itself') and the coastal areas, while the climate change adaptation strategy for the Baltic Sea Region was to focus on the entire macro-regional area. Within the project there was no agreement on what constituted a 'coastal area', whether it was 200 metres inland from the sea, two kilometres inland or 200 kilometres inland. This had a strong impact on the extent to which certain sectors (such as agriculture or biodiversity) would be covered by the strategy. The Baltadapt project was able to define its own geographic and functional scope as an example of a 'soft' territorial grouping alongside administrative boundaries. In the end, the geographic scope of the strategy was partly defined by the four focus sectors of the project (marine biodiversity and habitats, food supply – fisheries and agriculture, coastal infrastructure and coastal tourism). An integrated territorial dimension was only tacitly considered in the project due to the strong sectoral focus of the partners and experts involved in the process (personal communications 2013). The uncertainty about 'who' the strategy was actually addressed to was also a barrier to realising the territorial or place-based approach (personal communication 2013).

Territorial knowledge on climate change adaptation

Climate change impacts occur locally or regionally and can be rather specific to one locality or region. Within the Baltic Sea Region there are very different geologies and different levels of exposure to the impacts of sea level rise, extreme weather and natural disaster risk. A common climate change adaptation strategy for the Baltic Sea Region needs to take this into account. But policy interventions to address climate change adaptation are taken and implemented locally/regionally and deal very clearly with place-based specificities, threats and vulnerabilities. Thus the question is how much sense does a macro-regional climate change adaptation strategy make? Is it only contributing to an additional level of complexity? A distinction could be made between regulative policy and normative policy, whereby the strategy has a normative and inspirational character, providing the impetus to action when needed and a forum in which local experiences and knowledge could be exchanged and transferred (Van Well and Lange Scherbenske 2014). The added value of the macro-regional strategy could thus be seen in its normative function.

In terms of knowledge gathering for the strategy, the Baltadapt project attempted to avoid 'knowledge overlaps' by coordinating the myriad of technical and institutional knowledge, processes and tools that were already in place and surveying existing strategies and policies. The Baltadapt project was only able to start this process, which is now in the hands of the Horizontal Action for Climate. One of the concrete tools developed in connection with the project, was the 'Baltic Window' portal to provide 'one-stop-shop' information on climate change adaptation in the Baltic Sea Region, including

216 *Scherbenske and Van Well*

the relevant policy frameworks, impacts, vulnerability studies and a range of adaptation actions. This has been made available for the general public, but is focused on being a hub for decision-makers from transnational to local level. As such it was a pilot 'macro-region' element as part of the EU's adaptation portal Climate Adapt (Third Policy Forum 2013).

Conclusions

The Baltic Sea Region is often seen as forerunner region when it comes to macro-regional cooperation in general (Metzger and Schmitt 2012) and local and regional climate change adaptation in particular (Baltadapt 2013a), but it is not expected that a macro-regional strategy will have much influence on climate change adaptation work at local and regional level or the national level (personal communications 2013). The main problem is that there is still a gap between what is happening at the macro-regional and strategy level and concrete actions at the local level. This is very much a territorial issue and one of the goals is to employ the strategy not as a regulation ('governance of territories'), but as a normative tool to spur on climate adaptation actions and measures.

The process of developing a climate change adaptation strategy for the Baltic Sea Region was characterised by (informal) governance and consensus. While there is an EU Climate Change Adaptation Strategy for all member states and there are National Adaptation Strategies adopted by a number of Baltic Sea Region countries, they do not seem to play an important role in developing the macro-regional strategy. The strategy rather builds upon consensus between project partners who cooperate transnationally and partly cross-sectorally. The Horizontal Action for Climate under the guidance of CBSS/Baltic 21 is the outcome of a consensus between different member states and institutions who will further develop the strategy towards possible adoption.

The expected utility of the macro-regional climate change adaptation strategy for the Baltic Sea Region lies in the process of bringing together relevant stakeholders, and networks of experts. Its role can include helping to raise awareness about climate adaptation (personal communication 2013). The strategy can also be seen as a justification for action at the local and regional level when there is little support from the national level.

In the end, the elaboration and adoption of a climate change adaptation strategy at the level of the BSR is still a pioneering effort, but there are possibilities for transfer of lessons to other transnational cooperation strategies or to other 'macro-regions'. A number of experts emphasised the efforts of the Baltic Sea Region as 'forerunner' and 'model' in terms of regional climate change adaptation and this may give weight to the potential impact of the macro-regional climate change adaptation strategy.

References

Andersson L., Bohman A., van Well L., Jonsson A., Persson G. and Farelius J., 2015. *Underlag till kontrollstation 2015 för anpassning till ett förändrat klimat*. SMHI Klimatologi Nr 12, Norrköping: SMHI.

Baltadapt, 2013a. *Baltadapt Action Plan. Recommended actions and proposed guidelines for climate change adaptation in the Baltic Sea Region*. Available from: http://www.baltadapt.eu/index.php?option=com_content&view=article&id=94&Itemid=225 [Accessed 26 March 2015].

Baltadapt, 2013b. *Baltadapt Strategy for adaptation to climate change in the Baltic Sea Region*. Available from: http://www.baltadapt.eu/index.php?option=com_content&view=article&id=93&Itemid=224 [Accessed 26 March 2015].

CBSS/Baltic 21 – Council of the Baltic Sea States/Baltic 21), 2014. *Non-paper on a Future Framework for Cooperation in Climate Change Adaptation in the Baltic Sea Region, Draft 17th April 2014*. Internal working document.

CEC – Commission of the European Communities, 2007. *Green Paper from the Commission to the Council on Adapting to Climate Change in Europe – Pptions for EU Action*. Available from: http://eur-lex.europa.eu/legal-content/EN/TXT/PDF/?uri=CELEX:52007DC0354&from=EN [Accessed 20 February 2015].

CEC – Commission of the European Communities, 2009a. *European Union Strategy for the Baltic Sea Region – Action Plan*. Brussels: Commission of the European Communities.

CEC – Commission of the European Communities, 2009b. *White Paper – Adapting to Climate Change: Towards a European Framework for Action*. Available from: http://eur-lex.europa.eu/legal-content/EN/TXT/PDF/?uri=CELEX:52009DC0147&from=EN [Accessed 20 February 2015].

CEC – Commission of the European Communities, 2013a. *An EU Strategy on Adaptation to Climate Change*. Available from: http://ec.europa.eu/clima/publications/docs/eu_strategy_en.pdf, COM/2013/0216 final [Accessed 20 February 2015].

CEC – Commission of the European Communities, 2013b, *European Union Strategy for the Baltic Sea Region – Action Plan*. Available from: http://www.balticsea-region-strategy.eu/component/edocman/13-eusbsr-action-plan [Accessed 20 February 2015].

Dubois, A., Hedin, S., Schmitt, P., Sterling, J., 2009. *EU Macro-regions and Macro-regional Strategies: A Scoping Study*. Working Paper 2009:4, Stockholm: Nordregio.

EEA – European Environmental Agency, 2014. *National Adaptation Policy Processes in European Countries – 2014*. European Environmental Agency Report no. 4/2014, Available from: http://www.eea.europa.eu/publications/national-adaptation-policy-processes [Accessed 23 April 2015].

EEA – European Environmental Agency, 2015. *Overview of Climate Change Adaptation Platforms in Europe*. Technical report No 5/2015. Available from: http://www.eea.europa.eu/publications/overview-of-climate-change-adaptation [Accessed 28 May 2015].

Faludi, A., 2010. Centenary Paper: European Spatial Planning; Past, Present and Future. *Town Planning Review*, 81 (1), 1–22.

Glaas, E. and Juhola, S., 2013. New Levels of Climate Adaptation Policy: Analyzing the Institutional Interplay in the Baltic Sea Region. *Sustainability*, 5 (1), 256–275.

Lange Scherbenske, S., Van Well, L. and Tepecik, D.A., 2012. Transnational Cooperation on Climate Change Adaptation and Policy Implications. In: P. Schmidt-Thomé and J. Klein, eds. *BALTCICA: Climate Change Impacts, Costs and Adaptation in the Baltic Sea Region*. BaltCICA Final Report, 3–9. Available at: http://www.baltcica.org/documents/BaltCICA_Final_Report_Version_1_080512.pdf [Accessed 30 May 2015].

Lange Scherbenske, S. and Van Well, L., 2015, forthcoming. Transnational learning for climate change adaptation in the Baltic Sea Region. In: J. Knieling. *Climate Adaptation Governance – Theory, Concepts and Praxis in Cities and Regions*. Chichester: John Wiley & Sons Inc.

Metzger, J. and Schmitt P., 2012. When Soft Spaces Harden: The EU Strategy for the Baltic Sea Region. *Environment and Planning A,* 44 (2), 263–280.

Sterling J., 2008. The Baltic Sea Region Organisations. *Journal of Nordregio,* 1, 30–32.

Van Well L. and Lange Scherbenske, S., 2014. Towards a Macroregional Climate Change Adaptation Strategy in the Baltic Sea Region. *Environment and Planning C: Government and Policy,* 32(6), 1100–1116.

Wise, R.M., Fazey, I., Stafford Smith, M., Park, S.E., Eakin, H.C., Archer Van Garderen, E.R.M., Campbell, B., 2014. Reconceptualising Adaptation to Climate Change as Part of Pathways of Change and Response. *Global Environmental Change*, 28, 325–336.

First Policy Forum, 2012. *First Baltadapt Policy Forum on Climate Change Adaptation in the Baltic Sea Region*. 24 April 2012, Berlin, Germany. Available from: http://www.baltadapt.eu/index.php [Accessed 12 March 2015].

Second Policy Forum, 2012. *Second Baltadapt Policy Forum on Climate Change Adaptation in the Baltic Sea Region*. 10–11 December 2012, Stockholm, Sweden. Available from: http://www.baltadapt.eu/index.php [Accessed 12 March 2015].

Third Policy Forum, 2013. *Third Baltadapt Policy Forum on Climate Change Adaptation in the Baltic Sea Region*. 29–30 May 2013, Tallinn, Estonia. Available from: http://www.baltadapt.eu/index.php [Accessed 12 March 2015].

Part III

Prospects on territorial governance across Europe

16 Revisiting territorial governance
Twenty empirically informed components

Peter Schmitt and Lisa Van Well

Introduction

Each of the ten cases discussed in Part II have illustrated a number of different features of territorial governance at play. They include innovative practices for achieving novel results, or how certain barriers have (or have not) been overcome. These 'features', as mentioned in Chapter 5, have a more 'normative' function indicating some lessons for designing territorial governance and offer opportunities for the transferability of 'good territorial governance' (cf. Chapter 17).

In addition the ten case studies have provided a number of observations about the 'building blocks' of territorial governance. These have been called 'components of territorial governance'. These components were distilled by extracting the essence of each case study in terms of the observed practices, routines, but also mechanisms and structures of territorial governance along the five dimensions. In this light they are representative of the patterns and process-oriented facets of territorial governance and enable us to reflect on the concept of territorial governance in this volume (cf. Chapters 1, 4 and 5) from the vantage point of the empirical evidence provided by the case studies.

After presenting and discussing the distilled components we critically re-visit the five dimensions of territorial governance as the backbone and research framework of this book (see also Figure 5.2). In doing so, the interplay between the dimensions will be discussed as well as how our results inform the relationship between our conceptualisation of territorial governance and the prevailing notions of multi-level governance in the literature.

In the final section we argue that our framework offers various entry points from which to understand the main characteristics of territorial governance and thus adds clarity to the debate on 'what territorial governance is'. However based on our empirical and conceptual findings, our framework also offers a more practical access for doing territorial governance, in the form of checkpoints to help practitioners and policy-makers at any level in working with territorial governance.

Dimension 1: Coordinating actions of actors and institutions
1) Distributing power across levels
2) Distinguishing modes of leadership
3) Structures of coordination
4) Dealing with constraints to coordination
Dimension 2: Integrating policy sectors
5) Structural context for sectoral integration
6) Achieving synergies across sectors
7) Acknowledging sectoral conflicts
8) Dealing with sectoral conflicts
Dimension 3: Mobilising Stakeholder participation
9) Identification of stakeholders
10) Securing of democratic legitimacy and accountability
11) Integration of interests/viewpoints
12) Insights into territorial governance processes
Dimension 4: Being adaptive to changing contexts
13) Institutional learning.
14) Individual learning and reflection
15) Evidence of forward-looking actions
16) Scope of flexibility/experimentation
Dimension 5: Realising place-based/territorial specificities and impacts
17) Criteria/logic of defining intervention area
18) Coping with hard and soft/functional spaces
19) Utilisation of territorial (expert) knowledge
20) Integration of territorial analysis

Figure 16.1 The 20 components of territorial governance

Source: Own adaptation based on ESPON and Nordregio (2013, p. 28)

Re-conceptualising territorial governance I: '20 components' as empirically-informed facets of territorial governance across Europe'

In total, 20 components have been extracted from the case study observations (cf. Figure 16.1 and Van Well and Schmitt 2015, forthcoming). They structure the empirically-based synthesis of territorial governance at play across Europe, which will be presented and discussed in the following section. Below we present these components with reference to the relevant cases from which the components were observed.

Dimension 1: coordinating actions of actors and institutions

Distributing power across levels

The cases demonstrate that power relationships are seldom symmetrical in any territorial governance situation, particularly those involving several administrative levels of government or governance. There is a distinction between distribution of formal power (governmental rights and responsibilities) and informal power (structures and processes for influencing the decision-making process outside of statutory mandates). Transnational or cross-border actors tend to exercise informal power, rather than formal power (see 'Trilateral nature park' and 'Baltic Sea Region'). In most of the cases, particularly local and intra-regional ones, actors exhibited power relations that were a mixture of both. Territorial specificities may also dictate power relations; for instance in questions of water governance, an 'upstream' territory may have more muscle to influence governance processes than a 'downstream' territory (see 'Rhine river basin'). In an intra-regional or intra-municipal setting, the largest city generally has a greater chance of dictating the agenda than does a smaller settlement in the area (see 'South Loire Plan' and 'Manchester').

Distinguishing modes of leadership

In terms of transparency and acceptance, clear leadership appears to be a characteristic in the more successful cases of achieving a specific territorial development goal. This was so regardless of whether the leadership was formal, informal or even fluctuating. In the same vein, clear leadership appeared to be a contributing factor to the success of other dimensions of territorial governance, in particular cross-sectoral integration. Regarding those cases in which 'softer spaces' were addressed, consensus among actors characterised the main mode of decision-making (see 'Southern Randstad' and 'Baltic Sea Region'). On the flip side, those cases which failed to achieve the targeted development goals were marked by leadership which was unclear, contested (see e.g. Stockholm) or shifting between different actors and policy levels (see 'European Capital of Culture – Pécs' and 'Hungarian Structural Fund management').

Structures of coordination

The most common tool for coordinating actors and institutions at all levels was by organising forums (e.g. conferences and workshops) where actors on all levels and sectors could meet and discuss the actions that they are currently taking for the territorial goal at hand. These forums could be institutionalised as part of a project (see 'Stockholm' and 'Trilateral Nature Park') or within administrative structure (see 'South Loire Plan' and 'Manchester') or organised on a more *ad hoc* basis (see 'Southern Randstad'). However the various forums were not organised solely to coordinate actors and institutions, but had the additional goals to extend the current knowledge base, identify technical solutions (see 'Stockholm') or explore various courses of action (see 'Hyper-local planning in England' and 'Baltic Sea Region'). In the organisation of forums there is always the risk that relevant stakeholders may be neglected or forgotten, or that only those with sufficient financial, capacity, or power resources are able to participate (see 'European Capital of Culture – Pécs' and 'Hungarian Structural Fund management').

Dealing with constraints to coordination

The constraints to coordination largely centre on the lack of tools and methods to achieve governance on multi-levels. While many actors have the desire to work up and down levels, they may have few ideas about how to do this. Several constraints to coordination were of an ad hoc character (see 'European Capital of Culture – Pécs'). Others were diverging interests on the territorial development goal (e.g. due to political differences, see 'South Loire Plan') or diffuse or dissimilar objectives (see 'Stockholm'). However several enabling elements in the coordination of actors can be distinguished. These include previous cooperation among actors (see 'Manchester'), specific inter-municipal arrangements that help to scale-up regional issues to the attention of the national government (see 'Southern Randstad'), the adoption of a new, but politically well-embedded key actor (see 'Rhine river basin') or the desire to create and maintain a certain image to be presented to the outside world (see 'Stockholm').

Dimension 2: integrating policy sectors

Structural context for sectoral integration

The structural context for sectoral integration is especially evident with regard to those case studies that cover 'softer' territories whereby a regional, transnational or cross-border strategy or agreement forms the basis for cooperation among entities (see 'Southern Randstad', 'Rhine river basin' and 'Baltic Sea Region'). At the national or sub-national level, cross-sectoral integration is generally nested within the governmental/ administrative level that is responsible for planning processes. Here, as the case of 'Stockholm' shows, the 'silo effect' between different departments within the city's urban planning and development apparatus is a robust structural construct that makes cross-sectoral integration difficult. In general, the softer functional territories address cross-sectoral integration more explicitly than do the 'harder' spaces, since the softer ones often have a non-binding mandate which allows them to be more experimental in their approaches to sectoral integration.

Achieving synergies across sectors

The processes for achieving synergies across sectors varied. In one case these were mainly conducted through established channels and regulations, such as statutory planning processes and relating legal frameworks (see 'South Loire

Plan'). In other cases, working concretely for synergies often occurred through dialogue among networks or partnerships associated with the drafting of programmes or strategies among trans-regional, transnational or cross-border actors (see 'Baltic Sea Region' and 'Rhine river basin'). In cases where regional, municipal or local governance issues were addressed, synergies were facilitated by formal and informal structures (see 'Southern Randstad' and 'Manchester') to promote public-private partnerships and to gain a mutual understanding of common interest (see 'Stockholm' and 'Hyper-local planning in England'). Especially in transnational or cross-border cases, initial attempts to address synergies across sectors was achieved by exploiting windows of opportunities that gave the impetus for further exploration of issue areas and sectoral interaction (see 'Rhine river basin' and 'Trilateral Nature Park').

Acknowledging sectoral conflicts

The nature of each sectoral conflict was coloured by various economic, social and environmental interests. The specific types of conflicts spanned economic-environmental dichotomies, transport and spatial planning, water management as well as mobility and housing. In general the dominating sectors were those with a harder economic profile, such as construction development or tourism (see 'Stockholm' and 'Hyper-local planning in England') at the expense of softer goals such as culture or environment (see 'South Lore Plan' and 'European Capital of Culture – Pécs'). One exception is the 'Baltic Sea Region' case which was rather steered by an environmental rationale, largely due to the natural science expertise of the involved actors. In addition, there were also tensions between short-term political goals and longer-term territorial or sectoral goals (see 'European Capital of Culture – Pécs'). Tensions also became apparent with regard to the 'territorial aspects and specificities' that appeared to be side-lined by the dominance of purely sectoral thinking and when sectoral interests were omitted in favour of other political interests, as observed in the case of 'Hungarian Structural Fund Management'.

Dealing with sectoral conflicts

Cases presented several ways for dealing with conflicts among various sectors, even if some conflicts were not necessarily solvable. One way was in gathering information or knowledge about the sectors at hand, particularly those sectors that were not the dominant ones within the case. This was addressed through forums where actors with sectoral interests were requested to report on interests and positions (see 'South Loire Plan'). Another way to overcome the 'silo mentality' was to discuss in terms of issues or problem areas, rather than the sectors or topics (see 'Baltic Sea Region'). A third way was in the established traditions of cooperation and relational dialogue to overcome differences, and in informal discussions among local actors to create a win-win

226 *Peter Schmitt and Lisa Van Well*

situation (see 'Trilateral Nature Park'). Actors from various sectors often come from disparate professional and/or administrative cultures and sometimes spoke very different 'languages', which can give rise to misunderstandings or conflicts. Engaging in structured discussion was a method used to understand one another (see 'Trilateral Nature Park'). In addition, boosting institutional capacity of administrative units was seen as a way to deal more effectively and equitably with conflicting inter-sectoral interests (see 'Manchester'). Finally, greater decentralisation of powers to lower levels was also suggested as a way to increase the capacity of the localities to mobilise resources for addressing conflicts between sectors (see 'Hyper-local planning in England').

Dimension 3: mobilising stakeholder participation

Identification of stakeholders

The practices of identifying who is relevant and who should be allowed to actively participate in territorial governance are either dependent on established routines which show some degree of consistency or transparency (see 'South Loire Plan' and 'Stockholm') or in rather novel and/or soft territorial governance constellations. These novel practices were seen emerging within a 'learning by doing' approach (see 'Hyper-local planning in England' and 'Baltic Sea Region'). Public institutions and authorities are generally designated to select these stakeholders, possibly with some flexibility to integrate stakeholders that are relevant for the issue at hand (see 'Southern Randstad'). In other cases specific institutional arrangements (e.g. platforms) already existed to represent a range of stakeholders, so that it was felt that no further selection process was required (see 'Hungarian Structural Fund Management'). Limited resources also hindered some stakeholders that were identified as being relevant from participating in the various forums (see 'Baltic Sea Region').

Securing of democratic legitimacy and accountability

This component includes the extent to which the territorial governance arrangement reflects democratic principles and integrates clarification of ownership in the project, policy or programme under consideration. Specific structures and mechanisms may be in place, in particular at the municipal level (e.g. the planning and building code), but also as the regional level, as the 'Manchester' case shows, where a well-balanced approach was undertaken in terms of accountability and democratic representativeness. From the 'Trilateral Nature Park' case we understand that although the differing legal mechanisms of the three countries make governance unwieldy, it has not jeopardised the coordination and informal cross-border cooperation. It is a difficult tightrope walk of securing democratic legitimacy and accountability on the one hand, while involving a potentially exclusive group of stakeholders, experts and interest groups and citizens on the other hand. This is in particular a thorny issue in those territorial governance arrangements which are not congruent with jurisdictional boundaries and/ or are not (yet) represented by any governmental layer (cf. also Chapter 3). Another difficulty from the 'Manchester' case is that the technical and strategic decisions taken at the regional level are often too abstract and strategic for the general public to engage with. It seems that regardless of what type of space ('soft' or 'hard') this territorial governance component is concerned with, a silver bullet of linking democratic accountability with the involvement of additional stakeholders does not seem to be forthcoming. This is inevitably related to the respective normative notion of the level and scope of democracy within such policies, programmes and projects discussed in this book. Some cases show ways of coping with this 'dilemma' at the regional level by installing mechanisms to achieve a sort of 'delegated democratic legitimacy' (e.g. 'Manchester' and 'South Loire Plan') or 'substantive legitimacy' (e.g. 'Southern Randstad' and 'Manchester').

Integration of interests/viewpoints

How and to what extent interests and viewpoints are integrated into territorial governance processes differed within the cases. Certainly this is dependent on the degree of formality of the institutional level at hand (e.g. transnational multi-level cooperation structure or urban planning at the neighbourhood level) and the general ambition in terms of either 'informing' or even 'engaging' others. What is particularly noteworthy is the fact that even within those institutions leading territorial governance processes, there is little consistency in how the integration of interests is being dealt with (see 'Baltic Sea Region'). Here the question to what extent the intervention at hand is considered to be strategic or of high or low political importance determines how and to what extent various interests and viewpoints are taken into account (see 'Stockholm'). In addition, it seems that specific groups were side-lined if their interests were thought to cause unwanted conflicts (see 'European Capital of Culture – Pécs', 'South Loire Plan' and 'Hungarian Structural Fund management'). We can observe some dynamics in terms of widening the range of stakeholder viewpoints, either by trying out new tools such as online surveys, albeit rather sporadically and selectively (see 'European Capital of Culture – Pécs' and 'Stockholm'), or rather traditional consultation methods (see 'Hyper-local planning in England' and 'South Loire Plan').

Insights into territorial governance processes

The key issue here seems not only to be the question of transparency, but how the articulated viewpoints are being dealt with in the governance process. It is important to understand the whole territorial governance

228 *Peter Schmitt and Lisa Van Well*

process as such in order to assess where and when viewpoints might feed into it and what is their relative power to re-shape the policy, programme or project. Unclear or undefined procedures for stakeholder involvement (see 'Hungarian Structural Fund management') can hamper any further mobilisation of stakeholders. This is especially evident where the influence of stakeholders is intentionally selective as this can frustrate and isolate those that have a stake in the issue at hand (see 'European Capital of Culture – Pécs'). It was also reported that such processes might be very transparent for those who actively take part (or are allowed to do so) from the beginning. But as outsiders or as stakeholders, joining such processes at a later stage is rather difficult (see 'Southern Randstad' and 'Hungarian Structural Fund management'). Various media channels (online, radio, newspaper) seem to be powerful tools, in their function as civic institutions, to make territorial governance more visible in principle, but not necessarily more transparent, due to high levels of complexity (see 'South Loire Plan' and 'Manchester'). In other cases, reports or publications are used as vehicles for broadening the understanding of the issues at hand as such (see 'Baltic Sea Region' and 'Rhine river basin'), albeit these 'communicative tools' are often more directed to parties that already have insight in the issue.

Dimension 4: being adaptive to changing contexts

Institutional learning

Institutional learning is promoted by the extent of existing structures and routines. This is important as the achievement of territorial development goals often demand that specialised sorts of knowledge are addressed. How this knowledge is managed and secured for future purposes within institutions is a question of resources and/or capabilities (both are very limited in the case of 'European Capital of Culture – Pécs', for instance), scope for (individual) capacity-building as well as of existing mechanisms (largely not given in the case of 'South Loire Plan'). What is apparently also required is stability of institutional arrangements (as given in the case of 'European Capital of Culture – Pécs', but lacking in the 'Hyper-local planning in England' case for instance), various means to store, develop and integrate knowledge such as monitoring systems, annual reports, feedback-systems, commissioned research, (see 'Southern Randstad', 'Hungarian Structural Fund management' and 'Rhine river basin') and mechanisms to transfer knowledge from specific projects to others (see 'Stockholm'). It is also important to safeguard institutional knowledge due to the fluctuation of individual actors (see 'Hungarian Structural Fund Management'). However, in addition to such structural aspects, leadership continuity and styles as well as the level of collaborative culture and social capital (see 'Manchester') and general willingness to institutionalise 'learning machinery' (see 'Rhine river basin') can either promote or inhibit the opportunity for institutional learning.

Individual learning and reflection

Individual learning and reflection were felt as being important, in particular in 'soft' territorial governance arrangements. Here learning processes are set in-motion based on working within joint (international) projects (see 'Baltic Sea Region' and 'Trilateral Nature Park'). Inter-personnel networking and trust, as well as the degree of motivation and passion of individual actors seem to be central drivers (see 'Trilateral Nature Park'). Otherwise there were often too few possibilities for individual learning in daily routines. Frequently decision-makers are confronted with a substantial amount of information, but this is hardly transformed into knowledge, since routines and time for reflection are generally scarce (see 'Stockholm' and 'Hyper-local planning in England').

Evidence of forward-looking actions

Anticipating future developments and changing contexts and being able to include this knowledge into territorial governance actions is another component within this dimension. However, indicative practices or even routines to consider future courses of action have only been noted sporadically. To some extent, future developments are intrinsically built into the policy, programme or project under consideration (see 'Rhine river basin' and 'Baltic Sea Region') or are part of strategy, scenario and/or monitoring work (see 'Manchester' and 'Southern Randstad'). Only occasionally are opportunities for forward-looking or alternative actions given significant consideration. In one case it was reported that a strong belief in a principle such as continuous urban growth seems to make the consideration of other alternatives meaningless (see 'Stockholm').

Scope of flexibility/experimentation

As a general rule one can say the less the territorial governance arrangement at hand is formalised, the greater is the scope for flexibility or even experimentation. A prime example is the 'Baltic Sea Region' case, since the relatively minimal guidance from the EU and its non-binding character leaves room for experimentation and a higher degree of flexibility as regards policy design and implementation. Other factors promoting the scope of flexibility are the possibilities to integrate ad hoc debates (see 'Southern Randstad'), create new partnerships (see 'Hyper-local planning in England'), or switch to a 'plan B' (see 'Manchester'). A soft leadership-style that allows for corrective actions (see 'Baltic Sea Region') or a search for new solutions in light of overwhelming economic crisis (see 'Trilateral Nature Park') are also factors promoting flexibility. Limiting factors are scarce resources (see monetary and human, as in the case of the 'Hungarian Structural Fund management' for instance) and business-as-usual attitudes (see 'Stockholm').

230 *Peter Schmitt and Lisa Van Well*

Another item that could be discerned in some cases is the positive effect of robust institutional structures that are at the same time flexible enough to absorb the impacts of political changes.

Dimension 5: realising place-based/territorial specificities and impacts

Criteria/logic of defining intervention area

Two different types of intervention logics are observed in the cases: a) the territorial scope as pre-defined by the jurisdictional boundaries of the lead institution (e.g. municipality) and b) the territorial scope based on functional/ issue-based criteria (e.g. catchment area of river, nature conservation, labour market region). In some cases both logics are integrated, and this enormously complicates a number of previously discussed components of territorial governance. As regards functional criteria, the territorial scope can also be unclear depending on the issue area or sector that is being covered (see 'Baltic Sea Region') or even contested as it may favour the largest city in the region (as the cases 'South Loire Plan' and 'Manchester' indicate). However, in the 'Manchester' case this is tempered by a high degree of sensitivity of this imbalance when deciding upon prioritised projects and policies. Ambitious strategic objectives such as 'territorial integration within the region', 'balanced spatially distribution of investments' or the principle of 'zooming out' to a larger territorial context, may easily wither away if the goal is rather the realisation of more tangible and easily achievable (i.e. often 'local') and communicable objectives (see 'European Capital of Culture – Pécs', 'Hungarian Structural Fund management' and 'Stockholm').

Coping with hard and soft/functional spaces

There is a clear tension between the approaches to integrate 'soft' territorial governance practices with concrete interventions that are dealt within 'harder' administrative spaces. It seems that more functional approaches can challenge prevailing perceptions and routines of actors and institutions that are locked into 'hard' spaces and can contribute to a more relational territorial understanding (see 'Rhine river basin' and 'Trilateral Nature Park'). The 'Stockholm' case indicates that different logics and traditions are at play, which partly restricts policy integration and inter-municipal cooperation. More frequently, however, it seems that a soft or functional-based understanding in particular at the regional level is influencing the design of policies, programmes and projects. The key question is then to what extent such an understanding is integrated or formally institutionalised in the long run. Here again the 'Rhine river basin' case illustrates how 'functional dependencies' within flood management simply force the involved actors and institutions to cope with the inherent territorial relationality of the issue at stake. In other words, 'functional dependencies' can be a trigger for linking 'hard spaces' with 'soft spaces' (such as the territorial impacts of flooding), which has led to an advanced mode of cross-border territorial governance.

Utilisation of territorial (expert) knowledge

The utilisation of territorial (expert) knowledge has generally been characterised as being sufficient or high in the cases. In other words, it appears that today's territorial governance policy-makers and practitioners have access to an enormous body of knowledge. Some cases even reported that place-based/territorial knowledge has been the key to produce a holistic plan and to increase mutual understanding of the various actors about the issues at stake (see 'Trilateral Nature Park' and 'Hyper-local planning in England'). Others reported that the mutual generation of territorial knowledge was an outcome of the related territorial governance process rather than its guiding principle (see 'South Loire Plan'). Yet other cases failed to do so, due to the general low level of trust in sharing knowledge and in collective actions (see 'European Capital of Culture – Pécs'). An issue mentioned in many cases is the question of who collects and owns this knowledge (and thus becomes knowledgeable) and to what extent the various actors and institutions involved in the territorial governance work at hand are able (and willing) to share it.

Integration of territorial analysis

Although the provision of territorial (expert) knowledge is in general high across the case studies, we see rather strong variations as to the extent that this knowledge is being integrated in policy designs. For example, territorial analysis may be strongly considered at the local and regional level (see 'Southern Randstad'), but to a lesser extent at the transnational level. The cases of the 'Baltic Sea Region' and 'Trilateral Nature Park' have indicated the dependence on project-based funding in this respect. In other cases, ex-ante evaluations may have shaped the policy, programme or project at hand, but not necessarily the lessons taken from ex-post analysis. Evidently, although comprehensive analysis has been undertaken, in some cases the decision-making process was rather shaped by other rationales (see 'Hungarian Structural Fund Management'). Another issue that can be carved out from the cases is the question of continuity, as during the plan-making phase the integration of territorial analysis can be high, but rather low once the plan is adopted (see 'Hyper-local planning in England'). Examples for the latter are the selection of certain areas for territorial monitoring (see 'European Capital of Culture – Pécs') or the integration of territorial impact assessments only for strategic projects (those which get high political attention) (see 'Stockholm').

232 Peter Schmitt and Lisa Van Well

Re-conceptualising territorial governance II: exploring linkages between the five dimensions

Returning to our framework for (re-)conceptualising territorial governance we find that 'Coordinating actions of actors and institutions' (dimension 1) and 'Integrating policy sectors' (dimension 2) are often entangled within the scope of what is usually called 'governance'. Central for the strong interplay between these dimensions is the distribution of various sorts of power, including formal and informal as well as regulatory and normative power, and ways to overcome the barriers, constraints or gaps within the prevailing institutional structures. 'Mobilising stakeholder participation' (dimension 3) expands on the two aforementioned dimensions and functions, as our analysis shows, as a lynchpin for achieving both coordination among actors and sectoral integration. Although our empirical research was directed towards problematising the degree of democratic legitimacy in the various cases, the case studies show that legitimacy was not entirely secured within actions for dimensions 1 and 2. Thus, the thorny question remains how to mobilise in particular civil society and those actors with weak financial and/or institutional capacities and how their engagement can (or will) feed into dimensions 1 and 2.

We also detect a strong interplay between dimensions 1 and 2 as there is a high dependence on institutionalised structures to integrate both actors and sectors in various policy decisions (cf. Figure 16.1). This became evident when working with the case studies, as many researchers reported that the analytical distinction between dimensions 1 and 2 was somewhat challenging due to their tight interrelations. Examples are the way that power is distributed across levels (cf. component 1) which affects the structural context for sectoral integration (cf. component 5). The component 'acknowledging and dealing with sectoral conflicts' is also dependent on the 'modes of leadership' and how 'constraints to coordination' are dealt with (components 2 and 4). Between dimensions 1 and 3 the interplay is moderate. Here, for instance, the 'structure of coordination' (cf. component 2) often regulates the 'integration of interests/view points' (cf. component 11). Leadership styles (component 2) may also influence, at least to some extent, the general identification and inclusion of further stakeholders. Likewise the interplay between dimensions 2 and 3 is also rather moderate (compared to dimensions 1 and 2): the mobilisation of relevant stakeholders can support achieving synergies across sectors (component 6) and thus help to control and assess the design of policies, programmes or projects. Be this as it may, what all these linkages between dimensions 1, 2 and 3 have in common is the fact that they are characterised by 'coordination' as the overarching mechanism (see Figure 16.2).

However, when considering the linkages between 'Mobilising stakeholder participation' (dimension 3) and the dimensions 'Being adaptive to changing contexts' (dimension 4) and 'Realising place-based/territorial specificities and impacts' (dimension 5), we cannot discern that dimension 3 functions as a lynchpin. Rather it appears that this dimension is almost disconnected with the other two. This is perhaps because between dimensions 4 and 5 there is a different overarching mechanism at play, namely 'knowledge', rather than being based on representative coordination as are dimensions 1, 2 and 3. The uniting characteristic of dimensions 4 and 5 and their respective indicators and components is that they require consolidated knowledge capacities. The case studies show that in order to be adaptive to changing contexts it is necessary to have certain institutional structures in place to safeguard knowledge and ensure that individual learning is transposed into institutional learning (components 13 and 14). Knowledge also underpins the components of dimension 5 in particular regarding defining an area of intervention and the coping with 'softer' spaces. In particular the components 'institutional' and 'individual learning' seem to form the prerequisites for all four components under dimension 5. Hence, based on the empirical findings in our case studies we can also discern a strong interplay, if not correlation, between dimensions 4 and 5. The tracing of these dimensions in the case studies has shown that rather limited capacities are at play in many cases in regards to dimension 4, whereas within dimension 5 a number of structures and routines have been adopted. However, we can only discern to a very minor degree to what extent these two dimensions also flesh out into the coordination of dimensions 1 and 2.

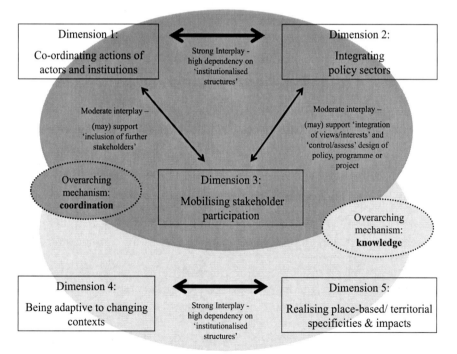

Figure 16.2 Inter-relations between the five dimensions of territorial governance
Source: Own adaptation based on ESPON and Nordregio (2013, p. 39)

One strong indication for this is that 'territorial elements' are only implicitly integrated in dimensions 1 and 2. In essence, these dimensions are not specifically 'territorial' but are important aspects of any governance or multi-level governance issue. The territorial element comes in if the composition of actors and institutions at hand as well as the represented policy sectors show a high sensitivity for a 'territorial' perspective. This might be expressed by discussing various territorial impacts for instance. This potential lack of territorial sensitivity or 'grounding' can be compensated to some extent within those practices and routines for integrating the interests and ideas of stakeholders that have been identified and discussed within dimension 3. In this vein, mobilising stakeholders can be also understood as investigating the responsiveness for a place-based or territorial approach.

The analysis of the cases also showed that what was sometimes hindering local, regional, national or transnational territorial governance was the fact that governance routines were not very adaptive to dealing with change. They often lacked the capacity to respond to unanticipated events or long-term challenges or work within 'softer' territorial groupings such as cross-border cooperation schemes or macro-regions. The necessity of the adaptability of institutions is not only limited to changing territorial contexts, as institutions need to adapt to a range of shifting circumstances such as declining population or the financial crisis. However the case studies found that adaptability became particularly important when knowledge about differing territorial conditions became apparent, such as the need for local or national institutions to adapt to new Structural Fund demands or the need for local climate change strategies to take into consideration a strategy at the level of the macro-region. Likewise, actors in several cases often were unsure how to actually use the expert knowledge, analyses and tools produced on territorial issues (such as local plans). They also lacked routines to incorporate local knowledge gleaned from stakeholders into their decision-making processes. Hence, the analysis of dimensions 4 and 5 reveals that different formations of territory-related 'knowledge' are central components for the design of policies, programmes and projects. In other words, the inclusion of dimensions 4 and 5 sheds light on the question whether 'relevant' territorial knowledge is created, maintained and applied to understand, assess or even envision the impacts and consequences that interventions may have.

The cases also show that utilisation of territorial knowledge was widespread, but how the knowledge is collected and 'stored' in the long-term can be more problematic, especially when dealing with knowledge accrued through short-term projects and programmes. Thus the question of 'ownership' and 'stewardship' of knowledge comes into play. The production and use of territorial knowledge also has a temporal dimension. From the work with the case studies we could also learn that often very comprehensive territorial knowledge is produced in the initial stages of a programme or project and evaluated through ex-ante procedures. But perhaps due to the prevalence of working towards territorial goals in project or programme form, it is not unusual that ex-post analyses receive less focus and thus territorial knowledge is not always fed back into the policy process.

Territorial governance as a specific 'extended' type of multi-level governance

When re-examining Figure 16.2, we can construe that the interplay between dimensions 1, 2 and 3 has been (largely) captured, although from a different starting point, by the concepts of 'regular' governance and/or 'multi-level' governance (e.g. Hooghe and Marks, 2003, 2010). Following Faludi's (2012) discussion of multi-level governance one can certainly assign the various case studies in Part II as examples of primarily 'Type I' or 'Type II' multi-level governance as suggested by Hooghe and Marks (2003) (cf. Table 1.1). Nonetheless, we argue that the territorial elements and the shift from 'multi-level-governance' to what we conceptualise as 'territorial governance' in this volume (see Figure 1.1) become most explicit when incorporating dimensions 4 and 5. Here the focus on the knowledge-related components within the case studies give evidence that helped us to move the analysis from 'multi-level governance' to 'territorial governance', echoing as Harrison (2013) postulates towards understanding territory and networks via processes of interaction that are specifically about the ways in which a territory develops. Only in this way do relational space as a social construct and categories such as 'place' and 'territory', factor into multi-level governance.

However, as discussed above, we discern a clear 'disconnect' or weak relationship between dimensions 1, 2 and 3 on the one hand and dimensions 4 and 5 on the other. It was hard in reality to find examples where the case studies specifically made conscious efforts to adapt their institutions to new or shifting territorial knowledge. This disconnect is mirrored in the theoretical discussions of (multi-level) governance whereby many contributions (e.g. Hooghe and Marks 2001, Howlett 2009 and Lidström 2007) discuss the 'vertical' and 'horizontal' dimensions of governance, but fewer have really honed in on how institutions can be adaptive and how they can realise place-based specificities (rudimentary approaches are to be found in for example Birkmann *et al.* 2010, Bulkeley and Kern 2006). We assert that this is one of the added value elements of the research presented in this book: based on our empirical evidence we argue that territorial governance includes not only dimensions 1, 2 and 3, but also dimensions 4 and 5 (and the related indicators and components extracted here), which truly distinguish it from multi-level governance by prominently including the adaptability and knowledge-based perspectives.

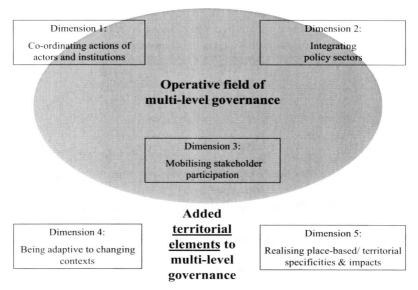

Figure 16.3 The operative field of multi-level governance and the 'added territorial elements to multi-level governance'

Source: Own adaptation based on ESPON and Nordregio (2013, p. 40)

Revisiting the framework of analysing territorial governance

We would further argue that the five dimensions as such constitute a robust framework to analyse territorial governance. The 12 indicators, the 42 core questions and 20 components (see Figure 5.2) have been helpful in tracing our study of territorial governance processes at play, rather than solely focusing on describing the institutional structures. Certainly, one can adapt these indicators and components depending on the specific focus of any follow-up investigations. The analytical framework could be further enlarged and/or revised by additional conceptual and empirical research. Overall, it offers a solid ground to make distinctions within the complex and nested field of territorial governance. In particular the framework helps to assess the extent to which the territorial dimension matters within regular (multi-level) governance and thus offers a holistic approach towards territorial governance.

To this end we also suggest that the five dimensions as such can constitute a simple framework or heuristic in which to actually 'promote' territorial governance. Policy-makers, decision-makers and practitioners that desire to take a territorial governance perspective in their work can use the five dimensions, 12 indicators and 20 components as checkpoints for thinking about what actions they can take that will facilitate the realisation of a territorial goal in an efficient, equitable and sustainable manner. In this sense, they serve as a reminder or a benchmark in particular for those who organise, manage or want to initiate territorial governance processes or basically to review current territorial governance situations.

In addition we underline that the framework presented here for analysing territorial governance is not a territorial development assessment tool. Rather it helps to 'think about' territorial governance processes. In doing so, it also provides a useful means to carve out a number of features of territorial governance and thus to make some further qualified investigations into the 'quality of processes' within territorial governance (cf. Chapter 17 and ESPON and Politecnico di Torino 2013).

References

Birkmann, J., Garschargen, M., Kraas, F. and Quang, N., 2010. Adaptive urban governance: new challenges for the second generation of urban adaptation strategies to climate change. *Sustainability Science*, 5 (2), 185–206.

Bulkeley, H. and Kern, K., 2006. Local government and climate change governance in the UK and Germany. *Urban Studies*, 43 (12), 2237–2259.

ESPON and Politecnico di Torino, 2013. *Towards Better Territorial Governance in Europe. A Guide for Practitioners, Policy and Decision Makers*. Available from: http://www.espon.eu/main/Menu_Publications/Menu_Guidance/ [Accessed 18 April 2015].

Faludi, A., 2012. Multi-level (territorial) governance: three criticisms. *Planning Theory & Practice*, 13 (2), 197–211.

Harrison, J., 2013. Configuring the new 'regional world': on being caught between territory and networks, *Regional Studies*, 47 (1), 55–74.

Hooghe, L. and Marks, G., 2001. *Multi-level Governance and European Integration*. Lanham, MD: Rowman & Littlefield.

Hooghe, L. and Marks, G., 2003. Unraveling the central state, but how? Types of multi-level governance. *The American Political Science Review*, 97 (2), 233–243.

Hooghe, L. and Marks, G., 2010. Types of multi-level governance. In: H. Enderlein, S. Wälti and M. Zürn, eds. *Types of Multilevel Governance*. Cheltenham: Elgar, 17–31.

Howlett, M., 2009. Governance modes, policy regimes and operational plans: a multi-level nested model of policy instrument choice and policy design. *Policy Sciences*, 42 (1), 73–89.

Lidström, A., 2007. Territorial governance in transition, *Regional and Federal Studies*, 17(4), 499–508.

Van Well, L. and Schmitt, P., 2015, forthcoming. Understanding Territorial Governance: Conceptual and practical implications, *Europa Regional*.

17 Transferring 'good' territorial governance across Europe
Opportunities and barriers

Giancarlo Cotella, Umberto Janin Rivolin and Marco Santangelo

Introduction

The idea that dissemination of good practices can lead to policy improvement 'has become an accepted wisdom within national policies and programmes, as well as in international arenas and networks' (Bulkeley 2006, p. 1030). In general terms, the concept of 'good practice' is related to the accumulation and application of knowledge about what is working or not working in different situations and contexts, implying a continual process of learning, feedback, reflection and analysis (what works, where, how and why) (Andrews 2010, Grindle 2011). Various global policies, programmes and initiatives illustrate that the identification and dissemination of good practices is widely considered to be an effective means for promoting policy transfer and learning (World Bank 2000, OECD 2001, UN-Habitat 2009). This is of particular value for the European Union (EU), a supranational context where policy progress and innovation are mostly based on mutual exchange of, and learning from, very diverse local experiences (CEC 2008).

Aimed at providing a contribution to the spreading of good territorial governance in Europe, one of the outcomes of the ESPON TANGO project was the delivery of a 'handbook with best practices for territorial governance', with the ambition of 'disseminating good territorial governance principles that lead to successful outcomes to stakeholders' (ESPON 2011, p. 10). The elaboration of this specific product, available on paper and online (ESPON and Politecnico di Torino 2013), proved to be a particularly mind-ravelling and challenging task. One main difficulty relates to the fact that territorial governance is not a 'policy' *per se*, but rather an integrative process of linking various policy sectors and intentions. As the case studies presented in Part II clearly show, territorial governance processes are intrinsically complex and made up of a number of key components. Hence, to define any territorial governance practice as entirely 'good' (or 'bad') would be highly questionable. Each case proves in fact to be a mix of successful and unsuccessful features: opportunities to be seized and barriers to be avoided.

The problem of spreading good territorial governance can thus be conceptualised in terms of identification and transferability of various 'features' emerging from the case studies, taking into account their capacity to either 'promote' or 'inhibit' the achievement of certain territorial development goals (for an extensive discussion of such 'promoters' and 'inhibitors' of good territorial governance, see: ESPON and Nordregio 2013, pp. 134–140, ESPON and Politecnico di Torino 2013). Whereas the previous chapter presented the 'components of territorial governance' which were distilled from the results of the case study analysis, this chapter focuses on the conditions of transferability of territorial governance features, which were also distilled from the case studies and a one-day workshop with 25 practitioners, policy-makers and decision-makers from various institutional levels around Europe. This means the questions 'through whom' and 'how' these features might be spread in the EU institutional context are in focus here. In other words, this chapter will not tackle the issues of defining what is 'good' in territorial governance, or of 'what exactly' should be transferred in this complex domain

In light of the well-known complexities concerning policy transfer (amongst others: Dolowitz and Marsh 1996, 2000, James and Lodge 2003), the model for transferability presented in the following sections (see also Janin Rivolin and Cotella 2014) assumes that specific characteristics of an institutional context are fundamental prerequisites for action, especially as far as territorial governance is concerned. Particularly building on previous reflections about Europeanisation of territorial governance (Böhme and Waterhout 2008, Cotella and Janin Rivolin 2010, 2011, Cotella *et al.* 2011), the proposed approach welcomes the assumption that, with regard to territorial governance, policy transfer in the EU and Europeanisation are arguably two sides of the same coin (Wishlade *et al.* 2003). From such a point of departure, this chapter focuses on the modalities of transfer, and particularly on the 'paths and means' through which the major opportunities and barriers for (good) territorial governance might be spread from one context to another.

Following this introduction, the chapter depicts the theoretical foundations of the proposed model, which is built upon an institutional approach to territorial governance. Then, it illustrates how this framework allows for the identification of three distinct modes for the spread of (good) territorial governance in Europe, a 'dialogic mode', an 'operational mode' and an 'institutional mode' respectively. The next section provides a brief synopsis of the identified transfer modes, explaining how they are addressed to various categories of stakeholders. Finally, a conclusive section rounds off the contribution, summarising its main findings and providing indications for future research and action.

Understanding European territorial governance as an institutional phenomenon: a conceptual framework

The transferability of territorial governance is characterised by a high degree of complexity, difficulty and risk of failure. Reasons behind this are primarily linked to the activity of policy transfer in general, and may refer to (i) the questionability of 'reproductive' assumptions behind the rhetoric of good practice transferability, especially where this concerns diversified institutional contexts (James and Lodge 2003, Vettoretto 2009, Stead 2012) and (ii) the lack of universal models for policy transfer, verified and tested, because of the high number of variables at stake (see Table 17.1). An additional and more specific complexity is related to the very nature of territorial governance, which is not a policy *per se*, but rather a complex multi-level and multi-actor process integrating several policy sectors and aimed at achieving multiple territorial development goals.

On the other hand, to address the issue in the EU context offers opportunities that are not given in other institutional contexts. As some authors have pointed out, policy transfer in Europe is intimately connected with the process of so-called 'Europeanisation', a specific phenomenon of institutionalisation composed of top-down, bottom-up and horizontal dynamics of influence (Knill and Lehmkuhl 1999, Wishlade *et al.* 2003, Radaelli 2004, Holzinger and Knill 2005). In other words, 'the [EU] apparatus of policy diffusion and development has transnationalised in such a profound and irreversible way as to render anachronistic the notion of independent, 'domestic' decision-making' (Peck 2011, p. 774).

Directing attention to the institutional characteristics of the EU is moreover consistent with the specific nature of territorial governance. Various discussions (among others: Alexander 1995, Healey 1999, 2006, Gualini 2001, Moulaert 2005, Verma 2007) highlighted indeed that territorial governance should be understood as an 'institutional phenomenon'. As such, it may be described as the end-product of a creative selection process of trial and error based on

> (i) first, the generation of variety (in particular, a variety of practices and rules); (ii) second, competition and reduction of the variety (of rules) via selection; (iii) third, propagation and some persistence of the solution (the system of rules) selected.
>
> (Moroni 2010, p. 279)

These considerations have been recently applied for the purpose of conceptualisation in comparative analysis for spatial planning (Nadin 2010), representing territorial governance as characterised by various dimensions that connect, in a given institutional context, the 'government system' with the 'territorial/spatial development system' (see Figure 17.1). In particular, the crucial role of 'practices' (p), as the primary source for the generation of variety, is complemented by the dimension of 'discourse' (d), which refers to the activity of territorial knowledge arenas (Adams *et al.* 2011) in 'competition and reduction of the variety via selection' (Moroni 2010, p. 279). The possible codification of certain rules may lead to the 'propagation and some persistence of the solution selected' (ibid.), and occurs through a modification of the 'structure' (s), the overall set of constitutional and legal provisions allowing for and determining the operation of territorial governance. A sort of 'descending phase' in the process continues from here, as systematic application of the established 'tools' (t) – namely various types of spatial plans and programmes, but also control devices, monitoring and evaluation procedures, forms of economic incentive, and so on – creates the operational conditions for (new) practices. Needless to say, this description does not have the ambition to explain in detail all possible outcomes of territorial governance, which are the result of an infinite variety of factors, circumstances and individual behaviours. Rather, it proposes an analytical approach to frame and discuss how territorial governance, as an institutional phenomenon, can be subject to social change.

These institutional and process-related dynamics which constantly change the framework conditions of territorial governance are however complemented by further external relations, as for instance the influence of supranational organisations, or the fluctuation of macroeconomic framework conditions, and so on. A reflection on the role of external relations inspired an extension of the framework to the context of European territorial governance (Cotella and Janin Rivolin 2010, 2011, Cotella *et al.* 2011). More in detail, as the European context is characterised by the simultaneous activity of one supranational process (the EU) embedding various national processes, possible changes in European territorial governance result in being simultaneously driven by: (a) relations occurring in national domains; (b) similar relations occurring in the whole EU domain; and (c) mutual relations between these two types of domains (see Figure 17.2).

Whereas this framework proved useful for explaining potential top-down, bottom-up and horizontal influences in the possible Europeanisation of territorial governance, the following sections explain how it can be used to identify possible modes for spreading good territorial governance in the EU.

Transferring good territorial governance in Europe: three potential modes

Building on the descriptive capacity of the above presented model, the identification of possible modes for spreading good territorial governance in Europe can be derived from the various 'paths' that policy transfer is expected to take from a given 'good practice' (p1, in a certain domestic context) to a new one replicated somewhere else (p2/n, in another or other domestic contexts). An important observation that the model suggests is that the initial step of these possible paths is always directed from p1 to D; that is from the supposed 'good' practice to the 'EU discourse'. The latter is the virtual place constituted by the sum of the 'knowledge arenas' in which the various social

Table 17.1 A policy transfer framework

Why transfer? Continuum Want to—Have to			Who is involved in transfer?	What is transferred?	From where?
Voluntary	Mixtures	Coercive			Past
Lesson drawing (Perfect rationality)	Lesson drawing (Bounded rationality)	Direct imposition	Elected officials	Policies (goals) (content) (instruments)	Internal
	International pressures		Bureaucrats Civil servants	Programmes	Global
	(Image) (Consensus) (Perceptions)				
	Externalities	Pressure groups	Institutions		
	Conditionality	Political parties	Ideology		
	(Loans) (Conditions attached to business activity)				
	Obligations	Policy entrepreneurs / experts	Attitudes / cultural values		
			Consultants Think Tanks Transnational corporations Supranational institutions	Negative lessons	

Source: Authors' own adaptation based on Dolowitz and Marsh (2000)

		Degrees of transfer	Constraints on transfer	How to demonstrate policy transfer	How transfer leads to policy failure
Within a nation	*Cross-national*				
State government	International organizations	Copying	Policy complexity (Newspaper) (Magazine) (TV) (Radio)	Media	Uniformed transfer
City government	Regional State Local governments	Emulation	Past policies	Reports	Incomplete transfer
				(Commissioned) (Not commissioned)	
Local authorities		Mixtures	Structural Institutional	Conferences	Inappropriate transfer
		Inspiration	Feasibility	Meetings / visits	
			(Ideology) (Cultural proximity) (Technology) (Economic) (Bureaucratic)		
			Language	Statements (Written) (Verbal)	
	Past relations				

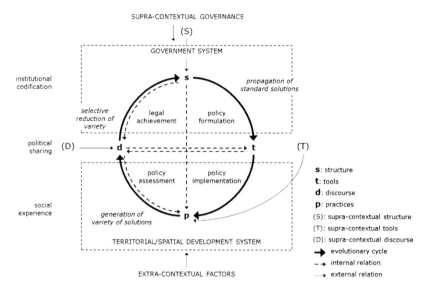

Figure 17.1 The dynamic and changing framework of territorial governance
Source: Own adaptation based on Janin Rivolin, (2012, p. 73)

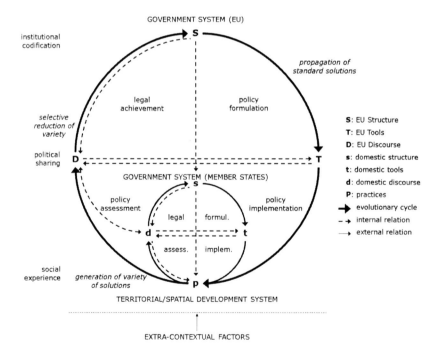

Figure 17.2 Process of change of 'European' territorial governance
Source: Own adaptation based on Cotella and Janin Rivolin (2010, p. 6)

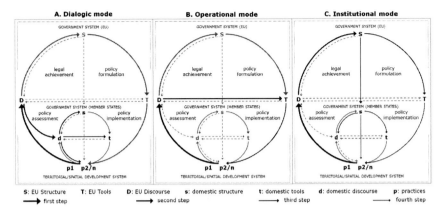

Figure 17.3 Modes for the transfer of (good) territorial governance in Europe
Source: Own adaptation based on Cotella and Janin Rivolin (2014, p. 17)

experiences are shared and filtered, via selection by policy assessment, in the form of ideas and proposals for good territorial governance at the EU level (e.g. the ESPON platform). This means that possible modes for spreading territorial governance in Europe are all pivoted on the activity of a more or less structured and coherent EU discourse, and are distinguishable for the different paths that ideas and proposals can take from here in order to reach and influence other social experiences (p2/n).

In particular, three distinct 'modes of transfer' are identifiable, as illustrated in the following sub-sections. These constituted the key perspectives adopted in the ESPON handbook for good territorial governance in Europe (ESPON and Politecnico di Torino 2013) on the basis of the assumption that the TANGO project and the cases presented in this book play an active role within the EU territorial governance discourse (D), due to their critical study of a number of original practices (p1, i.e. the case studies, see Chapters 6 to 15) in order to identify 'good' features to spread towards other practices in different domestic contexts (p2/n) (see Figure 17.3).

Dialogic mode of transfer

First, the influence of a 'dialogic mode' for the transfer of good territorial governance in Europe resides in the ability of the EU discourse to influence one or more domestic discourses (D → d2/n) and, from there, relevant practices in a direct or indirect way (i.e. via domestic tools or structures) (see Figure 17.3 A). This occurs when

> in its 'weakest' form, European policy [...] affects domestic arrangements [...] indirectly, namely by altering the beliefs and expectations of

domestic actors. [...] Hence, the domestic impact of European policies is primarily based on a cognitive logic.

(Knill and Lehmkuhl 1999, p. 2)

This kind of 'discursive integration' 'can be successful when there are strong policy communities active at European and national levels and direct links between them' (Böhme 2002, p. III). Therefore potential borrowers can exploit this opportunity of importing innovative solutions only up to the actual extent of integration of a domestic discourse (d2/n) with the EU discourse (D).

The most immediate manifestation of the dialogic mode of transfer is represented by the translation of good territorial governance features from the discursive arenas into practices (p2/n). The plethora of bilateral or multilateral projects and mutual learning exchanges instituted within the framework of the European territorial cooperation objective, be they cross-border, transnational or interregional in nature, are clear examples of this process (Dühr *et al.* 2007). In a second instance, domestic practices may also be influenced indirectly in the long run, assuming that the domestic discourse is able to have an effect on domestic structure (s2/n) or tools (t2/n).

Operational mode of transfer

Similarly, an *operational mode* for spreading good territorial governance in Europe (see Figure 17.3B) concerns the translation of insights elaborated in the EU discourse into the EU tools (D → T), which are then capable of influencing the territorial governance practices in various domestic contexts. This mode is effective insofar as 'European influence is confined to altering domestic opportunity structures, and hence the distribution of power and resources between domestic actors' (Knill and Lehmkuhl 1999, p. 1). In this mode, specific good territorial governance practices can provide inspiration for the functioning of EU territorial governance tools in terms of methods and techniques which, in turn, are transferred 'directly' to new potential experiences in various domestic contexts (p2/n) via economic conditionality, namely through the adoption of specific behaviours at the domestic level, in order to benefit from EU support.

One example in this regard is traceable in the EU establishment of the Territorial Employment Pacts in 1997, on the basis of the Italian experience of 'Territorial Pacts' (Law 662/1996) that was developed in the early 1990s as a new means for the support of depressed areas. This led to the launch of 89 pilot actions in various EU countries, and ended up in the adoption of a similar approach in the mainstream objectives of the Structural Funds programming period 2000–2006, in turn exerting an influence on domestic practices in all EU countries (Janin Rivolin 2003, 2012). A similar example concerns the well-known process that gave birth to the Urban Pilot Projects and, later on, to the Urban Community Initiative, taking inspiration from activities undertaken within the French domestic context (Janin Rivolin and Faludi 2005).

Institutional mode of transfer

Finally, an 'institutional mode' for spreading good territorial governance in Europe (see Figure 17.3C) occurs when elements from the EU discourse become codified within the EU structure (D → S), inducing changes into domestic structures and, from here, to respective practices, or into EU tools, with effects described in the previous section. In this case,

> European policy-making may trigger domestic change by defining concrete institutional requirements with which member states must comply; that is, EU policy 'positively' prescribes an institutional model to which domestic arrangements have to be adjusted.
>
> (Knill and Lehmkuhl 1999, p. 1)

This mode implies that good territorial governance practices, after being analysed in the EU discourse, provide inspiration for the definition of rules, codes and laws. Many local experiences may be reached this way through a more complex, 'enveloping' process of policy transfer, pivoted around mechanisms of legal conditionality filtered by domestic structures (s2/n) plus possible mechanisms of economic conditionality triggered by the EU tools (T).

A relevant example of this process is traceable in the increasingly widespread adoption of the principle of 'sustainable development' in territorial governance practices in Europe, which followed from the establishment of a series of EU directives (e.g. Habitat 92/43/CE, SEA 2001/42/CE). These have progressively transferred this principle via domestic structures, as well as through the influence of EU policy frameworks and initiatives (such as Cohesion Policy or the EU 2020 strategy).

Addressing different categories of stakeholders: towards a typology for action

One advantage of the proposed conceptualisation lies in its capacity to react to a criticism which is often raised in relation to policy transfer, namely that the latter is mostly addressed 'out on a limb', without enough attention to the most suitable 'means' and 'drivers' for transfer (Wolman and Page 2002). Indeed, the modes of transfer described above do not address all potential stakeholders active in the field of territorial governance in Europe in the same way and through the same means. Although the three modes are all construed as being key transmitters of policy change from a practice (p1) to others (p2n), each of them is in fact expected to achieve its own specific effectiveness by passing through distinct categories of means and stakeholders (see Table 17.2).

Following the approach of Wolman and Page (2002), who define policy transfer among local government as occurring through a communication and information framework including producers, senders, and facilitators of

248 Cotella, Janin Rivolin and Santangelo

information as well as recipients, the features of good territorial governance generated in this book can be translated indeed in distinct 'interactive resources', namely: (i) examples of practical application, (ii) techniques and methods for policy-making and (iii) rules for good territorial governance. These are, in turn, relevant for specific categories of stakeholders active in territorial governance, namely (i) practitioners, (ii) policy-makers and (iii) decision-makers.

In particular, the former are the private and public professionals that are engaged in various activities and scales of territorial governance in Europe, who are protagonists of the creation of interactive knowledge and possible innovation. Policy-makers of territorial governance are usually public authorities and officials in charge of, for instance, spatial planning and control activities at various administrative levels within a country as well as assigned to implement Cohesion Policy at the EU level (e.g. officials of the European Commission) or at national, regional and local levels. Decision-makers of territorial governance are those appointed by democratic vote, such as members of the EU Parliament and national parliaments or regional and municipal councils, often in charge of ministerial or departmental roles that are related to spatial planning and cohesion policy.

Against this backdrop, the 'dialogic mode' of transfer is particularly concerned with the territorial knowledge communities active in a specific domestic context, and especially in order to be able to 'filter' ideas, concepts and proposals to be utilised by the stakeholders of territorial governance in this context: decision-makers, policy-makers and practitioners. The 'operational mode' of transfer implies rather the opportunity for EU policy-makers (who prepare the operational tools at the EU level) to learn about specific activities. Finally, the 'institutional mode' of transfer addresses specifically the EU decision-makers (who establish rules and norms at the EU level).

An overall comparison suggests that the dialogic mode may occur more 'easily' than the others, because it tends to take shape in a voluntary way through processes of lesson drawing and progressive 'cognitive re-orientation' (Radaelli 2004). This means also that the dialogic mode may be less 'secure', because its only constraints depend on the willingness to adopt good governance lessons. Contrarily, the institutional mode has the potential to produce the deepest and widest impact through rather coercive processes of policy transfer based both on legal and economic conditionality (Knill and Lehmkuhl 1999). Its occurrence is however very difficult in practice, because the making of rules or codes with universal values poses higher transaction costs (Alexander 1992). In between, the operational mode is relatively complex, but apparently the most direct mode in stimulating the emergence of new practices in several domestic contexts.

Table 17.2 A typology for the transfer of good territorial governance in Europe

Transfer modes	Interactive resources	Direct beneficiaries	Pivotal dimensions	Main paths from provider (p1) to final user (p2n)	Influence mechanisms
Dialogic	Examples of practical application	Practitioners	Practices (p)	p1→D→d2n→p2n	Cognitive re-orientation
	Techniques and methods for policy-making	Domestic policy-makers	Domestic tools (t)	p1→D→d2n→t2n→p2n	Cognitive re-orientation
	Rules for good territorial governance	Domestic decision-makers	Domestic structure (s)	p1→D→d2n→s2n→p2n	Cognitive re-orientation
Operational	Techniques and methods for policy-making	EU policy-makers	EU Tools (T)	p1→D→T→p2n	Economic conditionality
Institutional	Rules for good territorial governance	EU decision-makers	EU Structure (S)	p1→D→S→s2n→p2n + p1→D→S→T→p2n	Legal conditionality + Economic conditionality

Source: Authors' own adaptation based on Cotella and Janin Rivolin (2014, p. 17)

Concluding remarks

By focusing on the conditions under which European experiences of good territorial governance may constitute a trigger for learning in other European contexts, this chapter has explained how a conceptual bridge can be built between the analysis of relevant case studies (see Part II of the book) and the production of dissemination outputs as for instance undertaken in the handbook 'Towards better territorial governance in Europe' (ESPON and Politecnico di Torino 2013).

However, when it comes to relevant policy implications, it is important to stress once more the strong context-dependence of territorial governance practices, in terms of issues and challenges at stake, territorial context, as well as territorial and political level(s) involved. Specifically, particular attention should be paid to identifying 'for whom' a specific territorial governance feature maybe considered to be 'good' or 'bad', because this raises particular challenges in relation to any in-depth discussion concerning the extent of its transferability into other contexts. Whereas the experiences collected in this volume allow for a preliminary identification of specific good territorial governance features that, in turn, may be addressed to a potential target audience, such operation is by no mean easy to perform, and requires further empirical research on the matter. More in detail, as various critiques addressed to theories of policy transfer and lesson drawing clearly remark, the 'filtering out' process of translating and combining features of good territorial governance from different contexts into one is a complex process that implies different degrees of adaptation (see for instance James and Lodge 2003, Bulkeley 2006, Vettoretto 2009, Peck 2011 and Stead 2012). In a similar way, the 'filtering in' process through which specific territorial governance features may be taken on board in a different domestic context appears to be related to two intertwined dimensions, namely a process of 'adoption', which gives origin to policies/actions according to new contextual forms or shapes, and a degree of 'territorialisation', that is the relationship between these possible policies/actions and specific place-based issues at stake.

For this reason, one main message of this book is that the improvement of territorial governance in Europe should not chase elusive 'one-size-fits-all' solutions. It is rather through a patient and progressive building of an evidence-based set of opportunities for innovation at different levels and/or in different contexts that various stakeholders may draw lessons according to their own peculiar needs. In addition, we argue that the overall operation of 'European' territorial governance is based on a process of articulated and interwoven forms of continuous policy transfer between the EU and domestic domains, which European stakeholders involved in territorial governance processes need to recognise.

Acknowledgements

The authors would like to express their gratitude to the transnational project group and to other members of the Politecnico di Torino local unit involved in the project, namely Nadia Caruso, Alberta De Luca and Francesca Governa, for the continuous proactive collaboration during the research.

References

Adams, N., Cotella, G. and Nunes, R., eds., 2011. *Territorial Development, Cohesion and Spatial Planning Knowledge and Policy Development in an Enlarged EU*. London: Routledge.

Alexander E.R., 1992. A Transaction Cost Theory of Planning, *Journal of the American Planning Association*, 58 (2), 190–200.

Alexander, E.R., 1995. *How Organizations Act Together*. Luxembourg: Gordon and Breach.

Andrews M., 2010. Good Government Means Different Things in Different Countries. *Governance: An International Journal of Policy, Administration, and Institutions*, 23 (1), 7–35.

Böhme, K., 2002. *Nordic Echoes of European Spatial Planning*. Stockholm: Nordregio.

Böhme, K. and Waterhout, B., 2008. The Europeanization of Planning. In: Faludi A. ed., *European Spatial Research and Planning*. Cambridge, MA: Lincoln Institute of Land Policy, 225–248.

Boudon, R., 1984. *La Place du désordre. Critique des théories du changement social*. Paris: PUF.

Bulkeley, H., 2006. Urban Sustainability: Learning from Best Practice? *Environment and Planning A*, 38 (6), 1029–1044.

CEC – Commission of the European Communities, 2008. *Communication from the Commission to the Council, the European Parliament, the Committee of the Regions and the European Economic and Social Committee. Green Paper on Territorial Cohesion: Turning Territorial Diversity into Strength*. COM (2008)616 Final. Luxembourg: Office for Official Publications of the European Communities.

Cotella, G. and Janin Rivolin, U., 2010. Institutions, Discourse and Practices: Towards a Multi-dimensional Understanding of EU Territorial Governance. Paper presented at the XXIV AESOP Congress: *Space is Luxury*, 7–10 July 2010, Helsinki.

Cotella, G. and Janin Rivolin, U., 2011. Europeanization of Spatial Planning through Discourse and Practice in Italy. *disP – The Planning Review*, 47 (186), 42–53.

Cotella G. and Janin Rivolin, U. 2014. Policy Transfer and Territorial Governance in the European Union, *Regions*, 296 (1), 16–18.

Cotella, G., Janin Rivolin, U. and Reimer, M., 2011. Structure, Tools, Discourse and Practices: A Multidimensional Comparative Approach to EU Territorial Governance. Paper presented at the 3rd World Planning Schools Congress, 4–8 July 2011, Perth (WA).

Dolowitz, D. and Marsh, D. 1996. Who Learns What from Whom: a Review of the Policy Transfer Literature. *Political Studies*, 44 (2), 343–357.

Dolowitz, D. and Marsh, D., 2000. Learning from Abroad: The Role of Policy Transfer in Contemporary Policy-making. *Governance*, 13 (1), 5–24.

252 Cotella, Janin Rivolin and Santangelo

Dühr, S., Stead, D. and Zonneveld, W., 2007. The Europeanization of Spatial Planning Through Territorial Cooperation, *Planning Practice & Research*, 22 (3), 291–471.

ESPON, 2011. *SPECIFICATION ESPON Applied Research Project 2013/1/21: Territorial Governance – Best Practices for New Perspectives (2011–2014)*. Available from: http://www.espon.eu/export/sites/default/Documents/Projects/AppliedResearch/ TANGO/Territorial_Governance.pdf [Accessed 20 December 2014].

ESPON and Nordregio, 2013. *ESPON TANGO–Territorial Approaches for New Governance*. Scientific Report. Available from: http://www.espon.eu/main/Menu_ Projects/Menu_AppliedResearch/tango.html [Accessed 12 March 2015].

ESPON and Politecnico di Torino, 2013. *Towards better Territorial Governance in Europe. A Guide for Practitioners, Policy and Decision Makers*. Available from: http://www.espon.eu/main/Menu_Publications/Menu_Guidance/ [Accessed 08 February 2015].

Grindle, M.S., 2011. Governance Reform: The New Analytics of Next Steps, *Governance: An International Journal of Policy, Administrations, and Institutions*, 24 (3), 415–418.

Gualini, E., 2001. *Planning and the Intelligence of Institutions. Interactive Approaches to Territorial Policy-making Between Institutional Design and Institution-building*. Aldershot: Ashgate.

Healey, P., 1999. Institutionalist Analysis, Communicative Planning and Shaping Places. *Journal of Planning Education & Research*, 19 (2), 111–122.

Healey, P., 2006. Transforming Governance: Challenges of Institutional Adaptation and a New Politics of Space. *European Planning Studies*, 14 (3), 299–320.

Holzinger, K. and Knill, C., 2005. Causes and Conditions of Cross-national Policy Convergence. *Journal of European Public Policy*, 12 (5), 775–796.

James, O. and Lodge, M., 2003. The Limitations of 'Policy Transfer' and 'Lesson Drawing' for Public Policy Research. *Political Studies Review*, 20 (1), 179–193.

Janin Rivolin, U., 2003. Shaping European Spatial Planning. How Italy's Experience Can Contribute. *Town Planning Review*, 74 (1), 51–76.

Janin Rivolin, U., 2010. EU Territorial Governance: Learning from Institutional Progress. *European Journal of Spatial Development*, refereed articles, April 2010, Available from: http://www.nordregio.se/EJSD/referred38, 1–28 [Accessed 12 February 2015].

Janin Rivolin, U., 2012. Planning Systems as Institutional Technologies: a Proposed Conceptualization and the Implications for Comparison. *Planning Practice and Research*, 27 (1), 63–85.

Janin Rivolin, U. and Faludi, A., 2005. The Hidden Face of European Spatial Planning: Innovations in Governance. *European Planning Studies*, 13 (2), 195–215.

Janin Rivolin, U. and Cotella, G., 2014. A Conceptual Device for Spreading (Good) Territorial Governance in Europe. In: ESPON, ed. *Second ESPON 2013 Scientific Report: Science in Support of European Territorial Development and Cohesion*. Luxembourg: ESPON, 175–179.

Kasper, W.K. and Streit, M.E., 1998. *Institutional Economics*. Cheltenham: Edward Elgar.

Knill, C. and Lehmkuhl, D., 1999. How Europe Matters. Different Mechanisms of Europeanization. *European Integration Online Papers*, 7 (3), Available from: http://eiop.or.at/eiop/texte/1999-007.htm [Accessed 12 January 2015].

Lenschow, A., 2006. Europeanization of Public Policy. In: Richardson, J., ed. *European Union. Power and Policy Making*. Abingdon: Routledge, 55–71.

Moroni S., 2010. An Evolutionary Theory of Institutions and a Dynamic Approach to Reform. *Planning Theory*, 9 (4), 275–297.

Moulaert, F., 2005. Institutional Economics and Planning Theory. A Partnership Between Ostriches. *Planning Theory*, 4 (1), 21–32.

Nadin, V., 2010. International Comparative Planning Methodology, *Planning Practice and Research*, 27 (1), 1–5.

North, D.C., 1990. *Institutions, Institutional Change and Economic Performance*. Cambridge: Cambridge University Press.

OECD – Organisation for Economic Co-operation and Development, 2001. *Best Practices in Local Development*. Paris: OECD.

Olsen, J.P., 2002. The Many faces of Europeanization. *Journal of Common Market Studies*, 40 (5), 921–952.

Peck J., 2011. Geographies of Policy: From Transfer-diffusion to Mobility-mutation. *Progress in Human Geography,* 35 (6), 773–797.

Radaelli, C.M., 2004. Europeanization: Solution or Problem? *European Integration Online Papers*, 8 (16), Available from: http://eiop.or.at/eiop/texte/2004-016.htm [Accessed 10 January 2015].

Servillo, L., 2010. Territorial Cohesion Discourses: Hegemonic Strategic Concepts in European Spatial Planning. *Planning Theory & Practice*, 11 (3), 397–416.

Stead, D., 2012. Best Practices and Policy transfer in spatial planning. *Planning Practice and Research*, 27 (1), 103–116.

Stoker, G., 1998. Governance as Theory: Five Propositions. *International Social Science Journal,* 50 (155), 17–18.

UN-Habitat, 2009. *Best Practices and Local Leadership Programme*. Nairobi: UN-Habitat.

Verma, N., ed., 2007. *Institutions and Planning*. Oxford: Elsevier.

Vettoretto, L., 2009. A Preliminary Critique of the Best and Good Practices Approach in European Spatial Planning and Policy-making. *European Planning Studies*, 17 (7), 1067–1083.

Wishlade, F., Yuill, D. and Mendez C., 2003. *Regional Policy in the EU: A Passing Phase of Europeanisation or a Complex Case of Policy Transfer?* European Policy Research Paper No. 50, Glasgow: European Policies Research Centre. Available from: http://www.eprc.strath.ac.uk/eprc/Documents/PDF_files/RIPR%2050%20 ESRC.pdf [Accessed 18 February 2015].

Wolman, H.L. and Page, E., 2002. Policy transfer among local governments. An Information Theory Approach. *Governance*, 15 (4), 477–501.

World Bank, 2000. *Local Economic Development: Good Practice from the European Union (and beyond)*. Unpublished paper, Washington, DC: World Bank.

18 Towards future territorial governance

Lisa Van Well, Simin Davoudi, Umberto Janin Rivolin, Ilona Pálné Kovács and Peter Schmitt

Introduction

The cases outlined in Part II document how territorial governance is being utilised to address some of the territorial challenges facing Europe today. While EU member states share many common challenges, the specific pre-conditions and contexts within each territory preclude the adoption of 'one-size-fits-all' solutions. EU Cohesion Policy's response to challenges such as long-term unemployment or economic recovery requires initiatives and actions at European, national, regional and local levels as well as across policy sectors and better inclusion of partners at all levels (CEC 2014). The so-called 'place-based approach' as defined in the Barca Report (Barca 2009) and the existence of good governance with a strong adaptive capacity are thus recognised in the last EU report on economic, social and territorial cohesion (CEC 2014) as critical factors in effectively addressing the agenda set by the 'Europe 2020' Strategy (CEC 2010). This was also reflected in the Territorial Agenda of the European Union 2020 from 2011 (Ministers responsible for Spatial Planning and Territorial Development of the European Union 2011) and the NTCCP (Network of Territorial Cohesion Contact Points) report from 2013 (NTCCP 2013); both of which called for a place-based, territorially sensitive and integrated approach to policies in order to improve performance on all levels and create synergies between different types of policy interventions.

The findings in Part II of this book assert that 'good' governance does matter, and territorial governance matters for achieving specific territorial development goals in an efficient, inclusive and sustainable manner. In the final stages of writing this book (early 2015), the territorial governance debate at the level of the EU Cohesion Policy appears to have gone somewhat quiet, perhaps due to the completion and acceptance of the 2014–2020 EU programmes. As can be seen in the Sixth Cohesion Report (CEC 2014), the focus appears to have shifted to 'good governance of territories' perhaps as a response to other pressing issues such as persistent financial and employment problems in many parts of Europe. At the same time, the various dimensions of territorial governance, as discussed in Chapters 1 and 16 of this book, seem to be both more relevant than ever in national, regional and local policy-making. Yet territorial governance takes different pathways across Europe given the diversity of long established spatial planning systems and cultures (Knieling and Othengrafen 2009, Reimer *et al.* 2014). For example, there seems to be a return to a more centralised mode of governance in many parts of Central and Eastern Europe even in those member states where the EU Cohesion Policy instruments have strong influence. The continued dominance of the national government level in the system of multi-level governance may be due to not only the financial crises, but also the enlargement process which has not exerted pressure for financial adaptation and Europeanisation (Ferry and McMaster 2013, Bouckaert *et al.* 2011). The 'urbanism tradition' established in Southern Europe, and pivoted on rigid local zoning (CEC 1997), also exhibits resistance against the new pathways for good territorial governance.

Against this backdrop, this book has argued that it may be possible to incorporate quite generalised territorial governance approaches into spatial planning and development at all levels while at the same time acknowledging the diversity of spatial planning systems in Europe. But this will be dependent on how future research approaches the concept.

The conclusions summed up in this final chapter are three-pronged. First, we discuss the prospects for territorial governance at various administrative levels, macro-regional, national, regional and local, in Europe as a whole. Second, we draw some conclusions about how a territorial governance approach can be employed generally in Northern Europe, Southern Europe, Central and Eastern Europe and in the UK and the Republic of Ireland. Finally the chapter ends with some ideas about the future prospects for territorial governance research.

Prospects for territorial governance at various levels

A place-based, territorially sensitive approach to spatial planning and Cohesion Policy at EU level can help realise the closer coordination of European Funds, as proposed by the Common Strategic Framework (CFS) 2014 to 2020 (CEC 2012). It can also maximise the impact of EU investments by the integration of various EU funds (the European Regional Development Fund the European Social Fund, the Cohesion Fund, the European Agricultural Fund for Rural Development and the European Maritime and Fisheries Fund). The Common Strategic Framework asserts that the various funds can be more efficiently pursued by avoiding overlaps and maximising potential synergies at the national, regional and local levels (CEC 2012). Thus national authorities and programme drafters have been challenged to take a more integrated approach in charting out their Cohesion Policy options. The 2014–2020 European Structural Fund programmes are now more streamlined in terms of thematic objectives and investment priorities and a territorial governance approach can facilitate

256 *Van Well et al.*

policy coherence and absorption of funding at the national and regional levels. The Common Strategic Framework does not specify how funds are to be integrated and the governance processes are left to the discretion of the states, regions or localities. Tools such as Community-led local development (CLLD) and Integrated Territorial investments (ITI) are proposed but not elaborated (ibid.). Yet the challenge remains for how individual projects within the Structural Fund programmes can take an adaptive, cross-sectoral approach to link with other EU funding opportunities including the LIFE programme, the EU's funding instrument for environmental investments, and the Horizon 2020 programme for research and innovation. In many member states and regions there may be a desire to apply territorial governance solutions in the utilisation of EU funding but, there is still a lack of good examples regarding how this would actually work. On the one hand we could assert that 'more Europe is needed' in the regulation of structural funds (as seen in Chapter 12 on Structural Fund management in Hungary). On the other hand, the 'more Europe' agenda is now being seriously contested by some member states, notably the UK. This book asserts that a territorial governance perspective provides an inroad into how synergies might be realised and overlaps reduced within the projects that are utilising various cohesion policy instruments and funds.

A focus on territorial governance is justified not just on the basis of 'which' goals should be pursued through territorial cohesion policy, but also 'how' they should be pursued. European regions are becoming increasingly interconnected and territorial challenges and opportunities transcend local, regional and national administrative demarcations. This has led, among other things, to the instigation of macro-regions for the Baltic Sea Region (BSR), the Danube Region, the Adriatic and Ionian Region and the initial elaboration of the Alpine Region as 'soft' territorial spaces for pursuing broader spatial policy and planning goals. In many ways, macro-regions and transnational or cross-border cooperation areas are fresh representations of territorial governance, as conceptualised in this book, rather than 'governance of territories' (cf. Chapter 1). Macro-regions are still in the process of carving out their roles in achieving territorial cohesion despite their lack of sovereignty and accountability. However, as seen in Chapter 15 which chronicles the process of developing a climate change adaptation strategy for the Baltic Sea Region, an essential role for macro-regions is knowledge-brokering and helping to gather and communicate knowledge and raise awareness of territorial issues to policy-makers at multiple levels. As such, it may be useful for actors working within the emerging macro-regions to consider the five dimensions of territorial governance, which are outlined in this book, as a way of working with the interception between territorial knowledge and stakeholders at all levels and sectors.

While macro-regions are rather new phenomena in the European landscape, territorial governance across borders has a longer history and has been developed within the established channels of working communities

Towards future territorial governance 257

and Euroregions as well as under the EU Cross-border and Transnational Cooperation programmes. As seen in the case of the trilateral nature park in Chapter 14, territorial governance can be challenging in these 'softer' territories when the nested administrative competencies in each country vary significantly. Thus many platforms and programmes mainly rely on project-based management to pursue their goals. The future challenge in terms of territorial governance is to find ways of institutionalising the outcomes of territorial cooperation projects so as to boost the institutional capacity of the partners. Macro-regional Action Plan entities (Priority Areas or Horizontal Actions) might be appropriate conduits for learning from project outcomes. It is important to note that institutional learning and territorial knowledgeability across borders is not just about exchanging experience about technical solutions and can include exchange about governance processes. For example, in Chapter 13, the case of flood management in the Rhine river basin has shown the limitations of taking a purely technical approach to flood control and alludes to the power of 'softer' territorial governance measures to facilitate normative cross-border and inter-sectoral actions.

At national level, territorial governance, with its focus on coordination of actors at all administrative levels, integration of various sectoral policies, inclusion of a variety of stakeholders, reliance on flexible institutions, and use of territorial knowledge, might be seen as a weak sparring partner compared to the more established forms of government practised by the nation-state, as Faludi asserts in Chapter 3. However, as demonstrated in Part II of the book, the way forward for territorial governance may be as a 'complement' to government, rather than as a 'contender'. Territorial governance approaches can be facilitated by working within (as well as without) the existing demarcated boundaries of the state and complementing place-based and content-related processes by the inclusion of new types of actors, new linkages between sectors, more flexible routines and new more context-oriented types of knowledge. At national level the main challenges of marrying territorial governance with more traditional 'governance of territories' are in ensuring transparency in responsibilities, delegation of power and use of financial instruments. As seen in Chapter 7 depicting the Pécs experience as a European Capital of Culture, the trap of an integrated approach in a centralised administrative system is that elements that should be integrated locally are instead controlled by different ministries at central level, hampering cooperation with other actors.

With regard to the regional level, we see fertile ground for a territorial governance perspective, as countries throughout Europe are looking towards more flexible solutions that transcend local and regional boundaries. This highlights the region's ever shifting role as a coordinator of actors and sectoral interests in a wide variety of configurations that reflect functional areas rather than strictly jurisdictional areas. It is perhaps here that territorial governance could have significant prospects, as regions often have responsibilities for coordinating cross-cutting territorial issues such as transport networks, regional (or rural) development or climate change adaptation. As discussed in Chapter 10 on the regional Stedenbaan initiative in the Netherlands, the lack of statutory powers and instruments make it difficult to steer development, particularly private development. Yet the soft instruments used provide a platform for coordination and informative functions which facilitate agreements among the various actors involved. But in the South Loire Plan for Territorial Cohesion, discussed in Chapter 9, even regional forums as soft instruments were insufficient for bringing important private interests into the process. In the case of the Greater Manchester Combined Authority in Chapter 11, new governance arrangements of varying types were possible and a number of public and private actors were involved because of the existing institutional capacity and social capital within the region.

Our conception of territorial governance is based on the processes involving place-based knowledge, the inclusion of local stakeholders and their interests and provision of a commonly expressed territorial goal. The example from the Neighbourhood Forum established with regard to the planning of the North Shields Fish Quay in Chapter 6 demonstrates how support from all types of stakeholders was essential, but not necessarily an end in itself. Rather it was important for local stakeholders to have a sufficient degree of civic capacity in order to participate in the planning process. Somewhat paradoxically, the local level may be the administrative level where territorial governance processes are most difficult to achieve. A valid explanation of such an apparent paradox is that the local level is where the implementation of many spatial planning measures takes place. It may be a relatively modest endeavour to discuss coordination of policy sectors and use of knowledge at EU, national, transnational, national or even regional levels where the focus is on strategic policy-making. But when it comes down to making and implementing actual decisions locally, the integration of sectoral interests may be unwieldy in a local policy environment characterised by tight budgets and lack of time, institutional capacity, and territorial tools, as well as inflexible administrative structures. Various statutes, laws and land-use regulations constrain the local level's room for manoeuvre for decision-taking and implementation. Mobilising stakeholder opinions around an issue may be utilised as a means to gain validation for planning decisions, but there is a risk that this is done in a rather inconsistent way as seen in Chapter 8 on resource efficient urban planning in Stockholm.

We can cautiously argue that prospects for territorial governance have thus far been more easily facilitated at the higher administrative levels where territorial goals are formulated and where the agenda is set for strategic policy-making. As the policy-making process becomes more concrete at the stage of decision-making, lofty rhetoric about the importance of coordination or use of knowledge might be disregarded in the course of bargaining or negotiating a decision. If policy decisions made at the EU, transnational, national or sometimes regional levels that are not attuned to local or place-based characteristics and specificities, it is difficult to see how local implementers of a spatial planning decision can have the capacity to consider all territorial governance dimensions. This can be particularly problematic in the European context, where the existence of distinct spatial planning systems and cultures results in very different approaches to the public control of local developments (Janin Rivolin 2008, Muñoz Gielen and Tasan-Kok 2010).

Prospects for territorial governance in different parts of Europe

We acknowledge that there is no one definitive recipe for using a territorial governance perspective as a tool for policy-making and planning. Rather there are different ways of employing a territorial governance perspective in different parts of Europe in such a way that it responds to their actual territorial challenges, experiences and contexts.

Prospects for territorial governance in Northern Europe

Migration and accessibility are two of the specific territorial challenges in the northern parts of Europe. Out-migration from rural areas characterises many of the German regions as well as regions in the Baltic countries and Northern Sweden and Finland (ESPON 2014). In-migration to primarily large urban agglomerations in the entire area, coupled with an aging and healthier population has led to shortages of affordable housing in cities and bottlenecks in transportation systems. Cities and regions in Northern Europe are also striving to adapt to the impacts of a changing climate, achieving sustainable planning and building practices, as well as innovation and employment goals as reflected in the Baltic Sea Region Programme 2014–2020. For example one of the challenges facing Sweden is to combine economic growth with a reduction of CO_2 emissions, particularly in domestic transport which represents a third of Sweden's CO_2 emissions (Swedish National OP 2015). The impacts of a changing climate also have various consequences for Sweden depending on the regional or territorial pre-conditions, as well as the ability to fund adaptation measures. It has been suggested that regions and municipalities could utilise the different Cohesion Policy funds, as well as environmental funding from the LIFE programme and research funding from Horizon 2020 for integrated investments in sustainable planning and building and climate adaptation measures to a much greater degree for their particular territorial conditions (Andersson *et al.* 2015).

The governance challenge for sustainable planning and building in the Nordic countries is to find ways to provide affordable housing, which is still economically viable and at the same time energy-efficient and resilient to the impacts of a changing climate. This will necessitate seeking ways to integrate diverging interests and sectors, as well as effective communication of territorial knowledge. It is not necessarily more knowledge on territorial

260   *Van Well et al.*

dynamics such as transport or commuting flows, coastal erosion or energy use that is needed, but rather how this knowledge is communicated to decision-makers and planners in a way that is understandable and can be mainstreamed into existing administrative routines (Andersson *et al.* 2015). Focusing on the 'knowledge' dimensions (dimensions 4 and 5 in, Figure 16.2) of the interplay between territorial pre-conditions and knowledge, and institutions that are adaptive, is an area where a territorial governance approach may be useful in the future.

Prospects for territorial governance in Southern Europe

Southern European countries are those most affected in Europe by the current economic crisis. One effect of this crisis is that in many countries, capital (i.e. wealth in the form of real estate property, financial assets, etc.) is currently growing at a faster pace than the economy, with an average growth rate of 4–5 per cent vs. 1–1.5 per cent per year (Piketty 2014). Urban markets play a crucial role in this process, as privatising gains and socialising losses is seen as a way to manage the crisis (Forrest and Yip 2011, Fujita 2011). When the economy expands more slowly than income, economic and social inequality will worsen and this can seriously undermine even the most solid of democracies (Fukuyama 2011). Apart from the most known and worrying case of Greece, in Italy the net wealth of households decreased by over 8 per cent from 2007 to 2013, while the concentration of net wealth grew so much that in 2012, the richest 10 per cent of the population owned 46.6 per cent of the wealth (Banca d'Italia 2014).

The more traditional operation of territorial governance in Southern European countries, which is still firmly rooted in the 'urbanism tradition', has had an impact on effects of the current crisis, especially as regards the social distribution of gains and losses on the urban markets. This somewhat dated approach to spatial planning pivots on 'a strong architectural flavour and concern with urban design, townscape and building control' to be 'undertaken through rigid zoning and codes' (CEC 1997, p. 37). The allegiance to binding zoning of a 'preventive' character (i.e. which assigns land-use rules and rights before the public control of development projects) in Southern European countries has proven to be harmful in terms of 'public-value capturing' (Muñoz Gielen and Tasan-Kok 2010). Despite expectations of better territorial governance, this system creates continuous property rights and incomes that prevent an equal distribution of gains and losses in spatial development and tends to inhibit new territorial governance strategies.

During the last 20–25 years, however, the evidence of innovative local practices of territorial governance triggered by the EU programmes and initiatives in Southern Europe (Giannakourou 2005) has begun to reveal how European territorial governance 'takes shape by passing through the prism of progressive and complex changes in planning practices. Even if Community-led, this is an eminently local and diversified process' (Janin

Rivolin and Faludi 2005, p. 211). This confirms that a process of policy transfer with respect to territorial governance is effective in Europe, as it tends to challenge 'the weakest link in the chain' of good territorial governance: obsolescent local spatial planning practices in Southern Europe. We are now able to distinguish an 'operational mode' of policy transfer and change (as seen in Chapter 17), acting via 'economic conditionality' in Southern Europe. The question remains if innovation instilled by practices will be effective enough to break the path-dependency of the spatial planning systems and the urbanism tradition established in Southern European countries. In the meantime, good territorial governance appears to concern rhetoric more than practice in Southern Europe.

Prospects for territorial governance in Central and Eastern Europe

Central and Eastern Europe is not a uniform block even from the point of view of territorial governance and regional policy. However some generalised challenges can be observed. Starting from an initial lagging behind economic situation, the relatively rapid economic development in the new member states was concentrated in the capital cities and in their immediate surroundings, enabling these urban agglomerations to compete internationally. This led to a deepening of regional disparities and a reduction of resources for 'catching up' with the rest of the country. Thus Central and Eastern European new member states are suffering from much sharper regional polarisation (Blokker-Dallago 2009). This group of countries also suffered intensely from the financial crisis, having insufficient space of movement and absorption capacity. The crisis in 2008 decreased the financial capacity of the sub-national levels due to the necessary budget constraints, which further deteriorated the absorption capacity especially in the lagging behind regions.

The explanation for the rather centralised Structural Fund management system in Central and Eastern Europe stems from the former EU programming periods. Although from 2007 onward there was a requirement to involve the regions in the decision-making, the EU Commission was ambivalent and had little trust in the regional government levels in Central and Eastern European countries. It thus supported sectoral Operational Programmes and a centralised model in managing the Structural Funds. The Sixth Cohesion Report (CEC 2014) also mentions that a smaller number of managing authorities can be advantageous in effective use of EU funds. This can be seen by central governments as justification for setting up centralised management systems. In spite of many reform attempts in Central and Eastern European countries, most regional reforms have been postponed or have failed and have not led to the creation of stronger, larger elected regions (Hendriks *et al.* 2011). The main problem in most of the Central and Eastern European countries is that they were unable to decentralise their public power system. At most they could only rescale it. The EU Cohesion Policy proved to be

262 Van Well et al.

an insufficient motivation in implementing real regional decentralisation reforms or modernisation (Yanakiev 2010, Pálné 2009).

It will most likely be important for the Central and Eastern European countries to strengthen the quality and capacity of territorial governance in order to use Structural Funds more efficiently. For example, instead of further administrative decentralisation or regionalisation, special measures are mentioned in order to make the management and administration more flexible, transparent, and business-friendly. The only exception is Poland where the regions will be important actors in regional development as a consequence of the successful regional reforms implemented in the last decade. Central and Eastern European governments are mostly convinced that a more focused use of Structural Funds needs more centralised management. The prospects of further decentralisation, especially of increasing the role of regions, are uncertain in Central and Eastern European countries since there are no firm official ambitions to strengthen the territorial governments. At most, larger cities will be empowered to implement integrated development programmes as islands in the hierarchical, rigid public administration.

Prospects for territorial governance in the UK and the Republic of Ireland

The United Kingdom (UK) and the Republic of Ireland, despite some similarities and shared history, cannot be considered as a unified block. Even in the UK, the devolution of power to Scotland, Wales and Northern Ireland has created important differences in territorial governance approaches of each devolved administration. As regards the variation between the UK and the Republic of Ireland, one revealing example is housing provision. In the latter, the debt-driven economic boom of the early 2000s led to a massive over-supply of housing, fuelled by speculative development, encouraged by the local governments' opportunistic revenue generation, and enabled by a lack of effective planning regulations. Following the 2008 economic crisis, the country had to face up to hundreds of thousands of empty houses in 'ghost towns' and a large financial burden for the government. In the UK, however, a similar debt-driven economic boom was coupled with a major shortage of housing supply, especially affordable housing, which is partly due to significant decline in the local governments' building schemes for social housing. Housing supply shortages, especially in the South East is one of the major challenges which, among other things, require coordinated territorial governance. Another important post-2008 challenge at the national level is the widening of regional disparities and the growing territorial imbalances. In the Republic of Ireland, the problem is mainly manifested in the monocentric concentrations of activities in the Greater Dublin Area (Davoudi and Wishardt 2005). In the UK, it is frequently characterised as 'the North-South divide'. While this has been a persistent feature of UK territory for more than a century, territorial disparities have been growing, even during the boom years of the 2000s.

The need for territorial rebalancing has been on and off the UK government's agenda and its associated regional policies and planning at least since the 1960s (Davoudi 2011) justified on the grounds of social cohesion, economic efficiency and environmental sustainability. The New Labour government's territorial governance response to this was to create regionally-elected levels of government with power and responsibility for, among other things, strategic spatial planning. This was rejected in a referendum in the North East on the grounds that it would create an additional layer of government bureaucracy. The Coalition government (Conservative and Liberal Democrat) which took office in 2010 dismantled all regional institutions and put the emphasis on localism (Davoudi and Madanipour 2015, see also Chapter 6). While empowering local communities is the backbone of democracy and hence widely applauded, localism can also lead to exclusionary practices and fragmentation of decision-making. Thus, the localism agenda has been paralleled with a renewed call for policy coordination and a renewed call for strategic level of decision-making beyond the local administrative boundaries. This plus the substantive issues of territorial disparities has led to a new initiative by the newly elected (in 2015) Conservative Government, called the 'Northern Powerhouse'. This is to encourage the creation of other agglomerations outside London, notably the Greater Manchester city-region or an even larger geographical concentrations such as the one made of four major cities (Manchester, Sheffield, Leeds and Liverpool) and termed 'ManSheffLeedsPool' (Parker and Bounds 2014). While rhetoric plays a big part in the idea of the 'Northern Powerhouse' and its effectiveness in addressing the UK's uneven and asymmetric decentralisation remains questionable, the initiative can be used as a window of opportunity to achieve better, more coordinated and place-based territorial governance which can mobilise placed-based knowledge generation, interconnect spatial and economic strategies in a coherent way, and respond to specific challenges and opportunities of the variable geometries of the 'North'.

Prospects for territorial governance research

Conclusions derived from the case studies in this volume give evidence that analysing territorial development on all levels in Europe could benefit from taking a territorial governance perspective as the five dimensions and 12 indicators discussed in this book provide a simple heuristic to guide research efforts. Chapter 16 points out the analytical prospects for territorial governance in research programmes while Chapter 17 shows that the means of policy transfer of the features of 'good' territorial governance are not self-evident. Above we discuss the prospects of territorial governance at different levels and in different parts of Europe in terms of the specific challenges, but

264 *Van Well et al.*

there are still some outstanding questions about how territorial governance research can help to address these challenges.

One of the aims of this book has been to stimulate debate and discussion on the overall relationship between good territorial governance in Europe and the operation of spatial planning systems in the EU countries. But do we have evidence that territorial governance and spatial planning are not just two sides of the same coin? In recent years some basic work has been undertaken in the field of comparing planning systems and conceptualising the notion of planning cultures across Europe (e.g. Knieling and Othengrafen 2009, Panagiotis 2012, Reimer *et al.* 2014). The results stemming from this exercise should be systematically compared with findings and conclusions from this book. A fruitful question for debate within the larger planning and policy community in Europe is how the two notions (territorial governance and spatial planning) can cross-fertilise each other, as Nuissl and Heinrichs (2011) have pointed out. In this light, the research could also give fuel to the debate about the robustness of the two concepts in research and policy. One way to approach this, for instance, could be the acknowledgement of distinct modes of policy transfer for territorial governance in Europe, each concerning different 'subjects' and 'objects' within an institutional contexts (Chapter 17), which sets the conceptual basis for a more conscious and targeted process of comparison between territorial governance and spatial planning processes.

Related to the 'subjects' and 'objects' of territorial governance studies, Chapter 3 of this volume wonders if the presented territorial governance framework conflates the notions of 'place' and 'territory'? From the cases presented here, we acknowledge that spatial planning processes are important sub-sets of a territorial governance processes, but territorial governance is not limited to defined boundaries the way traditional land-use planning (or 'hard planning') tends to be. In the same way we see 'place' as understood in the Barca Report (Barca, 2009) as spatial configuration that generally implies a relatively limited population and with a strong cohesive identity, such as a city or region. Spatial planning is generally done within 'places'. 'Territory', on the other hand is not just a larger area of jurisdiction or democratic accountability, such as a state, but relates to more loosely coupled identities, but with strong functional affinities and territorial specificities that matter at any geographic scope and policy level – from the neighbourhood to the macro-region. These functional affinities and territorial specificities may be at odds with 'harder' spatial planning jurisdictions, and these cases provide interesting areas of further research. One area of research as pointed out in this volume is the Central and Eastern European countries, where the territorial vision of the EU with its focus on 'softer' governance structures such as cities-agglomerations and macro-regions may be more of an obstacle than an opportunity in member states where inner territorial divisions of governance are still in flux.

Most research today focuses on governance or multi-level governance in the sense of tracing vertical and horizontal linkages and integrating new types of stakeholders and interests into decision-making and policy-making processes. Thus far, little attention has been paid to the 'territorial' dimensions of governance; or adaptability and use of territorial specificities and impacts, as this book has outlined. These dimensions are projected to become even more important in light of the proliferation of 'softer' territorial spaces across Europe that transcend national administrative boundaries such as macro-regions (cf. Allmendinger *et al.* 2015). In this light, research projects that intensively study how the two dimensions factor into territorial development within a specific territorial context (e.g. a city-region) will be relevant. The research-oriented challenge is how to make territorial knowledability more applicable for users and more attuned to the organisational/administrative pre-conditions of soft or hard territories. At the same time it is vital that institutions are able to be sufficiently flexible and capable so as to be able to absorb such knowledge (interplay between dimensions 4 and 5). Perhaps it is the role of the researcher or a bridging institution to make this transition between territorial governance in theory and territorial governance in practice visible.

References

Allmendinger, P., Haughton, G., Knieling, J. and Othengrafen, F., 2015. *Soft Spaces in Europe. Re-negotiating Governance, Boundaries and Borders.* Abingdon: Routledge.

Andersson, L., Bohman, A., van Well, L., Jonsson, A., Persson, G. and Farelius, J., 2015. *Underlag till kontrollstation 2015 för anpassning till ett förändrat klimat.* SMHI Klimatologi Nr 12, SMHI, Norrköping: SMHI.

Banca d'Italia, 2014. *La ricchezza delle famiglie italiane*, Supplementi al Bollettino Statistico, anno XXIV, n. 69, Roma: Banca d'Italia.

Barca, F., 2009. *An Agenda for a Reformed Cohesion Policy. A Place-based Approach to Meeting European Union Challenges and Expectations.* Independent report prepared at the request of Danuta Hübner, Commissioner for Regional Policy. Available from http://ec.europa.eu/regional_policy/archive/policy/future/pdf/report_barca_v0306.pdf [Accessed 26 April 2015].

Blokker, P. and Dallago, B., eds., 2009. *Regional Diversity and Local development in the New Member States.* Houndmills: Palgrave Macmillan.

Bouckaert, G., Nacrosis, V. and Nemec, J., 2011. Public Administration and Management Reforms in CEE: Main Trajectories and Results. *The NISPAcee Journal of Public Administration and Policy*, 4 (1), 9–32.

CEC – Commission of the European Communities, 1997. *The EU Compendium of Spatial Planning Systems and Policies.* Regional Development Studies, 28, Luxembourg: Office for Official Publication of the European Communities.

CEC – Commission of the European Communities, 2010. *Europe 2020. A Strategy for Smart, Sustainable and Inclusive Growth, Communication from the Commission.* Brussels, 3.3.2010 COM(2010) 2020 final, Available from http://eur-lex.europa.eu/LexUriServ/LexUriServ.do?uri=COM:2010:2020:FIN:EN:PDF [Accessed 14 April 2015].

CEC – Commission of the European Communities, 2012. *Elements for a Common Strategic Framework 2014 to 2020 the European Regional Development Fund the*

266 *Van Well et al.*

European Social Fund, the Cohesion Fund, the European Agricultural Fund for Rural Development and the European Maritime and Fisheries Fund. Commission Staff Working Document. SW(2012) 61 final, Brussels, 14 March 2012. Available from: http://ec.europa.eu/regional_policy/newsroom/detail.cfm?id=180 [Accessed 18 January 2014].

CEC – Commission of the European Communities, 2014. *Investment for Jobs and Growth. Promoting Development and Good Governance in EU Regions and Cities. Sixth Report on Economic, Social and Territorial Cohesion.* Available from: http://ec.europa.eu/regional_policy/sources/docoffic/official/reports/cohesion6/6cr_en.pdf. [Accessed 9 February 2015].

Davoudi, S., 2011. Localism and the Reform of the Planning System in England, *DiSP – The Planning Review*, 187 (4), 92–96.

Davoudi, S. and Wishardt, M., 2005. Polycentric Turn in the Irish Spatial Strategy. *Built Environment*, 31 (2), 122–132.

Davoudi, S. and Madanipour, A., eds., 2015, *Reconsidering localism*, Routledge: London.

ESPON, 2014. *A Territorial Monitoring Tool for a European Macro-region: The Example of the Baltic Sea Region.* Evidence Brief 8, April 2014. Available from: http://www.espon.eu/export/sites/default/Documents/Publications/EvidenceBriefs/EEB8_MonitoringBSR/ESPON_Evidence-Brief_8_Monitoring_tool_macro-region_BSR.pdf. [Accessed 12 April 2015].

Ferry, M. and McMaster, I., 2013. Cohesion Policy and the Evolution of Regional Policy in Central and Eastern Europe. *Europe-Asia Studies*, 65 (8), 1502–1528.

Forrest, R. and Yip, N.M., 2011. *Housing Markets and the Global Financial Crisis: The Uneven Impact on Households.* Cheltenham and Northampton, MA: Edward Elgar.

Fujita, K., ed., 2011. The Global Financial Crisis, State Regime Shifts, and Urban Theory. *Environment and Planning A*, 43(2), 265–327.

Fukuyama, F., 2011. Dealing with Inequality. *Journal of Democracy*, 22 (3), 79–89.

Giannakourou, G., 2005. Transforming Spatial Planning Policy in Mediterranean Countries: Europeanization and Domestic Change. *European Planning Studies*, 13 (2), 319–331.

Gorzelak, G., Bachtler, J. and Smetkowski, M., eds., 2010. *Regional Development in Central and Eastern Europe.* London: Routledge.

Hendriks, F., Loughlin, J. and Lidström, A., 2011. European Subnational Democracy: Comparative Reflections and Conclusions. In: J. Loughlin, F. Henriks and A. Lidström, *eds. Oxford Handbook of Local and Regional Democracy in Europe.* Oxford: University Press, 715–743.

Janin Rivolin, U., 2008. Conforming and Performing Planning Systems in Europe: An Unbearable Cohabitation. *Planning Practice & Research*, 23 (2), 167–186.

Janin Rivolin, U., 2010. EU Territorial Governance: Learning from Institutional Progress. *European Journal of Spatial Development*, Refereed Article, 38, 1–28, Available from: http://www.nordregio.se/Global/EJSD/Refereed%20articles/refereed38.pdf [Accessed 27 March 2015].

Janin Rivolin, U. and Faludi, A., 2005. The Hidden Face European Spatial Planning: Innovations in Governance. *European Planning Studies*, 13 (2), 195–215.

Knieling, J. and Othengrafen, F., eds., 2009. *Planning Cultures in Europe: Decoding Cultural Phenomena in Urban and Regional Planning.* Farnham: Ashgate.

Ministers of Urban Development and Territorial Cohesion of the European Union, 2011. *Territorial Agenda of the European Union 2020: Towards an Inclusive, Smart and Sustainable Europe of Diverse Regions*. Agreed at the Informal Ministerial Meeting of Ministers responsible for Spatial Planning and Territorial Development on 19 May 2011 Gödöllő, Hungary. Available from http://www.eu-territorial-agenda.eu/Reference%20Documents/Final%20TA2020.pdf [Accessed 17 January 2015].

Muñoz Gielen, D. and Tasan-Kok, T., 2010. Flexibility in Planning and the Consequences for Public-value Capturing in UK, Spain and the Netherlands. *European Planning Studies*, 18 (7), 1097–1131.

NTCCP (Network of Territorial Cohesion Contact Points), 2013. *Place-based Territorially sensitive and Integrated Approach*. Ministry of Regional Development, Warsaw, Poland.

Nuissl, H. and Heinrichs, D., 2011. Fresh Wind or Hot Air – Does the Governance Discourse Have Something to Offer Spatial Planning? *Journal of Planning Education and Research*, 31 (1), 47–59.

Pálné Kovács, I., 2009. Europeanisation of Territorial governance in Three Eastern/Central European countries. *Halduskultuur – Administrative Culture*, 10, 40–57.

Panagiotis, G., 2012. Comparing Spatial Planning Systems and Planning Cultures in Europe. The Need for a Multi-scalar Approach. *Planning Practice & Research*, 27 (1), 25–40.

Parker, G. and Bounds, A., 2014. Osborne to Back 'Northern Powerhouse'. *The Financial Times*, 23 October, The Financial Times: London.

Piketty, T., 2014. *Capital in the Twenty-First Century*. Cambridge, MA: Harvard University Press.

Reimer M., Getimis P. and Blotevogel H., eds., 2014. *Spatial Planning Systems and Practices in Europe*. London: Routledge.

Swedish OP for Investments in Employment and Growth, 2014. *Operativt Program Inom Målet Investering för Sysselsättning och Tillväxt, 2014*. 2014SE16RFOP009. Available from: http://eu.tillvaxtverket.se/download/18.63d855b314a67290039 86a31/1420641582575/OP+Nationellt+program.pdf [Accessed 12 April 2015].

Yanakiev, A., 2010. The Europeanization of Bulgarian Regional Policy: A Case of Strengthened Centralization. *Southeast European and Black Sea Studies*, 10 (1), 45–57.

Index

accessibility 81, 96, 106, 109, 117, 126–7, 132–3, 135, 137, 168, 185, 259

accountability 25, 44, 49, 51, 53–4, 57, 108, 138, 150–1, 155, 211, 222, 226–7, 256, 264

adaptability 10, 12, 50, 53–4, 57, 76, 121, 138, 148, 152, 184, 198, 234–5, 265

adaptive flood protection 184

administrative unit 25, 46, 51, 186, 226

Agency for the Economic Development of Loire 115

agenda-setting 131, 133

agriculture 117, 171, 187, 192, 194–5, 195–8, 201, 204, 208–10, 215

'Agglomeration Project' 111

Alps-Adriatic Working Community 189–90

aménagement du territoire 39

Association of Greater Manchester Authorities 145–6, 149–52,

Atlantic Arc 204

Austria 16, 189–97, 199, 201

'Autonomous change' 51

autonomy 27, 39, 50, 82, 90, 111–12, 142, 151

Baltadapt 204–16

Baltic Sea Region 16, 64–5, 204–8, 210–16, 223–31, 256, 259

'Baltic Sea Region Climate Change Dialogue Platform' 211

Baltic Sea Region Programme 2007–2013 204, 206

'Baltic Window' 205, 215

Baranya 159, 164

'Barca Report' 7, 254, 264

Barents Sea 199

Basque country 27

BBC 153

being adaptive to changing contexts 13, 40, 53–4, 57, 76, 89, 104–5, 109, 116, 120, 136, 152, 165, 184, 198, 212, 228, 232–3, 236

Berlin 206–7

Bern Convention 174–5

Berstein, Sir Howard 152

'best practices' 16, 103, 212, 238

Bestuurlijke Commissie 132

Bestuurlijk Platform Zuidvleugel (BPZ) 128

biodiversity 195–6, 207–8, 215

Bird Directive 176, 195

Blair, Tony 143

boundaries 9, 11, 23, 40, 43–4, 46, 64, 75, 78, 96, 98, 129, 147, 189–90, 257, 264; administrative boundaries 25, 54, 167, 171, 185, 189, 215, 263, 265; 'fuzzy boundaries' 24; institutional boundaries 23, 40; jurisdictional boundaries 10, 11, 36, 40–1, 64–5, 95, 214, 227, 230; municipal boundaries 98; national boundaries 28, 44; policy boundaries 23; regional boundaries 44, 257; territorial boundaries 9, 23, 41–2, 54

Budapest 81–2

Bulgaria 31

bureaucracy 31, 145, 150, 263

bureaucratic mission creep 131

Burgenland 191, 196

Business Leaders Council 146

business sector 28, 86, 88, 90, 165

capabilities 122, 228

capacity 4, 11, 36, 39, 49–52, 56, 74–5, 77, 79, 88, 105, 107, 109,

111, 120, 123, 142, 152, 154, 184, 192, 200–2, 208, 224, 226, 234, 239, 254, 259; absorption capacity 261; adaptive capacity 4, 50–1, 57, 208, 213; civic capacity 70, 79, 258; community capacity 79; coordination capacity 206; decision-making capacity 106; descriptive capacity 241; financial capacity 261; governance capacity 145, 176; 'governing capacity' 52, 54, 56, 108, 138, 191; individual capacity 106, 228; institutional capacity 52, 152, 154, 186, 226, 257–8; 'learning capacity' 51; 'reactive capacity' 121, 247; regional governance capacity 145, 149; territorial governance capacity 15, 16, 108, 142, 145, 147, 149

Carinthia 189

'cartography of social life' 42; non-territorialist cartography of social life 42

case studies 4–6, 13–14, 17, 41, 46, 48, 58, 63–6, 68–70, 76, 79, 95, 97, 104, 107, 142, 147, 150–3, 159, 221

Central and Eastern Europe 30–1, 157–9, 163, 190, 200, 255, 261–2, 264; countries 29–31, 157–9, 163, 261–2, 264

central state 29, 111, 115

centralisation 16, 26, 31, 161, 163, 167

Chazelles-sur-Lyon 113, 115

citizen 7, 9, 29, 38, 48–9, 52, 121, 227; citizen engagement 67, 104; citizen involvement 211; citizen participation 22

citizenship 37, 49

City Deals 145

'civic engagement' 49

civic groups 79

civic institution 151, 228

civic network 88

civic organisation 86

civic participation 89

civic sector 88, 90, 147

civic society 57

civil elite 86, 88

civil preparedness 204

civil (society) organisation 163–4,

civil servant 31, 181, 242

civil society 3, 48–9, 82, 85, 91, 183, 232

civil (society) sector 53, 89

climate change 3–4, 22, 50, 181–2, 205, 209, 211–14, 234; climate change adaptation 8, 16, 63–4, 204–13, 215–16, 258; climate change adaptation measures 211; climate change adaptation plan 211; climate change adaptation strategy 204–5, 208–16, 256; climate change adaptation work 216; impact of climate change 206, 215; climate change issues 208; climate change mitigation 208

Code de l'urbanisme 117

coherence 7, 49, 117, 134, 207, 256

Cohesion Fund 25, 255

cohesion goals 31

Cohesion Policy 4, 7, 28–9, 31–2, 82, 84, 91–2, 157–8, 160–1, 164, 247, 248, 254–6, 259, 261

Cohesion Report 254, 261

Colbert, Jean-Baptiste 38

Cold War 37

'collaboration' 50, 52, 123, 145, 151, 183, 195; collaborative culture 228; collaborative planning 120; collaborative projects 152; collaborative tradition 115; collaborative working 151

collective action 7, 23, 91, 111, 123, 231

collective commitment 87

collective decision-making 9

comité syndical 115–16, 118

Commissariat général à l'égalité des territoires 39

Commission for the Protection of the Alpine Regions (CIPRA) 189

Common Fisheries Policy 68

Common Strategic Framework 255–6

Commonwealth Games 152–3

Communautés d'agglomeration 115

Communautés de communes 115

'Community-led local developments' 92, 256

Community Strategic Guidelines 164

Conservative Party 70

Constitution of Europe 39

constructivism 43–5

contingency plan 199

cooperation 16, 22, 29, 88, 91, 96, 104, 106, 123, 128–9, 131, 165, 171–2, 174, 177, 183, 185–6, 189–90, 192–4, 196, 198, 200–2, 204–6, 212–13, 224–5, 257; cooperation arrangement 21–2, 28, 131; bilateral cooperation 200; cross-

270 *Index*

border cooperation 16, 172, 174, 185–6, 189, 198–201, 211, 226, 234, 256; cross-border cooperation programme 190, 200, 257; cross-border cooperation project 201, 213; horizontal cooperation 21; inter-institutional cooperation 112; inter-municipal cooperation 106, 120–1, 230; international cooperation 96; macro-regional cooperation 205, 216; multi-level cooperation 15, 227; regional cooperation 96, 129, 167; river cooperation 172; soft cooperation 181; territorial cooperation 24, 200, 202, 212–13, 257; transnational cooperation 205, 214, 256; transnational cooperation programme 257; transnational co-operation project 204; transnational cooperation strategy 216; trilateral cooperation 194; vertical cooperation 21

coordination 15, 39–40, 52–3, 100–1, 106, 108, 118–19, 131, 138, 154, 162, 165–6, 168, 195–6, 198, 200–2, 204–7, 223–4, 226, 232–3, 255, 258; co-ordinating actions of actors and institutions 10, 39, 69, 97, 131, 146, 159, 172, 191, 201, 205, 222, 232; coordination of actors and institutions 4, 40, 99, 123, 146, 168, 192, 201, 223–4, 232, 257; coordination mechanism 29, 198; cross-sectoral coordination 195, 196–7, 201; governmental coordination 162; horizontal coordination 10, 138; inter-municipal coordination 109, 120; international coordination 181; policy coordination 21, 138–9, 145–6, 263; project coordination 206; vertical coordination 10, 138, 161

corps d'Etat 38
cost-benefit analysis 51
Council of Europe 6, 25
Council of European Municipalities and Regions 26
Council of the Baltic Sea States/Baltic 21 (CBSS/Baltic 21) 205, 207–8, 211–12, 216
County Administrative Board 98–9, 101
crisis management 89
cross-sector objective 117
cross-sector synergy 53–4, 57, 102, 196, 209
cross-sectoral integration 4, 117–18, 195–6, 209, 223–4

Danish Meteorological Institute (DMI) 205
Danube Basin 204
Danube Region 256
De l'État-nation aux sociétés ingouvernable 39
decentralisation 9, 25–6, 29–30, 49, 83, 112, 128, 141–2, 159, 226, 262–3
decision-maker 14, 49, 57, 87, 89–90, 98, 124, 163, 205–6, 213, 216, 229, 236, 239, 248–9, 260
Delft-South 133
Delphi method 55
Delphi survey 14, 48, 55, 57–8
Delta Programme 181
democracy 21, 150, 227, 263; associative democracy 22; deliberative democracy 45; participative democracy 53, 197; participatory democracy 67; representative democracy 44; stakeholder democracy 22; democratic representativeness 226
Den Haag Laan van NOI 135
Denmark 26
deregulation 14
devolution 9, 56, 67, 141–3, 147, 262
'Devo Manc' 147
dialogic mode of transfer 245, 246, 248
Dordrecht 126, 128–9, 132
Drecht cities 129
Drôme 120

Eastern European countries 82
Eastern European political culture 91
Ecologic Institute 207
economic conditionality 246–9, 261
economic convergence 31
economic crisis 10, 31, 90, 134–6, 166, 198, 229, 260–2
economic disparities 28
education 28, 128, 148, 154, 191, 194
effectiveness 21, 49, 51, 57, 120, 247, 263
efficiency 7, 13, 22, 30, 40, 49–51, 57, 83, 131, 136, 148–9, 159, 168, 263
England 15, 45, 67–9, 142–3, 223, 225–9, 231
English Heritage 72, 75
English Regional Development Agencies 143

Environmental Audit Report 193
environmental management 26
environmental quality 13, 40, 198
EPURES 113, 115
equality 13, 38, 40
equity 7, 24, 49, 51
ESPON Coordination Unit 55
ESPON Monitoring Committee 55
ESPON National Contact Point 55
Établissement *Public de Cooperation Intercommunale* (EPCI) 112
EU budget 28
EU Cohesion Policy *see* Cohesion Policy
EU Cross-border and Transnational Cooperation programmes 257
EU directive 184, 186, 247
EU discourse 241, 245, 246–7
EU Habitat and Birds directive 195
EU member state 30, 176, 190, 254
EU Parliament *see* European Parliament
EU spatial policy discourse 6
EU Strategy for the Alpine Region 204
EU Strategy on Adaptation to Climate Change 205
EU White Paper 'Adapting to Climate Change: Towards a European Framework for Action' 205
EU White Paper on Governance 8, 40, 49
Euclidean planning 25
Eurocities 26
European Charter of Local Self-Government 25
European integration 3, 9, 22–3, 28, 38, 189
European territory 4, 51
Europe 2020 51, 142, 208, 247, 254
European Agricultural Fund for Rural Development 255
European Capital of Culture 15, 81–91, 223–5, 227–8, 230–1, 257
European Cohesion Policy *see* Cohesion Policy
European Commission 7, 29, 32, 206–7, 211, 214, 248
European Economic Community 171
European Green Belt initiative 194, 199
European Green Capital 95
European integration 3, 9, 22–3, 28, 38, 184
European Maritime and Fisheries Fund 255
European Parliament 81, 248
European Regional Development Fund 255

European Social Fund 255
European Structural Funds 81, 83, 85–7, 255
European Union 3, 15, 25, 28, 30–1, 48, 81, 158, 162–3, 171, 194, 200, 238
European Union Strategy for the Baltic Sea Region (EUSBSR) 204–5, 208, 210, 213
Europeanisation 82, 142, 239–41, 255
Eurotowns 26
evidence-based approach 153
ex-ante evaluation 107, 161, 231
ex-post evaluation 108
Exeter St James Forum 77
experimentation 105, 109, 166, 213–14, 229
Exploateringskontoret 97

Fastighetskontoret 105
feedback mechanism 53, 184
feedback routine 116
financial crises 255
fiscal reform 26
fish processing 71–2, 78
fishermen 69, 75, 78
fishing industry 68, 71, 74
flagship project 95, 102, 105, 107, 204
flexibility 10, 24, 50–1, 54, 83, 152, 184, 201, 213–14, 222, 226, 229
flood management 16, 171, 174, 184, 230, 257
flood plains 179–80
flooding 177–9, 182, 184, 186, 231
floods 16, 176, 179, 186
floods directive 171, 174–6, 182, 185
forward-looking actions 222, 229
France 15, 38, 111–12, 115, 121
Friuli-Venezia Giulia 189
'functional dependencies' 230–1
functional economic area 147, 153
functional space 9, 230
Färgfabriken 101

Geddes, Patrick 171
Gelderland 172, 175, 177–8
'Gemeinsame Erklärung' 175, 177
German–Dutch Working Group on High Water 16, 172, 174–5, 177, 178, 181, 186
German Federal Ministry for the Environment, Nature Conservation and Nuclear Safety (BMU) 207

272 *Index*

Germany 172, 177, 180, 182, 184–6
global transactions 42
globalisation 28, 37–8, 40, 142, 149
good practice 238, 240–1
Goričko-Raab-Őrség 16, 65, 189–91,
192–3, 200
Gouda 128–9, 135
governance 7–9; European governance
31, 39; 'fair governance' 51; 'good'
governance 8, 48–52, 248, 254;
governance arrangements 10, 21,
24, 27, 30, 36, 130, 212, 226–7,
229, 258; governance institution 16,
50, 68, 72, 141–3, 145–6, 150–4;
governance of territories 5–6, 11–12,
21–2, 117, 124, 216, 254, 256–7;
governance reform 28, 30, 159;
governance process 4, 10–11, 14–16,
51, 53, 56–8, 63, 66, 74, 111, 113–
15, 120–4, 182, 205, 212, 222–3,
227, 231, 236–8, 250, 256–8, 264;
governance structure 10, 22, 51,
79, 141, 143, 146–8, 150–4, 264;
local governance 84, 141, 225;
'multi-level' governance 3–5, 9–12,
25, 32, 43, 82, 89, 91, 205–6, 208,
210, 221, 234–6, 255, 264; 'regular
governance' 12–13, 235; regional
governance 16, 27, 45, 141–3, 145,
149, 154; 'soft governance arrangements' 130; water governance 223;
see also territorial governance
government 5-7, 9-10, 13-4, 21-32,
36-41, 43-46, 49, 63, 67-8, 77,
82, 84, 86-7, 106, 112, 127, 129,
132-4, 138-9, 141, 143, 145-6, 152,
153-4, 159, 162-8, 172, 177, 181,
183, 185, 191, 213-4, 223-4, 240,
245, 262-3; county government 159,
162; Government Commission for
Development Policy 162; Government Offices for the Regions 143;
government reform 26; governmental actor 21, 112, 162; intergovernmental actor 207; intergovernmental
organisation/body or actor 183, 186,
207; intergovernmentalism 3, 9;
local government 9, 26, 29, 32, 48,
83-6, 88-92, 107, 132, 143, 245,
247, 262; national government 9,
29-30, 74, 83, 87, 92, 96, 126-34,
138, 141, 146, 148, 150, 152, 191-
2, 197, 224, 255, 257; non-governmental actor or agency 21, 32, 112,

190; non-governmental organisation
(NGO) 21, 29, 146, 183, 195, 200,
210; regional government 9, 26-7,
135, 138, 143, 185, 189, 261; self-
government 25-6, 31, 84, 88, 127,
159; sub-national government 21,
26, 31-2
Greater London 142–3, 145; Greater
London Authority 143
Greater Manchester 16, 65, 142–3,
145–55, 263; Greater Manchester
Combined Authority 141, 144;
146–8, 150, 258; Greater Manchester County Council 143, 145
Greece 26, 260
'Grenelle II Law' 111–12, 121
gross domestic product 28

Haaglanden 129–30
Habitat Directive 180
Hammarby Sjöstad 96, 100, 105
hard spaces 24–5, 65, 230–1
hazard mitigation 50
Health and Wellbeing Commission 154
HELCOM (Helsinki Commission) 207,
213
Helsinki Water Convention 174
High Water Conference 183
*Hoogwatermagazine/Hochwassermaga-
zin* 183
Horizon 2020 programme for research
and innovation 256, 259
'horizontal actions' 208, 210, 215–16,
257
horizontal interaction 39
horizontal policy coordination 138
housing supply 122, 262
HS2020 105
Hull 142
human geography 37, 41, 44
Hungary 16, 31, 81–2, 157–61, 163,
166, 167–8, 189–99, 201, 256
hyper-local planning 15, 67–79, 223,
225–31

identity 26, 45, 117, 155; cohesive
identity 264; collective identity
39; cultural identity 153; historical identity 154; national identity
38; regional identity 85, 153, 167,
208; spatial identity 137; territorial
identity 38
'imitating countries' 159
IMMOCHAN 119

inclusive growth 51
inductive approach 5
industrial revolution 143
industrialisation 38
institutional context 64, 239–40, 264
institutional memory 51, 115
'institutional mode' of transfer 248
'institutional-cum-political-economic emphasis' 41
'Instrument for Pre-Accession Assistance' (IPA) 190
integrated coastal zone management 204
integrated territorial investments (ITI) 256
integrating policy sectors 10, 13, 40, 103, 146, 224
'interactive resources' 248
International Commission for the Protection of the Rhine (ICPR) 171, 175
International Convention on the Prevention of Chemical Pollution of the Rhine 174
international relations theory 36–7, 41
INTERREG 190
intervention area 230
IPO (association of provinces) 132
Ireland 26, 255, 262
Iron Curtain 190, 199
Italy 27, 189–90, 260

jurisdiction 9, 25, 37, 40, 44, 107, 214, 264

knowledge 3–4, 6–7, 11–12, 16–17, 43, 54, 63, 72, 79, 90, 105, 108, 118, 124, 152–3, 160, 165–6, 181, 185–6, 198, 201. 204–6, 213, 215, 223, 225, 228–9, 231, 233–5, 238, 248, 257–60, 265; collective knowledge 198; communicative knowledge 256; expert knowledge 107, 212, 222, 231, 234; formal knowledge 199; institutional knowledge 215, 228; knowledge arenas 241; knowledge broker 205, 212; knowledge overlaps 215; knowledge resources 52; knowledge transfer 104, 108, 186, 228; local knowledge 54, 79, 234; organisational knowledge 165; place-based knowledge 10, 79, 200–1, 231, 258; reciprocal knowledge 115; regional knowledge 16, 162, 166–7, 182; technical knowledge 4, 215; territorial knowledge 4,
13, 107, 109, 121–4, 201, 222, 231, 234–5, 241, 248, 256–7, 259; see also territorial knowledge arenas
Krajinski park Goričko 191

'La fin des territories' 37
Labour Party 70, 152
'Landscape in harmony' 198
land use 53, 134, 179, 186, 192, 199, 214, 260; planning 75, 99, 106, 264; regulation 36, 132
'leadership' 52, 56–7, 88, 99–100, 108, 116, 123, 147, 152, 207, 222–3
leadership continuity 228; consensual leadership 207; decentralised leadership 193, 200, 201; formal leadership 223; informal leadership 209, 223; modes of leadership 232; political leadership 30, 49; 'soft' leadership 193, 201, 229
learning 10–11,16, 51, 53, 89–90, 105, 108, 136, 184, 212–13, 238, 246, 250, 257; individual learning 199, 212, 222, 229, 233; institutional learning 120–1, 166, 184, 198, 212, 214, 222, 228, 233, 257; 'learning by doing' approach 226; learning capability 12; learning capacity 5; 'learning machines' 184; 'learning machinery' 228; learning process 10, 120, 229, 238; organisational learning 16, 90, 201; transnational learning 212
Leeds 142, 263
legal conditionality 247, 249
legal framework 57, 119, 185, 211, 22
legal mechanism 226
legal right 49
legitimacy 15, 38, 39, 45, 51, 53, 67, 70, 79, 85, 87, 89, 103, 150, 164, 211, 232; democratic legitimacy 14, 24, 37, 40, 44–6, 53–4, 57, 70, 108, 138, 147, 150, 197–8, 226–7, 232; substantive legitimacy 150, 227
Leiden 126, 128–9
Lesse, Sir Richard 152
liberalisation 38, 99, 108
LIFE programme 256, 259
light-rail transport system 126
Liverpool 142, 263
Lobith 182
'Local Agenda 21' 111
Localism 15, 67, 70, 72, 75, 141–2, 263

274 *Index*

Localism Act 67, 72, 145, 263
Local Enterprise Partnership 145, 147–9
Loire-Forez 113,
London 27, 263; *see also* Greater London
Louis XIV 38
Lyon 111, 113, 115, 117, 119, 122, 124

macro-region 14, 204–6, 213–16, 234, 255–6, 264–5
macro-regional Action Plan 257
macro-regional climate change adaptation strategy 211, 215–16
macro-regional strategy 37, 64, 204, 208, 210, 215–16
macro-regional strategy for the Baltic Sea Region 16
macro-regional territory 209
Manchester 142, 144, 152–4, 223, 224–30, 263; *see also* Greater Manchester
Manchester Independent Economic Review 149, 153
Manchester Investment Delivery Agency Service 146, 149
ManSheffLeedsPoo 263
marine environment 207, 209, 215
market economy 39
Marketing Manchester 146
marketisation 15, 25, 27, 31
Marseillaise 37
Mediterranean Sea 204
Meerjarenprogramma Infrastructuur, Ruimte en Transport (MIRT) 134
mega-region 171
Mercouri, Melina 81
'metageographies' 41–3
metropolitan region 8, 28, 131–3, 135–6, 154
micro-regions 164
Midden-Holland 129
Ministers responsible for Spatial Planning and Territorial Development of the European Union 7, 254
Ministry of Infrastructure and the Environment 134, 177
Ministry of the Agriculture and Environment 195–6, 198
mobilisation of stakeholder (participation) 138, 228
mobilising stakeholder participation 10, 13, 40, 53–4, 57, 73, 76, 87, 103,

108, 116, 119, 135, 150, 163, 182, 197, 210, 222, 226 232–4, 236, 258
mobility 99, 109, 112, 117–18, 133–4, 137, 225
mobility infrastructure 95
Mogersdorf 196
Monts du Pilat 113, 115, 120
multi-case study method 63
Mura 196

National Adaptation Strategies 216
national development agency 87, 160–5, 168
National Development Plan 81
National Health Service 148, 154
national spatial plans 196
National Strategic Reference Framework 157, 160–2, 164, 167
Natura 2000 180, 191, 194–6, 198–9
natural disaster risk 215
natural protection 63
natural resources 117, 189
nature protection 191–7, 201
nature protection directives 26
Naturpark Raab 189–202
Navarre 27
Neighbourhood Forum 67–79
neighbourhood planning 67–79
neighbourhood scale 15, 67–79
network approach 54, 106
Network of Territorial Cohesion Contact Points (NTCCP) 7, 254
'New Economy' 148–9
New Labour 143, 263
new public management 28, 31
NGO 21, 29, 183, 200, 210, 238, 245
NIMBYism 72
non-state networks 39
non-territorialist 41–3
North East of England 68, 143, 150
North Sea 174
North Sea-English Channel Area 204
North Shields (Fish Quay) 65, 67–79, 258
North Tyneside Council 70
Northern Europe 255, 259
Northern Ireland 27, 143, 145, 262
Northern Powerhouse 263
North-Rhine Westphalia 172, 177–8
NS (national rail operator) 126, 129–30, 132, 135

Objektschutz 182

OECD 6, 8
Ooij Polder 182
openness 49
operational mode of transfer 246, 248
organisational structure 88, 148, 185
Öriszentpéter 191, 194
Örsegi Némzeti Park 191
Osborne, George 147
Östergötland 27
outsourcing 27–8

parish councils 77, 79
participation of stakeholders (see mobilising stakeholder participation)
participatory planning 104
Partnership Agreement 191–4
partnership principle 30
Pécs 15, 65, 81–92, 223–38, 257
PHARE CBC programme 200
Pilat Regional Nature Park 115
place governance 37
place-based approach 24, 27–8, 91, 137, 154, 215, 254
place-based consistency 122
plan A 166
plan B 109, 166, 229
planning region 171
platform 21, 52, 88, 107–8, 111, 128, 138, 226, 257
Poland 168, 262
polarisation 28, 261
policies of liberalisation 38
policy design 229, 231
policy networks 9, 154
policy packaging 53, 54, 56, 85–6, 102, 124, 139, 195, 208
policy-maker 14, 119, 121, 124, 197, 204, 206, 211, 221, 231, 236, 239, 248–9, 256
policy-making 4, 8–10, 23, 28, 119, 121, 247–8, 255, 258–9
political and social actors 39
political regime 39
polity 44
polycentric region 130
post-structuralism 43
practical application 17, 248–9
practitioner 54, 124, 197, 221, 231, 236, 239, 248–9
Programma Beter Benutten 134
Programma Hoogfrequent Spoorvervoer 134
property crisis 136
proportionality 49

ProRail 132
Provinciale structuurvisie 132
Provinciale verordening 132
public accountability 53, 54, 57, 108, 138
public administration 22, 31–2, 84, 157–60, 167, 263
public consultation process 164
public domain 25, 27, 31
public organisations 27, 89
public policy 3, 13, 22, 54, 56, 117, 124, 138, 195–6
public transport 15, 63, 95–101, 106–7, 126–139, 157
public transport network 15, 126–8
Putnam, Robert 152

qualitative methods 63

Randstad 15, 65, 126–39, 223–31
Randstad Urgent Programme 133
'Randstad 2040 Structural Vision' 133
Raum für die Flüsse 180; *see also* 'room for the river'
realising place-based/territorial specificities and impacts 13, 54, 78, 91, 106, 121, 137, 153, 167, 185, 199, 230, 232
redundancy 50
reflexivity 53–57
regeneration 68, 69, 74, 86, 122
Regional Competitiveness Index 157
Regional Development Agency 83, 90, 143–5, 150–3, 159–67, 195–6, 199
Regional Development Council 115, 159, 161–7
Regional Operational Programme 16, 86, 91, 157–161
Regional Planning Office 101
regional policy decisions 29
regional selectivity 137
Regional Transport Authority 115
regionalisation 29, 30, 42, 202
regionalism 43, 44, 91, 143, 152
Regionalpläne 182
regulative power 176
relational conception of space 42
relational planning 25
relativist constructionism 43
representative democracy 44
republican model 38
rescaling 13, 21–32
resilience 10, 54, 59, 205
resource efficiency 15, 95–109

276 *Index*

resource-efficient urban planning 63
responsiveness 22, 51, 187, 234
Rhine river basin 16, 171–87
Rhône-Alpes Region 111, 115
Rijkswaterstaat 186
River Tyne 68
River Vecht 172
Romania 31
'room for the river' 179–86
'room for water' 179
Rotterdam 128–36, 180
rules for good territorial governance
    248–9
rural areas 128, 136
Russia 9, 206, 210

Saint Galmier 115–120
Saint Simon 38
Saint-Étienne 111–13, 116, 121–3
Salford Quays 153
Samfundet St. Erik 98
scale 9,11, 23–4, 32, 39, 51, 84, 95,
    128, 154, 248
Schéma de Coherence Territorial (SCOT)
    15, 111–124
Schiedam 133
Scotland 27, 142–3, 145, 262
Scrutiny Pool 148, 151
secondary cities 142
sectoral conflict 222, 225, 232
sectoral integration 25, 84, 224, 232
Sectoral Operational Programme 162,
    166, 168, 261
sectoral policy areas 63
security 39
settlements 42, 91, 119, 157, 159, 164
Sheffield 263
silo effect 102, 224
silo mentality 209, 214, 225
Sivom 120
Sixth Cohesion Report 254, 261
Skåne 27
Slovenia 16, 189–202
Slovenian Act on Nature Protection 191
small and medium-sized enterprises 88
smart growth 51
smart specialisation 142
social and economic segregation 28
social capital 15, 87–8, 152, 155, 200,
    228, 258
social cohesion 38, 263
social inequality 168, 260
social policies 38
societal challenges 3, 22, 28

Sociologie de l'action publique 39
soft spaces 24–5, 32, 64–5, 112, 231
solidarity 16, 37–8, 172, 176, 185, 208
Solidarity and Urban Renovation Law
    111, 124
Somogy 159, 164
South Loire 15, 65, 111–124
South Transdanubian Region 65,
    157–159
South Wing 128–9, 131–5, 137
Southern Europe 255, 260–1
southern Randstad 15, 65, 126–39,
    223–9, 231
sovereign state 36, 213
sovereignty 20, 36–8, 41, 43, 256
Spain 26, 27
spatiality 11, 43
spatial development 24, 30, 43, 122,
    133, 240, 260
spatial planning 4,5, 7–8, 14–17, 39,
    79, 115, 122, 127–8, 132–8, 143,
    145, 172, 179, 182, 187, 204, 208,
    210, 225, 240, 248, 254–5, 258–64
Stadsbyggnadskontoret 97
Stadsledningskontoret 97
Stadsregio Rotterdam 129–30
stakeholder mobilisation 4, 87, 103;
    see also mobilisation of stakeholder
    participation
Stedenbaan 15, 126–139
Stockholm 15, 65, 95–109, 206–7,
    223–31, 258
'Stockholm at large' 101
Stockholm Beauty Council 98
'Stockholm model' 98–9, 103, 108
Stockholm Royal Seaport 15, 95–109
Stockholms Skönhetsråd 98
Storstockholms Lokaltrafik 98, 106
Strategic Environmental Assessments
    (SEA) 197
strategic integrative planning 159
structural context 10, 12, 222, 224, 232
Structural Funds 16, 25–6, 29–30, 81,
    83, 85–7, 157–69, 223–245, 246,
    255–6, 261–2
sub-national government 21, 26, 31–2
subsidiarity 44, 49, 50, 52, 54, 56–7,
    67, 82, 108
substantive legitimacy 150, 227
Summer Olympics 152
supremacy 44
surface water 176, 186
Survey Monkey 55
'sustainability' 15, 49, 69, 85, 89, 90,

110, 263
sustainable development 22, 49, 51, 92, 117–18, 122, 194, 199, 208, 210, 247
sustainable growth 51
Sweden 26–7, 33, 95–109, 259
Swedish Meteorological and Hydrological Institute (SMHI) 207–8
Switzerland 171, 180
Syndicat Mixte 112–13, 117–18, 120–1, 125

TANGO project 51, 55, 238, 245
Territorial Agenda of the European Union 2020 7, 254
territorial analysis 122, 222, 231
territorial blindness 106
territorial cohesion 7, 10, 22, 39, 51, 168, 205, 254, 256
Territorial Cohesion Plan 15, 111–124
territorial constituencies 44
territorial context 63, 230, 234, 250, 265
territorial development goal 4, 63, 228, 239–40, 254
territorial dimensions 4, 11, 265
territorial distance 42
territorial diversity 11
Territorial Employment Pacts 246
territorial governance 10–13; components of territorial governance 17, 66, 221–2, 230, 239; cross-border territorial governance 201, 231; dimensions of territorial governance 17, 40, 54–55, 58, 63–4, 66, 79, 159, 221, 223, 233, 254, 256; European territorial governance 17, 240–2, 250, 260; features of territorial governance 66, 221, 237; 'good' territorial governance 5–6, 14, 17, 48–58, 64, 95–109, 168, 221, 238–51, 255, 261, 263–4; territorial governance practice 6, 11, 14, 17, 63, 95, 107, 230, 238, 246–7, 250; territorial development 10, 28, 36, 116–17, 120, 166, 171–2, 213; territorial development assessment tool 237; territorial development goal 4, 63, 66, 223–4, 228, 239–40, 254; territorial development policy 4; territorial dimension of governance 4, 11, 265; territorial governance capacity 15–16, 108, 142, 145; quality of territorial governance 14,

48, 51, 56, 58
territorial impacts 4, 54, 109, 176, 231, 234
territorial knowledge arenas 241
territorial knowledgeability 4, 54–5, 58, 168, 257
territorial objective 64
territorial pacts 21, 246
Territorial Planning Directive 111, 119, 122, 124
territorial realms 42
territorial relationality 54, 57–8, 106–7, 214, 230
territorial representation 45
territorial scope 65, 97, 113, 144, 158, 209, 214, 230
territorial specificities 4–5, 11–13, 16, 24, 40, 54, 57, 78, 91, 106, 119, 121, 124, 137, 139, 153, 163, 167–8, 199, 212, 214, 223, 230, 232–3, 236, 264–5
territorial strategies 50, 107
territorial trap 41
territorialisation 112, 186, 250
territorialism 42–6; absolutistic territorialism 43–6; statist territorialism 42–3
territorialist 41–3
territoriality 42, 44, 51, 139, 154
territory 45, 53–4, 56, 58, 97, 103, 106, 111–12, 117, 119, 122, 131, 135, 137, 147, 186, 189, 191, 209, 213–14, 235, 254, 263–4; 'downstream' territory 223; European territory 4; fixed territories 45; functional territory 12, 224; hard territories 265; national territory 38; soft territories 12, 113, 213, 215, 224, 234, 257, 265; 'upstream' territory 223
Thatcher, Margaret 143
The Hague 128–9, 131–3, 135–6
The Netherlands 15, 126–39, 171–87, 158
'The Walkable City: Stockholm City Plan' 96
Tillväxt- och regionplaneförvaltning 98
timeframes 51
Tolna 159, 164
tourism 63, 69, 71, 78, 87, 122, 191–2, 194–7, 199, 204, 208–10, 215, 225
Trafikkontoret 97
transboundary water 174–5
transfer 17, 23, 25–6, 66, 98, 104–5,

278 *Index*

108, 129, 134, 136, 172, 176, 186–7, 212, 215–16, 228, 238, 245–51
transferability 5–6, 66, 212, 221, 238–50
transit-oriented development 126
transparency 4, 21, 40, 49, 51, 53–4, 57, 77, 79, 89, 103, 108, 120, 151, 159, 223, 226–7, 257
Trilateral Nature Park 16, 189, 199, 223, 225–6, 229–31, 257
Trilateral Nature Park Goričko-Raab-Örség 16, 65, 189–202

United Cities and Local Governments 26
United Kingdom (UK) 16, 26–7, 45, 67–79, 71, 141–55, 255–6, 262–3
United Nations Development Programme (UNDP) 48–9
University of Linköping 207
University of Manchester 153
'upstream-downstream' 178
upward rescaling 26
Urban Community Initiative 246
urban culture 85
urban development 15, 81–4, 86 , 96–103, 105–7, 109
Urban Pilot Projects 246

urban planning 63, 95, 102, 107, 109, 111–124, 223–4, 227, 258
urbanism 255, 260–1
Utrecht 130, 132

VÁTI 161
'valley section' 171
vertical policy coordination 139
'Vision 2030' 96
VGN (association of municipalities) 132
Västra Götaland 27

Wales 15, 27, 68, 143, 145, 262
Water Framework Directive 174–6, 182, 195
water management 63, 171, 174, 176–180, 182, 185–7, 196, 204, 225
water quality 171, 174, 176–7, 185
water quantity 16, 171–2, 179
water storage capacity 179, 184
welfare state 27, 37, 39, 99
Western Europe 30–1, 58
Westphalian order 38
Windisch-Minihof 194

'Yes In My BackYard' (YIMBY) 98, 104

Zuid-Holland 129, 132, 137